UNDERSTANDING COLLEGE
AND UNIVERSITY ORGANIZATION

Volume I—The State of the System

UNDERSTANDING COLLEGE AND UNIVERSITY ORGANIZATION

Theories for Effective Policy and Practice

James L. Bess and Jay R. Dee

Foreword by D. Bruce Johnstone

Volume I—The State of the System

STERLING, VIRGINIA

COPYRIGHT © 2008, 2012 BY
STYLUS PUBLISHING, LLC.

Published by Stylus Publishing, LLC
22883 Quicksilver Drive
Sterling, Virginia 20166-2102

A hardcover edition of this book was published in 2008 by
Stylus Publishing, LLC.

**The Library of Congress has cataloged the hardcover
edition as follows:**
Bess, James L.
    Understanding college and university organization :
theories for effective policy and practice / James L. Bess and
Jay R. Dee ; foreword by D. Bruce Johnstone.
        p.   cm.
    Includes bibliographical references and index.
    ISBN 1-57922-131-9 (v. 1 : alk. paper)
    ISBN 1-57922-132-7 (v. 2 : alk. paper)
    1. Universities and colleges—Administration.
2. Organizational sociology.   I. Dee, Jay R.   II. Title.
LB2341.B4769   2007
378.1′01—dc22   2006033065

Volume I
ISBN: 978-1-57922-131-7 (cloth)
ISBN: 978-1-57922-768-5 (paper)
ISBN: 978-1-57922-771-5 (library networkable e-edition)
ISBN: 978-1-57922-773-9 (consumer e-edition)

Volume II
ISBN: 978-1-57922-132-4 (cloth)
ISBN: 978-1-57922-769-2 (paper)
ISBN: 978-1-57922-772-2 (library networkable e-edition)
ISBN: 978-1-57922-774-6 (consumer e-edition)

Two-Volume Sets
ISBN: 978-1-57922-197-3 (cloth)
ISBN: 978-1-57922-770-8 (paper)

Printed in the United States of America

All first editions printed on acid-free paper
that meets the American National Standards Institute
Z39-48 Standard.

Bulk Purchases

Quantity discounts are available for use in workshops
and for staff development.
Call 1-800-232-0223

First Paperback Edition, 2012

10 9 8 7 6 5 4 3 2

CONTENTS

VOLUME II: DYNAMICS OF THE SYSTEM

PROBLEM-TO-THEORY APPLICATION TABLE

The following are organizational problems college and university administrators typically encounter in their work. For each problem listed, reference is given to directly relevant theory and to conceptual frameworks that have been found to be effective by researchers and administrators.

We have presented these problems as illustrations of the utility of organizational theories. We do not, however, claim that the list of problems is comprehensive. Readers who seek theoretical solutions to problems not listed below should consult the index, whose entries provide access to the wide range of administrative issues and theoretical approaches covered by this book.

Organizational Problem	Related Theory or Conceptual Framework	Vol/Chap/Page
1. Competition and External Relations		
Need to conduct a comprehensive environmental scan.	General and Proximate Environments	V1, C5 (pp. 131–134)
	SWOT Analysis	V2, C7 (pp. 728–729)
Competition with other colleges and universities is intensifying.	Population Ecology Theory	V1, C5 (pp. 138–141)
	Adaptive Model of Strategy (including determining the organization's core competencies)	V2, C7 (pp. 726–729)
Pressures from external agencies (e.g., state government) demand a response.	Institutional Theory	V1, C5 (pp. 141–144)
	Planned Change Models	V2, C9 (pp. 798–808)
Organization is not well known or understood by external groups.	Organizational Image and Identity	V1, C5 (pp. 155–158)
	Symbolic Model of Strategy	V2, C7 (pp. 732–734)
Accreditation issues, standards from the professional associations (e.g., law, nursing, education, social work)	Institutional Theory	V1, C5 (pp. 141–144)

(continued)

Organizational Problem	Related Theory or Conceptual Framework	Vol/Chap/Page
Need to improve external relations	Identifying Stakeholders	V2, C7 (pp. 715–716)
	Boundary Spanning Personnel	V2, C7 (pp. 721–722)
Organization needs to demonstrate accountability to external agencies.	Goal Model of Effectiveness	V2, C8 (pp. 758–763)
2. Planning and Budgeting		
Resources are scarce (e.g., declining state revenue for public university and college budgets).	Resource Dependence Theory	V1, C5 (pp. 148–152)
	System Resource Model of Effectiveness	V2, C8 (pp. 764–765)
Plans and forecasts have failed to serve as an accurate guide for institutional decision making.	Chaos Theory	V1, C5 (pp. 158–161)
	Postmodern and Critical Perspectives on Change	V2, C9 (pp. 816–819)
Declining enrollment	Resource Dependence Theory	V1, C5 (pp. 148–152)
	Population Ecology Theory	V1, C5 (pp. 138–141)
The organization needs to make decisions regarding program expansion and/or contraction.	Decision Trees	V2, C5 (pp. 649–650)
Budget uncertainties	Strategic Contingencies Theory	V2, C3 (pp. 551–554)
Decisions are made too quickly without sufficient analysis of the problem.	Decision Making as a Process	V2, C4 (pp. 594–597)
	Group versus Individual Decision Making	V2, C4 (pp. 606–608)
	Shared Decision Making	V2, C4 (pp. 608–614)
Decisions are made too slowly; not all decisions require extensive discussion and analysis.	Modes of Decision Making in Organizations	V2, C4 (pp. 602–605)
	Group versus Individual Decision Making	V2, C4 (pp. 606–608)
	Shared Decision Making	V2, C4 (pp. 608–614)

Organizational Problem	Related Theory or Conceptual Framework	Vol/Chap/Page
The use of formal decision-making procedures does not improve the quality of decisions made within the organization.	Garbage Can Model of Decision Making	V2, C5 (pp. 634–637)
	Nondecision Making	V2, C5 (pp. 650–653)
	Postmodern Perspectives on Individual Decision Making	V2, C5 (pp. 653–655)
The organization struggles to find the "right" people to make different kinds of decisions under different types of circumstances; decision makers' skills are not a good match for the types of decisions that typically come to them.	Information Accessing Preferences and Information Processing Preferences	V2, C5 (pp. 639–643)
	Decisions and Information Use	V2, C5 (pp. 643–646)
Top-level leaders are too controlling of the planning process.	Dialectical Perspectives on Cultural Learning	V2, C6 (pp. 689–693)
	Postmodern Interpretations of Organizational Learning	V2, C6 (pp. 693–694)
	Postmodern Perspectives on Strategy	V2, C7 (pp. 734–736)
	Emergent Change Framework	V2, C9 (pp. 808–810)
Organization has difficulty using data to demonstrate its effectiveness; data are misunderstood or distorted, or too few data are used.	Social Construction Model of Organizational Effectiveness	V2, C8 (pp. 774–777)
3. Organizational Structure and Core Processes		
Organization is slow to respond to changes in the external environment.	Contingency Theory	V1, C5 (pp. 145–148)
	Adaptive Model of Strategy	V2, C7 (pp. 726–729)
Rules and procedures are interfering with the organization's ability to respond to changes in the external environment.	Matching Organizational Design and External Environment	V1, C6 (pp. 183–184)
Core organizational processes are not yielding effective outcomes.	Matching Organizational Design and Technology	V1, C6 (pp. 184–189)

(continued)

Organizational Problem	Related Theory or Conceptual Framework	Vol/Chap/Page
Student services (e.g., financial aid, advising) are too scattered across campus; the services are not convenient or well coordinated.	Functional Forms of Organization	V1, C7 (pp. 215–217)
Leaders of specialized units complain that centralized administrative functions (e.g., budget, fund raising) are not addressing their needs.	Product Forms of Organization	V1, C7 (pp. 217–219)
Interdisciplinary initiatives are difficult to implement.	Matrix Forms of Organization	V1, C7 (pp. 220–222)
	Loose Coupling Theory	V1, C7 (pp. 223–226)
Collaboration between student affairs and academic affairs divisions is rare.	Matrix Forms of Organization	V1, C7 (pp. 220–222)
	Loose Coupling Theory	V1, C7 (pp. 223–226)
	Collaborative Leadership	V2, C10 (pp. 869–871)
Restructuring initiatives have failed to improve organizational performance.	Structuration Theory	V1, C7 (pp. 226–228)
	Postmodern Views on Organizational Design	V1, C7 (pp. 228–231)
Formal procedures for resolving conflict do not improve unit or organizational performance.	Social Constructionist Perspectives on Conflict	V2, C2 (pp. 522–524)
	Postmodern Perspectives on Conflict	V2, C2 (pp. 524–526)
Organization fails to detect service problems until they reach near-crisis proportions.	Single- and Double-Loop Learning	V2, C6 (pp. 674–678)
Effective practices are concentrated in only a few units within the organization; good ideas to improve performance do not spread across the organization.	Shared Mental Models: The Nexus between Individual and Organizational Learning	V2, C6 (pp. 680–686)
	Adoption of Innovations	V2, C9 (pp. 800–801)
4. Managing Departments and Institutional Units		
Departments do not coordinate their work with other units, leading to unnecessary duplication.	Differentiation and Integration	V1, C6 (pp. 176–178)
	Pooled, Sequential, and Reciprocal Interdependence	V1, C6 (pp. 191–194)

Organizational Problem	Related Theory or Conceptual Framework	Vol/Chap/Page
Information is not being exchanged among units that need to coordinate their efforts.	Division of Labor	V1, C7 (pp. 205–206)
Lack of clear rules and procedures has led to inconsistent performance within and across units.	Procedural Specification	V1, C7 (pp. 206–208)
Too many people report to one supervisor.	Hierarchy–Span of Control	V1, C7 (pp. 210–212)
Organizational members report they receive mixed messages or conflicting instructions from their supervisors about how to do their jobs.	Role Conflict	V1, C8 (pp. 262–265)
Organizational members report they do not receive clear instructions from their supervisors.	Role Ambiguity	V1, C8 (pp. 265–266)
Lack of focus on task accomplishment; too much socializing among organizational members interferes with performance.	ERG Theory–Frustration-Regression Hypothesis Optimum Levels of Conflict	V1, C9 (pp. 292–294) V2, C2 (pp. 498–500)
Competition among departments for resources	Organizational Sources of Conflict Structural Approaches to Conflict Management Process Approaches to Conflict Management	V2, C2 (pp. 496–497) V2, C2 (pp. 517–518) V2, C2 (pp. 518–521)
Conflict between individuals	Conflict of Interest, Conflict of Understanding, Conflict of Ideology Structural Approaches to Conflict Management Process Approaches to Conflict Management	V2, C2 (p. 497) V2, C2 (pp. 517–518) V2, C2 (pp. 518–521)

(continued)

Organizational Problem	Related Theory or Conceptual Framework	Vol/Chap/Page
Organizational units continue to make the same errors repeatedly; they fail to improve over time.	How Organizational Learning May Be in Error	V2, C6 (pp. 667–668)
	Single- and Double-Loop Learning	V2, C6 (pp. 674–678)
Leaders do not do a good job of delegating responsibilities; too much micromanagement.	Situational Leadership	V2, C10 (pp. 852–853)
	Collaborative Leadership	V2, C10 (pp. 869–871)
Leaders tend to give projects to people who are not prepared to handle them; lack of mentoring.	Situational Leadership	V2, C10 (pp. 852–853)
5. Managing Groups and Teams		
Team members disagree about who should be in charge.	Authority of the Situation	V1, C10 (pp. 322–323)
Group/team/committee meetings tend to accomplish little.	Personal Roles in Groups	V1, C10 (pp. 333–334)
	Stages of Group Function and Development	V1, C10 (pp. 336–338)
	Social Construction, Groups, and Teams	V1, C10 (pp. 346–349)
Team members are not contributing equally toward group performance; a few members are doing most of the work.	Free Riding and Social Loafing	V1, C10 (pp. 342–343)
Groups and teams tend to shoot down new ideas.	Groupthink	V1, C10 (pp. 344–345)
Groups and teams tend to avoid tough decisions.	Groupthink	V1, C10 (pp. 344–345)
Groups and teams have difficulty making decisions.	Decision Making as a Process	V2, C4 (pp. 594–597)
	Symbolic Convergence Theory	V2, C4 (pp. 617–620)

Organizational Problem	*Related Theory or Conceptual Framework*	*Vol/Chap/Page*
6. Change Management and Organizational Growth		
Need to plan for organizational growth and expansion	Matching Organizational Design and Size	V1, C6 (p. 191)
Current values and assumptions impede organizational growth and development.	Cultural Typologies in Higher Education	V1, C11 (pp. 376–380)
Faculty and staff members often resist decisions by organizational leaders.	Downward Influence: How Authorities Attempt to Influence Partisans	V2, C3 (pp. 559–561)
	Zone of Acceptance	V2, C4 (pp. 614–615)
Organization is not innovative.	Dialectical Perspectives on Cultural Learning	V2, C6 (pp. 689–693)
	Implementing a Learning Organization	V2, C6 (pp. 696–698)
	Emergent Model of Strategy	V2, C7 (pp. 730–732)
	Adoption of Innovations	V2, C9 (pp. 800–801)
	Sociotechnical Theories of Change	V2, C9 (pp. 801–805)
	Emergent Change Framework	V2, C9 (pp. 808–810)
Change initiatives get stalled, lose momentum, and fail to accomplish their intended goals.	Central Problems in the Management of Change	V2, C9 (pp. 796–797)
	Planned Change Models	V2, C9 (pp. 798–808)
Organization needs to implement new technology more extensively in distance education; need to encourage more faculty members to use the technology.	Planned Change Models	V2, C9 (pp. 798–808)
	Adoption of Innovations	V2, C9 (pp. 800–801)
Faculty and staff are resistant to changing their behaviors.	Force Field Analysis of Change	V2, C9 (pp. 805–807)

(continued)

Organizational Problem	*Related Theory or Conceptual Framework*	*Vol/Chap/Page*
7. Personnel Management		
Orientation programs do not prepare new employees effectively to be successful in their jobs.	Role Socialization	V1, C8 (pp. 258–260)
The organization needs to improve faculty development and evaluation systems.	Job Characteristics Theory	V1, C9 (pp. 302–306)
Salary ratcheting issues: Senior faculty and staff complain that incoming junior-level faculty and staff are earning nearly as much as (or more than) they do.	Equity Theory	V1, C9 (pp. 299–302)
Demands for higher salaries	Upward Influence: How Partisans Attempt to Influence Authorities (Influencing, Shaping, and Determining Others' Objectives)	V2, C3 (pp. 557–559)
Unions and collective bargaining difficulties	Upward Influence: How Partisans Attempt to Influence Authorities	V2, C3 (pp. 557–559)
	Downward Influence: How Authorities Attempt to Influence Partisans	V2, C3 (pp. 559–561)
8. Mission, Vision, and Goals for the Organization		
Need to develop new goals for department, unit, or whole organization	Matching Organizational Design and Goals	V1, C6 (pp. 189–190)
	Goal Model of Effectiveness	V2, C8 (pp. 758–763)
New leaders (e.g., a newly hired president) need to learn as much as possible about the organization.	Schein's Organizational Culture Framework	V1, C11 (pp. 364–372)
	Using Positivist, Social Constructionist, and Postmodern Approaches for Analyzing Organizational Culture	V1, C11 (pp. 389–390)

Organizational Problem	Related Theory or Conceptual Framework	Vol/Chap/Page
Inefficiency: Organizational efforts are not clearly linked to the institution's mission; too many disconnected initiatives	Linear Model of Strategy	V2, C7 (pp. 723–726)
Organizational drift: The institution's key values and purposes are not known or not clearly articulated.	Symbolic Model of Strategy	V2, C7 (pp. 732–734)
9. Diversity and Quality of Work Life		
Women and racial/ethnic minorities report that their contributions are not valued as highly.	Postmodern and Feminist Perspectives on Roles	V1, C8 (pp. 260–262)
	Sex and Gender Issues in Leadership	V2, C10 (pp. 871–874)
Organizational morale is low; job dissatisfaction is high.	Two-Factor Theory	V1, C9 (pp. 289–291)
Organizational members lack motivation; they experience high levels of burnout and frustration.	Expectancy Theory	V1, C9 (pp. 294–296)
	Goal Theory	V1, C9 (pp. 296–299)
	Job Characteristics Theory	V1, C9 (pp. 302–306)
	Path-Goal Theory	V2, C10 (pp. 854–859)
Organizational members complain they are treated unfairly and other people in the organization receive more rewards for the same or less effort.	Equity Theory	V1, C9 (pp. 299–302)
Organization is not as welcoming as it should be for students, faculty, and staff from traditionally underrepresented groups.	Critical Theory and Organizational Culture	V1, C11 (pp. 385–386)
	Postmodern Perspectives on Organizational Culture	V1, C11 (pp. 386–388)
	Culture and Difference	V1, C11 (pp. 388–389)
Lack of trust between administration and faculty, or between administration and staff	Continuum of Trust	V2, C3 (pp. 556–557)

FOREWORD

I n this monumental two-volume study, *Understanding College and University Organization*, Jim Bess and Jay Dee have produced a reference (really, a text) that is highly theoretical, eminently practical, and like no other work to date on the complex topic of how and why colleges and universities behave as they do and how to lead (and follow) for a more humane, appropriately responsive, and cost-effective institution. The sweep of their coverage draws on decades of theoretical and empirical work, not just on colleges and universities, but on organizations of all forms and from the disciplinary vantages of sociology, psychology, management, and organizational behavior as well as the extensive and growing body of literature on higher education itself, to which both authors have made major contributions.

If there can be an overriding theme to a work of this scope, it is found in their subtitle: *Theories for Effective Policy and Practice*. Theory, however abstract and increasingly contested (that is, between positivist, social-constructionist, and post-modern paradigms), is essential not only for understanding these complex organizations, but also for their more effective design and leadership. Although the paradigmatic tilt is definitely positivist, the authors provide sympathetic, learned, and nuanced explanations of the more recent social constructionist and postmodern approaches and illustrate the fundamental complementarities of these ontologically and epistemologically different strands of scholarship.

Whether a graduate student given these two volumes as a text in a doctoral level course on higher education organization and governance or a scholar aspiring to an administrative career will become a *better* college dean or university president is beside the point. Anyone caring to become immersed in the nature of organizational theory, liberally illustrated by realistic cases, will better understand from these volumes what has happened—not only to a particular college or university at a point in time, but to the public's and politician's important and not always favorable perceptions of, and behaviors toward, the more than four thousand U.S. colleges and universities.

As a former college and university administrator (vice president for administration at the University of Pennsylvania, president of Buffalo State College, and chancellor of the State University of New York system, and for the most recent thirteen years as University Professor of higher and comparative education, I have attempted to fathom answers to questions such as:

- Why is it that many or most presidents (and virtually all members of college and university boards) lament what they perceive to be the excessive power of the faculty, especially to thwart the president's efforts to change the institution in directions that are more fiscally prudent and responsive to the changing needs of the students and the society that is to be served, while most faculty lament the fact that they have little or no *real* authority and that sooner or later the president (or the dean or the board) will have their way?

- And why is it that politicians and the press are convinced that colleges and universities "almost never change," which they invariably perceive as a kind of organizational pathology, while by most measures, the institutions that truly need to change do so quite profoundly (e.g., from a Roman Catholic liberal arts college for women to a co-educational college serving largely part-time and nontraditional students in preparation for careers in business and the health professions) and those institutions that are most resistant to change (e.g., a well-endowed, selective liberal arts college or university with a deep applicant pool and considerable socioeconomic and ethnic diversity in the entering classes) probably do not and almost certainly should not?

- Why do large lectures and smaller "discussion" classes continue to meet for two or three sessions a week for two annual semesters of thirteen weeks (mainly from mid-morning to mid-afternoon Monday through Thursday) in spite of advances in instructional technology that could provide synchronous and asynchronous learning opportunities for students to move at their own paces at home or elsewhere?

- Why do politicians and the press (and more than a few students and parents) see nothing but waste and incompetence in average yearly tuition increases that exceed the prevailing rates of inflation when a rate of inflation is nothing but an average of many price increases, roughly one-half of which perforce will be above the average, and when whether a price increase is in the "above" or the "below" half is a function mainly of the degree to which capital can replace labor—which is rarely the case in traditional higher education?

I read many books in my administrative career and gave more than a few lectures and wrote many chapters and articles for the edification of other higher education leaders, all in an attempt not so much to figure out what to do, but to better understand what happened when I did what I did and why other people seem to so misunderstand us. Later in my career as a professor of higher and comparative education, specializing in higher education

finance, governance, and policy in both domestic and international comparative perspectives, I searched for works that would help my students better
understand the wonderful complexities of these organizations we term "colleges and universities." Alas, I was never quite satisfied. I wish Professors Bess
and Dee had completed this work, say, thirty years earlier. But then, it would
have missed the last three decades' worth of theoretical and empirical work
that the authors so adroitly draw on. So I will never know, and perhaps it is
just as well, what I might have done differently had I had the advantage of
Jim Bess's and Jay Dee's learning earlier in one of my careers in higher education. But I predict that many years will pass before these two volumes are
surpassed.

D. Bruce Johnstone
Buffalo, New York

ABOUT THE AUTHORS

James L. Bess is professor emeritus at New York University and a consultant to colleges and universities throughout the world. He conducts research on organizational and faculty issues and is completing several books and papers on matters of higher education policy.

Dr. Bess's education includes degrees from Cornell, Harvard, New York University, and the University of California at Berkeley. He has written or edited eight books, including *Collegiality and Bureaucracy in the Modern University* and, most recently, *Teaching Alone/Teaching Together: Transforming the Structure of Teams for Teaching*. He has published more than 60 articles and book chapters, many on the organization of colleges and universities, faculty motivation, and issues of tenure.

Dr. Bess has received grants from the U.S. Department of Education, Exxon Education Foundation, TIAA-CREF, and a number of organizations in Japan, where he and his family spent two sabbatical years and subsequent shorter periods with the support of a Fulbright research grant.

Jay R. Dee is associate professor at the University of Massachusetts, Boston, where he also directs the doctoral program in higher education administration. He earned a Ph.D. from the University of Iowa, and his research interests include organizational change, faculty development, and governance. He has published more than twenty studies of college and university organization and leadership with particular attention to how institutional cultures and external accountability pressures shape organizational behavior.

In 2004, Dr. Dee received a grant from the Ford Foundation to work with colleges and universities in New England to improve faculty development programs. Under the auspices of this grant, he worked with faculty at eight institutions to create the New England Center for Inclusive Teaching, a faculty development network that promotes pedagogical and curricular change to serve diverse student populations.

Dr. Dee also teaches in the Leadership in Urban Schools Doctoral Program at the University of Massachusetts, Boston, and he has written extensively on teams and teamwork in school organizations.

ACKNOWLEDGMENTS

Writing books is no picnic except when the readers find the intellectual "food" tasty and nutritional and the "conversation" with the author stimulating. We hope that our readers will find sustenance and enjoyment from reading this book. But preparing for a picnic is also no picnic, and in this case, we owe to many our deep thanks for making important, substantive contributions of different kinds.

Both authors are grateful for the generosity of the reviewers whose names appear at the beginning of each chapter. We also owe a special debt of gratitude to Sharon McDade at George Washington University, who provided a thorough and thoughtful critique of the cases presented in each chapter. In addition, we are especially appreciative of our conversations with Adrianna Kezar at the University of Southern California and Joseph Berger at the University of Massachusetts, Amherst. Both of these colleagues shared with us insights and observations on organizational theory—and on the teaching of organizational theory—that enriched our perspectives for the book.

We also thank the doctoral students and graduates from the University of Massachusetts, Boston who provided equally insightful reviews of many of the chapters in this book: Mirtha Crisostomo (Emmanuel College), Cheryl Daly (University of New Hampshire), Paul DiFrancesco (Massachusetts College of Pharmacy and Health Sciences), Roxanne Gonzales (Colorado State University), Ralph Kidder (Newbury College), and Helen Page (Harvard University).

We are especially grateful to Bruce Johnstone for a generous and informative foreword. We owe debts as well to the many unnamed colleagues, mentors, students, and contributors to the body of literature from which we liberally borrowed ideas, old and new. Finally, together, we thank our publisher, John von Knorring, whose demeanor and tact matched his command of our field and led us to avoid many false steps that he anticipated with great insight.

Individually, James L. Bess would like to acknowledge the 35-year "gift" of his spouse, Nancy Moore Bess, who permitted him to be himself, despite his frequent idiosyncratic, irascible departures from reason and obligations to family life. How she managed her own professional life (she's a textile craftsperson) while tending to me is a wonderful mystery. She had help from our two sons, Isaac and Ivan, whose own professional and personal lives distracted me felicitously from my cocoon and enlivened my days. To them and other family and friends, I give my grateful thanks.

Jay Dee extends sincere thanks and gratitude to family, friends, and colleagues who have been patient and supportive during the writing process, including but not limited to Steve Backhaus, Alan Henkin, and Tim and Cinda Dee.

T his book was written with two audiences in mind. The first audience comprises graduate students studying to become upper-level administrators, leaders, and policy makers in higher education. The second includes those persons currently employed in institutions of higher learning as administrative and faculty leaders.

The reason we felt such a book was necessary was not that there are insufficient resources in the literature that are relevant to contemporary practice. Rather, we believe that the literature is fragmented and not well organized. Readers of this book, probably as a regular practice, read the *Chronicle of Higher Education* and perhaps some other highly regarded periodicals, such as *Academe, Change, About Campus*, and other high-quality newsletters and periodicals of a more specialized nature. Relatively little of this literature, however, is grounded in **organizational theory**—the knowledge base that informs the practice of leadership and management.

Theory, as social psychologist Kurt Lewin said, is the best practice. Without theory, organizational leaders are forced to treat each problem that they encounter as unique—as if it were encountered for the first time. While leaders may have some experience with a particular problem, their solutions are usually not informed by the accumulated wisdom of others who have already encountered and solved similar problems, perhaps with much greater efficiency and effectiveness. Building theory in higher education results in a heuristic approach to problem solving that uses validated, proven theoretical relationships among independent and dependent variables (which are often causes and effects of phenomena). Having theory in mind, organizational leaders can determine whether the extant theory works for them. We hope with this book to provide a large number of systematically organized theories that can be applied in many typical situations. Ours is a pragmatic approach. Here are some possible answers to organizational problems that are suggested by theory. Try them out.

On the other hand, we hasten to add that the book is not a "how to" guidebook for managers. Many such management texts offer the latest techniques in organizational efficiency. Instead, we offer deeper, more sophisticated theories that will allow readers to develop their *own* management techniques and to evaluate intelligently contemporaneous approaches that are put forth regularly in magazines and management workshops.

In an effort to provide initial linkages between established theories and pressing problems being experienced by readers, we offer a **Problem-to-Theory Application Table** (see pages xiii–xxi). The table offers a range of typical problems (by no means an exhaustive list) with references to chapters and pages in the book where applicable theories can be found.

We have attempted as far as possible to speak plainly, avoiding jargon wherever possible. This is difficult when dealing with theory, since its linguistic mode tends to be abstract. Nevertheless, we hope that the reader will be able to follow our reasoning about the theories. In virtually all cases, we support our own explanations with references to literature that either amplifies what we have written or offers alternative perspectives. For pedagogical purposes, we also provide case material to which the theories can be applied and discussions of the application modes conducted. Working with theory requires practice, and skill development is cumulative. It is difficult at the start, but it becomes somewhat easier as one learns how to make the theory relevant to problems at hand.

The reader will discover quickly that we have approached the theory of the organization and administration of colleges and universities from three quite different perspectives, each relying on different assumptions about how human beings apprehend reality—or believe they do. Readers should be able to learn about their organizations from all three perspectives. On occasion, the approaches may appear to yield contradictory directives about which actions to take. We believe that this conclusion is largely a result of the fundamental philosophic assumptions about the most important characteristics of human life that underlie all behavior and projections of behavior in organizations, including colleges and universities. Each perspective—we call them paradigms rather than perspectives—has its own validity, but each does not automatically lead to immediately practical solutions to problems. They do, however, highlight phenomena that require attention if the institution is ultimately to be considered successful. We also argue that success needs to be measured in many ways, including not only the traditional criteria of student, faculty, and administrative achievement, but also the social and ethical goals of the larger society.

Indeed, we wish finally to underline our commitment to these goals. Individual human behavior in all domains—for example, home, market, school, work—is driven at least partially by each individual's underlying and often unexamined, deeply held beliefs about human nature, about the morality of interpersonal interactions in general, and about the meaning and purposes of human life. While we cannot examine all of the assumptions and presumptions that lie behind each of the theories we present in this book about the application of organizational theory in colleges and universities, we do wish to make explicit our view about the ethical posture to which all organizations, including those in our field—perhaps especially those—should adhere.

We take as an essential good the integrity and worth of each human being—each organizational member—regardless of position or authority in the organizational structure. Such a perspective requires the organization to deal with each individual with dignity and respect. It recognizes the need for each person to be enabled to continue to develop and grow in different ways—intellectual, practical, and psychological. The organization thus represents an environment for learning and personal growth. It means, in addition, that organizations do not have a reason for being in and of themselves in which they intentionally or unintentionally use employees as mechanical tools to further either alleged organizational goals or the goals of the organizations' more powerful executives.

We are not, however, so naïve as to ignore the practical necessity for organizations to be "in the real world." Every organization must be able to survive, especially to compete successfully. To do so, it must be perceived by clients as making meaningful contributions to them, individually and collectively. This sustained pressure on organizations from the external, competitive environment places great burdens on leaders who must transform that force, often transmitted downward in the organization, into the need to be efficient and effective—requirements for sustained successful competition.

Our aim in this book is to elucidate how administration can be made more efficient and effective through rational decision making, but not at the risk of sacrificing humanistic values. There may be occasions when demands for efficiency or effectiveness of organizational outcomes appear to give priority to dehumanization of workers. Our own ethical standards suggest, however, that morally conscious and conscientious administrators must be persistently and diligently sensitive to such proclivities and must exercise their power and influence to create a strong cultural norm with action consequences that uphold the integrity and dignity of every human being. Our presentation of multiple alternative paradigms should give conceptual support and moral grounding for these orientations and actions.

What the reader will find, therefore, in each of the chapters in this book are theories drawn from the literature that address the human condition in organizational life. It will invariably be the case that the theories will be cast at least as having the potential for providing organizational members with opportunities for becoming more active, energetic, enthusiastic, and satisfied with their organizational lives. We believe that such an objective can readily be accomplished within the parameters of achieving with sustained high quality the important goals of colleges and universities.

INTRODUCTION

Organization of the Book by Chapter

In this first volume of *Understanding College and University Organization*, we endeavor to portray and analyze theoretically many of the more stable and enduring conditions of colleges and universities and the behavior of their various constituents—both inside and outside the organization. In the second volume, we address the more dynamic relationships among the parts and the ingredients that influence the institution's effectiveness and efficiency. We encourage the reader to become familiar with Figure A, which indicates the central focus of each of the chapters in both Volume I and Volume II, and shows the relationships among the contents of the chapters.

As will be clear later in our discussion of systems theory, each component and each process in an organization has either a direct or indirect relationship to all of the others. Thus, a change in any one component or process will have an impact on some or all of the others. Almost all of the arrows in Figure A are bidirectional, signifying mutual influences. In some cases (e.g., organizational learning, strategy, leadership, and change), however, we imply by the single-direction arrow that the relationships between the elements are more powerful in one direction, though there are usually mutual influences in these cases as well.

In the first chapter of Volume I, we introduce the various dimensions of college and university organizations that are explored in depth later in individual chapters. These include the external environment, the structure of colleges and universities, the interpersonal challenges, and the culture—indeed, the multiple cultures—of higher education institutions. Perhaps most important in this first chapter is our position on the use of theory in understanding organizational phenomena. In particular, we outline the argument of higher education scholar Robert Zemsky (2001) that the theoretical principles that are used in profit-making organizations are usually quite suitable for colleges and universities. Zemsky (2001) notes:

> Colleges and universities tend to see themselves as entities that differ fundamentally from other organizations, but the reality is that the managerial skills required are very similar to those of other organizations. (ERIC Abstract No. ED450664).

Our argument throughout both volumes of the book is that theory is not simply an abstraction without value in the practical affairs of organizations, including colleges and universities. When applied correctly, theory can be

FIGURE A
Organization of the Book by Chapters*

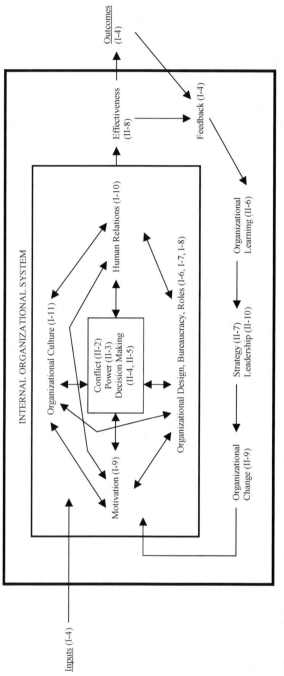

*Volume and chapter numbers appear in parentheses. Arrows refer to interactions among components.

used to identify the conceptual foundations of common problems that occur in organizations. Too often, organizational members tend to believe that each problem at their particular institution is totally unlike that at other, similar institutions. However, because theory has been established on the basis of empirical research at many other such institutions, its precepts and predictions generally provide guidance in particular instances. As has often been noted, theory can be eminently practical when used correctly.

Theory is not easy to understand or to apply, however. It requires precision in thinking and an understanding of the limitations of theories. Nevertheless, it is most often a much better guide than chance and intuition or even personal experience.

Our first chapter in this volume introduces the reader to three alternative perspectives or **paradigms** for understanding organizational theory—positivism, social constructionism, and postmodernism—that will be found extrapolated in all of the chapters as these positions are applied to real situations. At first glance, the paradigms would seem to be mutually exclusive, since the underlying philosophies on which each is based are quite different. In our view, the different perspectives can be complementary. The book is based primarily on a positivist paradigm. Its premises suggest that it is possible and desirable—indeed, essential—to seek and achieve consensus among interested parties (e.g., organizational participants) on the objective realities (e.g., problems and issues) that present themselves in the organization. Only positivism permits the scientific application of most of the theories that we present. Nevertheless, in this book we give considerable credence to the position that realities perceived by different individuals are frequently social constructions that reflect personal experience, beliefs, or ideology. Indeed, we assert that one danger of positivist theories to which college and university leaders must pay vigilant attention is the subtle, usually unintended but sometimes intended, implications embedded in the theories that exploit individuals or classes of individuals.

In chapter 2 of this volume, we give a description of the most common structures of colleges and universities and of some other typical activities in which units of the institutions engage. For many readers of this book, especially those who are employed in institutions of higher education, this chapter may not be necessary or may serve as a refresher. Needless to say, although institutions of higher education are among the most enduring of all social institutions, they have undergone substantial changes in their modes of operation, particularly in recent years. The reader will have to be attentive to other current literature that may modify the basic descriptions in this chapter.

Since three paradigms undergird our explanatory modes in all of the chapters, readers need to be thoroughly familiar with each. In chapter 3, we present the origins of the paradigms, the arguments put forth by contemporary adherents of each, and the current controversies surrounding the use of one or another. After reading this chapter, readers should be able to draw their own conclusions about their personal preferences for applying the paradigms.

Chapter 4 comprises the central conceptual framework for the positivist perspectives in the book. General systems theory and social systems theory have long guided the development not only of omnibus theories of organizations but of many if not most empirically based specific theories of organization—that is, theories in each of the other chapters in the book. The main thesis of general systems theory is that any action in any part of the system has an impact on the other parts of the system. The main benefit of the extensive treatment of systems theory in this book is that it provides a vocabulary for discussion of the theories put forth later in the book. Thus, for example, when we discuss the external environment in chapter 5, the reader will have already come to understand how the environment is conceived in general. The concepts introduced in this chapter also can (and should) be used as stimuli to organizational members seeking to understand phenomena of particular interest to them. It is helpful, in other words, to use the list of key concepts as a checklist for predicting the impact of different decision options on the organization.

Social systems theory is introduced to remind the reader that all organizational behavior is a product of both environment and personality. It is easy to overlook one or the other and to blame either the organization or the individual for problems encountered. As Bolman and Deal (2003) note, "faulting people blocks us from seeing system weaknesses and offers few workable options" (p. 38). Similarly, blaming the organization ignores the fact that people created the organization in the first place, and they can change the organization if they desire. Social systems theory encourages us to consider both people and organizational conditions in the assessment of organizational problems.

The increasing use of electronic media that instantaneously connect organizations to the worlds outside their boundaries has stimulated researchers to look deeply into the characteristics of different external environments—the subject matter of chapter 5. Many different theories have emerged, each of which conceivably could be used in understanding the relationships of colleges and universities to their varied outside constituencies. As we demonstrate in this chapter, the dynamic relationship between institution and environment depends in part on history, but also on a more fundamental understanding of how organizations in a competitive setting initiate organization-environment relationships or react to them. Indeed, as some of the theories discussed in this chapter reveal, there is some question about the degree of freedom organizations such as colleges and universities have to develop unique and productive relationships with supportive and/or competitive systems. The ultimate irony of some theories that we introduce is the position that understanding the environment from a rational perspective may not always be possible.

In chapter 6, we introduce models of organizational design. Essential to understanding this chapter is the principle that all organizations must balance their needs for differentiation and integration. For purposes of efficiency, organizations typically divide labor into more specialized tasks that trained individuals can perform better than generalists—though some theories argue that under certain circumstances generalists are more valuable. Once labor is divided, however, there must be a mechanism for integrating the separated parts. Both the division of labor and the integration of the subunits are part of what we call organizational design. As we point out in this chapter, quite a number of independent variables contribute singly and in combination to decisions about how to "package" the work that needs to be done. In higher education, for the most part we have opted for a system that groups faculty together who have common knowledge backgrounds.

A number of other possibilities for performing the work of higher education—for example, undergraduate teaching—call for combinations of human resources with quite different knowledge backgrounds in departments guided by either technology or goals or special environmental conditions, or a combination of them. Of late, pressures from the external environment for greater accountability have resulted in the formation of units whose productivity can be measured quantitatively. Many would say that such design reformation is more responsive to short-run economic considerations than to long-term institutional creativity and effectiveness.

Chapter 7 focuses on one of the most common organizational designs—bureaucracy. Although colleges and universities are made up of both academic professionals and administrators, the principles of bureaucracy can be seen as fundamentally guiding the design of virtually all institutions. Hence, it is important to know what bureaucracy is, what its advantages are, and how it breaks down when its essential principles are violated. In this chapter, we discuss the components of bureaucracies and their common alternative configurations. We also introduce some alternative perspectives on organizational design that differ significantly from bureaucracies—in particular, the social construction perspective and postmodernism.

While organizational designs describe the dimensions and configurations of organizational subunits that are formally connected for the purpose of accomplishing institutional goals, they do not address the individual level of analysis—that is, the roles that individuals play within those units. In chapter 8, we take up the modes by which organizational functions are divided into roles. As we point out, roles frequently are defined ambiguously, again sometimes intentionally and to good effect, while in other cases, they are overly prescribed. Since role behavior is a function of both a sent role and a received role, there are many opportunities for misapprehensions about what was sent and received, and the chapter addresses the reasons these misapprehensions arise. Role conflict and role ambiguity, for example, are common problems in colleges and universities; in this chapter, we discuss the origins of both phenomena.

The final three substantive chapters in Volume I address individual, group, and organizational relationships in colleges and universities. We start at the individual level, with a chapter on motivation, move up a level to group dynamics, and then still further up and wider to organizational culture. In chapter 9, we consider the individual actor in organizations and consider such concepts as personality, self-concept, goals, and values. Two general theories of human motivation are introduced: content theories and process theories. The complexity of the notion of motivation requires that we present a fairly large number of theories that allege to explain human behavior. While there is some overlap among the theories, in our view, each theory uniquely adds another mode for examining the ways that human beings in organizations initiate and/or respond to stimuli.

At the group level, we explain in chapter 10 how human behavior is shaped by the nature of individual participation in collective settings. Collaboration is becoming increasingly more common. Group activity in research teams, academic departments, student affairs divisions, and other collections of individuals constitutes a lively and omnipresent influence on organizational behavior. Some of that influence is obviously visible through formal role assignments, but the pressures of group norms often represent even stronger incentives and constraints on how organizational members go about their business. Groups, as we point out, can be beneficial when cohesiveness is used in the service of common goals. On the other hand, when group norms become overly powerful, members of groups either become victims of "group think"—that is, adhering to one and only one accepted direction or value—or find expression of differences of opinion difficult and sometimes punished.

Similar phenomena occur, one level up, in the culture of organizations. Colleges and universities often develop "sagas" that are so powerful they influence virtually all institutional behavior. On the other hand, in some organizations, the culture is divided or fragmented, leaving organizational participants without a firm foundation of beliefs and values on which to base their behavior. Since so much organizational behavior is *not* prescribed in manuals of procedure, it remains for the individual to fill in the blanks—to make personal interpretations of what is expected. Absent a core of values that are promulgated and institutionalized, different individuals and different parts of the organization may act in ways that are not mutually supportive or that do not advance the goals of the organization. The cliché of "being on the same page" describes an essential component of effective organizational performance. Understanding organizational culture from the theoretical perspectives presented in chapter 11 points the way to making it possible for all organizational participants to act autonomously without undue fear of violating institutional values and norms. This chapter also acknowledges that on occasion organizational values and norms are dysfunctional, and fundamental changes in culture and ways of relating to others in the organization are necessary. Hence, we offer social constructionist and postmodern perspectives to amplify the alternatives available for assessing and changing organizational culture.

The Pedagogical Approach of the Book

The substantive chapters of the book are organized in ways that we hope will be useful for the reader's own learning and application of organizational theories. Here are the main ingredients of the pedagogical approaches that are used in the book:

1. Chapter Preview: After the table of contents, each chapter begins with a summary of the main points in the chapter. The purpose of the preview is to alert (and perhaps intrigue) the reader to key theoretical concerns that will appear later in the chapter.
2. Case Context: Each chapter is further introduced with a practical example of one or more of the organizational dilemmas with which a higher education administrator might be faced and to which some of the theories in the chapter can be applied. The primary reason for the case is to illustrate the complexity of the contexts of most organizational problems. Almost invariably what are identified in theories as "variables" are immersed in personal, structural, temporal, financial, and ethical circumstances. It takes practice to isolate the key influences in organizational behavior. While situations differ in different organizations, the skills needed to identify and utilize variables and theories can be practiced with the case provided. [Note that

all of the cases are fictitious. Institutions and characters referenced in the cases are not intended to represent actual locations or persons. The organizational problems described in the cases, however, do reflect common issues encountered in higher education institutions.]

3. Introduction: Each chapter also has an introductory section in which the central theoretical themes and dilemmas of the chapter are laid out, as are the various approaches to problem solving through the use of the theories in the chapter.

4. Presentation of Theories: Each chapter presents a selection of theories drawn from a very large number available in the literature. It is obviously impossible to cover all theories comprehensively, nor even the selections chosen here with sufficient depth to provide full examples and applications of each. Nevertheless, we have elected to explicate those theories that we have found either commonly in use (as cited by many reputable sources) or others that seem to us to be innovative but are still emerging. These latter may be controversial, but nevertheless worthy of consideration. In many cases, for two reasons, we have criticized and/or modified extant theories. The first is, hopefully, to improve them—to add to their predictive validity and/or explanatory value. The second is to translate them into modes that more readily can be adapted to the field of higher education.

5. Review Questions: At the conclusion of each chapter is a series of multiple choice questions about the various theories presented in the chapter. The answers to each question are designed to require the reader to understand all of the theories presented in the chapter before a correct choice can be made. In a number of cases, more than one answer may be correct. We have found that allowing readers to separate into groups of no more than five individuals gives opportunities for each participant to voice both questions and opinions about the answers. When used in the full classroom, it has been our finding that for the most part only the students who know the answers (or think they do) will volunteer, while those with doubts will be inhibited from raising them.

6. Case Discussion Questions: These questions are raised to assist the reader in analyzing the case presented at the beginning of the chapter. They are not posed in theoretical terms—for example, with independent and dependent variables clearly identified—but more in terms of practical problems that the case indicates may be present. Discussions among readers will evoke analyses of practical dilemmas being faced and will lead in turn to the search for theory-based solutions.

7. References: References to all of the theories are provided, as are, on

occasion, published commentaries on the theories. For the most part, original sources are cited, though when there have been amplifications or changes in the theories, the latest or best source is offered.

8. Index: Two indexes appear at the ends of both volumes. The indexes contain references to both volumes, not just to the volume in which they appear, since often terms and/or authors appear in both volumes. The two indexes are by author and topic. In the latter case, the topics are further broken down into subtopics.

In sum, Volume I of this book is replete with theories that help explain how colleges and universities operate and, equally important, the ways in which they succeed and fail. Again, Volume I describes the more stable elements in college and university organizations. In Volume II, we take up the

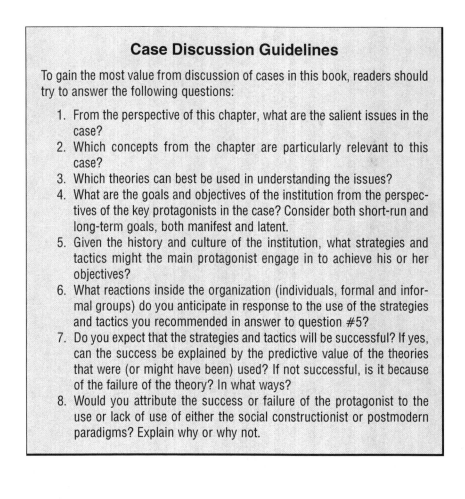

Case Discussion Guidelines

To gain the most value from discussion of cases in this book, readers should try to answer the following questions:

1. From the perspective of this chapter, what are the salient issues in the case?
2. Which concepts from the chapter are particularly relevant to this case?
3. Which theories can best be used in understanding the issues?
4. What are the goals and objectives of the institution from the perspectives of the key protagonists in the case? Consider both short-run and long-term goals, both manifest and latent.
5. Given the history and culture of the institution, what strategies and tactics might the main protagonist engage in to achieve his or her objectives?
6. What reactions inside the organization (individuals, formal and informal groups) do you anticipate in response to the use of the strategies and tactics you recommended in answer to question #5?
7. Do you expect that the strategies and tactics will be successful? If yes, can the success be explained by the predictive value of the theories that were (or might have been) used? If not successful, is it because of the failure of the theory? In what ways?
8. Would you attribute the success or failure of the protagonist to the use or lack of use of either the social constructionist or postmodern paradigms? Explain why or why not.

more dynamic conditions that intersect with these stable features and cause them to be either disrupted and/or changed.

References

Bolman, L., & Deal, T. (2003). *Reframing organizations: Artistry, choice, and leadership* (3rd ed.). San Francisco: Jossey-Bass.

Zemsky, R. (2001, March). Inside out. *Policy Perspectives, 10*(1), 1–12.

I

THE APPLICATION OF ORGANIZATIONAL THEORY TO COLLEGES AND UNIVERSITIES

CONTENTS

Preview

- Higher education institutions can be viewed as complex organizations.
- Colleges and universities confront a range of organizational challenges.
- Environmental challenge: how to be accountable without becoming too diffuse.
- Structural challenge: how to coordinate the work of highly specialized experts.
- Interpersonal challenge: how to address the needs of organizational members who have a wide variety of skills, abilities, and interests.
- Cultural challenge: how to build an organizational identity that still enables expressions of difference.
- Organizational theory can be used as a tool for developing frameworks for understanding, analyzing, and leading colleges and universities.
- Organizational theory can help leaders identify patterns, engage in reflection, analyze problems, and think of the organization as a system.
- Three prominent patterns of theorizing have emerged in organizational theory: positivism, social constructionism, and postmodernism.
- The positivist perspective suggests that theory can be used to explain, predict, and control organizational activity.
- The social constructionist perspective emphasizes the importance of communication, interpretation, and perceptual frames for making sense of organizational life.
- The postmodern perspective suggests that theory can help organizational members better understand and alleviate conditions of oppression and alienation.

Colleges and Universities as Complex Organizations

Colleges and universities are complex organizations operating in a diverse and ever-changing environment with shifting values, varying states of economic prosperity, and obscure permutations of political power. Yet they have endured—constituting a remarkably resilient organizational form and one of the oldest in human history. They predate the great commercial trading companies of the 16th century, the smokestack factories of the Industrial Revolution, and the multinational corporations and high-tech firms of the 20th and 21st centuries. Their missions have expanded from educating the elite for positions of community leadership to providing the primary vehicle for economic and social mobility to all strata of society. Colleges and universities are places of discovery and are sources of new technologies that improve human life. They are also places of learning; they empower people for lifelong learning, civic engagement, and spiritual fulfillment.

Many features of the first universities—founded in Europe in the 11th and 12th centuries—remain evident today. We still encounter the robes and hoods of academic regalia, the faculty lecture, and exams for students. Early universities even had a rudimentary form of academic freedom. But the modern roles of colleges and universities in society have changed dramatically. Enrollments, for example, are mass rather than elite. Over half of all Americans now have at least some college education ("Educational Attainment of the U.S. Population," 2005). As a result, the internal modes for carrying out higher education's role have similarly shifted. In teaching, pedagogy has diversified beyond the didactic lecture. The disciplines have proliferated, and the knowledge base has expanded enormously. With respect to research, universities have developed extensive external linkages that make institutions far more intimately connected to the industrial sector. Most colleges and universities, especially land-grant institutions, have found significant new public service responsibilities. Community colleges, responding to the priorities of state governments, now have large roles in developmental education and workforce training.

In serving the public in its many roles, however, higher education does not act as a monopoly. It is immersed in an often competitive environment that requires continual vigilance and constant attention to the quality of its products and its modes of operation.

To understand the significant and intriguing complexity of this major social institution requires both advanced knowledge and sophisticated tools of analysis. The primary objective of this book is to assist readers in understanding and using organizational theories that explicate the structures and processes of higher education. We present a wide variety of theories as potentially illuminating responses to the numerous organizational challenges facing higher education leaders. The challenges have been grouped into four important and related categories: environmental, structural, interpersonal, and cultural.

Environmental Challenges

Institutional legitimacy and continued financial support may depend on the extent to which colleges and universities are accountable and responsive to their environments. Institutions have developed elaborate assessment systems to demonstrate the high quality of teaching and learning outcomes. Financial control systems have been put in place to ensure that research grants and state and federal funds are spent appropriately. Institutions also face pressures to meet specific economic and social needs, such as workforce training and developmental education for academically underprepared students. Thus, many institutions have formed partnerships with local businesses and K–12 school systems.

As the external environment has become increasingly complex, the internal operations of colleges and universities have also become correspondingly complicated and sometimes convoluted. New departments, programs, and procedures have been developed to respond to a rapidly changing environment. Continuous expansion of institutions, however, may not be tenable. Most institutions have limited resources and cannot address every environmental need. Expansion, in many instances, can lead to mission drift and excessive diffuseness as well as to financial distress. Hence, institutions are challenged to assess their environments intelligently so that internal structures can be accountable, effective, and efficient. Put simply, this challenge is to determine how an institution of higher education can be responsive without wasting its resources in attempting to become all things to all people.

Structural Challenges

Colleges and universities are highly specialized organizations. The organizational chart is typically differentiated into academic affairs, student affairs, and administration and finance. In large institutions, the academic affairs unit is usually divided into relatively autonomous schools and colleges. Nearly every college, regardless of size, is divided into academic departments or divisions, where faculty members call upon specialized expertise related to their academic disciplines. In community colleges, workforce training is further differentiated from general education divisions.

Specialization enables colleges and universities to aggregate a vast array of skills and talents more efficiently into functional work units. If some people are enabled to specialize in certain tasks, others become free to perform different duties, and the organization can achieve more than would have been possible otherwise. Specialization, however, produces many centrifugal forces in the organization that make coordination of the separated units more difficult. The danger here is that uncoordinated units will lose touch with each other and perhaps drift from the institutional mission. In addition, uncoordinated units may develop similar or overlapping programs, leading to redundancy and inefficiency. Or they may develop programs that work at cross-purposes, thus diminishing institutional effectiveness. The challenge of structure, then, is to design efficient clusters of like-minded professionals, then to find ways to develop coordination mechanisms across these clusters that integrate the outputs of the separated groups but do not impinge upon the work of the highly trained specialists. In other words, how can leaders create viable specialized units that ensure that the work advances the overall institutional mission? Or, as Bolman and Deal (2003) ask, how do you hold an organization together without holding it back?

Interpersonal Challenges

Higher education institutions are more than organizational charts and role descriptions. They are webs of human interaction. They enable people to meet personal needs for achievement, satisfaction, and autonomy while at the same time achieving organizational goals.

One of the keys to organizational success is maintaining high levels of motivation, commitment, and trust among members. Thus, a central challenge for leaders is to understand the informal, interpersonal side of organizational life and to support essential prerequisites that faculty and staff members perceive as incentives for their work. Leaders must address the needs of a wide variety of workers at different levels of skill and maturity and with diverse roles and responsibilities.

Cultural Challenges

The rituals and symbols of a college, when widely held, give it a sense of coherence and unity that is important to both organizational members and the outside publics they serve. Various events and structures generate and propagate organizational culture. New student orientation, residence hall programming, athletic events, and graduation ceremonies, for example, may create a distinctive culture that attracts students to the institution and retains them after they enroll. Similarly, faculty may be attracted to an institution based on its values and academic traditions. Further, institutional ties to a religious denomination or the espousal of a mission directed toward access for traditionally underrepresented groups can unite a faculty around a set of core values and beliefs.

Organizational culture can provide a sense of stability, consistency, and direction during times of stress or crisis, as the "wagons" circle around common values and orientations. In many instances, however, the dominant culture of a college can excessively homogenize the educational experience in such a way that it represses differences, stifles innovation, and breeds an insular and defensive posture. The challenge in this case is to create a common organizational identity and a supportive culture, yet one that is open enough to encourage expression of an optimum level of differences in beliefs and values.

In sum, colleges and universities as organizations face formidable key challenges that compete for leader and follower attention (see summary in Table 1.1) and that must be addressed for high-quality performance to result.

Objectives of the Book

Helping readers understand the complexity of higher education institutions in light of the organizational challenges noted above is the primary objective

TABLE 1.1
Organizational Challenges

- **Environmental:** how to be accountable without becoming too diffuse

- **Structural:** how to coordinate the work of highly specialized experts

- **Interpersonal:** how to address the needs of organizational members who have a wide variety of skills, abilities, and interests

- **Cultural:** how to build an organizational identity that still enables expressions of difference

of this book. To accomplish this purpose, it is necessary to try to make sense of the complexity without oversimplifying important relationships among the parts. Social science and its theories are tools for making sense out of complex organizational phenomena, and it is these mechanisms that are used here. We use a range of theories from the very broad and general that provide orienting frameworks, to "middle range" theory, to narrowly specialized theory that explains quite specific phenomena. The theories are drawn largely from different social science fields, but especially from **organizational theory**—an applied discipline used by scholars to understand work organizations, including for-profit corporations, nonprofit associations, government agencies, and educational institutions (both for-profit and nonprofit).

In addition to promoting a general understanding of organizational theory, the book has several other important objectives. First, it is intended to equip graduate students in higher education and practicing administrators with a repertoire of well-tested, accepted theories that can be applied to the organizational challenges that they are currently experiencing or will experience. Second, it is meant to provide practice in the skills of organizational analysis and diagnosis of organizational problems. Third, it introduces researchers and graduate students to a range of contemporary theories that can be used in research about higher education organizations.

There is currently a considerable amount of confusion, disagreement, conflict, overlap, and inconsistency in the field of organizational theory. That is part of what makes it exciting for both beginning and advanced scholars. There is also relatively little agreement about what is basic or essential to know. Hence, the material in this book constitutes a considered selection of old and new theories that we believe are especially relevant to higher education issues. It is not, however, an exhaustive survey of the field of organizational theory, and readers are invited to explore other potentially fruitful avenues.

Theory

Many people, especially busy administrators, express some doubt about the practical utility of theory. As Hoy and Miskel (2005, p. 2) noted, "[T]o many individuals, including educational administrators, facts and theories are antonyms; that is, facts are real and their meanings self-evident, and theories are speculations or dreams."

Theories may seem abstract and removed from our concrete day-to-day experience, but that is partly what makes them useful. Consider, for example, the problem of encouraging faculty members to participate more fully in the assessment of key student learning outcomes. One way to approach the problem is to search for solutions that have worked well in other institutions. What was effective in one organization, however, may be a poor fit for the circumstances of another institution. What worked well at Harvard University may not be as successful at the Community College of Denver and vice versa. When we attempt to generalize a solution from one institution to another, we often encounter problems of fit. The degree to which another institution's solution to a problem precisely fits our own organization's needs is unlikely to be optimal.

Does this mean that we can learn nothing from the experience of others? Certainly not. Instead of searching for concrete solutions, we can attempt to discover organizational principles related to the problem of interest that apply across many different contexts. Theory helps leaders become aware of and sensitive to what is useful and important, and then place the important ideas into a framework that can be used to understand, predict, and allow effective and timely intervention.

As another example, consider the problem of low staff morale and diminished job satisfaction. Suppose that an administrator chose to duplicate a reward system that was successful at her previous institution—for example, double compensatory time off for extra effort during heavy workload periods. At her new institution, however, because workload was spread out fairly evenly, such a program was a poor match with staff needs. The generalization of a concrete solution at one institution to another would not be successful here.

An alternative approach is to use a theoretical perspective to understand the underlying problem of low morale. Researchers have produced theories that identify a range of organizational concepts that have been found to be related to morale; for example, autonomy, collegial communication, and opportunities for professional development. These abstract concepts can be generalized from one institution to another, because they are removed from the specific, concrete context of particular organizations. The administrator can use these concepts to examine morale problems in her institution. She may study whether restricted autonomy, poor communication, limited professional development opportunities, or some combination of the three is affecting morale. After coming to a theoretical understanding of the problem in her institution, she is better equipped to address the problem with an institutional reward system that meets the human needs of the staff at her new organization.

Can Theory Be Taught, and Is It Useful?

A great deal of research has been conducted on organizations. Hence, we now know quite a bit about how organizations work. The theories in this book have been built on the findings from that research. There is some question, however, about whether those theories should be taught at all. Why should not administrators just "fumble" through, until they become accustomed to the "ropes"? After all, each situation may very well be unique in circumstances, people, and financial conditions, among other factors. It is said, for example, that administrators are never faced with exactly the same problem twice.

Some scholars and leaders argue very strongly for this position—that is, wisdom and habit are adequate guidelines for action. Rules of thumb in this view are in essence intuitive heuristics that have been shown to work. When administrators have acquired skills over time that enable them to understand situations and to deal with people in organizations, they will have become adequately trained, especially when these skills are combined with innate leadership ability—or so the argument goes.

On the other hand, organizational theorists argue, as all educators do, that there ought to be a way to avoid having to learn "by the seat of your pants," making unnecessary mistakes along the way. The alternative is to use theory. Basically, the argument is that while some problems are unique and require unique solutions, it is more often the case that they only *appear* that way to those involved. Indeed, both problems and solutions, and the circumstances that surround them, usually fall into patterns or categories that persist or recur frequently. Organizational theorists, through research, have identified many of the factors that are involved in organizational problem solving and decision making, and they have formally categorized or classified them. Sometimes this classification constitutes a comprehensive theory that does not require people to add special case contingencies. Other times, the theoretical categories are tentative and broad—in which case they are more helpful as heuristics; that is, as introductions to potential new ways of thinking about organizations that may or may not be applicable in a particular situation.

In sum, while higher education administration is, or at least should be, an experimental, trial-and-error process, some patterns and routines are repetitive and common to almost all organizations and people who work in them. This book presents a fairly large number of empirically verified relationships among phenomena that can be used as tools for analysis of commonly occurring problems that arise in administration.

The above is not to suggest that there is nothing new to be experienced in organizations. Indeed, new technologies and changes in social and economic conditions force managers and leaders to deal with unique situations quite frequently. Suffice it to say that, if administrators can gain understanding and control over the routine, then they will have more time and creative energy to deal with the unusual.

Definition of Theory

A theory is "a set of well-developed concepts related through statements of relationship, which together constitute an integrated framework that can be used to explain or predict phenomena" (Strauss & Corbin, 1998, p. 15). Each component of this definition requires some explanation.

Theories Consist of Concepts

A concept is an interpretation or image of a particular phenomenon such as a process, event, or object (Knezevich, 1984). Concepts are generated from observations and experiences. That is, as we look at a group of behaviors in an organization and ask, "What is going on," we can abstract from the particulars of a given situation and give it a name—however tentatively. The name of the concept thus represents the observed phenomenon. For example, *autonomy* is a concept that represents self-determination of behavior, and *job satisfaction* is a concept that represents an emotional orientation toward one's work roles within an organization.

Concepts are derived largely from systematic, scientific observation. We observe people and groups of people in action and formulate ways to talk about their actions.

Concepts are developed in two ways. The first derives from the habit of having it frequently associated with the phenomena under observation. We can call this an **inductive** method of establishing meaning. In other words, if we see a great deal of a particular activity in an organization, and we call it X and keep calling it X, soon observers will understand that X refers to the phenomena at hand. The second method of establishing meaning is by relating it to other known concepts. Hence, we can say that when someone is "aggressive," it means something like "abusive" or "hostile" or "ambitious" or "active."

That is, we define the concept by using other concepts that have phenomenological referents—that is, they refer to other phenomena. We call this a **deductive** method of determining meaning. Thus, theories are composed of concepts whose meaning is established either inductively or deductively.

Concepts Are Made Useful Through Statements of Relationships Among Them

Theories use two or more concepts that are related in a specific way. The stated connection establishes a probable value or condition of one concept given the value or condition of the other concept. For example, regarding job satisfaction, theory may state that opportunities for professional development are positively associated with satisfaction. As professional development opportunities increase (that is, take on a higher value), job satisfaction also tends to increase (also taking on a greater value). The relationships between concepts are usually not called a theory until they have been scientifically tested and verified over time.

It is important to remember that conceptual relationships do not necessarily imply causality. To assert that a high value of one concept "causes" a different value in another concept requires a rigorous research validation that most theories do not undergo. Practitioners who use theories, therefore, must be cautious in claiming causality. Other extenuating and/or unexamined conditions could be responsible for what appears to be a causal relationship. Nevertheless, relationships among concepts that are set in a theory tell the user that there are consistent interactions between and among organizational phenomena that the user would be wise to consider in developing policy and in taking administrative or leadership action.

Organizational Theory

Organizational theory is an eclectic field, drawing on many other fields, mostly in the basic social sciences such as psychology, sociology, and economics. Ultimately, organizational theory is intended to be useful. Theories can be used to identify patterns, engage in reflection, think systemically, analyze problems, and take action effectively.

Identification of Patterns

Theories provide categories for sorting and organizing experience. People can use theory to identify patterns and connections in organizational life. Once a pattern has been identified, people can assign a name to the problem or issue that they are facing.

The classification or categorization of phenomena allows organizational members to deal with them more efficiently. Rather than seeing a multiplicity of organizational inputs as unique each time they are encountered, people can deal with them as categories of problems, events, and practical solutions that have been shown consistently through research to have occurred together in the past with sufficient frequency to be ruled out as unique or chance occurrences. So, from a practical standpoint, it becomes possible to say, "Here is another of the *X* phenomenon coming along. We've seen that before."

Identifying and naming a problem can also be empowering. People come to realize that they are not alone in facing the problem; other leaders and organizations have experienced similar dilemmas. Once a pattern has been identified, leaders can convey a coherent vision of the problem to relevant constituencies. In other words, through the use of a theoretical perspective, leaders can help others "see" the problem, too.

Reflective Practice

Practitioners gain some distance from a problem when they use theory to analyze the situation. The problem becomes less personalized when people attempt to understand it through a theoretical framework. They are less likely to blame the problem on people or personalities, or to believe that problems are caused by external forces over which they have no control. Ultimately, using theories to analyze problems is more constructive than blaming people or merely accepting that one's fate is determined by forces beyond one's control.

Systemic Thinking

A theoretical approach helps leaders see beyond their functional roles and positions and begin to take note of relationships across the organization and between the organization and its environment. Leslie and Fretwell (1996, p. 30) suggest that many higher education administrators "do not see the convergence of many unrelated trends and factors until they have reason to. [Instead] they focus on their specific jobs and responsibilities within the institution." Knowledge of organizational theory helps administrators transcend these narrow perspectives. The outcome of gaining theoretical knowledge is not just doing the same job better; it involves seeing the organization *as a whole* in a different light.

Tools for Analysis

When theory becomes a working tool of the practicing administrator, it contributes importantly to improved decision making. Theory helps leaders transcend the "one best way" approach by showing that the same problem can be viewed in many different ways. Knowing multiple theories helps leaders understand how their organizations work (or don't) and how to diagnose organizational problems. A theoretical approach provides leaders with greater maneuverability and a broader range of choices when confronted with difficult situations. In contrast, without a solid base of theoretical knowledge, leaders are often forced into reactive responses, relying on intuition and guesswork.

It is inappropriate, however, to expect theory to reveal what *should* be done. There is a difference between description and prescription. Each person acts on certain value premises that tell him or her which theories to choose and if and how to act when using a particular theory. The theory may predict which outcomes are most likely, but those outcomes may not be valued or desired. For example, a theory may suggest how to make an organization more efficient, but it may be at the expense of faculty, staff, or students.

Organizational theory will reduce the number of action options that leaders will want to try, but there will still be options. Some theories simply will not work in all circumstances. Sometimes different theories will suggest contradictory actions. In this book, a substantial number of theories are provided. If one does not work in practice—because there are hidden contingencies not accounted for—perhaps another will.

Three Perspectives on Organizational Theory

Three patterns of theorizing—also known as paradigms—have emerged in social science: positivism, social constructionism, and postmodernism. Each of these paradigms has influenced organizational theory, research, and leadership practice. We consider each of these below briefly and at greater length in chapter 3.

The Positivist Perspective

The positivist paradigm suggests that there is an objective organizational reality independent of the observer's perspective that can be discovered through observation, analysis, and verification by others. In this view, mind and body, psychological state, and the real world are different and separable. Through careful observation, valid and meaningful conclusions about that outside world can be drawn. Valid explanation about "external" reality— that is, explanation that accurately captures that reality—allows inferences to be made about cause-and-effect relationships, and permits the prediction of future organizational occurrences. Thus, the purpose of positivist research is threefold:

1. *To explain* scientifically the phenomenon of interest—for example, individual or group behavior, beliefs, and attitudes. Positivists attempt to explore the possible explanations of various outcomes such as organizational performance or job satisfaction. The ability to isolate the potential or probable cause of a particular outcome enables organizational leaders to explain why certain outcomes prevail and others don't. A positivist explanation may suggest, for example, that after a department switched to team-based decision making, its performance improved. Or, after budget cuts were implemented, job satisfaction declined.

2. *To predict* what is likely to follow from observations in order to anticipate problems and issues. Positivist research permits us to place a statistical probability on the likelihood of our predictions being accurate over a given number of times that the theory is applied. From a positivist perspective, theories are sets of principles that seem to predict or account for events with a level of accuracy better than chance. Such possibilities for prediction, needless to say, are of enormous value to leaders in planning. If we know that certain decision-making structures such as teams are likely to improve performance, then we can predict that when teamwork is implemented appropriately, performance is likely to be enhanced. Similarly, if we know that salary and work conditions are the key to job satisfaction, then organizational leaders can take concrete steps to improve organizational morale.

3. *To control or intervene,* by designing policies and practices, again based on observations, that may lead to changes in individual and organizational behavior. If future events can, indeed, be predicted, then organizational leaders can have an impact on the future by controlling what seem to be random events. Once leaders can predict the likely outcomes of alternative courses of action, they can select options that lead to enhanced individual and organizational performance. As Nadler and Tushman (1997) explained:

> In many senses, the task of the manager is to influence behavior in a desired direction, usually toward the accomplishment of a specific task or performance goal. Given this definition of the managerial role, skills in the diagnosis of patterns of organizational behavior become vital. Specifically, the manager needs to be able to understand the patterns of behavior that are observed, to predict in what direction behavior will

move (particularly in light of managerial action), and to use this knowledge to control behavior over the course of time. (p. 85)

The Social Construction Perspective

While the positivist approach suggests that organizational phenomena are "objective," exist independent of human cognition, and are the same for different individuals, the social construction approach, in contrast, suggests that the organizational world is a human creation achieved individually and in groups (Berger & Luckmann, 1966; Weick, 1969, 1995). Organizational reality is created and recreated every day through interpersonal interactions.

The social constructionist perspective suggests that perceptual frames or "mental maps" shape how we think about organizations and how we enact the reality in which we live (Bolman & Deal, 2003; Senge, 1990). Each organizational member has a frame of reference that consists of his or her set of values, concepts, and ideas. These perceptual frames affect what we take note of, what we ignore, and how we interpret what we experience. Some elements of the different frames of reference overlap across individuals, but many do not (Bormann, 1996). Organizational members, therefore, will construct and interpret reality in a variety of ways. Hence, leaders can expect to encounter resistance to directives that reflect only the perspectives of top management or only the traditional way of "doing business." The social constructionist perspective thus acts as a caution to those using positivist approaches by forcing recognition that positivist thinkers' so-called "objective" reality may not be shared by all members of the organization.

The Postmodern Perspective

The postmodern paradigm extends beyond the social constructionist critique of the objective knowledge claims of positivism. In addition to rejecting positivist assumptions about an objective reality, postmodernism calls into question a vast array of concepts that have been considered foundational to modern life, including science, progress, and rationality. Postmodern theorists suggest that human experience is fragmented. Knowledge is produced in so many bits and pieces that it cannot be aggregated into a unitary understanding of human experience that can be generalized across different contexts. Accurate prediction of the future from presumed understandings of the past and present is not possible under the assumptions of postmodernism.

Postmodernists, therefore, do not use theory to predict or control behavior. Instead, postmodern theorists try to identify alienation, apathy, and cynicism in organizations, especially when the source of these conditions is an asymmetry in power and power use. Postmodern perspectives can help leaders identify conditions of oppression in organizations, challenge underlying assumptions, and reconstruct the organization based on values of openness, participation, and empowerment in a context of nonhierarchical leadership (Hirschhorn, 1997).

We should note here that it is not necessarily the case that those who take positivist approaches to organizational design and leadership are evil and malicious. Indeed, it is entirely possible to design organizations with hierarchical patterns of control and authority that are open and participative and that preserve the dignity of the individual. In later chapters, we examine the challenges of developing such an organization in an academic setting.

Applying the Three Perspectives

Consider, for example, a liberal arts college that is experiencing enrollment decline. From a *positivist* perspective, organizational leaders could use theory to develop the most accurate explanation of the problem—their view of the most accurate representation of reality. They would conduct an analysis of the college, its environment, and the views of organizational members to determine the factors that most likely contributed to enrollment decline. Once these factors were identified, organizational leaders would seek to manipulate (control) those factors in ways that could reverse the enrollment trend. It should be noted that "control" is used here in the sense that the variables identified as contributing to the decline could be manipulated—not that leaders would unilaterally force members to conform to their particular view. The positivist perspective is theoretically neutral in its underlying epistemological assumptions. Those assumptions, however, can be distorted by inept or unethical administrators to advance their own perspectives.

The *social constructionist* perspective suggests that organizations are characterized by multiple interpretations of reality. These multiple interpretations are revealed in the language that people use to discuss the problem. To gain a better understanding of the problem, therefore, college leaders could provide venues for dialogue. They would attempt to understand the various ways that people interpret the enrollment problem. Leaders could engage in dialogue with a range of constituency groups until a consensus interpretation of the problem is constructed and a common course of action is agreed upon. Alternatively, leaders could allow people to hold multiple (even conflicting) interpretations and engage simultaneously in a broad range of different strategies to address the problem.

From a *postmodern* perspective, leaders could deconstruct organizational assumptions about enrollment and access. Postmodern writings would lead people to question how rigid, systemic structures and their underlying cultures may cause some students to be disadvantaged by existing recruitment strategies, admissions policies, curricular foci, and pedagogical approaches (Bensimon, 2004). This may lead to further analysis regarding whether the college provides educational venues for the academic success of students from diverse backgrounds. New strategies and policies can then be constructed to address institutionalized practices that tend to oppress certain groups of students.

As is probably evident, understanding and applying organizational theory is not easy. Since readers at this point may not yet have had much formal exposure to organizational theories, the procedures may appear daunting. As readers gain experience with theory and its use, however, comprehension and application will become progressively easier.

Summary

Colleges and universities have become increasingly complex since they have expanded their roles in modern society. These complexities derive from (1) the interactions of institutions with the varying demands of their external environments; (2) the increased structural differentiation and specialization of functions of academic and nonacademic departments; (3) the variations in expectations and human needs of workers in and clients of the institution; and (4) the variations in norms and values within an institution.

This chapter introduced the nature of theory and its utility in unraveling the above complexities. Theories consist of concepts that have an abstract relationship to the phenomena they are meant to explain. Two or more concepts that consistently have been found to be related to one another in the same way as the phenomena they explain may comprise a theory.

Theories help administrators identify patterns, understand problems, think systemically, and intervene in organizational actions in a timely way. There are three prominent perspectives—or paradigms—on organizational theory. The positivist perspective suggests that theories can explain organizational phenomena that are assumed to exist independent of the observer. The social construction perspective argues that people—individually and jointly—construct frames of reference to interpret organizational reality. Sometimes people share a common or similar frame of reference, but many times they do not. Organizations consist, therefore, of multiple constructions of reality, and it may not be necessary for all participants to agree on any one interpretation. The postmodern perspective argues that theories used to explain organizational phenomena have historically tended to come from the point of view of managers who frequently are not sensitive to the needs of organizational members who are not in positions of authority or power.

Some readers may find the technical jargon associated with each perspective more or less irrelevant to the "real world." On the other hand, those who are engaged in organizational research and analysis or who plan to be should find this material of considerable use. It is also especially valuable in interpreting publications where research and theory are used to explicate organizational phenomena. Practitioners, too, should find the clarification of concepts used to explain organizational phenomena of considerable value not only in organizational analysis, but also in explaining to colleagues complex ideas to be used in policy analysis and planning.

References

Bensimon, E. (2004). The diversity scorecard: A learning approach to institutional change. *Change, 36*(1), 45–52.

Berger, P., & Luckmann, T. (1966). *The social construction of reality.* Garden City, NJ: Doubleday.

Bolman, L., & Deal, T. (2003). *Reframing organizations: Artistry, choice, and leadership* (3rd ed.). San Francisco: Jossey-Bass.

Bormann, E. (1996). Symbolic convergence theory and communication in group decision making. In R. Hirokawa & M. Poole (Eds.), *Communication and group decision making* (2nd ed., pp. 81–113). Thousand Oaks, CA: Sage.

Educational attainment of the U.S. population by racial and ethnic group. (2005, August 26). *Chronicle of Higher Education, 52*(1), 25.

Hirschhorn, L. (1997). *Reworking authority: Leading and following in a postmodern organization.* Cambridge, MA: MIT Press.

Hoy, W., & Miskel, C. (2005). *Educational administration: Theory, research, and practice* (7th ed.). New York: McGraw-Hill.

Knezevich, S. J. (1984). *Administration of public education* (4th ed.). New York: Harper & Row.

Leslie, D., & Fretwell, E. (1996). *Wise moves in hard times: Creating and managing resilient colleges and universities.* San Francisco: Jossey-Bass.

Nadler, D. A., & Tushman, M. L. (1997). A general diagnostic model for organizational behavior: Applying a congruence perspective. In J. R. Hackman, E. E. Lawler III, & L. W. Porter (Eds.), *Perspectives on behavior in organizations* (2nd ed., pp. 112–124). New York: McGraw-Hill.

Senge, P. (1990). *The fifth discipline: The art and practice of the learning organization.* New York: Currency, Doubleday.

Strauss, A., & Corbin, J. (1998). *Basics of qualitative research: Grounded theory procedures and techniques* (2nd ed.). Thousand Oaks, CA: Sage.

Weick, K. (1969). *The social psychology of organizing* (1st ed.). Reading, MA: Addison-Wesley.

Weick, K. (1995). *Sensemaking in organizations.* Thousand Oaks, CA: Sage.

2

COLLEGES AND UNIVERSITIES AS COMPLEX ORGANIZATIONS

CONTENTS

Preview

- Colleges and universities in the United States constitutionally fall under the jurisdiction of the governments of each of the 50 states. Public institutions receive some proportion of their funding directly from the state government, and are obligated to comply with state statutes on issues ranging from setting tuition levels to demonstrating accountability on performance benchmarks.
- College presidents have complex roles that include working with trustees to set the general direction and strategy of the institution, meeting with external constituents to shape the public image of the institution, and leading an administrative staff of vice presidents and other senior-level administrators for day-to-day policy making.
- Faculty members are organized into academic departments, which are led by department chairs. Academic departments are often grouped into different divisions, schools, or colleges (e.g., the Division of Allied Health, Medical School, College of Arts and Sciences).
- A system of shared governance on many campuses provides opportunities for faculty members to become directly involved in decision making and policy development, especially in areas related to their teaching, research, and service roles.
- Faculty members in tenure-eligible positions undergo a multilevel review during their sixth year of initial employment. The results of this review determine whether the faculty member receives tenure. If tenure is granted, then the faculty member is guaranteed academic freedom and lifetime employment at the institution. If tenure is denied, then the faculty member is not reappointed, and he or she must seek work elsewhere.

Introduction

This chapter is for readers who may not be familiar with the basic structure, functions, typical operations, and common issues that arise in colleges and universities in the United States. The chapter is not theoretical and is intended to provide background material for the remaining chapters. Readers interested in more extensive overviews of the field should refer to Bess and Webster (1999), Birnbaum (1988), and McGee (1971).

The primary characteristics of the U.S. system of higher education are described in the following sections. In particular, the discussion includes the organization and administration of colleges and universities, including the roles and responsibilities of each of the major officers of administration and of the faculty. Also included is a discussion of the nature of the faculty career. To illustrate a common decision-making procedure, tenure decisions for faculty are explored, showing in particular which officers and decision-making bodies are involved and at what times. The chapter concludes with a discussion of the value of tenure as contrasted with an alternative system of limited term, renewable contracts.

Roles and Functions of Colleges and Universities

Higher education in the United States is extremely diverse. There are more than 4,300 institutions of higher education (Carnegie Foundation, 2006). These institutions can be differentiated from one another in a number of ways, such as institutional goals, clients served, control (public versus private), and funding. For example, community colleges, which have two-year curricular programs, most commonly aim at vocational preparation of students as well as general education to improve academic skills of incoming students and/or to prepare students for transfer to the four-year sector for baccalaureate degree opportunities. These colleges are predominantly publicly controlled, partly by the state and partly by local communities. Approximately 37% of a community college's budget is derived from state appropriations; local appropriations account for an additional 17% of revenues, and tuition and fees account for slightly less than 20% of community college revenues ("Finances of Colleges and Universities," 2004). The remaining revenue streams are associated primarily with federal and state grants.

A contrasting kind of institution is a research university, which seeks to provide an education for undergraduate students that is somewhat broader in curricular scope and for graduate students at advanced levels. Research universities also seek to produce new knowledge through both basic and applied scholarship. Funding for private research universities comes from student tuition and an accumulated surplus of funds, called an endowment. Public research universities, in contrast, derive a proportion of their revenues from state government appropriations. The national average is approximately 31% for public four-year institutions ("Finances of Colleges and Universities," 2004). This proportion has been declining over the past several years. When state governments decrease their funding for higher education, public institutions often raise tuition levels to make up the difference. Public institutions are also becoming more dependent on endowment revenue, as the proportion of state support continues to decline. Additional sources of funds for both private and public universities come from the federal government, foundations, and corporations.

College and University National Organization

Colleges and universities in the United States constitutionally fall under the jurisdiction of the governments of each of the 50 states. Public and private institutions of higher education differ somewhat in their operating policies. State-governed institutions tend to be more bureaucratic, with more rules and regulations. Policy decisions are made at the state level and are carried out by state agencies in consultation with the institutional administrative personnel (not usually with the faculty) of the state institutions. Broad policies such as tuition rates and hiring procedures are often set by state legislatures or state boards of higher education, but campus presidents, trustees, and administrators may have discretion in how they implement state policies, and some policy-making domains are actually reverting away from the states and back to the campuses, a decentralization trend (McLendon, 2003).

Faculty members have little or no contact with the state officials who develop and execute institutional policy. However, they do retain significant authority for curriculum decisions, personnel actions (faculty hiring and promotion), and departmental decision making.

Faculty personnel policies include the following: (1) terms of employment; (2) salaries and fringe benefits; and (3) roles and responsibilities. Terms of employment refer to the periods of time that faculty may be employed. For example, new, beginning faculty are usually offered a six-year contract. At the end of that period, a decision is made about whether that person will be awarded tenure; that is, the opportunity for lifetime employment at that institution. If the decision is negative, the person must look for a position at another institution. If the decision is positive, the person continues to be employed by the tenure-awarding institution. Increasingly of late, many institutions are offering long-term, renewable contracts instead of tenure, and are relying more extensively on adjunct faculty appointments. In fact, more than half of all new faculty members are hired into positions that are not eligible for tenure (Schuster, 2003).

Before discussing the faculty role and career at length, however, we first consider the organizational structure of a typical college or university. It is only in the context of the organization that we can understand the progression of career stages and the processes that are required to take place before the faculty member can advance from one stage to another.

Internal Organization of Colleges and Universities

As noted above, colleges and universities have several distinguishing characteristics. They can be differentiated on the basis of their public or private status; their role as universities, four-year colleges, or community colleges; and their size and age. For example, a large, private research university is organized and governed differently from a public community college. In the former case, the faculty have substantial input into faculty personnel policy, while in the latter, partly because of the funding sources, there are more diverse influences on the development of policy.

There is variety, however, even within the different institutional classifications. Each institution is unique. Each has a history, which determines the traditions that partially guide policy. Public higher education, for example, did not become prominent in the United States until the 1950s, and these somewhat newer institutions are much more subject to standardization and bureaucratization than are the older private universities and colleges.

Because public and private differences are important, it is necessary to describe each separately, though there are many parallels. Public institutions in each state are chartered by the legislatures of each state. Since a portion of the funding comes from the state treasury, each institution must prepare an annual budget and submit it to the part of the government that has responsibility for higher education.

Nearly half of the states have a **coordinating board** for public higher education. Coordinating boards, which have policy-making authority for all sectors of public higher education (universities, comprehensive colleges, and community colleges), can present a unified voice for public higher education. They also seek to reduce budgetary competition among institutions and between the two-year and four-year sectors. The governor of the state typically appoints coordinating board members.

Half of the states do not have coordinating boards. Instead, these states have **governing boards**—often called Boards of Regents—that focus on *only one sector* of the higher education system. For example, a state may have a Board of Regents that governs its universities, while another board may have authority for the state's community colleges. In many states, community colleges are governed by the same board that administers K–12 education.

Statewide governing boards seek to ensure responsible use of public resources. They aim to prevent redundancy within a particular sector of higher education. For example, in the area of curriculum, a governing board may dictate that for the next ten years, there will be no expansion in the number of medical schools that can be established in the state. Or, they may say that there will be an evaluation of the fiscal and educational viability of each Ph.D. program in every university to ensure that the state's money is not being spent for duplicative services. Similarly, the governing board for the state's community colleges may not allow an institution to establish a branch campus in an area already being served by another community college.

The governing board—or board of regents—also has primary responsibility for the selection of the chief executive officers of all institutions within a particular sector. Often they recruit the CEO through specially formed subcommittees. Board members have final approval over all proposed presidential appointments.

Statewide governing boards also ensure that institutions meet established standards for quality. They may require institutions to report on a range of performance indicators, such as student retention, degree completion rates, and faculty productivity. The governor typically appoints the members of state-wide governing boards.

Coordinating boards and state-wide governing boards operate at the "macro" level. They establish policies that affect all public institutions (coordinating boards) or policies that affect entire sectors of public higher education (statewide governing boards). Individual public colleges and universities often have their own **board of trustees**, which is responsible for policy at the "micro" level; in other words, boards of trustees set policies that apply to particular institutions. The campus board is responsible for assuring the fiscal stability of the institution. Board members work with the campus president to assess institutional performance and develop strategic plans to advance the institution's mission.

Turning to the typical internal organization of a public institution, roles in the administrative sector of colleges and universities are arranged in order of hierarchical authority. Figure 2.1 represents an organization chart for a large state university. The chart for a private university is not too different, except that instead of a coordinating board or statewide governing board, the central governing body is the board of trustees.

The Role of the President

College and university presidents have as a primary role securing a firm financial future for their institutions. Usually, they turn over the responsibilities for day-to-day policy making in administrative and academic areas to executive vice presidents. Presidents work closely with the board of trustees, which may meet four to eight times a year. The board itself may have many subcommittees paralleling the committees of the faculty and the officers of the administration. Each of these subcommittees attempts to oversee the domain under its jurisdiction without becoming so intimately involved in daily activities that it interferes with the roles played by the faculty and administrators.

The president may devote most of the working day to external affairs—to talking with alumni, potential financial contributors, state legislators, local community leaders, parents, and other constituencies concerned

FIGURE 2.1
Typical Organization Chart for a Large State University

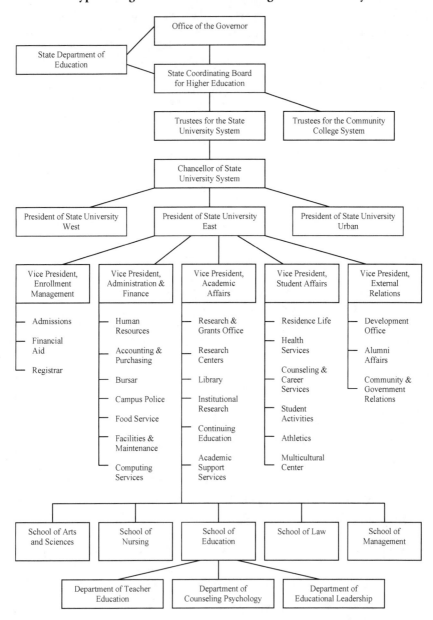

with the performance of the institution. The president tries to clarify to the public the image of the institution—what it stands for philosophically and pragmatically—so that those outside can predict with reasonable certainty what the institution can be counted on to produce. Of course, the clarity of the institutional image also makes it possible for internal members of the college or university—employees and students—to identify with institutional goals and to take pride in the institution's achievements.

Role of the Executive Vice President

The executive vice president, sometimes called a "provost," is usually in charge of the internal affairs of the institution. He or she must assemble and direct the administrative staff of the institution. Although the president may be the titular leader of the various decision-making groups (e.g., the faculty council, the senate, and the executive staff), it is the Executive Vice President who is most responsible in practice. The planning, coordinating, and reviewing of the activities of each of the executive staff officers is part of the role of the executive vice president.

Roles of the Administrative Staff Officers

The roles of the other staff officers are fairly obvious from the functions indicated in their job titles; however, not every institution provides the same title for the same role. Some administrative offices, for example, are almost always led by a vice president. Most institutions designate the chief academic officer as a vice president for academic affairs. The same may be true for the chief student affairs officer and the chief financial officer. Other functions may or may not have the vice presidential designation. A large research institution may have a vice president for research, but a smaller institution may call that position the director of research. The vice presidential designation means that the officer reports directly to the president, although director-level officers may have the opportunity to meet frequently with the president on issues that pertain to their jurisdiction. In this section, we discuss some of the more common administrative offices.

The vice president for student affairs is an important position in colleges and universities. He or she is responsible for the provision of student services that attend to both basic needs (e.g., cafeterias, student residences) and opportunities for learning outside the formal classroom setting. The vice president for student affairs usually has a large staff to cover the many areas in which students are involved.

A related officer in most institutions is the vice president for enrollment management, who is, in essence, the institution's marketing manager. This vice president addresses the needs of the institution for maintaining or increasing enrollments. This job is quite complex. Staff in this office must calculate the number of students to be offered admission to obtain the desired total enrollment for the institution, given expected returning student and transfer student enrollments. They must also design and offer sufficient financial aid packages to remain competitive with other institutions, yet not discount the tuition so significantly as to affect the institution's financial health negatively.

The vice president for administration and finance is also charged with responsibilities related to financial well being. This vice president organizes and supervises the institution's budget. Those who manage the institution's investment portfolio—buying and selling stocks and bonds and overseeing the real estate holdings—also report to this vice president. Other administrative areas under his or her jurisdiction may include safety and security, personnel management, payroll, facilities and maintenance, purchasing, and other services that are provided to members of the institution.

If an institution has a strong research function, then those activities may be under the supervision of a vice president for research. This person establishes close relations with state and federal governments, which provide funds for research purposes. Preparing grant proposals now involves an enormous amount of paperwork and may necessitate hiring people who have special expertise in the technical requirements for submitting proposals. This vice president may also be in charge of the research institutes and centers on a campus, with the directors of each institute reporting directly to him or her.

The vice president for development is the chief administrator for managing external relations. He or she organizes an office that maintains close communication with the institution's alumni and organizes fund-raising drives to solicit gifts to the institution. Institutional publications that are sent outside of campus may also be reviewed by this officer.

Some institutions have a vice president for planning who analyzes data, often from the university's office of institutional research, which collects data of many kinds for internal use and external reporting. Assessment has become important in U.S. colleges and universities, and the office of institutional research or other special offices collect demographic, cognitive achievement, and affective growth data on students when they arrive and when they leave the institution.

Finally we turn to the vice president for academic affairs. This person is the chief academic officer in the institution, responsible for all matters having to do with the faculty and curriculum (Bess, 2002). Of course, students are not neglected, since their engagement with the curriculum and the faculty is the focus of the teaching function of the college or university.

All of the deans who lead schools and colleges in the institution (with the general exception of medical and dental schools) report to the vice president for academic affairs. Each school or college is focused on a curricular or knowledge-based theme or vocational objective such as education, engineering, social work, and law, among many others. The deans are responsible for developing budgets and policies for the school or college. Most schools operate independently of each other or are only loosely connected. Hence, there are often faculty in the different schools who teach similar courses and belong to the same discipline but seldom interact due to the highly differentiated structure of the typical academic organization. An alternative organizational mode, rarely practiced, is for all faculty in the same field to be organized by department, with the departments serving the needs of all of the schools. An applied statistics department, for example, could provide research methods courses for students from a variety of schools. This is called a "matrix" design (see chapter 6). The schools then would offer courses only in their particular specialization.

Within each school, there are many departments, each with a department chair. The definition of the department chair position is ambiguous, and duties and authority vary greatly across different institutions. Some chairs have considerable authority; others have relatively little. Some chairs speak for their faculty members; others speak to their faculty members on behalf of the dean. In other words, sometimes a chair is considered as a member of the administration, sometimes as a member of the faculty. Often he or she is both, and the expectations of the dean and the faculty are at odds from time to time with one another. Department chairs, therefore, frequently experience conflict and stress in their roles (Gmelch, 2004).

Faculty Roles and Faculty Organization

Faculty in colleges and universities are directly involved in organization and administration at all levels through their membership in academic departments and through other faculty and institutional decision-making bodies. In academic departments, faculty engage in decision making about matters of direct concern to their primary common activities—curriculum and teaching—but less often about research, which is more individualized. Decision making about research is conducted by individual faculty members or in voluntary collaborations, which are more common in the scientific fields. The mode of decision making by faculty is almost invariably by consensus.

Faculty also serve on departmental committees and on school- and institution-wide committees that address a wide variety of educational concerns, including curriculum, grading standards, and personnel issues. In larger institutions, a faculty council or senate (variously named at different colleges and universities) is the representative body for the discussion of matters of cross-departmental or cross-school concern to faculty in the institution. Faculty representatives from the departments are elected by their peers, and faculty representatives at-large may be chosen by the entire faculty as well. This body generates a number of committees that are concerned with the various domains of faculty jurisdiction.

The extent of faculty involvement in institutional decision making tends to vary among institutional types. Community college leadership, for example, has traditionally been viewed as more authoritarian and "top-down" than has leadership in other sectors, and faculty participation in governing and changing these institutions may be limited (Kezar, 1998; Thaxter & Graham, 1999). Significant pressures for accountability to external entities may explain the tendency toward centralized decision making in this sector.

We should also note that faculty participation in governance is especially complex on unionized campuses, due to collective bargaining agreements and formal grievance procedures. The decision-making bodies of the various unions engage in bilateral negotiations with the administration on issues of wages and working conditions. Where faculty are unionized, areas of union jurisdiction may overlap or intersect with the responsibilities of a formal faculty organizational unit, such as a faculty senate. Thus, on unionized campuses, faculty have two entities that represent their interests—the union and the faculty senate. These two entities are challenged to find ways to work together to advance faculty interests. For illustrative purposes, the next two sections take up two types of decisions that are critical in any organization—budgets and personnel.

Budget Making in Academic Institutions

Now that we have laid out the organizational structure of the typical college or university, we can consider how budgets are established. The process is different in public and private institutions. In the former, there is quite a long "lead time"—the time required by the state to review the college or university's budget submissions. The process is not unusual to budget making in general, although there are interesting variations in institutions throughout the United States. Some states ask institutions to justify all budget items; others require an overall rationale for continuing the old budget (adding cost-of-living increments) plus a justification for new items only.

Budget preparation begins at the departmental level. Proposals by department chairs are reviewed by deans. The deans then submit their budget proposals to the academic vice president who, after a review, submits it to the president, who then asks for approval from the board of regents or trustees. Throughout this process, committees and persons with interests in the results are consulted so that their concerns can be represented. As with any budget-making process, there are differences of opinion. The faculty can exercise a significant influence. (For a description of this process, see Schuster, Smith, Corak, & Yamada, 1994, pp. 49–63.) Formal, final authority over the budget, however, ultimately resides with the administrators and trustees, not the faculty or students.

Personnel Decisions

Decisions about whom to employ and whom to promote are among the most important decisions made in all organizations, especially colleges and universities, which are so heavily labor intensive. These decisions directly affect the quality of the enterprise, because if the wrong person is chosen, then that person may not fit into the overall cultural practices of the institution, school, or department. He or she may not produce at the levels expected. In either case, there will be resentment and lower levels of cooperation among colleagues. Since the personnel decision may involve lifetime employment (say, 40 years), the institution's investment (in terms of today's dollar) can be more than $3,000,000. Accordingly, many individuals and decision-making bodies are involved in the final decision.

The academic career ladder in the United States is quite simple. There are only three faculty ranks—assistant professor, associate professor, and full professor. There has been some research on what influences the decision to become a college teacher, but the data are still tentative and inconclusive. It is likely that successful undergraduate students pursuing their bachelor's degrees are rewarded with high grades and high praise by the faculty. They are encouraged to go on to graduate school because they have demonstrated interest and competence in the subject matter area.

Most college and university graduates do not attend graduate school at the same institution where they pursued their undergraduate degrees, and most do not take positions as faculty members at the institutions where they earned their doctorates. In fact, many institutions prohibit hiring faculty directly from their own graduate schools, preferring that the graduates gain some experience at other institutions first. They can then be recruited and hired after they have had the benefit of experience elsewhere.

Recruitment of students to graduate school is a function of the individual academic departments. In general, they look for candidates who display the promise of successful research careers. It is rare that graduate students are selected because they are likely to be good teachers. For those who plan careers in institutions of higher education, the perception is that significant professional satisfaction is more likely to be forthcoming from noteworthy research productivity. Good teachers, in contrast, rarely become "famous," certainly not outside of their own institutions, while good researchers do. The high productivity and visibility of excellent researchers eventually brings credit to the faculty in the department, school, and institution that recruited the student and then educated him or her. Hence, potential research productivity, not potential teaching excellence, is given higher priority in recruitment and selection decisions.

After receiving their degrees (or shortly before), graduating students seek employment as assistant professors. The positions for which they apply are available as six-year contracts, after which their achievements are reviewed, and a decision is made about whether they should be employed by the institution for the rest of their working lives. The six-year probationary period can be extremely stressful, as there is enormous competition for a declining number of full-time, tenured positions in U.S. higher education. Indeed, now more than 45% of all U.S. faculty are employed in part-time positions, and more than 50% of all new full-time faculty are appointed to positions for which tenure is not a possibility (Schuster & Finkelstein, 2006). College and university administrations are not openly averse to hiring part-time and nontenure-eligible, full-time faculty, since these faculty may not be eligible for fringe benefits such as medical insurance, life insurance, and sabbatical leaves, among others. They also receive far lower salaries than do full-time, tenured faculty, and they need not be continued in their employment if the demand for their services declines.

While allegedly advantageous for the hiring institution, the rising number of part-time faculty can have several negative consequences. In the first place, because of limited rewards, part-time employment may seriously discourage faculty from pursuing their careers. Part-time faculty may have to teach at three or four different institutions just to earn enough to survive. Because they are so busy preparing for class and commuting to different campuses, these faculty have little time for the research and publication that might provide them with the credentials to be appointed full time.

The higher education institutions also suffer. Part-time faculty typically have no voting rights in the organizational decision-making structure. They may seldom attend faculty meetings and participate infrequently in decisions about important faculty or institutional matters. Partly as a result, they may not be fully committed to promoting the interests of the institution. Their involvement in the life of the institution—for example, advising students or participating in institutional events and ceremonies—is limited.

Appointment as Assistant Professor

The procedure by which initial appointments to the assistant professor position are made involves a number of members of the organization. First, of course, the position itself must be available, because a faculty member has retired, has moved to another job, or it has been determined that the department needs to expand to permit the addition of another faculty member. In most cases, since budget factors are involved, the department chair and the dean must request permission for another "faculty line" in the budget—an additional allocation for salary and fringe benefits. These increments in departmental size are usually cleared through the office of the academic vice president.

During the probationary six-year period, assistant professors are often reviewed annually or at least biannually. A report may be written, called "progress toward tenure," that performs two functions. First, it gives important information to the candidate on the degree to which his or her current efforts are likely to result in tenure and on the changes perceived by the current faculty and administration as necessary to achieve tenure. Second, it protects the institution from later accusations (if not legal redress) that it failed to convey its expectations adequately.

At the end of the fifth year, the candidate must prepare an application for tenure. The application provides evidence of achievements to date, including publications, publications in process, evaluations of teaching by students, peer evaluations of contributions to the department, and any other credentials that may add to the likelihood of achieving tenure.

Evaluation of the candidate takes place during his or her sixth year of employment. To perform the evaluation of the candidate, a committee is formed within the department. Or, if the department is large, a standing committee undertakes the review. The department chair usually selects the members of the review committee, though sometimes the faculty elect the members, and sometimes both faculty and chair have equal rights of selection. The committee meets in closed session and reviews all of the papers prepared by the candidate. At the end of the sixth year, the candidate is notified whether tenure is granted. According to informally accepted traditions in the academic world, if a faculty member is denied tenure, he or she is granted one additional year of employment, during which time the faculty member can seek employment elsewhere. Thus, faculty members receive one year's notice of intention of nonreappointment.

If the committee recommends tenure, a separate decision is usually made with respect to promotion. Almost invariably, the decision to award tenure is accompanied by a decision to promote the candidate to the associate professor rank. An increase in salary is also typical. But the process does not end with the decision of the departmental faculty committee. The faculty committee makes its recommendation to the chair of the department *and* to the Promotion and Tenure Committee of the school. Each school usually has a standing committee (an ongoing, rather than an ad hoc, committee) to review tenure and promotion recommendations from the separate departments. This school-wide review body functions to prevent weak departments from perpetuating their weakness. It also ensures uniformity of quality across the different departments in the school.

Thus, the paperwork and the recommendation of the department's personnel committee are reviewed simultaneously—in the administrative structure (by the chairperson) and in the faculty structure (by the school-wide faculty committee). The chair makes an independent judgment and forwards the paperwork to the dean. The school-wide committee also makes its judgment and informs the dean. Thus, the dean has separate input from several independent sources—the chairperson and two faculty committees. The dean then makes a recommendation and sends it simultaneously to the vice president for academic affairs and in some cases to an institution-wide faculty personnel committee. The role of the latter is similar to the school-wide committee in that it ensures that the quality of all of the schools is relatively uniform. The institution-wide personnel committee makes its recommendation to the vice president for academic affairs, who renders his or her judgment and forwards it to the executive vice president or provost and then on to the president. Again a judgment is made. The president's recommendation is sent to the board of regents or board of trustees, where the final decision is made.

It is unusual for a president to reverse the decisions of the prior reviewing committees and/or the academic vice president. If a negative decision is made, it will come primarily at the school level, when the dean determines either that the candidate is unqualified or that the economic circumstances in the particular department or school do not justify appointment of another tenured professor. It is also extremely rare, though not without precedent, for a board of trustees or regents to overturn the recommendation of the president.

Promotion to Full Professor

A similar review is performed for faculty members who are being considered for promotion from associate to full professor. In this case, the faculty member initiates the request when he or she feels that there has been sufficient achievement to warrant promotion. That is, there is no fixed time after which all associate professors must apply for full professorship. In fact, some faculty members remain at the associate professor level for their entire careers. As with the assistant professor promotion procedure, the paperwork moves through the various committees and administrative offices until a final decision is made by the board of regents or board of trustees.

The Criteria for Tenure and Promotion

For both tenure and promotion decisions, the same general evaluation criteria are used. These include aspects of teaching, research, and service to the institution, to professional associations, and to civic communities.

Candidates for tenure and promotion must collect evidence of their success in teaching. At most colleges and universities, at the end of each semester in every course, evaluation data are collected from students. Sometimes the data collection activity is organized by the administration, sometimes by faculty. Which one depends on the type of institution. Community colleges may be dominated by administrative oversight, while the process in research universities is often controlled by the faculty.

Student data in the form of evaluation questionnaires are submitted by candidates for tenure and promotion. Often a summary of the evaluations is offered. Data on teaching effectiveness tend to be more important in institutions where teaching is the primary activity and less so in institutions where research is more important. In the latter instance, satisfactory teaching—that is, neither extraordinarily good nor bad—may be sufficient in the promotion decision, since research and publication are often deemed more important. In institutions where teaching is more important, a poor research publication record may be ignored, while a moderate or good publication record may offset some deficiencies in teaching ability.

The data on teaching effectiveness are collected in both undergraduate and graduate classes. In addition, candidates submit evidence of their productivity in working with master's and doctoral students, particularly as it relates to supervising theses and dissertations. Candidates may also be observed in the classroom by tenure and promotion committee members to gain a firsthand understanding of their teaching performance.

Candidates for tenure and promotion must also gather evidence of their research and publication productivity. This paperwork includes published books, book chapters, and journal articles, as well as papers presented at annual professional meetings, and other evidence of scholarly activity. If it can be determined that the sponsor of the publication (book publisher or journal) is highly reputed and relies on professional, peer review processes to determine acceptability for publication, the candidate provides evidence of this as well. In other words, when the candidate can prove not only that he or she has published material, but that the quality of the publisher is high, the publications count for more in the eyes of the personnel committees and others reviewing the candidate's credentials.

Finally, the candidate presents evidence of service, which may include work on national professional organizations, work on college or university committees, or work in the local community on civic projects. While it might seem that this last activity is not relevant to the candidate's qualifications for promotion, in point of fact, most institutions of higher education like to have their faculty visible in the local community, since it brings credit to the institution.

In almost all U.S. institutions, tenured faculty members are permitted to take sabbatical leaves every seven years. Faculty members present plans for the sabbatical to faculty peer committees and to the administration. The plans include the faculty member's intentions to improve his or her competencies and/or to engage in work that is in accordance with institutional objectives. Thus, some faculty do research either to improve their teaching or to produce new knowledge. The work may be performed at their home institution, but faculty often go to another institution. Faculty are paid only a portion of their salary during the sabbatical, and most faculty supplement that remuneration with other work.

In general, faculty members typically are paid for the nine-month, two-semester work period, but distribution of salary is prorated across 12 months. The sabbatical and summer months provide opportunities for faculty to depart from routine activities. These departures may encourage development of new skills and better morale, and offer opportunities for supplementary income. Institutional salaries paid during the sabbatical are usually reduced by 25–50%.

Tenure and Academic Freedom

The establishment of tenure in the United States did not become an important movement until the early part of the 20th century. It arose as a result of the efforts of owners of private colleges and universities to impose their ideological perspectives on the activities and public expressions of the faculty. When the faculty refused to succumb to the particular philosophic or conceptual perspective of the "owner," the faculty were summarily dismissed.

In 1915, the American Association of University Professors (AAUP) was formed to help protect academic freedom by securing the employment of U.S. college faculty. A set of policy statements was prepared (now published annually—see AAUP, 2005) that outlined the conditions under which faculty members could be fired from their positions. First, if a faculty member engages in immoral activity, especially with students, then the institution has a right to dismiss him or her. Second, evidence of gross incompetence is also a cause for dismissal, though proof of such incompetence is difficult to ascertain. Moreover, faculty are reluctant to expose such incompetence lest it be revealed that they, too, lack the skills they claim are lacking in a colleague.

A third cause for dismissal comes not because of personal behavior, but because of external circumstances. If the institution can demonstrate that continuation of the faculty member in his or her position will cause critical damage to the budget of the institution, then the faculty member can be dismissed. However, faculty members usually are deemed to have tenure in the larger college or university as a whole, not the specific department or school. So, if a department is closed, the institution may be obligated to try to find a position in another part of the college or university. This is often difficult, since the dismissed faculty member's qualifications may not match the requirements of other departments.

Sometimes administrations use the excuse of financial exigency to try to remove poorly performing faculty or whole departments. Since the process is long and elaborate, administrations usually must be very certain of their positions, or faculty members may seek through legal means to retain their positions.

The original reason for instituting a tenure system, then, was to prevent administrators (actually private owners of the institution) from interfering in the academic work of the faculty. The argument for tenure was that it permitted freedom of speech or academic freedom. That is, it allowed a faculty member to be completely free to express ideas that may be initially seen as ideologically or conceptually deviant. Such a feeling of protection from outside interference encouraged faculty members to explore new ways of thinking rather than simply to pursue old ideas. Since one of the functions of the modern college or university is to pursue the new knowledge, it is believed that academic freedom must be in place. And to ensure that academic freedom is both a strong value and a legally protected quality, tenure is necessary. That is, through the mechanism of lifetime employment, tenure guarantees that academic freedom is permitted and that personal expression of belief will not be cause for dismissal.

But there is a latent psychological benefit to tenure as well. People may desire the assurance of continuity that comes with job security. The feeling of security that permanent employment conveys satisfies a basic human need. When job security is in question, creativity may not be as forthcoming.

Student Participation in Decision Making

Another decision-making body is the student government, which is composed entirely of students who are elected by their peers. Again, a set of committees is usually mandated. Some, but not all, of the committees parallel the concerns of faculty. While the faculty senate can be a potent political force on the campus, most student government bodies are primarily care-taker institutions that are not usually held in high regard by the majority of students. This situation changes, however, when critical issues affecting students require decisions. For example, during the Vietnam War, student councils became extremely important conduits between the college or university administration and the student body.

Summary

The organization of higher education in the United States differs dramatically from that of most profit-making corporations. Perhaps most important of the differences is the separation of the roles of academic and administrative personnel and the sharing of authority and responsibility. Colleges and universities are both bureaucracies and political entities rendering efficient decision making difficult and time consuming. Recent concerns of the general public about the apparent lack of efficiency of colleges and universities—and the rising costs associated with it—for the most part do not take into account the complications of decision making in these kinds of institutions.

References

American Association of University Professors (AAUP). (2005). *Policy documents and reports* (17th ed.). Washington, DC: Author.

Bess, J. L. (2002). Academic administration. In J. Forest & K. Kinser (Eds.), *Higher education in the United States: An encyclopedia*. Washington, DC: ABC-CLIO Publishers.

Bess, J. L., & Webster, D. (1999). *Foundations of American higher education* (2nd ed.). Needham, MA: Simon & Schuster Custom Publishers.

Birnbaum, R. (1988). *How colleges work, The cybernetics of academic organization and leadership*. San Francisco: Jossey-Bass.

Carnegie Foundation. (2006). *Classification descriptions*. Retrieved July 1, 2006, from www.carnegiefoundation.org

Finances of colleges and universities. (2004, August 27). *Chronicle of Higher Education, 52*(1), 25.

Gmelch, W. (2004). The department chair's balancing act. *New Directions for Higher Education, 126*, 69–84. San Francisco: Jossey-Bass.

Kezar, A. (1998). Exploring new avenues for leading community colleges: The paradox of participatory models. *Community College Review, 25*(4), 75–88.

McGee, R. (1971). *Academic Janus*. San Francisco: Jossey-Bass.

McLendon, M. (2003). Setting the governmental agenda for state decentralization of higher education. *Journal of Higher Education, 74*(5), 479–515.

Schuster, J. (2003). The faculty makeover: What does it mean for students? *New Directions for Higher Education, 123*, 15–22. San Francisco: Jossey-Bass.

Schuster, J., & Finkelstein, M. (2006). *The American faculty: The restructuring of academic work and careers.* Baltimore, MD: Johns Hopkins University Press.

Schuster, J., Smith, D., Corak, K., & Yamada, M. (1994). *Strategic governance: How to make big decisions better.* Washington, DC: Oryx Press.

Thaxter, L., & Graham, S. (1999). Community college faculty involvement in decision making. *Community College Journal of Research and Practice, 23*(7), 655–674.

3

APPROACHES TO ORGANIZATIONAL ANALYSIS: THREE PARADIGMS

CONTENTS

The authors are most grateful for the critical comments on an early draft of this chapter by Pamela Eddy, Central Michigan University. The final version, of course, is our own and may or may not reflect the perspective of the reviewer.

Preview

- To understand the complexity of higher education institutions, it is necessary to consider organizations from the perspective of multiple paradigms.
- Paradigms are sets of assumptions, practices, and agreements that guide a research community.
- This chapter examines three of the most common and powerful paradigms in social science today: positivist, social constructionist, and postmodern.
- **Positivism** is a philosophic belief in the existence of an objective reality independent of the observer's perspective. Through careful observation, conclusions about reality can be drawn and shared meaningfully with those of other observers.
- Positivist researchers seek to identify independent variables that predict or explain outcomes for a dependent variable of interest to organizational leaders and policy makers.
- Systems theory and contingency theory are examples of positivist theorizing.
- The **social construction paradigm** draws attention to how beliefs about organizational phenomena are "constructed" through interpersonal interaction and human cognition.
- The social construction perspective suggests that organizations consist of multiple constructions of reality.
- The theory of social construction suggests that people are not (or need not be) passive recipients of organizational and environmental constraints. Instead people are (or can be) active agents who produce the context in which they live and work.
- **Postmodernism** has been conceptualized as a historical era, an intellectual and philosophic perspective, and a critique of social values.
- As a historical era, postmodernism reflects massive changes in society and culture, especially trends that indicate an increasing disconnect among diverse elements.
- Philosophically, postmodernism casts doubt on the traditional reliance of social systems and individuals on science, rationality, and the possibility of planned change and progress.
- As an intellectual perspective, postmodernism also frequently takes value positions on social inequities and seeks to deconstruct the latent abuses of hierarchies in organizations. It looks deeply and critically at the relationships between knowledge and power.
- Postmodernism calls for a critical reassessment of institutional priorities and individual philosophic positions on value-based action.

———————————————————— CASE CONTEXT ————————————————————

Challenges for Warren College

Warren College was struggling. This small liberal arts college had been the destination of choice for local families to send their prep-school-educated sons and daughters. But the demographics of the area changed rapidly, beginning in the 1970s. Wealthier families relocated and began sending their college-age children to more prestigious institutions farther away from home. The area became more working class. Older neighborhoods were revitalized, but newcomers to the area, who were more ethnically and racially diverse than their predecessors, felt no connection to Warren College. Instead, they were more likely to enroll in the nearby state college or the community college that had opened recently in one of the working class neighborhoods.

The financial picture for Warren College was bleak. Enrollment had fallen from a high of 1,900 students in 1954 to only 420 students. The institution routinely dipped into its limited endowment for operating expenses, sometimes just to meet payroll. Five years ago, the college launched a continuing education division in a desperate attempt to increase revenue. Many faculty opposed the initiative as a deviation from the traditional liberal arts focus of the college. After significant investments in marketing and technology-enhanced classrooms, the continuing education division flopped. Revenues never exceeded expenses, and the programs were quietly eliminated or folded into other academic departments.

John Kenwood, the college's president, convened a group of senior faculty members to discuss the financial crisis. They gathered in the president's office on a Friday afternoon in December. The early-setting sun cast long shadows across the campus quad; a perfect metaphor for this meeting, the president thought to himself.

"The first thing you need to do is fix the administrative structure of this place," blurted the head of the biology program, even before the others had taken their seats. "Budget decisions are being made without any faculty input. Continuing education was a fiasco. We have no strategic plan to speak of, and we have been coasting for far too long."

The biology professor, who saw himself as a tell-it-like-it-is kind of guy, pointed to the president. "You've been here for three years, and I can't say that things have improved much. We need a systematic assessment of the whole college, top to bottom. Find out what's not working. Make it better or get rid of it."

"There's been too much talk and not enough action," continued the biology professor. "The culture of this place is dysfunctional."

"Well, it's not so dysfunctional that the senior faculty can't have an honest conversation with the president," joked a senior professor of history. "We've been giving him hell for the last ten minutes."

The history professor had been at the institution longer than anyone else in the room, and she was well respected across campus for her keen insight and sharp sense of humor. After some laughter, the history professor continued. "Actually, I disagree that there's been too much talk. We've really been talking around the problem for the past several years, complaining about our situation and arguing with each other. That's not the kind of talk we need. Instead, we need a conversation about our mission. Who are we as an institution? What do we do, and why do we do it? What are our values, and how are they revealed in our teaching and curriculum? Right now, we're all over the place; we're not communicating about ourselves in a very clear way. Why would a student want to come here if we aren't clear about who we are?"

"Well, we did have that committee to update the mission statement," replied President Kenwood.

"That's not what I mean," responded the history professor. "That whole process was top-down and driven by marketing. What I'm talking about is a college-wide conversation about values and how we see ourselves in the world."

"We don't have time for that nonsense," retorted the biology professor. "The ship is already sinking."

"But if we aren't clear about our mission and values," responded the history professor, "then what you propose to do is just rearrange the deck chairs on the *Titanic*. Whichever way you reorganize the college, it's still going down."

The open conflict created an awkward silence that the political science professor, a well-known community organizer and activist, was all too happy to fill. "I have a real skepticism about this call for conversation. How many of us will really engage in a conversation about our basic assumptions? How many of us will really attempt to see our position in the world? I believe that is a conversation few of us have the appetite for, because it's likely to reveal how irrelevant we are in an age of rampant capitalism and consumerism. I mean, really, how many students come to us because they have a love of liberal learning? They go to college to get ahead in life, and that means financially ahead. Where does that leave a traditional liberal arts college? It leaves us struggling and foundering. Corporate interests and consumerism drive our society, and we are left in the margins."

"Are you suggesting that the situation is hopeless?" asked President Kenwood.

"No, it isn't hopeless, but we need to confront and challenge the dominant paradigm," responded the political scientist. "Otherwise we either go
out of business or become just another corporate training center."

Introduction

This chapter is intended to introduce three significant paradigms that
have emerged in social science research: positivist, social constructionist, and postmodern. Each of these paradigms has influenced organizational theory, research, and leadership practice. All three vary
importantly in philosophic assumptions, beliefs about human capacities and
prototypical behavior, motivation, and purpose of life (both in and out of
organizations). And their differences are important in understanding changes
in higher education—those that have occurred, those in which we are currently immersed, and those that comprise the possibilities for the future.

We have chosen to offer these three paradigms as complementary approaches to understanding college and university organization. Our intent is
to provide the reader with an understanding of the paradigms as well as the
tools for using them constructively in practice. Each paradigm has much to
offer those who study and lead higher education organizations, especially in
light of rapid changes in both the external environments of colleges and universities and the organizational designs of the institutions that have changed
to address those environments. Colleges and universities are in the process of
undergoing a paradigm shift (Lincoln, 1985) that reflects significant changes
in society. We now have many different ways of observing and understanding
how organizations operate, especially colleges and universities, which are different from our usual interpretations of behavior in traditional bureaucracies.

The application of different paradigms in organizational analysis is a skill
that requires considerable practice. Hence, first attempts may be difficult,
while later efforts may proceed more easily. (The reader who wishes a more
concrete and technical understanding of problem diagnosis and analysis for
practical use in administrative problem solving should refer to the appendix.)

Paradigms Defined

A **paradigm** consists of the assumptions, practices, and agreements that
guide a scholarly community (Lewis & Grimes, 1999). As Burrell (1996)
notes, paradigms "are the words (and sometimes even the concepts) that we
use to describe how we approach and confront our subject matter" (p. 643).
Paradigms reflect world views—ways of looking at and interpreting our
worlds. They are shaped by sets of beliefs (Lincoln, 1985).

Paradigms reflect different forms of practitioner knowledge and may account for differences in organizational members' behaviors and approaches to leadership (Argyris & Schön, 1992; Schön, 1983). The preference of an administrator for a particular paradigm, though usually not a conscious choice or prominent concern, may provide an important, almost ineluctable path to the ways that decisions are made. An organizational member who, consciously or unconsciously, adopts one or another of the paradigms is likely to make quite different policy decisions and to take different actions in meeting perceived organizational needs. Leaders who favor bureaucratic forms of decision making, for example, are guided by paradigmatic assumptions that differ substantially from those of leaders who seek collaboration and promote team-based approaches to solving organizational problems.

For the researcher, paradigms are inherent in the discipline being followed. They are very likely to guide choices regarding research topics, theoretical perspectives, and methodological approaches (e.g., quantitative versus qualitative). Thus, to understand the complex nature of college and university organization and its practices, scholars and practitioners need to be well versed in the multiplicity of approaches to organizational analysis, leadership assumptions, theories, and frameworks associated with multiple paradigms.

Approaches to Paradigmatic Use

Thomas Kuhn (1922–1996), an influential philosopher of science, is often recognized as the first scholar to conceptualize paradigm differences. Kuhn's ideas challenged the prevailing understandings of scientific practices. According to the tenets of scientific method, researchers were assumed to stand on the proverbial shoulders of giants in their field of study and extend the boundaries of knowledge through incremental additions to previous research findings. In contrast, Kuhn argued that scientific fields experience long periods of stability that are punctuated occasionally by radical, discontinuous shifts in the basic assumptions held by members of that field. When the new assumptions are widely embraced by the members of that field, then the field has experienced a paradigm shift.

Kuhn (1962, 1970) claimed that scientific fields are guided by paradigms that supply "puzzles" for scientists to solve. The paradigms also provide tools—theories, methods—for solving those puzzles. The process of scientific puzzle solving is analogous to doing crossword puzzles. The puzzle is viewed as potentially solvable, solving the puzzle largely depends on the skills of the puzzle solver, and the methods for solving the puzzle are well known.

Occasionally, however, scientists encounter a puzzle that cannot be solved through the methods of the current paradigm. This type of puzzle, called an **anomaly**, generates a crisis in confidence regarding the current paradigm. The crisis is followed by a revolutionary period characterized by competition among differing ideas about how to restructure the field of study. Through this competition of ideas, a new paradigm may displace the old, if the scientific community agrees that the new paradigm has greater puzzle-solving power than did the old paradigm. Thus, paradigm shifts occur through a perceived lack of potency of the current paradigm, and through an agreement that an alternative set of assumptions and practices is more likely to solve emerging puzzles in the field. As Hassard and Kelemen (2002) noted, "[T]his process involves sociological consensus as much as scientific experimentation" (p. 335).

Kuhn's historical analysis examined fields in the natural sciences, but social scientists readily embraced his ideas and adapted them to their disciplines. Burrell and Morgan (1979), for example, were among the first to specify paradigm differences in the field of organizational theory. They identified four paradigms that differ in their assumptions about the nature of reality (objective versus subjective) and in their preferences for stability or change (see Table 3.1).

1. The functionalist paradigm is based on an objective view of reality and a preference for regulation and control.
2. The interpretivist paradigm views reality as a set of subjective interpretations and demonstrates a preference for stability.
3. The radical humanist paradigm is based on a subjectivist view of reality and is oriented toward change.
4. Finally, the radical structuralist paradigm conceptualizes an objective reality and prefers change.

TABLE 3.1
Burrell and Morgan's Typology

		Assumptions about reality	
		Objective	Subjective
Ideological orientation	Stability	Functionalist	Interpretivist
	Change	Radical structuralist	Radical humanist

Burrell and Morgan (1979) claimed that these four paradigms are so different from each other that meaningful conversation among them is impossible: "[O]ne cannot operate in more than one paradigm at any given point in time, since in accepting the assumptions of one, we defy the assumptions of all the others" (p. 25). Their argument was consistent with Kuhn's earlier writings. Kuhn argued that theories developed under different paradigms are **incommensurable**—that is, they have no common criteria for adjudicating differences between different perspectives (Scherer & Steinmann, 1999). Differences among paradigms, according to this view, cannot be accommodated through the use of rational logic. Specifically, Kuhn noted three forms of incommensurability:

1. **Methodological incommensurability**: different paradigms use different research methods; therefore, they do not share a common measure upon which comparisons can be made.
2. **Observational incommensurability**: different paradigms cause researchers to "see" different things, even if they are observing the same phenomenon.
3. **Semantic incommensurability**: new paradigms develop new concepts and theoretical languages that adherents to other paradigms may not be able to understand.

Kuhn's ideas about incommensurability have been quite controversial, with some scholars arguing that the boundaries between paradigms are not as rigid as Kuhn suggests. Kuhn's writings focused primarily on physical sciences such as physics and chemistry, which seek to find the best interpretation of relatively unchanging phenomena, such as energy and matter. In contrast, the objects of study in social science—social systems—are themselves constantly changing and open to ongoing reinterpretation. The paradigmatic boundaries in social science are more fluid than they are in physical science. The hard/soft distinction that we often apply to characterizing various scientific disciplines refers, in part, to the boundaries of the paradigms in those fields (Biglan, 1973). Hard sciences have relatively well-formed paradigms with less permeable boundaries, and soft sciences contain more flexible paradigms with relatively open boundaries. As a result, scholarly discourse in the soft sciences tends to be characterized by more conflict than it is in the hard sciences, where consensus and agreement on a single dominant paradigm is more likely (Hearn & Anderson, 2002).

Some researchers, such as Jeffrey Pfeffer (1993), argue that theorists ought to unite around a single, strong paradigm to establish the legitimacy of the field of organizational studies. Similarly, Lex Donaldson (1995) claims that the development of multiple paradigms has fragmented the field and made organizational theory less useful for practitioners.

We are convinced, however, by strong counterarguments that the use of multiple paradigms is well suited for studying multifaceted problems in complex, rapidly changing organizations (Lewis & Grimes, 1999). Whereas earlier, the dominant vision of organizational phenomena was oriented toward the management of large bureaucratic organizations, today observers and organizational theorists recognize that no unified paradigm or conceptual framework satisfactorily represents contemporary explanations of the diversity of extant organizations (Abrahamson, 2002; Eckensberger, 2002). As Gioia and Pitre (1990) argue, the traditional approaches to organizational research "have tended to produce valuable, but nonetheless incomplete, views of organizational knowledge, mainly because they have been predicated predominantly on the tenets of one major paradigm" (p. 584).

Analyses that rely on more than one paradigm enable organizational researchers to explore multifaceted phenomena from the vantage point of multiple theories, and enable organizational leaders to create policies that reflect the underlying complexity of issues (Kezar, Carducci, & Contreras-McGavin, 2006). In contrast, organizational analyses based on a single paradigm may have limited power to explain complex problems that are nested within multiple levels of abstraction. Lewis and Grimes (1999), for example, suggest that multiparadigm analyses may be necessary to unravel the difficulties and complications associated with organizational environments, power, culture, and leadership. Moreover, Martin (1992) argues that "all too often the views of lower-ranking employees, women, and/or minorities have not been sought, deeply understood, or fully incorporated into theories of organization" (p. 5). By using multiple paradigms, researchers and practitioners can be informed by different voices and perspectives, and thus may "see" the organization more easily from multiple vantage points.

In this book, we use a three-paradigm framework to understand college and university organization. Specifically, our framework includes positivist, social constructionist, and postmodern perspectives. In this chapter, we present first an overview of the paradigms, and then a more intensive look at each.

Three Paradigms: An Overview

Positivists

Positivists believe that there is one (and only one) "reality." It exists independent of any one observer's perspective and includes the whole gamut of organizational phenomena. Positivists seek to find and accurately describe that external reality for the benefit of the organization. Once that reality is identi-fied, positivists believe that it is possible and useful to disaggregate its many parts and to understand how the parts relate to each other. For positivists, the relationships among the parts conform to rational, knowable patterns, and the parts relate to each other in much the same way that Newton de-scribed the physical action of one object on another—with predictability. While not all positivists agree with one another about what the reality is, they do agree that it is possible to discover it and to classify the terms used to label its parts. This knowledge base can then be used to plan and organize so that the organization is as efficient and effective as possible.

Social Constructionists

Organizational members who espouse this position deny that there is any *one* reality out there to be discovered. Indeed, since there is no objective reality, it is necessary for members of any working community to construct it on the basis of their own experience and beliefs. In contrast to the positivists, social constructionists seek to reconcile different conceptualizations of "reality" to forge a workable set of beliefs on which organizational action can be based. This more relativistic conceptualization requires much more discussion and communication than does the positivist position. It requires also more flexi-bility and adaptability, since differing positions demand mutual accommo-dation as organizational participants encounter problems and experience different pressures.

Instead of relying on universal principals, as positivists do, social con-structionists seek localized contextual knowledge, which may not necessarily be generalizable to other organizations. Knowledge is created and used in an organization through unique socialization processes that transmit the collec-tive "know-how" of a particular group to newcomers who, in turn, reshape the collective knowledge base of the social system that they entered (Cook & Yanow, 1996). The collective knowledge base of the organization is transmit-ted to new members, but it is changed—perhaps expanded or updated—in the process.

Postmodernists

For members of college and university organizations who take this position, the differing conceptualizations of reality allegedly revealed to social con-structionists are ineluctably irreconcilable. It is not possible, in other words, to negotiate among participants to find a mutually agreeable understanding of reality or to reach a workable compromise on organizational policy or action that would follow from it. Moreover, postmodernists do not take a

Newtonian position—that parts of reality are necessarily related to one another, and that one part is predictable from the other. The future, in fact, cannot be predicted based on observations of the past because future changes will be discontinuous and radically different from previous experience. Change will not reflect a linear extension of previous accomplishments. As Bloland (2005) notes, "[T]he postmodern position can alert us to be skeptical of unexamined claims regarding linear progress, and it directs us to search out and surface the implications and consequences of such claims" (p. 124). A certain amount of uncertainty and chaos are, therefore, inevitable in postmodern organizations, and conflict is viewed as a necessary concomitant of the postmodern position.

Given nonrational and unpredictable elements in postmodern organizations, higher education institutions are largely inscrutable and not capable of being organized rationally (Bloland, 2005). The inability to plan rationally, however, does not mean that leadership is irrelevant. Instead, the roles of leadership shift from planning and controlling to empowering organizational members so they can innovate and improvise in the context of chaotic, constantly changing conditions. This form of postmodern leadership is exceptionally challenging, however, because it requires leaders to question standard operating procedures, to take risks with untested ideas, and periodically to challenge the dominant mode of thinking within the organization.

Finally, some postmodernists not only take the position that organizational conflict reflects basic ontological and epistemological differences, but they also believe that some perspectives and the organizational policies and actions that follow from them are unethical. Hence, postmodernists often believe that positivist conclusions about an objective reality, which lead them to structural and personnel decisions, are likely to be biased by personal preferences, which favor those in power.

Paradigm Use in Higher Education

The positivist paradigm represents many of the frameworks that researchers have used to study college and university governance, leadership, and decision making (Baldridge, 1971; Bess, 1988; Keller, 1983). The positivist paradigm also guides many of the practitioner-oriented publications that seek to provide specific recommendations for college and university leaders (Balderston, 1995; Fisher & Koch, 1996; Marchese, 1997; Schuster, Smith, Corak, & Yamada, 1994). The social constructionist paradigm reflects some of the new and emerging frameworks for understanding higher education organizations, including cultural and symbolic frameworks for understanding and enacting leadership (Bergquist, 1992; Birnbaum, 1992; Kezar & Eckel, 2002). Social constructionist assumptions have also led to practices that emphasize collaborative, team-based approaches to leadership and change (Bensimon & Neumann, 1993; Kezar, 2002). Finally, the postmodern perspective captures the essence of many critiques of higher education and provides frameworks for radically restructuring colleges and universities (Bloland, 1995, 2005; Tierney, 1992).

Many observers of higher education believe that to understand colleges and universities from the perspective of multiple levels and roles (faculty, staff, administration) and across multiple sectors (two-year and four-year; public, private, and for-profit), researchers and practitioners need to frame their work around multiple paradigms (Kezar & Dee, 2006). Researchers and practitioners need to analyze organizational problems from positivist, social constructionist, and postmodern lenses to understand the complexity, diversity, and richness of organizational life in colleges and universities. As Gareth Morgan (1986) notes, "[A]ny realistic approach to organizational analysis must start from the premise that organizations can be many things at one and the same time" (p. 321). Positivism, social constructionism, and postmodernism each illuminate different dimensions of organizational life, and when considered together, the three paradigms present a more comprehensive picture of the organization. We view the three-paradigm framework, therefore, as a useful heuristic device to organize the vast array of perspectives used in the study of college and university organization.

It should be noted that the predominant position of most administrators and faculty in colleges and universities is positivist. They believe that it is possible to come to agreement about the "truth" of what is happening to and in their institutions, and to formulate rational plans to make the organization efficient and effective and, indeed, more humanistic in its treatment of workers. For most of this book, consequently, we attempt to portray how higher education is perceived and conceived by both researchers and practitioners—how they put their positivist positions to work. However, because the social constructionist and postmodern positions have received much attention and appear to have validity in the eyes of a significant number of thinkers in higher education, we offer observations about where these positions may be leading. The challenge of these alternatives may force a rethinking of the predominant positivist paradigm or may lead to new theoretical developments that strengthen it.

To this point, we have introduced three paradigms for understanding organizations: positivist, social constructionist, and postmodern. Each of the three paradigms has a rich history, and each offers a sophisticated conceptualization of how organizations work. Each carries its own assumptions about organizations and, equally important, its own methods for finding out how they work. Our belief is that all three perspectives can contribute to understanding organizations, especially organizations like colleges and universities, but to be useful, their separate strengths cannot be merged in a murky ad hoc, "let's see what works" approach. A more systematic, integrated approach is necessary. For each of the three paradigms, therefore, we first outline the underlying philosophic premises. This is followed by an exposition of the key terms of the paradigm—their meaning and use. Finally, the techniques for application of the paradigms, including implications for leadership, are discussed.

Our coverage of the positivist paradigm in this chapter is somewhat more limited than what we offer for the other two paradigms. This is because chapter 4 is devoted entirely to systems theory, which applies positivist assumptions toward the understanding of social systems such as organizations.

Positivist Paradigm

Foundations of the Positivist Perspective

Positivism is usually traced to Auguste Comte (1798–1857), though it can be argued that its origins date to the notions of scientific method and observation advanced by Isaac Newton (1642–1727). Comte claimed that we can have verifiable knowledge about events and phenomena that we observe. Indeed, such scientifically ordered knowledge should, Comte insisted, permit the abandonment of philosophic musings, especially metaphysics, which lacks substance and content. The foundations of positivism were elaborated more extensively in the 1930s and 1940s by a group of philosophers known as the Vienna Circle. This group devised a pattern of thinking, called "logical positivism," as a way to build theory through observation. The members of this "school" (there actually was no uniform approach) were particularly attentive to the "meaningfulness" of statements about reality. Their "verification principle" stated that ideas were meaningful only if their truth could logically be tested empirically (Giddens, 1978).

As communications researcher James Anderson (1996) notes, "[P]ositivism depends on valid observation being necessarily true and on the independence of theory and observation . . . If our observations are necessarily true, then we can have positive knowledge of our observations. Given this positive knowledge, theory can be corrected when it contradicts what is known to be observationally true" (p. 106). Positivist researchers, consequently, are especially interested in developing valid measurements that provide accurate ("true") observations of reality.

Emerging from these philosophic positivist perspectives were two unifying, overlapping frameworks that profoundly influenced theories about how organizational behavior and performance could be understood. One is called **systems theory**. (Chapter 4 explores this theory in depth.) Basically, by virtue of the belief in the verifiability of all organizational phenomena, systems theory posits that everything that happens in organizations is linked. It is not possible to act on one part of the organization without affecting all of its other parts.

Systems theory focuses on the relationship between a system (e.g., an organization) and its environment (i.e., everything that is not part of the system). Systems import energy from their environments to forestall progression toward entropy; that is, complete randomness, loss of energy, and eventual death. The system uses imported energy to produce some type of product, which it then exports to the environment in exchange for new energy imports. In systems theory, we can conceive therefore of an organization as an open, adaptive system that exists in an environment, interacts with elements of that environment, and engages in the transformation of inputs into outputs that, in turn, have some effect on the environment (Adams, 1980).

Systems theory conceptualizes the organization-environment relationship as an input/output exchange. William Evan's **organizational set** theory (1972) illustrates the basic input/output model (see Figure 3.1). Evan diagnoses both sides of the system external to the boundary in terms of "sets" of inputs and outputs. The **input set** is the group of organizations that provides resources to the focal organization. In the case of higher education, these include feeder high schools, financial contributors, agencies awarding research grants, and, in the public sector, state legislatures, among other sources. The **output set** consists of all organizations that receive goods and services from the focal organization. For colleges and universities, these include employers of graduates, clients of institutional services, recipients of research findings, and the external community at-large.

FIGURE 3.1
Evan's Organizational Set Theory*

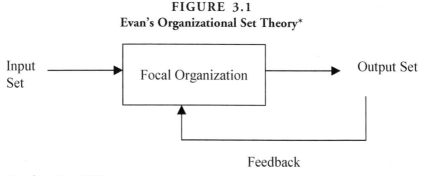

*Based on Evan, 1972.

Following systems theory further, Evan suggests that it is important to examine and use feedback from the recipients of organizational outputs concerning the adequacy and quality of these outputs. The communication of such information is critical to understanding how organizations can better adapt to their environments. Evan's theory suggests that it is critical to understand the dynamics of organization-environment relations not simply as a series of one-to-one connections between the focal organization and environmental components. Rather, the entire network of communications must be taken into account to understand the relation of any one organization to its environment.

Systems theory emerged in the 1930s and 1940s as an attempt to open disciplinary boundaries and create a general theory for explaining biological, social, and cognitive phenomena. By the 1960s, systems theory generated a shift in organizational studies. Theoretical examinations of internal bureaucratic structures (Taylor, 1911; Weber, 1924) and of informal work groups (Mayo, 1945; Roethlisberger & Dickson, 1939) became less salient as the focus on organization-environment interactions gained importance (Katz & Kahn, 1978; Thompson, 1967). Systems theory suggests that external environments partly determine the types of internal structures that organizations develop. These structures, in turn, shape individual and group behaviors (Blau, 1973; Parsons, 1951).

The other positivist orienting theory for this book is called **contingency theory**. Essentially, this approach takes into account a large number of factors that can affect the relationship between two or more aspects of organizations. That is, before it can be determined that one special solution will solve an organizational problem, it is necessary to consider various contingencies that may also affect the relationship between the problem being encountered and its proposed solution (Burns & Stalker, 1961). These contingencies constitute the subtle and sometimes hidden conditions in an organization that are often ignored, yet may make a difference in assessing cause and effect. For example, it is tempting to argue that whenever an employee is not performing "up to standards," it is necessary to "crack down" to make certain that the employee's work improves. But, as is obvious (to some, at any rate), there may be extenuating circumstances that caused the problem, or some idiosyncratic personal attributes may suggest modifications in the proposed solution. For college and university administrators to deal effectively with campus problems requires an awareness of what prior research has shown to be important—that is, the more subtle contingencies to be considered in solving problems of this sort.

But to return to systems theory and contingency theory, some might ask, "so what?" Any good administrator will try to identify all of the elements in a situation and try to anticipate what will happen by virtue of alternative action scenarios. However, here is where theory may be helpful. It permits understanding, prediction, and intervention in organizational affairs in more scientific and sophisticated ways. In other words, since theory evolves through systematic scientific research, its use removes some of the guesswork about what will happen and about what contingencies there are. In the next section, we provide an overview of the processes associated with applying theory from a positivist perspective.

Implications for Leadership Using the Positivist Perspective

The first step in applying theory is to identify a specific problematic situation that the organization needs to address to improve efficiency and/or effectiveness. Problem identification also involves the selection of an appropriate **unit of analysis**, which refers to the level of the system to be analyzed. According to systems theory, a problem at one level of an organization likely affects several other levels. For example, a structural problem such as poor coordination among organizational subunits may lead to conflict over roles and responsibilities between two staff members. It may be necessary, therefore, to analyze organizational problems from the vantage point of multiple system levels (e.g., at the level of individuals, groups, and whole organizations). This multilevel analysis, however, will likely require the application of multiple theories. Different theories apply to different units of analysis; structural theories relate to the organization as a whole, for example, and human relations theories pertain to the interpersonal and group levels of the system. Therefore, even though a particular problem may affect multiple system levels, separate analyses are needed for each level.

After the problem has been identified, the second step is to locate concepts from an organizational theory that describe or reflect the problem. In the example above, lack of structural integration appears to be producing role ambiguity among staff members. In this case, we have stated a hypothesis that reflects a relationship between two variables. Specifically, lower levels of structural integration produce higher levels of role ambiguity. The independent variable (structural integration) predicts outcomes on the dependent variable (role ambiguity)

To test this hypothesis, organizational leaders could manipulate the independent variable to change outcomes on the dependent variable. In this example, the college could implement new cross-functional teams to promote better integration among different units. If the result were fewer conflicts over roles and responsibilities, then the hypothesis would be deemed valid, and the institution would be justified in maintaining the cross-functional structure.

In sum, the underlying assumption of positivist analysis is that organizations are composites of multiple variables that can take on different values or strengths—and that *before* action can be taken, it is necessary to try to account for as many of the contingencies as possible that might affect the object or objects of the action (Van de Ven & Drazin, 1985). Further, it is necessary to anticipate the action and its effects across multiple system levels, including individuals, groups, and whole organizations, as well as beyond the organization's boundary to include potential impact on the external environment. Unfortunately, there are several reasons why a hypothesis may be discovered to be invalid for a particular organizational problem.

- The theory itself is not valid, and alternative theories need to be explored.
- The selected concepts do not actually reflect the problem; other concepts need to be identified to explain the problem.
- The selected concepts may be necessary but insufficient for explaining the problem; more variables need to be considered.
- All of the relevant units of analysis were not considered; the problem needs to be located at either a higher macrolevel (e.g., organization-environment relationships) or a lower microlevel (e.g., a staff member with limited skills).

Even though the positivist process for theory application is complex, it can identify useful ways for organizational leaders to intervene and improve situations for the betterment of the entire organization. For a more extensive discussion of this process, see the appendix.

Alternatives to the Positivist Approach

Positivist research and analysis seek to measure organizational variables accurately and then make decisions based on those measurements. In contrast, some observers of organizations suggest that the organizational context is a human creation that is constructed in a multitude of ways. As such, the emphasis shifts from accurate measurement of variables to developing an understanding of multiple constructions (interpretations) of issues and problems. These ideas reflect some of the basic tenets of the social constructionist perspective, which are taken up in the following section.

The Social Construction Paradigm

From a positivist perspective, reality is waiting to be observed and discovered. With valid and reliable measurement tools, we can assess organizational conditions and make decisions based on objective data. Organizational leaders who use a positivist lens attempt to assess internal and external conditions accurately, and then make changes to work roles and structures to improve the performance of the system. The social construction paradigm, in contrast, suggests that organizational phenomena are created through ongoing communication and negotiation of meaning and purpose. Social constructionists argue that all dimensions of an organization—its external environment, its internal structures, its cultural characteristics (to name but a few examples)—are created through ongoing action, negotiation, and social agreement among organizational members (Giddens, 1984; Weick, 1995).

An important implication of the social constructionist paradigm is that subjective impressions, mental maps, and interpretations are often more powerful than objective data in shaping the overall direction of an organization (Senge, 1990). Higher education researcher Anna Neumann (1995), for example, found that college presidents can inadvertently create perceptions of financial stress even when fiscal conditions are good. One president generated anxiety among faculty and staff even when the college's finances were relatively sound. Conversely, Neumann found that some campus leaders, through their interpretation of the situation, were able to alleviate financial stress even during serious fiscal downturns. Specifically, on one campus, the president constructed an organizational culture with pervasive optimistic values that enabled faculty and staff to transcend financial difficulties. In these cases, the objective financial data were less important than the socially constructed, consensus-driven understandings of the colleges' resources.

Social Constructionist Assumptions

Although there are many historical and philosophical predecessors, German sociologists Peter Berger and Thomas Luckmann (1966) introduced the theory of the social construction of reality in opposition to many of the prevailing assumptions of positivist research. In particular, the social construction paradigm rejects the positivist notions of a dualistic ontology and an objectivist epistemology (Sandberg, 2001).

Dualistic Ontology

Ontology refers to a person's set of beliefs about the nature of reality. Positivist researchers embrace a dualistic ontology in which the subject and object of research are two separate, independent entities. Studies of higher education leadership that are based on a dualistic ontology, for example, treat the leader and the organizational setting as two independent concepts. Researchers try either to identify the leader characteristics and behaviors that produce effective leadership or to focus on situational factors such as the difficulty of the task or the characteristics of those being led.

Social constructionists, however, view subject and object as inseparable. Subject and object are not independent entities. The study of reality, according to social constructionists, cannot be separated from the subject's experience of that reality. Thus, reality is apprehended through the lens of individual experience.

As Sandberg (2001) notes, "[N]ot only is reality mediated through our lived experience, but it is also mediated through the specific culture, historical time, and language in which we are situated" (p. 31). Therefore, social constructionists argue, the study of higher education leadership cannot focus only on leader behaviors or situational factors. The leader and the situation cannot be separated in the analysis. Instead, organizational researchers are challenged to explain how leaders shape the situation, and how the situation also reframes the leader's perspectives and behaviors. The focus shifts, moreover, from the leader to the interactions between leaders and followers (Rost, 1991). We need to understand how both leaders and followers construct leadership, and how these constructions of leadership are mediated by the culture, history, and language of a particular organizational setting (Fairhurst & Sarr, 1996).

When we reject a dualistic ontology, we challenge the idea that reality can be organized into discrete, measurable categories that are subject to common interpretation. Instead, reality is understood through the lived experiences of people in particular historical, cultural, and social contexts. Rather than attempt to isolate variables that are conceptually and empirically independent, the goal of social constructionist research is to develop "thick descriptions" that convey the richness of human experience (Geertz, 1973).

Objectivist Epistemology

Social constructionists also differ from positivists in their epistemological assumptions. Epistemology refers to a person's beliefs about the nature of knowledge. Is knowledge waiting for us to discover it? Or is knowledge produced through complex interactions that involve both the researcher and those being studied? Norwegian methodologist Steinar Kvale (1996) offers interesting metaphors for understanding epistemological differences.

> In the miner metaphor, knowledge is understood as buried metal and the [organizational leader] is a miner who unearths the valuable metal. Some miners seek objective facts to be quantified, others seek nuggets of essential meaning. In both conceptions the knowledge is waiting in the subjects' interior to be uncovered, uncontaminated by the miner. (p. 3)

The alternative traveler metaphor understands the [organizational leader] as a traveler on a journey that leads to a tale to be told upon returning home . . . The traveler explores the many domains of the country, as unknown territory or with maps, roaming freely around the territory . . . What the traveling reporter hears and sees is described qualitatively and is reconstructed as stories to be told . . . the tales are remolded into new narratives, which are convincing in their aesthetic form and are validated through their impact upon the listeners. (p. 4)

The miner metaphor reflects a positivist epistemology. The researcher or practitioner assumes that an objective reality exists beyond human consciousness. Through scientific observation and the development of more accurate measurement tools, we can come closer to the "true" picture of reality. This metaphor applies both to researchers who study organizations and to organizational leaders who attempt to make data-based decisions (i.e., decisions based on objective information, rather than intuition or guesswork).

The traveler metaphor describes a social constructionist epistemology. Knowledge is produced through an interactive process that involves communication, reflection, and the reframing of experience. The goal is not to unearth uncontaminated "truth." Instead, researchers and practitioners seek knowledge through interactions with others. Knowledge production, therefore, is a social process, rather than a solitary endeavor. "Social interactions between individuals, rather than the individual mind, is the primary vehicle for developing knowledge" (Sandberg, 2001, p. 32).

Social constructionists argue that knowledge is produced and reproduced socially through communication. Research knowledge is created through communication among researchers and between researchers and study participants. Practitioner knowledge is produced through communication between long-term employees and new hires. Cultural knowledge is generated through dialogues that occur in families, schools, religious institutions, and political venues, to name but a few examples.

In the social constructionist paradigm, communication is not conceptualized as the one-way transmission of knowledge. Knowledge is not created in the individual mind to be passed along to others (e.g., a faculty member depositing knowledge into students' heads). Instead, knowledge creation is a social process, and all parties in that process have the ability to shape what is created.

The Social Construction of Reality

The social construction of reality depends on some degree of overlap or correspondence regarding how people interpret experiences. If the constructed realities of two people are quite different, then they will find it difficult to understand each other, to learn from each other, and to create knowledge together. Through communication and shared experiences, people begin to develop common constructions of reality. Think of spouses who finish each other's sentences. Their psychological and cognitive worlds overlap so much that they seem to know what the other person is thinking. Communications researcher Ernest Bormann (1996) refers to this process as **symbolic convergence**. The separate cognitive worlds of different individuals begin to overlap or converge. As a result, people begin to construct and reconstruct reality in ways that are more similar than they are different.

This type of convergence occurs at both the macro and micro levels. It occurs across societies, within organizations, and among members of smaller subsystems such as academic departments or student affairs divisions. At the macro level, whole societies can converge around a particular construction of reality. In smaller social systems, such as work organizations, members tend to construct reality in ways that are consistent with the system's culture. Social constructions, therefore, are guided by the norms, values, and beliefs that characterize membership in a particular social system. Socially constructed realities at Vassar College, the University of Texas at Austin, and the Community College of Philadelphia, for example, reflect the cultures of these institutions. Socially constructed realities, in turn, serve as the means through which these norms, values, and beliefs are perpetuated. The cultures of Vassar, Texas, and the Community College of Philadelphia are produced and reproduced through the social construction process.

To illustrate the process of social construction, Sandberg (2001) uses the example of Daylight Saving Time, where entire nations have agreed to move the clock ahead one hour for several months. Clock time is not an objective reality that has a fixed meaning. We can move the clock forward and backward based on a social consensus regarding how to allocate clock time to available daylight. Therefore, Daylight Saving Time represents a particular social construction of clock time. But Daylight Saving Time becomes an objective fact of life for those who live in nations that abide by this construction of clock time. The subjective construction of clock time becomes an objective reality when there is a strong correspondence across a number of socially constructed realities. If we do not abide by this construction of clock time, then we will be out of sync with most of society. As Sandberg notes, "If my subjective construction of clock time deviates considerably from the general construction of clock time, I encounter difficulties in getting by" (p. 38).

The social construction of reality primarily entails ongoing social reproduction of reality, rather than idiosyncratic production of different realities by individuals. If people were persistently to create their own realities, then they would likely be viewed as distant, disconnected, or even abnormal. In the case of Daylight Saving Time, people would persistently be late or early for meetings and other appointments, thus making it difficult to participate in a social system.

Correspondence among multiple constructed realities emerges in part through two forms of socialization: primary and secondary. Through **primary socialization**, we internalize the basic constructions of reality that guide most of our activities and interactions with others. These include constructions of language, family, gender, and race and ethnicity, among others. Through **secondary socialization**, our cognitive worlds begin to converge with other members of the social systems to which we belong, including work organizations. We become conversant, and eventually participate, in the ongoing social construction of reality in a particular organization, such as a college or university. The socialization process often takes many years, given the complexities and intricacies of socially constructed reality. It is not as simple as learning a few rules and fulfilling a job description. Instead, we must internalize the customs and thought patterns of others. Socialization allows us to "internalize the reality in which others already act and live" (Sandberg, 2001, p. 40).

It is important to keep in mind, however, that the level of cognitive overlap across individuals never reaches 100%. Given differences in background and experience, members of a social system never think entirely alike, even after extensive communication and extended periods of socialization. Sandberg (2001) identifies three reasons why social constructions of reality differ:

1. The division of labor in organizations means that people experience the organization in different ways. By virtue of the different tasks and responsibilities they perform, organizational members construct reality differently. For example, even if faculty and administrators agree that the curriculum needs to be revised, their understandings of the problem and their ideas about potential solutions are likely to differ.

2. Social and cultural constructs mediate the ways that people construct reality. Gender, ethnicity, language, socioeconomic status, and sexual orientation are only a few of the many constructs that affect the social construction of reality. Students and faculty from working-class backgrounds, for example, may experience the institution in ways that are quite different from those with middle- and upper-class backgrounds. As a result, their constructions of reality differ. Where

one group interprets the campus climate as receptive, for example, another may find it neutral or hostile.

3. Other personal factors such as geographic location (e.g., urban-rural, West Coast, South), family status (partnered or single), and age may lead to a lower level of correspondence between different socially constructed realities.

These differences ensure that people construct reality in different ways even if they share some of the same experiences. There is some degree of overlap, but there are also substantial differences in how others view the organization and their role in it. In colleges and universities, many of which tend to be decentralized with unconnected academic departments, realities are often constructed according to disciplinary training, making social constructions of a commonly understood reality difficult. Even across the three primary academic fields of study—science, social science, and humanities— social constructions of reality may be attempted, but rather than resulting in a common understanding, the process often leads to a compromise—an agreement to disagree. Therefore, from a social constructionist perspective, there is no "true" picture of reality. As Bolman and Deal (1997, p. 13) note, "Organizations are filled with people who have different interpretations of what is happening and what should be happening . . . No single story is comprehensive enough to make an organization truly understandable and manageable." Some parts of the different stories overlap, but other parts are quite different. The role of researchers and practitioners is not to identify which story is most accurate, but, instead, to attempt to assign meaning to areas of convergence and divergence. Social constructionist researchers, for example, may seek to understand why faculty and administrators on a particular campus share a common understanding of the college's mission. Or they may attempt to uncover why student affairs and academic affairs divisions understand the college's learning goals differently.

Similar implications apply to college leaders. The goal is not to achieve 100% overlap in how people interpret the organization. Such correspondence could lead to "groupthink" and an inability to detect errors in judgment (Janis, 1982; Weick, 1993). Instead, college leaders who use a social constructionist framework attempt to understand a diverse array of interpretations of organizational life. They seek to make sense of patterns and experiences that may appear disparate and disconnected. They seek meaning in experience and communicate a sense of purpose that inspires commitment to both personal and organizational goals.

Higher education researcher Matthew Hartley (2003), for example, studied three struggling liberal arts colleges, each of which was in financial trouble and on the brink of crisis. In each case, college presidents and other campus leaders were able to reinvigorate their institutions through the construction of compelling new images and frameworks that inspired high levels of faculty and staff commitment. These leaders were able to communicate a vision for the future that was also rooted in their institution's heritage. On one campus, the faculty rallied around the college's traditional commitment to civic engagement. The president of another campus inspired commitment to the college's founding principles of social justice and access for women and people of color. These images of the organization were compelling because they connected with faculty and staff members' personal values and commitments. The campus leaders did not attempt to get all faculty and staff to think alike. Instead, they constructed images that resonated with most organizational members. In other words, these leaders found a "thread" that connected the multiple constructions of reality found within their organizations. This theme or thread did not enforce uniform thinking; instead, it allowed individuals to construct their own personal relationship to that vision.

Implications for Applying the Social Constructionist Perspective

The social constructionist perspective suggests that communication is the basic unit of organization; it is the process through which the organization and its environment are created and reproduced over time. This assertion suggests several implications for organizational leadership. First, it suggests that organizations are malleable. "If organizations are social constructions, then we reconstruct them continuously and could, if we were conscious of these processes, change them in the reconstruction process" (Hatch, 1997, p. 42). Organizations, in other words, are not at the mercy of external demands. Leaders can reconstruct their situations based on new concepts and interpretations. Second, it suggests that meaning is negotiated among organizational members, and that all members of an organization play a role in the social construction of organizational reality. It is important to note, however, that critical theorists point out that certain individuals have far greater influence in constructing organizational reality than do others (Deetz, 1992; Mumby, 1988). Finally, given that multiple interpretations of organizational reality are possible, leaders may expect to encounter some degree of conflict, particularly when organizational membership is diverse in its perspectives and ideologies. Thus, leaders need to be able to see a problem through a variety of frames or lenses, and then facilitate collaborative approaches to decision making that do not minimize or marginalize different points of view.

The social constructionist perspective "may help us see and understand more as we research and as we lead, but it does not necessarily make us better people" (Neumann, 1995, p. 27). Campus leaders have the power to construct organizations that are caring, collaborative, and empowering. But, just as easily, they can construct reality in ways that are selfish, controlling, and abusive. Indeed, some theorists postulate that powerful groups and individuals exploit others in the organization, and powerful organizations dominate the less powerful. Critical theorists and some feminist scholars take this position, which considers the moral and ethical implications of socially constructed reality.

Critical Theory

Critical theory interprets the scientific emphases of positivism as having embedded in them a bias of their own—the domination of the rationality of science itself, to the exclusion of values and subjectivity, even when there may be some social justification for it. Thus, organizations, as the embodiment of hyperrationality, may lack moral consciousness.

More specifically, critical theorists suggest that organizations are multilevel constructions that consist of a deep structure, a surface structure, and an ideology that obscures the relationship between the deep structure and the surface structure (Deetz, 1992; Mumby, 1988). **Deep structure** refers to an organization's unexamined values and assumptions that affect how meaning is produced. Deep structure reflects the dominant way of thinking in a particular organization, and people tend to construct reality in ways that are consistent with this established frame of reference. Put simply, we tend to see what we want to see. Certain ways of thinking are endorsed by the social systems to which we belong. These frames of reference affect what we attend to and may account for what we do not notice. Some issues are never raised in an organization, because they are not consistent with the values and assumptions of most organizational members (Bachrach & Baratz, 1962). College leaders, for example, may perceive that their institution does not have a "race problem" because issues of race never surface in campus discussions. However, if silence around race is part of the deep structure of the organization, then racial issues may not be raised. As a result, White administrators, faculty, and students may be completely unaware of the complex racial dynamics of their campuses.

Deep structure gives rise to the surface structure, which includes the language, goals, and structural arrangements of the organization. The **surface structure** is the visible, observable manifestation of a socially constructed reality that was shaped by the deep structure (i.e., by the organization's dominant set of values and assumptions). Pedagogical practices in colleges and universities are examples of surface structure artifacts that reflect a particular deep structure; service learning, for example, may reflect values that favor civic engagement and active student participation in the community. Promotion and tenure requirements for faculty are also surface structures that in this case reflect deep structure values regarding the relative importance of teaching, research, and service.

According to critical theorists, organizational members are seldom aware of the deep structure values that shape socially constructed reality (Kezar, 2000). A compelling organizational ideology often forestalls serious reflection about or questioning of the institution's dominant values. **Ideology** can be defined as the doctrine, myth, or belief system that guides individual or collective behavior. The ideology of "meritocracy," for example, suggests that success and failure are explainable through individual effort and ability. If we hold strong beliefs in meritocracy, then we may not reflect on systemic inequities that limit access to educational resources, mentors, and other forms of cultural capital that facilitate educational attainment (Stanton-Salazar, 1997). To extend this example further, faculty members may blame students for poor academic performance, but they fail to reflect on an institutional value system (deep structure) that rewards faculty members' development as researchers but does not promote pedagogical and curricular change to accommodate the needs of diverse learners.

Ideology thus hides the deep structure of the organization. Instead, attention is drawn to the visible surface structure. Organizational members may focus on and argue about goals and resource allocations (surface structure), but fail to question the power relationships that privilege certain goals and allocations over others (deep structure). Consider, for example, a student affairs division that must continually justify to college budget officers why it needs additional funds for its programs. Each year the division competes with academic units for scarce institutional resources. In some years, the student affairs division is able to acquire additional resources. In other years, it bears the brunt of budget cuts. But college leaders—even those in the student affairs division—may not reflect on or question why student affairs programs are continually viewed as separate from the academic core of the institution, and why the division's programs are typically first on the "chopping block" when budgets become tight (Hartley, 2001). Student affairs leaders may work to develop better programs and assessment tools, but fail to challenge the deep structure values that assign less importance to student affairs functions.

Critical theory has made important contributions to the study of socially constructed realities. The theory highlights how power and ideology shape the social construction process. Critical theorists explain that the social construction of reality is not an arbitrary construction. Certain constructions are privileged in that they may be intentionally created and endorsed by those in positions of power (Calas & Smircich, 1992; Kezar, 2000). Ideologies constructed by those in power may be so compelling that alternative social constructions are not considered, even by those who are disadvantaged by the prevailing construction of reality.

Critical theorists also emphasize the ethical dimensions of socially constructed reality. They pose difficult but important questions for organizational leaders. Are certain groups or individuals marginalized by the dominant ideology of the organization? Are certain constructions of reality privileged over others? How does the organization address the multiplicity of socially constructed realities? Are alternative voices valued or silenced?

Feminist Perspectives on Organizations

Feminist theorists pose similar questions. They examine how gender is socially constructed, and how certain constructions of gender may subordinate women (Glazer-Raymo, 1999). Historian Linda Kerber (1975) has traced the evolution of "separate spheres" of influence for men and women in the United States. Women traditionally had influence in the home, while men were influential in the spheres of work, religion, and politics. As the U.S. economy shifted from agrarian to industrial, men's work became linked to the monetary economy, while women's work remained unremunerated. Given the importance of the monetary economy, social constructions of work began to equate monetary value with personal value. Since women's work in the home was typically not compensated financially, women's work became viewed as less valuable.

The "separate spheres" of men's work and women's work were endorsed in the 1950s by functionalist sociologists who believed that women fulfilled internal functions such as caregiving, while men fulfilled external functions such as providing income (Parsons & Bales, 1955). These arrangements were said to promote family stability and decrease conflict within the home. Beginning in the 1960s, however, feminist scholars and activists began to challenge these differentiated roles. Betty Friedan (1963), for example, argued that many women felt trapped by roles that left them in a subservient position.

According to feminist theorists, socially constructed gender roles have contributed to a system of **patriarchy**, which is defined as an ideology that promotes an unequal distribution of power between men and women (Lorber, 1994). Under conditions of patriarchy, men have more power than women, and they use that power to maintain the status quo. In a patriarchal organization, members are rewarded for enacting gender-typical role behaviors that reinforce male dominance. To get ahead, female members of the organization may feel that it is necessary to behave in a stereotypically feminine way (e.g., act as a "mother figure" for students) or to behave in a more masculine way (i.e., become tough and aggressive) rather than attempt to disrupt the patriarchal structures that reinforce these rigid gender differences.

Patriarchal constructions of gender are likely to have detrimental effects on both women and men. Women are boxed into positions of subservience to others, or they are compelled to adopt the same patriarchal behaviors that subordinate their female colleagues. Consider, for example, an aggressive, controlling female college president who may be just as disempowering of women as is a similar male president. Men may also encounter stress and conflict related to enacting gender-typical male behaviors. Norms that discourage the expression of male emotions, for example, may make it difficult for men to negotiate interpersonal difficulties in the workplace. Conversely, both men and women may benefit from the deconstruction of patriarchy and the reconstruction of gender relationships that are built on collaboration and nonhierarchical forms of leadership, rather than on command and control.

Like the critical theorists, feminist theorists highlight the ethical and political dimensions of social construction. Feminist scholars point out that women continue to be underrepresented in the ranks of senior leadership in higher education. Only 22% of college presidents are women ("Characteristics of College Presidents," 2004). Unequal distributions of power and rigid gender roles are likely to constrain organizational performance for both men and women (Powell & Graves, 2003). Feminist theorists call for a reexamination of gender in organizations and a reformation of gender roles (Acker, 1992). The implications of feminist theory can be extended to other groups that have been marginalized by society or by higher education institutions in particular. Marginalized groups are also of central concern to postmodernists.

Postmodern Perspectives on Organizations

Postmodernism stands apart from positivist and social constructionist perspectives as a decidedly different viewpoint on society, social systems, and organizational activity. Similar to social constructionists, postmodernists reject the positivist assumptions of a dualistic ontology and an objectivist epistemology. But their critique extends far beyond that of social constructionists. The postmodern critique affects every aspect of society, culture, economics, and politics.

Postmodernism has been conceptualized in two ways: as a historical era and as an intellectual perspective (Bloland, 1995, 2005). As a historical era, postmodernism reflects a significant break from the past. Rapid advances in technology and changing beliefs about social institutions such as government, family, and work have produced new forms of social organization that differ significantly from those of an earlier era. As an intellectual perspective, postmodernism offers a new lens for organizational analysis and leadership. Given changes associated with a postmodern era, new forms of organization and leadership are needed, and the postmodern lens provides important insights for operating in this changed environment.

Postmodernism as a Historical Era

Some scholars have suggested that we are now living in a postmodern era characterized by large-scale social, cultural, economic, and political changes (Gergen, 1992; Hirschhorn, 1997). Some of these large-scale changes include globalization, the rise of multinational corporations, the shift from a production economy to a consumption society, and rapid advances in communications technology.

1. **Globalization** refers to the mobility of goods, services, technology, labor, and capital across national boundaries. Higher education has long been a global industry, given exchanges involving international students and faculty. However, the production and dissemination of knowledge is no longer bound by national borders; ideas flow instantly around the globe through cyberspace. When colleges and universities compete in global markets for students, faculty, and ideas, they find that speed and efficiency in decision making assume added importance. Pressure to make quick decisions to gain competitive advantage may lead colleges and universities toward more hierarchical models of governance that bypass faculty and staff input. Therefore, postmodernists raise concerns that higher education institutions may have adopted corporate practices that displace broader considerations of ethics, access, and equity. Have colleges and universities become soulless enterprises that have lost sight of the deeper meanings and transformations associated with higher education?

2. **Multinational corporations** now represent 52 of the world's 100 largest economies, and their business sales exceed the gross domestic product (GDP) of many nations. Wal-Mart is the 19th largest "economy" in the world; its sales exceed the GDP of Sweden ($246 billion versus $229 billion). Revenues for ExxonMobil exceed the gross domestic product of Turkey ($184 billion versus $183 billion); Honda's revenues are greater than the economy of Chile ($65 billion versus $64 billion); and Home Depot's sales surpass the gross domestic

product of New Zealand ($58.3 billion versus $58.2 billion) (Anderson & Cavanaugh, 2005). Postmodernists are concerned that corporate power may compromise the independence and autonomy of higher education institutions, especially if state power continues to erode. Higher education scholar Harland Bloland (1995), for example, commented on the growing unwillingness of states to increase taxes to support higher education, thereby making many colleges and universities more dependent on the corporate sector for support.

3. Postmodernists have noted a **shift from a production economy to a consumption society**. U.S. economic and tax policy, for example, is often designed to increase consumer spending to boost economic growth. Corporations, moreover, attempt to develop compelling brand images that fulfill consumers' psychological needs and desires. Postmodernists argue that our own identities are shaped by the products we buy and the services that we consume. For colleges and universities, this means that students are more likely to view themselves as consumers and, therefore, may have high expectations for customer satisfaction and service quality. A positive outcome from this development may be the realization that colleges and universities can no longer treat their students as passive recipients of knowledge, but must, instead, consider the unique needs of individual learners (Chaffee, 1998). A potential downside, however, is that academic quality may be diminished in favor of providing a pleasant but not very challenging college experience. Given this scenario, higher education is viewed as simply another commodity. Hence, the focus is on higher education as a private good that accrues to individuals, rather than a public good that benefits society at large (Labaree, 1997).

4. **Rapid changes in technology** have ushered in an era of instantaneous communication where ideas and information can be shared immediately around the globe. These developments make it more difficult to centralize the control of information. Rapid transmission of information makes top-down control exceptionally difficult. If the creation and dissemination of knowledge can be nearly simultaneous, then nearly everyone can have access to the information, and it becomes nearly impossible for organizations to control employees through withholding information (i.e., by providing information on a "need to know" basis only). But these developments also make organizations vulnerable to computer viruses and other threats to confidentiality and data security. Instantaneous communication has also enabled people to telecommute and interact with colleagues without

leaving their homes. Telecommuting may enable workers to spend more time with children or care for a family member; however, such developments also mean that people can be reached anywhere at any time. Constant communication through e-mail and cell phones may continue to erode the separation between home life and work life.

Postmodernism offers a cautionary tale of the potentially negative effects of globalization, corporatization, consumerism, and technology. But the postmodern era also represents liberation from the strictures of a rationalist, functionalist social order with prescribed roles and rigid expectations. Some view postmodernism "as a basis for the organization of a new, freer, more open society, capable of allowing the individual to create his/her own life in ways that have not been conceived of previously, picking and choosing parts of lifestyles that appear everywhere" (Bloland, 1995, p. 542). To understand the implications of living in a postmodern era, however, we must first examine modernism.

Postmodern Era Contrasted with Modernism

The postmodern perspective critiques many of the tenets of modern life, including scientific methods, faith in reason, and belief in progress. Modernism is rooted in intellectual and scientific developments in Western Europe during the 17th and 18th centuries. These developments include:

- Enlightenment thought from political philosophers such as Thomas Hobbes (1588–1679), René Descartes (1596–1650), John Locke (1632–1704), and Jean-Jacques Rousseau (1712–1778)
- The scientific revolution associated with the work of Francis Bacon (1561–1626) and Isaac Newton (1642–1727)
- The industrial revolution that converted agrarian economies into factory-based systems of production, as described by Adam Smith (1723–1790)

Enlightenment political thought, scientific methods, and industrial organization produced radical changes in Western society, including the advent of representative democracy, the rise of modern medicine, the development of an educated middle class, and the invention of the corporation. Modernist thought was solidified further in the 19th century through Charles Darwin's (1809–1882) theories of evolution and natural selection, and in the early 20th century by Max Weber's (1864–1920) theories of social organization based on bureaucracy and merit, rather than on tradition or inheritance. It is important to note that Weber's work had a significant influence on functionalist sociologists in the United States, such as Talcott Parsons (1951) (1902–1979).

According to Gergen (1992), the main components of modernist thought are the following:

1. The world is rational and can be understood through the use of reason and empirical observation.
2. The world is machine-like, predictable, and hence governable. We can manipulate and engineer society and social systems to improve performance.
3. Human history is largely a narrative of human progress. Through additional research and technological development, we are constantly moving toward a better future.

Obviously, these tenets of modernist thought remain strongly endorsed today in many fields of study and continue to reflect many commonplace assumptions in Western society, especially the belief that science will lead to progress, and that human life is rational, understandable, and controllable. Therefore, it is important to keep in mind that although society is now characterized by many postmodern tendencies, modernism remains a dominant force that continues to guide social organization, research, and theory.

Postmodernism, however, provides an important alternative to the modernist framework. As Bloland (1995) notes, "To see postmodernism as a way of understanding the limits of modernism is to view our world in the midst of profound change and to concentrate on the disillusionment we are experiencing with some of our deepest assumptions and cherished hopes relating to our most important institutions" (p. 525). Bloland (2005) argues that our faith in reason, science, and progress has been shaken in recent years. Science may now be associated as much with catastrophe and environmental damage as with progress, and rational explanations seem elusive in an era of terrorism, massive natural disasters, and global epidemics such as AIDS—all of which appear to be beyond the control of leaders, scientists, and policy makers.

Given our disillusionment and skepticism with modern institutions, we need new frameworks for enacting different forms of social organization in the postmodern era. The postmodern intellectual perspective attempts to address this call for new theories that can illuminate new paths for leadership.

Postmodernism as an Intellectual Perspective

Postmodernism as an intellectual perspective traces its roots to the work of French literary critic Jacques Derrida (1930–2004) and French philosopher

Michel Foucault (1926–1984). Both Derrida and Foucault developed sophisticated critiques of modernism. Derrida focused his attack on modernist assumptions about language and reality. Foucault critiqued the modernist belief in objective science and argued that all research is inherently political.

Derrida challenged the modernist assumption that language serves as a symbolic representation of an objective reality that exists prior to communication (Sandberg, 2001). Both Derrida and the social constructionists rejected the idea that language is used to represent an objective reality. But Derrida extended this argument and focused on the indeterminacy of language. Rather than view language as a representational system, Derrida argued that language and word meanings are constantly in flux and difficult to control.

Communication, therefore, is not simply defined as the transmission of knowledge from one mind to another. Instead, communication is a venue for the ongoing negotiation and renegotiation of word meanings. Concepts such as merit, equality, and freedom, for example, do not have fixed definitions; instead, their meanings are unsettled and open for interpretation.

Since word meanings are negotiable rather than fixed, they can be manipulated in ways that maintain advantages of power and status. Modernist uses of language, Derrida argued, reinforce hierarchical differences that omit and devalue alternative constructions of language. Specifically, Derrida criticized the modernist tendency to construct word meanings around binary oppositions such as:

- truth versus untruth;
- science versus nonscience;
- rational versus irrational; and
- in-group versus out-group.

Much of higher education, Derrida argued, is organized around the principle of determining binary distinctions between:

- what is science and what is not;
- what is high culture and what is not;
- which ideas are part of an academic discipline's knowledge base and which are not;
- which texts are in the literary canon and which are not;
- what is a legitimate credential and what is not; and
- who is a qualified student and who is not.

These binary distinctions push some individuals, groups, and ideas to the margins of society. Derrida (1976) sought to bring these people, groups, and ideas to the center of discourse through a process called **deconstruction**. Recall that if word meanings are indeterminate, they can be manipulated to maintain status hierarchies, but that indeterminacy also means that word meanings can be deconstructed to reveal inconsistencies and hidden hierarchies. In literary criticism, deconstruction means seeing beyond the literal meaning of a text and looking, instead, for what has been excluded or withheld. In a college or university, deconstruction entails close scrutiny of the dominant assumptions of organizational members and critical efforts to delegitimize hierarchies that privilege certain ideas over others. These efforts entail "harsh questioning of universities and colleges about their reward structures, the purposes and practices in which they are engaged, and the claims of those now in positions of power and responsibility to their right of office. If the hierarchies of academia are falsely assembled, are arbitrary, and illegitimate, the question becomes why are these particular professors and administrators, rather than others, now sitting in their superior positions benefiting from the modernist academic hierarchies?" (Bloland, 1995, p. 528).

Postmodernism argues that hierarchical distinctions are not based on inherent, universalistic principles such as merit, truth, or reason. Higher education in the United States, for example, is often held in greater esteem than K–12 education. Public school systems are held accountable for far more rules and regulations than are higher education institutions. School districts are mandated to demonstrate how teachers' instruction results in student learning as manifest in standardized test scores. But colleges and universities are largely free from such burdens. The work of colleges and universities is viewed as more complex and more scientific. Institutions of higher education have been granted more autonomy by governments and the courts than K–12 schools have received (though in recent years, that autonomy has increasingly been abridged by powerful government interests). It can be argued, however, that the work of teaching a six-year-old to read is vastly more complex than teaching a college student molecular biology. Moreover, the social and economic costs of failure (i.e., producing illiterate adults) may be far higher than the potential costs of failure in higher education (producing poorly trained biologists). Why is one type of work viewed more important and more prestigious than the other? Through the application of a different set of criteria, this status hierarchy can conceivably be reversed.

Postmodernists argue that there is no rational basis for giving preference to higher education over K–12 education, or for putting research above teaching, or for assigning more importance to physical sciences over the social sciences and humanities. Nevertheless, these status hierarchies prevail throughout education. The reason for this is not because one system has inherently better ideas or is inherently more worthy. As Hutcheon (1988) notes, there are no "natural" hierarchies. Hierarchies are socially constructed, and power relations are deeply implicated in the ongoing reproduction of status differences that "serve to put other ideas and people on the margin or exclude them entirely" (Bloland, 1995, p. 527). To illustrate this point further, we turn our attention to Foucault's postmodern conceptualization of power.

Foucault and Power

Foucault argued that power—rather than merit, truth, or reason—explains why certain people, organizations, and ideas are privileged in society. As critical theorists and feminist scholars also note, power relations in society affect the ongoing social construction of reality. Powerful groups and individuals are able to construct and maintain hierarchies that serve their own interests. A group of faculty members in the hard sciences, for example, may have attained great prominence in the 1950s and 1960s because the federal government endorsed their research agenda with significant funding related to national defense. These faculty members may have used their initial privileged position to secure even greater prominence within their fields of study and their institutions. As a result, alternative research agendas failed to achieve notice because (1) the dominant faculty now serve as grant proposal reviewers and restrict access only to those researchers who endorse their perspectives; (2) the dominant faculty now train doctoral students and other future faculty; (3) the dominant faculty now serve on the search committees that hire new faculty; and (4) the dominant faculty now serve as editors and reviewers for the major journals in the field.

This example illustrates how power is inextricably linked to knowledge. Those with power are able to determine the rules that designate what constitutes knowledge. And those with knowledge are better able to navigate the political waters of particular discourse communities such as those associated with academic disciplines or professional associations. In the previous example, the hard sciences faculty members had the power to define the parameters of knowledge creation through their control over grant proposal reviews and journal publication decisions. By defining knowledge in ways consistent with their own perspective, they reinforced their own positions of power.

Foucault's conceptualization of knowledge is radically different from the modernist idea that knowledge, especially through higher education, leads to empowerment and personal fulfillment. In contrast, Foucault argued that knowledge has become a mode of control and regulation. Dominant groups use knowledge to control less dominant groups. Even within a dominant group, knowledge claims are used to regulate and sanction behaviors that deviate from accepted practices. For example, some scholars argue that tenure and promotion processes marginalize faculty members whose research and teaching deviate from the conventions of their academic disciplines (Tierney & Bensimon, 1996). Faculty behavior that deviates from accepted conventions may be sanctioned through denying tenure and/or promotion. Similarly, reliance on standardized test scores to make admissions decisions privileges certain ways of knowing, but marginalizes others. Knowledge (or lack thereof) is used to exclude certain students from the academy.

If power, knowledge, and control are inextricably linked, then organizational leaders need a thorough understanding of **micropolitics**, or the politics of everyday life. Foucault was less interested in the macrolevel politics of political parties and national and state governments. Instead, his micropolitical perspective focused on small groups at the periphery of society or at the margins of social institutions.

Foucault's micropolitics focuses on organizational conflict and the striving of interest groups within organizations. However, unlike positivist perspectives on these same issues, Foucault was not interested in resolving conflict or forging a new consensus among competing interests. Instead, he sought to maintain conflict and permit the free expression of difference. Foucault's goal was not to bring together dominant and marginal groups as one united community. Instead, he argued, organizations should seek to empower marginal groups and enable them to be distinctively different from the mainstream. Higher education scholar William Tierney (1992) made a similar argument regarding colleges and universities; he claimed that consensus models of organizational leadership are inappropriate for governing higher education institutions. Instead, "[W]e need to develop a leadership style that allows conflict to be heard and honored, that allows differences to be visible and viable" (p. 17). This type of leadership style may be at odds with the preferences of some college leaders who seek to portray calm and promote unity. But Tierney notes that tendencies to resolve conflict and forge consensus can lead to the marginalization of certain groups and individuals who feel that they are no longer able to express themselves in opposition to the dominant consensus. Under such conditions, Tierney argues, innovative ideas are squelched and those at the margins of organizations feel disenfranchised.

Foucault's postmodern conceptualization of power and Tierney's analysis of conflict and consensus suggest two important implications for higher education leadership. The first relates to how higher education views diversity, and the second suggests the importance of learning about and leading within the context of conflict and paradox.

Postmodernist Implications for Higher Education

Postmodernism raises concerns about the potential for consensus to disenfranchise and alienate people and groups on the margins of institutions. Consensus around the literary canon, for example, may exclude books and ideas that minority faculty value. Similarly, adjunct faculty may be excluded from a consensus formed by tenured faculty regarding appropriate workloads.

Instead of resolving conflict and forging consensus, postmodern theorists urge higher education leaders to preserve healthy tensions within the organization. They argue that individual and group differences can strengthen an organization by making it more creative, lively, energetic, and innovative. This viewpoint suggests a radically different way of understanding and promoting diversity.

Diversity

The modernist idea of promoting diversity emphasizes locating similarities across differences. Organizational leaders attempt to build community and unite people around common themes. The postmodern perspective, however, rejects such efforts to smooth over differences and, instead, promotes diversity by highlighting the ways that people are different. There is no effort to merge different groups into one community; instead, historically marginal groups such as women, gays and lesbians, and persons of color are allowed to "claim space" within higher education institutions.

Consider, for example, a university committee on the status of gays and lesbians in the institution. After a year of assessing the campus climate, members of the committee learn that their group will be merged into a campuswide diversity committee that includes representatives from other committees that deal with gender, race, and ethnicity. The intent behind merging these committees was to promote unity and build a diverse community. However, gays, lesbians, and their allies may feel that their issues will now be marginalized and subordinated to other concerns related to gender, race, and ethnicity. They no longer have their own "space" to explore issues and advocate for change.

Some have argued that giving space and voice to diverse groups has led to a "Balkanization" within higher education where students and faculty engage in identity politics rather than knowledge creation (D'Souza, 1991). These scholars lament the decline of the notion of colleges and universities as scholarly communities united around common principles. However, higher education researcher Robert Rhoads (1998) studied five student protest movements that focused on issues of race, gender, and sexual orientation.

These protests did not lead to further isolation or polarization within the student body. Instead, protests that began as a movement involving a specific underrepresented group elicited support from a broad coalition of students of color, gays and lesbians, and majority White students. As Rhoads noted, "The notion that African Americans, Chicanos, American Indians, or gays are somehow isolating themselves from others as a result of separatist philosophies does not hold up when put to close scrutiny" (p. 644).

As Rhoads found, the postmodern notion of rejecting consensus and promoting difference does not necessarily mean that the very fabric of the institution will be torn apart. In fact, providing space for difference—rather than forging consensus or unity—can engender free expression and empower new voices in institutional decision making.

Paradox

In addition to thinking differently about diversity, postmodernism encourages us to reconceptualize conflict and paradox. Recall Derrida's concern regarding the modernist tendency to establish binary distinctions such as true/false or qualified/unqualified. These binary distinctions force people to make definitive distinctions in organizational life:

- Is the research scholarly or overly practical?
- Is the book objective or biased?
- Is the student qualified or unprepared?

In many instances, however, forcing a choice between two binary categories may not be appropriate and, as Derrida (1976) noted, is likely to lead to marginalization through the creation of in-groups and out-groups.

Alternatively, we can shift our thinking from either/or dichotomies to frameworks that embrace both/and. Both/and thinking requires a shift from binary categories to multivariable matrices (Bobko, 1985). Dee (2006), for example, argues that higher education leaders have tended to conceptualize relationships between public institutions and state governments in terms of an either/or tug-of-war between campus interests in autonomy and state concerns about accountability. Campus leaders and state policy makers have tended to conceptualize accountability and autonomy as opposing points on a single continuum. Some campus leaders have considered any increment in additional accountability as coming at the expense of autonomy, and state leaders may view efforts to protect institutional autonomy as attempts to circumvent public accountability. But this either/or dichotomy "reinforces the notion that higher education institutions and external actors have separate interests, rather than a common interest in the public good" (p. 134). Dee suggests that "campus leaders and state policymakers can work together to develop shared commitments and build trust-based relationships that maintain high levels of both public accountability and institutional autonomy" (p. 134).

Embracing both/and thinking means that we have learned to live with paradox and ambiguity (Bess, 2006). Hatch (1997) refers to **paradox** as a seemingly contradictory opposition within a social system. Paradox is central to several theoretical traditions, including Marxism, which identifies organizational contradictions that are typically resolved in favor of managerial interests (Braverman, 1974; Burawoy, 1982). Positivist theories such as functionalism offer specific strategies to forge consensus through "win-win" approaches that attempt to resolve contradictory views and eliminate paradox (Fisher & Ury, 1981; Galbraith, 1977). Unlike Marxism and functionalism, however, postmodernism seeks to preserve the interdependent relationship between oppositions (Baxter & Montgomery, 1996). This dialectical perspective suggests that organizations can maintain apparent contradictions—for example, a college can be both highly autonomous and highly accountable. Postmodernism's embrace of paradox stands in stark contrast to functionalist approaches that seek to resolve contradictions in favor of one opposition or the other.

Postmodern perspectives suggest that higher education leaders need to understand and learn to lead within the context of paradox. As Tierney (1992) notes, "The dichotomous character of higher education is evident on any number of fronts. We are called on to make painful budget cuts and increase services to diverse constituents. We want to lessen hateful speech on campus, yet maintain academic freedom. We desire improvements in classroom teaching but find that our reward structure favors research" (p. 16).

Learning to lead within the context of paradox, therefore, will continue to be an important challenge for college and university leaders.

Postmodernist Implications for Leadership

A common critique is that the postmodern paradigm provides intellectual fodder for abstract debates, ideological discussions, and critical assessments of underlying assumptions, but practically speaking, does not provide very many suggestions for leadership action. Indeed some postmodern theorists, such as Derrida, hesitate to offer alternative forms of organization for fear that these new structures will be corrupted as well by hierarchical tendencies that simply reproduce marginalization through a different means. Postmodernists, as well as critical theorists, for example, are suspicious of employee involvement programs such as self-managed teams and quality circles, and argue that these allegedly more participatory structures simply reproduce the biases and hierarchical divisions that maintain the status quo (Deetz, 1992). But other postmodern works have suggested a range of recommendations for organizational leadership (Delanty, 2001; Hirschhorn, 1997). Some of these include:

1. **Take nothing for granted**. Do not assume that there is one best way or that the current state of affairs is a necessary condition.
2. **Engage in deconstruction**. Reduce an argument to its basic assumptions, deny those assumptions by asserting their negation, and consider the implications for the original argument.
3. **Determine who benefits from particular ways of thinking about the organization**. For example, the positivist approach suggests that managers who use rational techniques to guide their organizations are effective, efficient, and produce more benefits for society. Alternatively, postmodernists suggest that giving managers more power to make the organization more rational simply reproduces and reinforces the dominance of those managers who use that power.
4. **Give voice to traditionally silenced groups**. Seek higher levels of participation from traditionally underrepresented members.
5. **Embrace paradox**. Positivist theorizing suggests that managers should seek to reduce ambiguity and eliminate contradictions to improve the functioning of the organizational system. Postmodern theorizing, however, highlights the utility of ambiguity and contradiction. Organizations, when presented with a contradiction, can hold both concepts as values. For example, organizations can strive for both accountability to their environment and autonomy from it.

Applying the Three Paradigms

Using all three of the paradigms in a complementary way remains a challenge for higher education scholars and practitioners. But there does seem to be promise, especially through mutual exploration across divergent paradigmatic standpoints in the same study (Poropat, 2002). Lewis and Grimes (1999), for example, identified three emerging approaches that use multiple paradigms in organizational analysis.

1. *Multiparadigm reviews* seek to identify transition zones between the paradigms. Transition zones serve as bridges between different paradigmatic traditions. For example, there are many studies of organizational structure within the positivist tradition, but social constructionists have also studied the processes through which structures

emerge. Therefore, the concept of structure can serve as a bridge or transition zone between positivist and social constructionist perspectives (Gioia & Pitre, 1990). By identifying transition zones, researchers and practitioners can venture beyond their initial paradigmatic preferences and explore connections to different ontological and epistemological standpoints. A leader who tends to rely on the assumptions of the positivist paradigm, for example, can explore the idea of structure from multiple paradigms, thus enlarging his or her perspective on the organization (Martin, 1992).

2. *Multiparadigm research* applies the methodological assumptions of different paradigms either sequentially or in parallel analyses. In the sequential strategy, a researcher begins the study from the perspective of one paradigm, and then switches to another paradigm to extend the initial findings. In the parallel strategy, different paradigms are applied with roughly equal emphasis, rather than in succession. Martin's (1992) study of corporate culture, for example, generated parallel analyses based in positivist, social constructionist, and postmodern perspectives.

3. *Metaparadigm theory building* attempts to transcend the initial "starting points" of the respective paradigms and generate new conceptual frameworks by weaving together insights from multiple paradigmatic traditions. Using positivist and postmodern perspectives, for example, a researcher could develop a new theory related to the uses and abuses of power in higher education organizations. Or, based on the "transition zone" associated with organizational structure, positivists and social constructionists could create a new theory associated with the ongoing production and reproduction of college and university structures. Developments in metaparadigm theory building remain limited in organizational theory and in higher education, but this technique holds great promise for producing new theories to explain the rapidly changing context of college and university organization.

Summary

In this chapter, three paradigms for understanding organizations were examined: positivist, social constructionist, and postmodern. Within each framework, the modes of organizational analysis and theory application were presented.

The positivist paradigm makes assumptions about a reality external to the individual that can be discovered through scientific methods. Positivism for organizational theory developed via two overlapping nodes—systems theory and contingency theory. Systems theory has been useful in identifying the energies that organizations use to transform inputs into finished products. The theory also highlights the importance of analyzing problems at multiple system levels and of considering the effects of organizational decisions on stakeholders in the external environment. The second approach of the positivist school is contingency theory. Through this theory, researchers and practitioners learn to avoid reductionism and to begin to look for the ways that many different variables are often involved in understanding and predicting outcomes.

Those who use positivist approaches to organizational analysis have developed a specialized vocabulary to enable scientific and precise measurement of variables. In research and organizational analysis, variables are placed in predictive relationships to one another. Thus, one variable, the independent variable, is used to predict the other, the dependent variable. Predictions of relationships between variables that over time have come to be seen as reliable are called theories.

Positivist approaches to organizational analysis are useful for leaders in capturing the history of relationships among organizational phenomena and using those that have endured to understand and make predictions about similar relationships in the present and future. It is important as well to recognize that, on the administrative side of college and university organization, positivist approaches to understanding organizational phenomena are by far the strongest paradigm in use, partly for historical reasons and partly because the outside world (businesspeople, parents, government officials) also use this paradigm and are more comfortable asking college and university personnel to respond to them in positivist terms.

The social constructionist paradigm assumes that reality is a human creation. People construct reality individually and in conjunction with others. Social construction theory suggests that organizations consist of multiple interpretations of reality, and leaders are advised to consider problems from multiple frames of reference. From a social construction perspective, theoretical concepts are not objectively "real" phenomena. Instead, concepts are constructed through communication and interpersonal agreement regarding meanings. These constructions may be mediated by such factors as how narrowly or broadly the institution interprets its mission, the institution's history, and the interpretive systems that people bring with them to their organizations.

The postmodern paradigm suggests that control-oriented management is outdated. Postmodernists offer alternative organizational practices that emphasize questioning basic assumptions and giving voice to people from traditionally underrepresented groups.

Review Questions

1. An administrator who emphasizes the need to align all activities with clearly defined goals and objectives tends to rely on assumptions based in which paradigm?
   a. Positivist
   b. Social constructionist
   c. Postmodern

2. Consider an administrator who identified an organizational problem, applied an organizational theory to address that problem, and took corrective action on the basis of that analysis. Unfortunately, the actions did not resolve the problem. What may explain this outcome?
   a. The administrator did not clearly specify the organizational problem.
   b. The theory does not account for all of the contingencies in this organization.
   c. The administrator is trying to solve the problem at the wrong level of the system.
   d. All of the above

3. An administrator who emphasizes collaborative problem solving and who encourages colleagues to consider the historical and social context of their institution as they make decisions tends to rely on assumptions based in which paradigm?
   a. Positivist
   b. Social constructionist
   c. Postmodern

4. Identify the differences between the "miner" and "traveler" metaphors regarding positivist and social constructionist epistemology.
   a. Miners attempt to unearth the "truth" about an objective reality; travelers attempt to know multiple "truths" through their interactions with others.
   b. Miners seek to deconstruct assumptions about issues of power in organizations; travelers seek to dismantle patriarchy.
   c. Miners rely on intuition to find "nuggets" of truth; travelers assign highest importance to rationality and reason.
   d. All of the above

5. Which of the following describes the social construction of reality?
   a. A symbolic convergence in which the separate cognitive worlds of different individuals begin to overlap to some degree

   b. Primary socialization into a particular culture or society in which members have similar understandings of language, family, gender, race, and ethnicity

   c. Secondary socialization into social systems such as work organizations

   d. Variety in social constructions due to division of labor, social and cultural constructs, and other personal factors such as age and geographic location

   e. All of the above

6. Which of the following is a characteristic of the postmodern era?
   a. The erosion of the boundary between home life and work life due to the pervasiveness of communications technology

   b. A growing consumerism among students

   c. Higher education's increasing dependence on corporate support in response to decreasing state support

   d. A globally accessible marketplace of ideas

   e. All of the above

7. The postmodern intellectual perspective emphasizes which of the following?
   a. Deconstruction of hierarchy

   b. Suppression of micropolitics

   c. Promotion of consensus and unity

   d. Quick resolution of conflict

Case Discussion Questions

Consider the Warren College case presented at the beginning of this chapter.

1. Assess the paradigmatic assumptions of the professors from biology, history, and political science. How were positivist assumptions manifest in their conversations with President Kenwood? Social constructionist assumptions? Postmodern assumptions?

2. Put yourself in the role of the president of Warren College. How would you continue the conversation with these senior faculty members? What would be your next step as an institutional leader? What type of data could you use to address the concerns and worldviews of the three professors?

References

Abrahamson, E. (2002). Disorganization theory and disorganizational behavior: Towards an etiology of messes. In B. M. Staw & R. M. Kramer (Eds.), *Research in organizational behavior* (pp. 139–180). Kidlington, Oxford, UK: Elsevier Science.

Acker, J. (1992). Gendering organizational theory. In A. Mills & P. Tanered (Eds.), *Gendering organizational theory* (pp. 248–260). Newbury Park, CA: Sage.

Adams, J. S. (1980). *Research in organizational behavior* (vol. 2). Greenwich, CT: JAI Press, 321–355.

Anderson, J. (1996). *Communication theory: Epistemological foundations.* New York: Guilford Press.

Anderson, S., & Cavanaugh, J. (2005). *Field guide to the global economy* (2nd ed.). New York: Free Press.

Argyris, C., & Schön, D. (1992). *Theory in practice: Increasing professional effectiveness.* San Francisco: Jossey-Bass.

Bachrach, P., & Baratz, M. (1962). The two faces of power. *American Political Science Review, 56,* 947–952.

Balderston, F. (1995). *Managing today's university* (2nd ed.). San Francisco: Jossey-Bass.

Baldridge, J. V. (1971). *Power and conflict in the university.* New York: John Wiley & Sons.

Baxter, L., & Montgomery, B. (1996). *Relating: Dialogues and dialectics.* New York: Guilford Press.

Bensimon, E., & Neumann, A. (1993). *Redesigning collegiate leadership: Teams and teamwork in higher education.* Baltimore, MD: Johns Hopkins University Press.

Berger, P., & Luckmann, T. (1966). *The social construction of reality.* Garden City, NY: Doubleday.

Bergquist, W. (1992). *The four cultures of the academy: Insights and strategies for improving leadership in collegiate organizations.* San Francisco: Jossey-Bass.

Bess, J. (1988). *Collegiality and bureaucracy in the modern university.* New York: Teachers College Press, Columbia University.

Bess, J. (2006). Strategic ambiguity: Antidote to managerialism in academia. In J. Smart (Ed.), *Higher education: Handbook of theory and research* (pp. 491–533). Dordrecht, Netherlands: Kluwer Press.

Biglan, A. (1973). The characteristics of subject matter in different academic areas. *Journal of Applied Psychology, 57*(3), 195–203.

Birnbaum, R. (1992). *How academic leadership works: Understanding success and failure in the college presidency.* San Francisco: Jossey-Bass.

Blau, P. (1973). *The organization of academic work.* New York: John Wiley & Sons.

Bloland, H. (1995). Postmodernism and higher education. *Journal of Higher Education, 66*(5), 521–559.

Bloland, H. (2005). Whatever happened to postmodernism in higher education? No requiem in the new millennium. *Journal of Higher Education, 76*(2), 121–150.

Bobko, P. (1985). Removing assumptions of bipolarity: Towards variation and circularity. *Academy of Management Review, 10,* 99–108.

Bolman, L., & Deal, T. (1997). *Reframing organizations: Artistry, choice, and leadership* (2nd ed.). San Francisco: Jossey-Bass.

Bormann, E. (1996). Symbolic convergence theory and communication in group decision making. In R. Hirokawa & M. Poole (Eds.), *Communication and group decision making* (2nd ed., pp. 81–113). Thousand Oaks, CA: Sage.

Braverman, H. (1974). *Labor and monopoly capital: The degradation of work in the twentieth century.* New York: Monthly Review Press.

Burawoy, M. (1982). Introduction: The resurgence of Marxism in American sociology. In M. Burawoy & T. Skocpol (Eds.), *Marxist inquiries: Studies of labor, class, and states.* Supplement to the *American Journal of Sociology, 88,* S1–S30.

Burns, T., & Stalker, G. (1961). *The management of innovation* (1st ed.). London: Tavistock Publications.

Burrell, G. (1996). Normal science, paradigms, metaphors, discourses and genealogies of analysis. In S. Clegg, C. Hardy, & W. Nord (Eds.), *Handbook of organization studies* (pp. 643–658). Thousand Oaks, CA: Sage.

Burrell, G., & Morgan, G. (1979). *Sociological paradigms and organizational analysis.* London: Heinemann.

Calas, M., & Smircich, L. (1992). Re-writing gender into organizational theorizing: Directions from feminist perspectives. In M. Reed & M. Hughes (Eds.), *Rethinking organization: New directions in organization theory and analysis* (pp. 227–253). Newbury Park, CA: Sage.

Chaffee, E. (1998). Listening to the people we serve. In W. Tierney (Ed.), *The responsive university: Restructuring for high performance* (pp. 13–37). Baltimore, MD: Johns Hopkins University Press.

Characteristics of college presidents. (2004, August 27). *Chronicle of Higher Education, 51*(1), 28.

Cook, S., & Yanow, D. (1996). Culture and organizational learning. In M. Cohen & L. Sproull (Eds.), *Organizational learning* (pp. 430–459). Thousand Oaks, CA: Sage

Dee, J. (2006). Institutional autonomy and state-level accountability: Loosely-coupled governance and the public good. In W. Tierney (Ed.), *Governance and the public good* (pp. 133–155). Albany, NY: State University of New York Press.

Deetz, S. (1992). *Democracy in an age of corporate colonization: Developments in communication and the politics of everyday life.* Albany, NY: State University of New York Press.

Delanty, G. (2001). *Challenging knowledge: The university in the knowledge society.* Philadelphia: SRHE and Open University Press.

Derrida, J. (1976). *Of grammatology.* Baltimore, MD: Johns Hopkins University Press.

Donaldson, L. (1995). *American anti-management theories of organization: A critique of paradigm proliferation.* Cambridge, UK: Cambridge University Press.

D'Souza, D. (1991). *Illiberal education: The politics of race and sex on campus.* New York: Free Press.

Eckensberger, L. H. (2002). Paradigms revisited: From incommensurability to respected complementarity. In H. Heller, Y. Poortinga, & A. Schölmerich (Eds.),

Between culture and biology: Perspectives on ontogenetic development. New York: Cambridge University Press.

Evan, W. (1972). An organization-set model of interorganizational relations. In M. F. Tuite, M. Radnor, & R. K. Chisholm (Eds.), *Interorganizational decision making* (pp. 181–200). Chicago: Aldine-Atherton Publishing.

Fairhurst, G. T., & Sarr, R. A. (1996). *The art of framing: Managing the language of leadership.* San Francisco: Jossey-Bass.

Fisher, J., & Koch, J. (1996). *Presidential leadership: Making a difference.* Phoenix, AZ: Oryx Press.

Fisher, R., & Ury, W. (1981). *Getting to yes.* Boston: Houghton Mifflin.

Friedan, B. (1963). *The feminine mystique.* New York: Norton.

Galbraith, J. (1977). *Organization design.* Reading, MA: Addison-Wesley.

Geertz, C. (1973). *Interpretation of cultures.* New York: Basic Books.

Gergen, K. (1992). Organization theory in the postmodern era. In M. Reed & M. Hughes (Eds.), *Rethinking organization: New directions in organization theory and analysis* (pp. 207–226). Newbury Park, CA: Sage.

Giddens, A. (1978). Positivism and its critics. In T. Bottomore & R. Nisbet (Eds.), *A history of sociological analysis* (pp. 237–286). New York: Basic Books.

Giddens, A. (1984). *The constitution of society.* Berkeley, CA: University of California Press.

Gioia, D., & Pitre, E. (1990). Multiparadigm perspectives on theory building. *Academy of Management Review, 15*(4), 584–602.

Glazer-Raymo, J. (1999). *Shattering the myths: Women in academe.* Baltimore, MD: Johns Hopkins University Press.

Hartley, M. (2001). Student learning as a framework for student affairs: Rhetoric or reality. *NASPA Journal, 38*(2), 224–237.

Hartley, M. (2003). "There is no way without a because": Revitalization of purpose at three liberal arts colleges. *Review of Higher Education, 27*(1), 75–102.

Hassard, J., & Kelemen, M. (2002, May). Production and consumption in organizational knowledge: The case of the paradigms debate. *Organization, 9*(2), 331–355.

Hatch, M. (1997). *Organization theory: Modern, symbolic, and postmodern perspectives.* New York: Oxford University Press.

Hearn, J., & Anderson, M. (2002). Conflict in academic departments: An analysis of disputes over faculty promotion and tenure. *Research in Higher Education, 43*(5), 503–529.

Hirschhorn, L. (1997). *Reworking authority: Leading and following in a postmodern organization.* Cambridge, MA: MIT Press.

Hutcheon, L. (1988). *A poetics of postmodernism.* London: Routledge.

Janis, I. (1982). *Groupthink: Psychological studies of policy decisions and fiascoes.* Boston: Houghton Mifflin.

Katz, D., & Kahn, R. L. (1978). *The social psychology of organizations* (2nd ed.). New York: John Wiley & Sons.

Keller, G. (1983). *Academic strategy: The management revolution in higher education.* Baltimore, MD: Johns Hopkins University Press.

Kerber, L. (1975). Separate spheres, female world, woman's place: The rhetoric of women's history. *Journal of American History, 75*, 9–37.

Kezar, A. (2000). Pluralistic leadership: Incorporating diverse voices. *Journal of Higher Education, 71*(6): 722–743.

Kezar, A. (2002). Reconstructing exclusive and static images of leadership: An application of positionality theory. *The Journal of Leadership Studies, 3*(3): 94–109.

Kezar, A., Carducci, R., & Contreras-McGavin, M. (2006). *Rethinking the "L" word in higher education: The revolution of research on leadership.* San Francisco: Jossey-Bass.

Kezar, A., & Dee, J. (2006, April). *Conducting multiple paradigm analyses of higher education organizations: Transforming the study of colleges and universities.* Paper presented at the annual meeting of the American Educational Research Association (AERA), San Francisco.

Kezar, A., & Eckel, P. (2002). The effects of institutional culture on change strategies in higher education: Universal principles or culturally responsive concepts. *Journal of Higher Education, 73*(4), 443–460.

Kuhn, T. S. (1962). *The structure of scientific revolutions* (1st ed.). Chicago: University of Chicago Press.

Kuhn, T. S. (1970). *The structure of scientific revolutions* (2nd ed.). Chicago: University of Chicago Press.

Kvale, S. (1996). *InterViews: An introduction to qualitative research interviewing.* Thousand Oaks, CA: Sage.

Labaree, D. (1997). *How to succeed in school without really learning.* New Haven, CT: Yale University Press.

Lewis, M., & Grimes, A. (1999). Metatriangulation: Building theory from multiple paradigms. *Academy of Management Review, 24*(4), 672–690.

Lincoln, Y. (Ed.). (1985). Introduction. In *Organizational theory and inquiry: The paradigm revolution* (pp. 29–40). Beverly Hills, CA: Sage Publications.

Lorber, J. (1994). *Paradoxes of gender.* New Haven, CT: Yale University Press.

Marchese, T. (1997). Sustaining quality enhancement in academic and managerial life. In M. Peterson, D. Dill, & L. Mets (Eds.), *Planning and management for a changing environment: A handbook on redesigning postsecondary institutions.* San Francisco: Jossey-Bass.

Martin, J. (1992). *Cultures in organizations: Three perspectives.* New York: Oxford University Press.

Mayo, E. (1945). *The social problems of an industrial civilization.* Boston: Harvard University Graduate School of Business Administration.

Morgan, G. (1986). *Images of organization.* Newbury Park, CA: Sage.

Mumby, D. (1988). *Communication and power in organizations: Discourse, ideology, and domination.* Norwood, NJ: Ablex.

Neumann, A. (1995). On the making of hard times and good times: The social construction of resource stress. *Journal of Higher Education, 66*(1), 3–31.

Parsons, T. (1951). *The social system.* New York: The Free Press.

Parsons, T., & Bales, R. (1955). *Family socialization and interaction process.* Glencoe, IL: Free Press.

Pfeffer, J. (1993). Barriers to the advance of organizational science: Paradigm development as a dependent variable. *Academy of Management Review, 18*(4), 559–620.

Poropat, A. (2002). Apples and oranges: Incommensurable paradigms and their implications for teaching organizational development. *Organizational Development Journal, 20*(3), 74–86.

Powell, G., & Graves, L. (2003). *Women and men in management.* Thousand Oaks, CA: Sage.

Rhoads, R. (1998). Student protest and multicultural reform: Making sense of campus unrest in the 1990s. *Journal of Higher Education, 69*(6), 621–646.

Roethlisberger, F. J., & Dickson, W. J. (1939). *Management and the worker.* Cambridge, MA: Harvard University Press.

Rost, J. C. (1991). *Leadership for the twenty-first century.* New York: Simon & Schuster.

Sandberg, J. (2001). The constructions of social constructionism. In S.-E. Sjöstrand, J. Sandberg, & M. Tyrstrup (Eds.), *Invisible management: The social construction of leadership* (pp. 28–48). London: Thomson Learning, Berkshire House.

Scherer, A., & Steinmann, H. (1999). Some remarks on the problem of incommensurability in organization studies. *Organization Studies, 20*(3), 519–544.

Schön, D. (1983). *The reflective practitioner.* New York: Basic Books.

Schuster, J., Smith, D., Corak, K., & Yamada, M. (1994). *Strategic governance: How to make big decisions better.* Phoenix, AZ: American Council on Education, Oryx Press.

Senge, P. (1990). *The fifth discipline: The art and practice of the learning organization.* New York: Currency, Doubleday.

Stanton-Salazar, R. (1997). A social capital framework for understanding the socialization of racial minority children and youths. *Harvard Educational Review, 67*(1), 1–40.

Taylor, F. W. (1911). *The principles of scientific management.* New York: Harper.

Thompson, J. D. (1967). *Organizations in action.* New York: McGraw-Hill Book Company.

Tierney, W. (1992). Cultural leadership and the search for community. *Liberal Education, 78*(5), 16–21.

Tierney, W., & Bensimon, E. (1996). *Promotion and tenure: Community and socialization in academe.* Albany, NY: State University of New York Press.

Van de Ven, A., & Drazin, R. (1985). The concept of fit in contingency theory. *Research in Organizational Behavior, 7,* 333–365.

Weber, M. (1924). *The theory of social and economic organizations* (A. M. Henderson & T. Parsons, Trans.; T. Parsons, Ed.). New York: Free Press.

Weick, K. (1993). The collapse of sensemaking in organizations: The Mann Gulch disaster. *Administrative Science Quarterly, 38,* 628–652.

Weick, K. (1995). *Sensemaking in organizations.* Thousand Oaks, CA: Sage.

4

GENERAL AND SOCIAL SYSTEMS THEORY

CONTENTS

The authors are most grateful for the critical comments on an early draft of this chapter by Marc Cutright, Ohio University. The final version, of course, is our own and may or may not reflect the perspective of the reviewer.

Preview

- Colleges and universities interact with and are affected by complex external systems. These external systems include other organized entities, including governments, industry, and religious and nonprofit organizations. These entities reflect and reproduce cultural and economic values in the larger social system.
- Internally, colleges and universities operate as complex systems where various academic and administrative functions transform inputs (e.g., students, new knowledge) into outputs that achieve the mission of the institution (e.g., socially responsible students, socially beneficial advances in research).
- Each functional area within the institution (e.g., academic departments, student affairs divisions) operates as a system within the larger organizational system. The rest of the organization is the "environment" for each subunit.
- Each organizational member is also a system. Some individuals operate primarily within the internal systems of the organization. Others are boundary spanners who interact with systems beyond the organization's boundary.
- General systems theory (GST) explains in broad terms the relationship between an organized entity and its external environment.
- GST explains how systems develop structures to deal with the complexity of their external environments and suggests that structures become more differentiated and specialized when systems grow and when environments become more complex.
- GST draws attention to the transformation processes of a system; however, it is necessary to use other theories to see inside the "black box" of systems processes.
- Social systems theory (SST) conceptualizes individuals as systems. People interact with and are affected by external "social environments." Individuals themselves are composed of cognitive and affective systems (e.g., personality) that interact in ways that shape behavior.
- SST explains individual behavior as a function of the interaction between the environment surrounding the individual and his or her internal systems (e.g., cognitive and affective systems, including personality).

──────────────────── CASE CONTEXT ────────────────────

Student Behavior at Mammoth State University

The bars and nightclubs that ring Mammoth State University's campus were filled to capacity with fans who watched their men's basketball team win the national championship. When the bars closed at 1:00 am, students streamed into the streets and sidewalks outside the nightclubs. Many continued to consume alcohol that they had purchased before "last call." The situation became dangerous when several students began to climb traffic lights and jump onto parked cars.

The celebration turned violent when students confronted police who were attempting to disperse the crowd. Eight students were injured in the ensuing brawl. Several local businesses sustained property damage when students broke windows and looted merchandise.

The university's president responded swiftly. The morning after the melee, she called together all of the university's vice presidents, the chief of police, a representative from the mayor's office, and three local bar owners.

"Fortunately, none of the students' injuries are life threatening," reported the vice president for student affairs. "All of their families have been contacted. Of course, we will initiate campus judicial action, and there will likely be criminal charges."

"The university will cooperate fully with the police department," indicated the president. "But the reason that I called you here today is to develop a rapid response plan so that we can avoid these types of incidents in the future. The media attention has been devastating. It makes us look like a 'party school,' and we have been trying to shed that image for years. We now have more endowed faculty chairs and honors scholarships than any other school in the state. But the only time we make the front page of the papers is when there is some type of brawl."

"Well, I am glad that the bar owners are here," said the vice president for academic affairs. "I would really like to hear what they are doing to curb excessive drinking, because it is causing real damage to the academic reputation of the university."

"Your comment assumes that *we* are the problem," responded one of the bar owners. "We have been doing the responsible thing for years. We moved last call back to 1:00 am. We've been promoting designated drivers. What has the university been doing? Nothing. This is the first time that I have ever been invited to the university, and I've been in business for twenty years. The only time you want to talk to me is when there's a problem."

"It's not true that we do nothing," responded the vice president for student affairs. "We have alcohol awareness and prevention programs. But one obvious area where we need to do better is coordinating our alcohol programs with the bars and nightclubs. I guess before this incident we always thought of you guys as the enemy—that is, stay away from the bars.

But students are going to go there, regardless of what we do. Maybe there are ways that we can find common solutions."

"And don't forget about the environments where these students live," contributed the mayor's representative. "I lived in a fraternity in college. I *know* what goes on." The group laughed, easing the tension. "Those kids get a lot of peer pressure to drink and act out. What are you doing to make the students' experience more academically focused?"

"That's exactly what we need," responded the president. "We need a broader perspective. This isn't just a town-gown problem between the university and the bars. We need to think about the whole student experience. What messages are they getting in the residence halls and fraternities and sororities? What messages are they getting from faculty and staff about the importance of academics? What opportunities do they have to interact around academic issues, rather than sports and alcohol? We need to think about how all of these components contribute to the problem."

Introduction

Colleges and universities are surrounded by a variety of forces that induce the organization to respond in some way. External constituencies (e.g., state governments, parents, granting agencies) provide resources for higher education and also set formal and informal expectations for institutional outputs (e.g., values, skills, and competencies in graduating students and new knowledge that can be used in social, commercial, and esthetic ventures). Because of these influences, institutions develop and execute both strategic and practical plans that accommodate the evolving needs of society and fluctuating resource availability. Within institutions of higher education, organizational members in professional and administrative positions process a variety of inputs (e.g., students and new knowledge) that is intentionally or unintentionally received. Workers attempt to "transform" the inputs into outputs that are acceptable to the receiving public. The institutions thus send out knowledgeable and skilled graduates, and they produce research-validated new knowledge that is of use in a variety of public and private sectors.

So, too, at the individual level, each college and university employee is immersed in social, economic, and emotional contexts outside of him or herself—contexts both within and outside the employing organization. Organizational members receive inputs from their immediate work environments, transform them into usable forms, and take actions intended to be well received by peers, supervisors, and clients.

Systems theory comprises a broad conceptual framework that permits the identification of key inputs, outputs, and transformative processes in organizations such as colleges and universities at both the institutional and individual levels. The theory introduces a vocabulary for making more meaningful other theories of organization, somewhat narrower in scope, which are discussed in later chapters. The concepts used in systems theory have virtually universal definitions. These concepts, therefore, comprise both a unified way of thinking about all organizations, including colleges and universities, and useful tools that allow busy administrators and researchers to communicate quickly and accurately about organizational phenomena.

The application of systems theory facilitates the understanding and classification of the more basic forces at work in and around organizations. Systems theory consists of two theoretical traditions—general systems theory (GST) and social systems theory (SST)—which permit better understanding of phenomena at the organizational and individual levels, respectively (Figure 4.1). Both general and social systems theory are considered in this chapter. First, however, we briefly describe the history and foundations of systems theory.

History of Systems Theory

Systems theory has developed over the past 50 or more years in a wide variety of fields, including biology, mathematics, computer science, communications, education, sociology, and psychology. The conceptual frameworks

FIGURE 4.1
The Relation of General and Social Systems

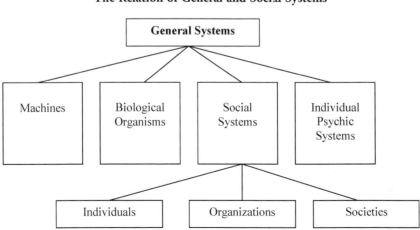

were originated by Ludwig von Bertalanffy (1968) and Kenneth Berrien (1968), particularly in the latter's application of general systems theory to problems in social psychology. (For a concise review of the history of systems theory, see Conway, 1988; Young, 1980.) Another branch of systems theory, based in sociology and sometimes labeled "grand theory," stems from the work of Talcott Parsons (1951), whose broad focus was social systems as a whole and the nature and relationships of their component parts. At about the same time Berrien was doing his work, several others were thinking and writing about systems, including Walter Buckley, C. West Churchman, Norbert Wiener, and Kenneth Boulding. What follows is a synthesis of their ideas. We use parts of all of these approaches in later chapters.

Systems theory begins at the most elemental level and progresses hierarchically to increasing levels of complexity (Boulding, 1953, 1956). For example, at the start of the universe, one could speculate that there were much simpler systems of organization, essentially nonorganic, molecular matter. Today, in addition to chemical interactions, there are human ones—many orders of magnitude more complex. Berrien suggests that the principles that governed the earlier inanimate systems also have a bearing on human systems (though the principles can be used with far less precision).

Systems theory lays the groundwork for all of the positivist theories that follow in this book. Despite many criticisms that systems theory is biased toward preserving the status quo (see, for example, Burrell & Morgan, 1979), its promise as a comprehensive model for integrating the disparate parts of organizational theory and behavior argues for its becoming one of the three primary orienting frameworks for this book. (Readers wishing to explore alternative perspectives on classical systems theory should refer to Berrien, 1968; Churchman, 1968; Hills, 1968; and Monane, 1967. For more contemporary views, see Bailey, 1994, 2005; Galliers, Mingers, & Jackson, 1997; and Luhmann, 1995, 2006. For practical applications, see Corea, 2005, and Weimer-Jehie, 2006.)

As noted above, most conceptualizations of systems theory are positivist in paradigmatic focus and emphasize rational rather than normative language (Abrahamson, 1997). Other, more specific theories within the positivist paradigm are embedded in and/or embraced by systems theory.

Because systems theory is quite broad and general, its *practical* utility is somewhat limited. For example, using systems theory, we are unable to make precise predictions of future events in institutions of higher education or to intervene propitiously to solve organizational problems. It is also difficult to be effective immediately on the microorganizational level—that is, understanding, predicting, and influencing individual behavior in specific settings such as academic departments.

Nevertheless, systems theory does permit us to make very broad generalizations about the character of an organization or a worker and his or her activities. It avoids some of the problems of localized, disconnected attention to subproblems. By providing a broad-brush picture of what is happening and why, it directs our attention to essential elements in organizations that are stable and to those whose relationships to one another are changing (Boulding, 1956). We can learn, for example, how the environment outside a college or university has an important bearing on what happens inside. Or, we can explain a person's behavior by understanding the complex pressures from office staff that affect his or her job performance. This may not sound very profound, but it is surprising how often the many different possibilities for understanding social or organizational phenomena are never even considered. In fact, the straightforwardness of systems theory is what makes it useful as a diagnostic device for beginning to understand organizational phenomena. For example, once we locate the environment as a source of the problem, we can then use other theories to provide further guidance for action. Alternatively, if we identify the internal components of the organization as part of the problem, we are then directed for solutions to yet another group of theories that may be useful.

Systems theory, then, is helpful in analyzing and explaining the behavior of two fundamental complex institutions in all societies—organizations and individuals. Both organizational and individual systems operate well when they are successful in balancing the often competing forces influencing them. The primary forces affecting them are both inside and outside the system. An organization must address the demands and expectations of the recipients of its outputs—its products and services—while at the same time attending to its need to link and coordinate its internal component parts—departments and people. Individuals, similarly, must be concerned with balancing the expectations of elements outside themselves against the requirement that their internal needs be met.

In this chapter, we identify and describe the elements that are important in the process of adjudicating the claims from outside and inside for both organizations and individuals. A number of theories suggest that there is an optimum "fit" between a focal unit and the external environment outside its boundaries (Donaldson, 2001; O'Reilly, Chatman, & Caldwell, 1991), and there is an optimum "fit" among the components within the focal unit (Burton, 2004). It should be understood, however, that these two "fits" may not always be synchronized (Nadler & Tushman, 1977; Olsen, 1968).

General Systems Theory

The early systems theorists working in the 1950s (e.g., Bertalanffy, Boulding) argued that scientists could use a set of *general* principals to explain both natural and social phenomena. **General systems theory** was conceptualized at a very high level of abstraction so that it could apply to systems as diverse as single cells within organisms or complex human societies. Proponents of general systems theory hoped that these broad conceptualizations would dismantle some of the barriers between academic fields and promote cross-disciplinary research as a way to solve complex, interrelated problems.

In this section, we examine the basic concepts that comprise general systems theory. At the conclusion of this discussion, we provide a schematic for viewing the concepts in an integrated model.

System

A **system** is a set of components or elements that are interrelated, interactive, and interdependent (Hall & Fagen, 1980). The relationships among the components comprise a structure designed to carry out the functions needed to maintain and enhance the system's well-being vis-à-vis its environment. The environment is simply everything that is not part of the system (Luhmann, 1995). Environments are invariably more complex and more differentiated than the system itself.

Since all of the components of a system are interdependent, changes in one component have repercussions in the others, although in some systems, when the components are more loosely coupled, there is greater independence of action among the components. In thinking about colleges and universities, it is easy to see how seemingly innocuous changes in one part of the system often result in unanticipated consequences elsewhere. Changes in admissions standards, for example, may have important effects on the number of developmental English sections and/or the number of residential housing units that are needed. On the other hand, it is also clear that academic departments, as system components, are freer to act independently than might be the case for departments in a commercial enterprise. A negative accreditation review in a nursing program, for example, would have little immediate or direct effect on the fine arts department.

Just as a college may be regarded as a system, so is the system within which it operates considered a system. Thus, one could imagine a college town as a system, or a state university with its constituent campuses as a system, or all U.S. colleges and universities as a system. Further, each of these systems' components themselves comprise systems. Hence, the office of the vice president for student affairs is a system, as is a residence hall, to name a few examples.

Boundary

Systems are separated from their environments by boundaries. The **boundary** is that part of a system that separates it from other systems, allows the system to define its identity, provides protection for the system through its filtering or selection mechanism, and acts as a point of contact and exchange with other systems in the environment. By drawing a boundary around an activity, others outside are able to perceive that activity as a whole—that is, as a collection of activities that represents something (Fombrun & Shanley, 1990). The system comes to have an "external identity," sometimes called the organization's public image (Gioia & Thomas, 1996). Organizational members in higher education institutions who cross boundaries to enact their roles in the surrounding environment—the "boundary spanners"—play key parts in maintaining the flow of energy in and out of the institution and in establishing and maintaining a clear image of the institution for the outside publics. Members of a college's admissions office and marketing department most obviously perform this function, but so do college lobbyists, athletics coaches, nationally recognized research scientists, and purchasing agents.

The boundary also allows workers *within* the system to relate to and identify with the system—to be part of it and separate from other systems. The system thus has an "internal identity." One's personal identity may be closely tied to the identity of the organization to which one belongs. As a result, organizational members in effective colleges and universities may develop strong allegiances to the institutions in which they work.

Boundaries are not necessarily physical—like a campus wall. Kuhn (1975) suggests that there are three kinds of boundaries: spatial, functional, and analytic. For example, a spatial boundary for a college might comprise an imaginary circumference around all of the buildings that the college owns. A functional boundary may encompass the route that the campus bus runs, or the market from which students are recruited. The boundary is delineated by the scope of the functions that the system performs. An analytic boundary, in contrast, reflects a classificatory distinction that identifies members of the system. The designation of being a student or not, for example, separates people by their "studenthood" from others who are not students. Thus, a classificatory boundary separates them.

Different systems have boundaries that are more or less open or closed to their environments. That is, it may be relatively easy or difficult for elements outside the system to enter. Some small colleges are relatively self-contained organizations of faculty and students, while some universities are extensively involved with local communities and national constituencies.

A system that can carry out exchanges with the environment more easily is an **open system** (Bertalanffy, 1968), and a system that restricts exchanges is a **closed system**. Closed systems must rely completely on their own resources to carry out all of the required system functions. For example, a terrarium allegedly contains all the necessary ingredients to function indefinitely, since the plants and environment engage in a symbiotic, mutually supportive exchange. (Obviously, even a terrarium is not completely closed, since sunlight is imported.) Living systems tend to be more open, but there are examples of relatively closed living systems. A prison, for example, has almost impermeable boundaries, but even it is not a completely closed system, since food, guards, and information (e.g., through television) are taken in. Different kinds of colleges and universities are relatively open or closed. Prestigious selective institutions, for example, tend to restrict enrollments (relatively closed boundaries), whereas community colleges may have open admissions (relatively open boundaries). Thus, control of the boundaries of colleges and universities becomes a significant policy issue.

Boundary Permeability

Open and closed systems are differentiated by the permeability of their boundaries. Boundary permeability varies across different systems and is related to the system's vitality and energy consumption. The optimum condition of the boundary is not necessarily completely open (see Figure 4.2). To accomplish their missions, some systems are better partially closed—as, for example, religious seminaries or military academies. But the effectiveness of all types of organizations may be restricted by conditions of "overboundedness" or "underboundedness."

FIGURE 4.2
Relationship Between System Vitality and Boundary Permeability

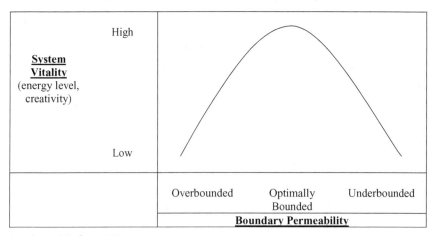

Based on Alderfer, 1976.

In "overbounded" systems, much energy (in the form of resources expended) is consumed in keeping people or things in or out. In "underbounded" systems, much energy (again, resources that might be used productively internally) leaks out or is used unproductively. Or more energy is inputted than can be used efficiently, and funds are wasted as a result. Even a prison has an optimum level of boundary permeability. If it is overbounded, too much energy at considerable cost is used to exercise more control than may be necessary to accomplish the incarceration goal. If it is underbounded, prisoners may escape.

A college campus can be overbounded—for example, when National Guard troops were called in on many campuses during the Vietnam War protests, some said that the system (in this case, a state) tended to be become less efficient. It was spending too much on control and not enough on education. On the other hand, when there is high boundary permeability, there may be little distinction between students and nonstudents, and much of the system's identity and energy may be lost. Some say this happened during the free speech movement in the 1960s at the University of California at Berkeley.

In recent years, the idea of boundaries between systems like colleges and universities and their environments has become somewhat more difficult to apply. Many institutions of higher education have established cooperative linkages with government agencies, community organizations, and industries. These boundary-spanning subsystems are subject to dual controls as they are simultaneously part of two separate systems and, in effect, become part of a larger macrosystem. Similarly, trends toward outsourcing institutional functions such as food service and transportation make it difficult to determine system boundaries and complicate efforts to address problems or improve performance.

Interface

Interface is the space through which exchanges between systems must pass. It is an area of separation. The size and qualitative character of the interface may say something about how the system operates. It may be useful, therefore, to analyze geographic, physical, or psychological distance. One might ask, for example, what is the interface between the college's residential life staff and the faculty (two subsystems, each with its own boundaries)? Are they physically and/or psychologically distant or close? Or, how big is the interface between a college and the citizens of the city or town in which it is located?

Understanding exchanges across subsystem interfaces is a critical component of higher education leadership. The effectiveness of campus governance, for example, may depend on the quality of exchanges between administrative subsystems that operate on principles of bureaucratic authority and faculty subsystems that rely on professional authority (Birnbaum, 1988; Del Favero, 2003).

Environment

Environment includes everything beyond the boundary of the system. A system is surrounded by other systems, forces, and conditions of varying types and strengths from which inputs to the organization originate and to which outputs are directed. In higher education, there are markets, buyers, clients, competitors, suppliers, state regulators, parents, and community members. Each of these has a potential impact on the structure and functioning of the organization (Crosson, 1984; Peterson, 1998). The specific modes by which that impact may take place are the subject of chapter 5.

Inputs

Inputs are the energy elements from the environment that are absorbed through the boundary. Some kinds of energy are kinetic, others potential. That is, some of the energy constitutes actual physical exchanges that can be put into action immediately within the organization, while some energy is in the form of accumulated surpluses that can be put into action at a later time. At the individual level, air is an input that is used immediately; food is stored as energy for later use. For organizations like colleges and universities, tuition income is an input that is stored until it is needed to compensate faculty, pay utility bills, buy equipment, or acquire other materials to be used in the transformation process.

Organizational inputs take many forms (Nadler & Tushman, 1977; Trice & Beyer, 1993). These include products, raw materials, human resources, information, technology, cultural expectations, and even human predispositions (e.g., past managerial behavior patterns that a newly hired administrator brings with him or her to a new institution). For diagnostic purposes, inputs can be classified into two types:

1. *Maintenance inputs* provide the system with the capacity to perform the requisite tasks to transform raw material into more complex forms suitable for output. Maintenance inputs, which enable the system to operate, include such things as money, instructional materials, students, research equipment, and new staff, among other resources.

2. *Signal inputs* are bits of information to be used by the system for decision making about how it should behave, both internally and

across its boundaries. Signal inputs include, for example, data on demographic changes in the high school population (Milliken, 1990), the jobs students get after college, or the graduate schools they attend.

New research findings and technological developments that are published in academic journals may constitute signal *or* maintenance inputs. They are signal inputs when faculty members are alerted to advances in the discipline to which attention must be paid. They are maintenance inputs when faculty members actually use the research findings to design their own studies in hopes of creating even more sophisticated forms of knowledge.

At the organizational level, it is important to account and plan for these different kinds of inputs in understanding how organizations operate and how effective they are in maintaining continuity of external support. The "just-in-time" (JIT) inventory system, for example, regulates the boundaries, the interface, and the environment in such a way that less investment in inventory is needed. Organizations do this through carefully articulated rapid purchasing and quick delivery arrangements with long-standing suppliers, which permit them to keep less inventory stored on the premises. A parallel in higher education is the use of adjunct faculty who can be considered as energy that is employed through a JIT-like system. The institution leaves them outside the system until needed. As a result, the institution does not commit itself to employing a potential excess of faculty. Some scholars, however, have raised concerns about the proportion of adjunct, nontenured faculty presently serving students. Schuster (2003), for example, argues that a modicum of tenured, full-time faculty is necessary to sustain the continuity of internal maintenance and transformational activities of the organization. Academic programs may be better staffed by those with some institutional memory and a closer connection to the campus culture.

Storage and Memory

Systems are not always immediately capable of processing inputs when they are received. Inputs may exceed the system's current capacity to use them, or there may be a temporary backup in the system's functioning that overloads the communication circuits. As a consequence, inputs must frequently be stored. Maintenance inputs can be stored in various ways. Surplus funds, for example, obviously can be banked. Student applications for admission can be kept either physically in files or stored in computers.

Signal inputs can also be stored in institutional memory banks (e.g., in files, archives, or the memories of longtime employees). Berrien (1968) defines **memory** as any relatively permanent record of inputs to a system that subsequently affects the processing of other inputs. Suppose, for example, that a community college receives word that because a new corporate office is opening nearby, there will be needs for workforce training and development. Since this information is needed for future planning purposes, it must be stored until it can be acted on. Failure to store it in the system's memory may cause it to be ignored, distorted, or discarded.

Needless to say, individuals as systems also have storage and memory needs and capacities. Students who listen to a lecture, for example, may record notes to be reviewed later.

Components or Subsystems

Components are the basic units of the system. They may be a single item or a grouping of items within a system that carries out a specific function or task. Examples of components at the organizational level in higher education include student affairs divisions, academic departments, information technology offices, research centers, and intercollegiate athletics, to name but a few. Note that components are, in effect, miniature systems complete with their own components and relationships among them. So, for example, the campus computer center has boundaries, inputs, storage and memory (lots of it!), and components.

A number of subsystems can be said to be generic—that is, they are present in some form in all organizations (Katz & Kahn, 1978, p. 51). These include:

1. *Production or technical subsystems*—units concerned with processing raw material
2. *Supportive subsystems*—units directed at aiding the production subsystem—for example, by procuring necessary materials for transformation processes
3. *Maintenance subsystems*—units oriented toward facilitating the human dynamics in getting the work done, including subsystems for personnel selection, rewards, and compensation, among others
4. *Adaptive subsystems*—units that consider and act on the long-range survival of the organization, such as market research, planning, and research and development
5. *Managerial subsystems*—units that define the decision-making authority of the system and whose roles include organizing, controlling, and coordinating.

Structure

Structure is the pattern of relationships among components that exists at any given time. This pattern provides order and coherence for members of the system. As Luhmann (1995) notes, "Structure transforms unstructured complexity into structured complexity" (p. 282). The more static character of structure offers organizational members a snapshot perspective on the components of an organization at any one time. This snapshot reveals the relationships among the components of a system, including authority relationships, power and information flows, and transfers of inputs (e.g., students "flowing" between departments). Some of the relationships are more long-standing; others are dynamic and constantly changing. Organizations need to be attentive to both—to how things stand at any one time and to how they may be changing. Over time, the snapshots can be considered as historical records of both manifest and subtle change.

Systems theory does not give us specific information about the qualitative nature of relationships among components (such as authority relationships or interdepartmental collaborations), but it does direct our attention to the structural patterns that persist over time, the flow of activities, and the flow and direction of communications. In a college or university, one can understand much about what is considered important by tracking the activities and interactions among faculty, academic departments, and various offices occupied by members of the administration. From an analysis of these ongoing and/or changing conditions, it is possible to infer the formal and informal relationships that exist in the organization. The *formal* organizational chart, however, may not necessarily reflect the *operative* structure of the organization. Connections among organizational units are at least somewhat ambiguous as a result of increased size and division of labor, and this ambiguity cannot be overcome with formal hierarchical oversight. Indeed, some would say that colleges and universities are not subject to systems analysis because they are anarchic and only partially analyzable from the structural perspective of systems theory (March & Olsen, 1976).

Differentiation and Specialization

One of the most basic of problems in systems such as formal organizations is the balancing of differentiation and integration—separating people or organizational units into specialized roles where expertise can be exercised, but then finding ways to connect them both organizationally and attitudinally (Lawrence & Lorsch, 1969). As systems grow, they tend to become more diversified and internally elaborated, with the components taking on more differentiated, specialized functions. Land-grant universities, for example, began as relatively small colleges that focused on agriculture and engineering. Over time, they became larger, added new functions, and developed highly differentiated internal structures composed of specialized academic departments and service and outreach units. Similarly, normal schools were founded in the 1800s with a teacher education mission, but nearly 200 of these institutions later became comprehensive state colleges and universities as they added more departments in the liberal arts and sciences (Ogren, 2005).

Clearly, this evolutionary process creates new problems to which the organizational system must be attentive. With increasing specialization, the newly specialized components must be integrated more carefully. If not, they will not be able to work together. The outputs from one component may not be acceptable as inputs to another (Katz & Kahn, 1978). On the other hand, too close a coupling may hamper the ability of individual units to respond quickly to local conditions. Nor will each component necessarily strive to maximize the benefits of the organization as a whole. This process— known as **suboptimization**—reflects the tendency of subsystems to try to maximize their own, rather than the larger organization's objectives.

Transformations

When inputs enter a system, they can be stored, as noted earlier, or they can be transformed through the use of different technologies. When transformed, the inputs undergo a change that converts them from raw material into finished products. Multiple technological processes may be involved in the transformation.

In colleges and universities, there are at least two important kinds of transformations. First, institutions admit students at different developmental stages; add to and change their cognitive skills, content knowledge, values, and attitudes; and then send them out transformed with value added—one hopes for the better. Processes of teaching in both curricular and extracurricular activities are technologies used in the transformation processes that facilitate growth in students.

A second type of transformation occurs when conducting research. Faculty members take in and transform raw data into more complex forms of knowledge. Research methods are the technology for the transformation process governing growth in knowledge.

A third set of technologies may emerge in some institutions with strong public service missions. Public service outreach often requires the application of specialized knowledge to the practical problems of agriculture, industry, education, health care, and environmental protection. Transforming theoretical knowledge into practical applications requires a complex set of skills, roles, and structures (Boyer, 1990; Lynton, 1995).

"Black Box"

The actual concrete acts of the transformation process, however, *cannot* be described using systems theory. The specific processes—for example, the dynamic interactions among the components in a system—are simply not open to scrutiny using systems theory. General systems theory does not address itself to these transactions. Hence, general systems theory always deals with phenomena that exist in what systems theorists call a "black box" (Klir, 1969). It is assumed that we are not able to get *inside* of the system with sufficient diagnostic accuracy to determine precisely what activities are taking place. We must use other theories to examine what occurs inside a system (Scott, 1998).

An example of a "black box" from the physical sciences may elucidate this idea. A telephone is a black box. We know that sound goes in and sound comes out. We can describe the communication system in general, but when we take an instrument apart to analyze the internal mechanism, we must use other tools, both conceptual and physical, to understand how it works. It is helpful to understand the telephone simply as a communication system, however, even without comprehending the theories from physics that explain its operation. When a system does not work, we can look to the elements comprising it that may account for the problem. We might check first to see if the inputs are being received. Is the telephone line plugged into the jack? We might listen to the earpiece. Is sound coming out? Is there output? What is its quality?

Human beings are and always will be "black boxes." Despite advances in science, the mystery of human beings as idiosyncratic entities will remain. It is helpful, therefore, to use systems theory to understand the larger parameters of organizational and human behavior to identify better which *other* theories may help explain the phenomena.

State of the System

The state of the system reflects the degree of openness of the system, the adaptability and variability of the system, and the stability and equilibrium of the system. To determine the state of the system, one must examine the present pattern of relationships among the components (its structure) and the filtering condition of the boundary (the rate and type of input/output flow). These characteristics determine what the system will accept as inputs as well as the manner in which it will process inputs and, perhaps, some characteristics of the output.

It is important to have this kind of information about a college. For example, admissions policy sets the boundaries for admission and filters out certain would-be inputs. It is a screening device. The criteria for admission (perhaps a high school diploma for a community college or high standardized test scores for a university) constitute a kind of boundary condition. The college may be patterned to continue this behavior, with different components regularly performing required activities.

Equilibrium and Homeostasis

In the positivist perspective, all systems must be in some kind of a balanced state or must be moving toward it (Buckley, 1967; Smart & Spalding, 1970). Otherwise, they either will die from lack of available energy or explode from too much. The balanced state or the movement toward it connotes a condition of **equilibrium**—that is, the stability of a system at a particular time (Berrien, 1980).

There are two types of equilibrium. One is called "static"—a steady state of the system in which there is an approximate balance among the parts of the system. This occurs when system inputs in general are adequate to meet transformation requirements and when system components are arranged in efficient internal input/output exchanges. The other kind of equilibrium is called "dynamic" in which either the component parts are temporarily not synchronized or the inputs and/or outputs are less or more than appropriate. In a dynamic equilibrium, both the components and the system as a whole are moving toward a new balance.

Dynamic systems have a natural tendency to move toward equilibrium. This tendency, known as **homeostasis**, entails continuous internal adjustments to remain in balance or harmony with the environment. Systems that exist in turbulent environments must constantly change their internal processes to attain a new balance with the outside world. Colleges and universities, for example, may continually create new academic programs and update curricular offerings in emerging fields. These changes bring the institution into balance with the expectations of the external environment. Some postmodern theorists, however, (e.g., Lyotard, 1984) would assert that there is no "total" system equilibrium—only **local determinism**, which dismisses the attempt to understand systemic relationships and posits instead that organizations and other social institutions are fragmented and that cohesive system-like behavior can only be found in localized "patches" within the organization.

In contrast to local determinism, systems theorists argue that organizations as a whole have systemic characteristics, and it may be useful to assess the state of *total* system equilibrium, since adjustments in any of the system components can be understood in that context. As a college reforms its internal structure to adapt to changing external conditions, for example, it may be perceived as operating inefficiently if viewed from a perspective of static equilibrium. When the college is seen in a transitional state, however, alleged inefficiencies will be conceived as a normal process of dynamic equilibrium.

Equifinality

The principle of **equifinality** "suggests that systems can reach the same end from different initial positions and through different paths" (Hoy & Miskel,

2005, p. 22). No two organizations need to have structures or transformation processes that are exactly alike to achieve the same ends. Apple and IBM both produced good computers using different operating systems in the early days of the computer era. Two colleges can help students grow and develop in quite different but equally effective ways. The concept of equifinality in systems theory (Gresov & Drazin, 1997) is particularly important, as there is a tendency to believe that prestigious colleges are models of educational policy and practice that must be copied. Similar pressures to adopt "best practices" may be based on thinking that there is "one best way" to achieve high-level performance. Equifinality suggests, however, that institutions can pursue multiple paths to success. This concept provides significant leeway for higher education leaders to develop policies and practices that are uniquely suited to the mission, size, history, and culture of their institution.

Outputs

Outputs are exported products of the system. They vary in their usefulness, depending on the criteria and needs of the receiving suprasystems. Clearly, educated graduates of colleges are generally useful to society at-large, while graduates produced with outmoded skills or intolerant attitudes will provide less benefit to society.

Many conceptualizations of organizational effectiveness suggest that success is a matter of the continued acceptability of the system's outputs. Sometimes called a **functionalist** perspective, this notion considers the role the organization plays as serving a function in a larger system. An organization is functional when it meets the larger system's needs. A college, for example, may be considered functional when it fulfills expectations for providing well-educated workers and civically engaged citizens.

Organizational subsystems also produce outputs that remain *within* the organization and are used by other subsystems. A human resources office, for example, produces outputs (services) that are directed almost entirely to other subsystems (departments) within the organization. Attention to this type of internal output encourages organizational members to think of their internal customers—that is, those people or units within the organization that receive the output from another internal subsystem.

Another form of internal output includes individual or group satisfaction, which often affects motivation levels and overall work performance. Affective states among employees are critical to organizational effectiveness. In colleges and universities, the production of internal outputs such as intrinsic satisfaction for faculty and staff is seen as critical to the institution's success.

Feedback

Feedback is a means for organizations to determine how outputs compare with goals and how well outputs are received in the environment (Bogart, 1980; Scott, 1998). Effective organizations have sensing mechanisms *outside* their boundaries that provide information about the system's behavior. They also have internal antennae tuned to those sensing mechanisms, and they are able to learn from the messages (Argyris, 1990; Senge, 1990). So, to obtain feedback, there must be a way to evaluate the impact of the organization *and* a mode of communication by which that information can be (and is) attended to inside.

Often the feedback triggers some adaptive reaction by the organization. The feedback mechanism to accomplish this is similar to the role played by a home thermostat. When an air conditioner reduces the temperature in a room, the thermostat senses the change, and this information is then fed back to the air conditioner switch to turn it off when the desired temperature is reached.

Colleges and universities have many means of sensing the acceptability of their outputs and their general images with the public. A signal input that is used for moderating college policy and procedures might be the report of a placement office on the success of the college's graduates in obtaining jobs. Such data provide information on whether and how to change the inputs, the transformation processes, or the cross-boundary processes (e.g., placement) that bridge the interface between the system and the recipients of its outputs.

Entropy

Earlier, we noted that as systems grow, they become more differentiated. But when systems become large, there is also a tendency for systems as a whole to lose energy and "run down." This is especially true of relatively closed systems that have few sources of new energy from the outside (Rifkin, 1980). The concept of **entropy**, which describes the tendencies of systems to drift toward disorder, is derived from the second law of thermodynamics in physics, which states that all systems unavoidably produce certain amounts of decay, depletion, and chaos. In the context of an organizational system, differentiated structures may become so diffuse and disconnected that they enter a state of entropy—a random arrangement of the components with maximum disorder and no possibility of predicting the particular functions of any one. Roles and responsibilities tend to become blurred, and it is more difficult to identify precisely what each component does. For example, when the admissions office and the faculty start keeping their own records for new applicants, functions are not unique, and energy is wasted. Similarly, over time, it may become unclear who in a community college is responsible for developing new articulation agreements: the faculty who interact with their counterparts at the four-year institutions, the transfer counselors who work with the admissions staff at the four-year institutions, or the academic administrators who coordinate the community college's wide array of programs. In this context, it becomes difficult to identify who is responsible for a particular function.

In each of these cases, the formerly differentiated functions become increasingly randomly distributed within the system and, hence, less predictably accountable for their behavior. It becomes more and more difficult to tell who is responsible for what. When this happens, the system begins to become less efficient, since specialization of functions is reduced as each unit does many things that others do, and much energy is spent or misspent in inefficient allocation of work.

To counteract the decreased efficiency, more energy inputs of greater complexity can be imported from the environment and used to reinvigorate and upgrade the internal system. This process—known as "negative entropy"—reverses the entropic tendency. As Katz and Kahn (1978) note: "To survive, open systems must reverse the entropic process; they must acquire negative entropy. The entropic process is a universal law of nature in which all forms of organization move toward disorganization or death. By importing more energy from its environment than it expends, the open system can store energy and acquire negative entropy" (p. 25). Thus, despite the apparent pessimism of the inevitability of decay in increasingly differentiated systems, it is not necessary to abandon hope for the future. Adaptive organizations continually restructure themselves to retain and enhance their vitality and energy. Dynamic equilibrium brings the system into a new balance with the environment, but it also requires a redistribution of the energies within the system.

Summary of General Systems Theory

General systems theory reveals connections among various components of a system and its environment. These relationships are displayed in Figure 4.3.

Colleges and universities fit well into this framework. Systems models reveal critical domains of organizational structure and function to which leaders must be sensitive, and for organizations to be successful, they must recognize each of the system components and the dynamic nature of their interactions. Indeed, as Talcott Parsons (1951) noted, the relationships among the parts of a system and their interactions must be organized in particular ways at different times for effective organizational functioning. Sometimes,

FIGURE 4.3
Elements in a Systems Framework*

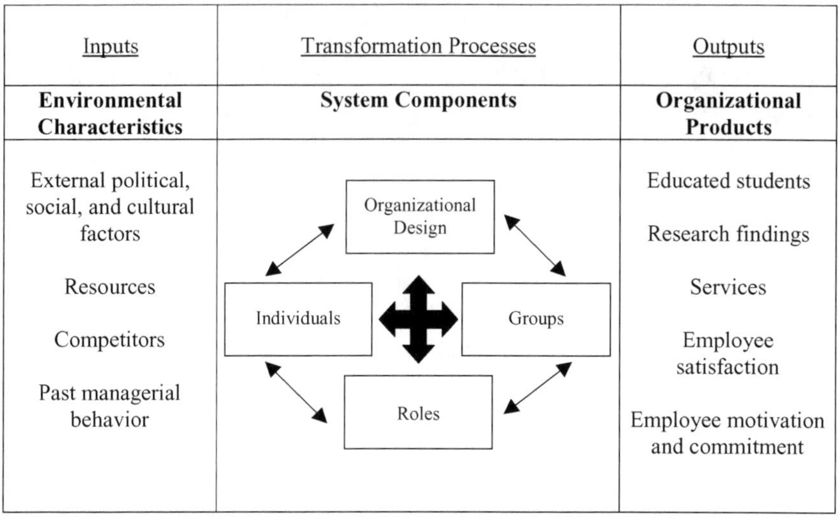

Inputs	Transformation Processes	Outputs
Environmental Characteristics	**System Components**	**Organizational Products**
External political, social, and cultural factors Resources Competitors Past managerial behavior	Organizational Design Individuals Groups Roles	Educated students Research findings Services Employee satisfaction Employee motivation and commitment

*Based on Hills, 1968, p. 21.

for example, more attention needs to be paid to the external environment. On other occasions, leaders need to focus their attention internally. In addition, organizations may alternate between periods when members focus on the ends or outputs of the system, and times when emphasis is placed on the means or transformation processes for doing the work. Considering a distinction between external and internal issues, and one between ends and means, Parsons suggests that there are four organizational **prerequisites** that all systems must attend to (Table 4.1).

1. **Adaptation** focuses on the system's exchanges with the environment. The exchanges focus primarily on acquiring sufficient resources from the environment to sustain the system. Organizational members in higher education fulfill this function when they recruit new faculty and staff, admit students, and acquire grant funding.

2. **Goal attainment** "refers to the necessity of every organization to establish a relatively stable relation with its environment through which both the organization and environment can achieve their ends" (Bess, 1988, p. 134). Staff in a development office, for example, seek to attain the institution's fund-raising goals, but in doing so, make sure that donors feel that their desires have been satisfied as well—perhaps by recognition through the naming of a building or scholarship fund.

TABLE 4.1
Functional Prerequisites of Systems*

	Instrumental ("means")	Consummatory ("ends")
External	Adaptation • securing adequate resources from the environment and distributing those resources efficiently	Goal Attainment • setting and achieving goals; demonstrating to the environment that system outputs are useful and of high quality
Internal	Latency • continuity and stability over time in working relations among units; achieved through socialization processes and communicating the system's values	Integration • maintaining solidarity or coordination among the subunits, and encouraging contributions to the effective functioning of the system as a whole

* Based on Parsons, 1951.

3. The **integration** function fulfills the need for mutual support and collaboration toward common goals. Collective action of some sort is required for nearly all organizational activity. An organizational member fulfilling this function might encourage faculty and staff to discuss how their work connects to related objectives.

4. Finally, **latency** provides the stability and continuity among system components needed for organized activity. Constant uncertainty and chaos can be demoralizing and can undermine effective performance. Stable structures and common values, in contrast, can ensure reliability and promote trust in relationships across system components. Organizational members can fulfill the latency function by facilitating consistent patterns of communication across the subsystems of the institution, and by promoting the norms and values of the organization.

Social Systems Theory

Next we move to a smaller unit of analysis than the total organization or its subunits—namely, to the individual as a system and to the systems contained within the individual. Called **social systems theory**, this is a self-contained set of concepts that fits *within* general systems theory and can be useful in understanding how human beings as bounded systems interact with their environments. Like general systems theory, social systems theory is also a general orientation model and is not intended to provide highly accurate predictions of human behavior. Other, more specific theories deal conceptually with those issues, and those theories are the focus of subsequent chapters in this book.

The main "system" in social systems theory is the *individual*, not the organization. Social systems theory is concerned with the juxtaposition of the two systems with which individuals are involved. One is the environment *outside* the individual's boundary—the individual's "social environment" or social system. The other is the set of subsystems or components *within* the individual—especially the personality subsystem (Roe & Siegelman, 1964). (Other subsystems or components within the individual are biological, physical, and cognitive.) For an illustration, see Figure 4.4.

Social systems theory examines the interaction of the external environment and the components of the individual's internal subsystems to explain individual behavior. This is similar to the interactive relationships of organizations and their environments. **Observed behavior** (OB) of individuals is thus a function (f) of the interaction of the inputs from the individual's **external social environment** (E) and **personal characteristics** (P). Symbolically, this can be represented by the following formula: OB = f(E, P). In organizations, the external social environment can be defined in terms of the roles

FIGURE 4.4.
The Individual as a System

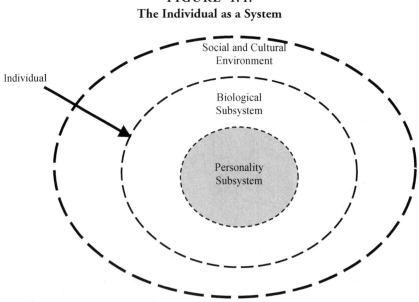

and expectations sent by the organization to the member. These roles and expectations include not only the formal job description but also the informal norms and social agreements prevalent in an organization. Consequently, behavior in organizations is a function of the interaction of organizational role and personal characteristics such as personality, beliefs, and needs, as well as individual cognition and emotions.

All too often, organizational members seeking solutions to pending problems tend to attribute alleged dysfunctional behavior to only *one* of these influences and ignore the other. A vice president, for example, may place the blame for poor enrollment planning exclusively on the enrollment manager. Social systems theory urges us to consider both the individual and his or her environment. In this case, the vice president also could look carefully at the variety of environmental factors that affect enrollment, going from the demographics of the market to the dynamics of the enrollment manager's office. In addition, it is important to consider the antecedent conditions that led to the current condition of the individual (the enrollment manager) and the system—and the history of circumstances that may explain the result of the interaction of the individual and the social system.

As further illustrations, consider a dean facing faculty resistance to change, a faculty member thinking about students' lack of motivation, and a vice president worrying about a subordinate's failure to observe rules. All of these require consideration of the simultaneous effects of personal characteristics and social environments on the behavior of organizational members. Social systems theory is thus oriented toward understanding the inevitably dynamic nature of the interactions between individuals and their organizations.

The Social Systems Model

According to social systems theory, two parallel tracks are used to explain human behavior—the **nomothetic** and **idiographic** (see Figure 4.5). The components of these forces are the organizational system, roles, and expectations (the nomothetic side), and personality, learned beliefs, and individual needs (the idiographic side). By identifying as clearly as possible the nature and strength of both organizational expectations and personal needs, it is possible (using positivist terminology) to *understand, predict,* and *intervene* in the ways a person behaves or is likely to behave.

The Nomothetic Dimension: The External Side

The nomothetic track comprises the forces external to the individual (Getzels, Lipham, & Campbell, 1968). These forces constitute the environment for the individual. For diagnostic purposes, this area is broken down into

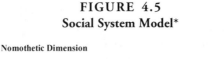

FIGURE 4.5
Social System Model*

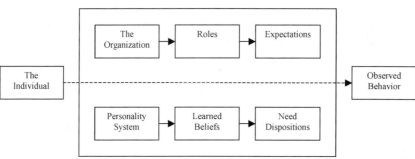

*Based on Getzels and Guba, 1957.

three interrelated parts—organization, roles, and expectations. Here are some abbreviated explanations of these terms.

An **organization** is a human system in which members pursue goals and satisfactions—sometimes collectively, sometimes individually. In a work organization, members enact a set of roles (a job) for pay among other rewards. **Roles** are positions in an organization that are set in an interlocking context, usually hierarchical. They can be diffuse or specific (i.e., either vague or quite concrete in specification of duties and responsibilities). Roles exist in complementary relationships. That is, any one role exists *only* in relation to at least one other role whose relationship is also defined at least partially by the first role. For example, there can be no teacher role without a companion student role. Neither makes sense without the other.

Roles are defined by the organization, and their definitions are impersonal—that is, not uniquely defined for each person. Organizationally defined roles are promulgated by administrative officers in terms of expected rights and responsibilities—for example, the right of a faculty member to make assignments for students and the expectation that the faculty member will provide a syllabus, hold office hours, and submit grades in a timely manner. Thus, the role connotes a set of **expected behaviors**.

The Idiographic Dimension: The Individual Side

The theory also uses three elements to describe the input to behavior from *inside* the individual: personality, individual beliefs, and need disposition.

For our purposes, **personality** refers to the dynamic organization of various psychological systems within an individual that determine his or her unique adjustments to his or her external environment (Allport, 1937). It is a relatively stable predisposition to behave with some degree of consistency or predictability across situations and time. Some individuals, for example, consistently respond optimistically to their environments, while others tend to have a more pessimistic view. Introversion and extroversion are also important personality domains. Extroverts are outgoing, adaptable, and confident in unfamiliar situations. Introverts are shy, reflective, and hesitant to act in unfamiliar settings.

Each individual also acquires a set of **beliefs** as he or she grows and develops. These beliefs are partly culturally induced and partly influenced by environmental circumstances. Over time, individuals acquire an understanding of personally acceptable ways of interacting with others. Out of personality and beliefs comes a corresponding unique combination of **needs** (Parsons & Shils, 1951). Examples of needs are those for achievement, security, risk, acceptance, and competency. Together, needs direct the individual to expect and desire features of the organizational system that will maintain equilibrium. When those expectations and desires are met, the individual achieves balance among internal and external forces.

Expanded Social Systems Model

Individuals are affected by internal forces other than just personality, beliefs, and need dispositions. On the idiographic side, biological needs—for sleep, food, and warmth, for example—also may press for certain kinds of behavior. On the nomothetic side, in addition to organizationally defined roles and expectations, there are two extremely important inputs to behavior to which an individual must attend. In addition to formal role expectations, there is a persistent set of informal expectations that emerges from the settings in which individuals work. The norms and values of the work group, for example, constrain behavior and must be taken into account in the explanation of observed behavior at work (see chapter 10). So, too, the culture of the organization as a whole (see chapter 11) has an impact on behavior. Still further outside the individual is a variety of values, all of which are generated by the culture of the nation and locality in which the organization is set. These, too, affect behavior and must be reviewed to understand individual behavior in organizations. To picture the total range of influences on individual behavior, see Figure 4.6.

FIGURE 4.6
The Expanded Social System Model*

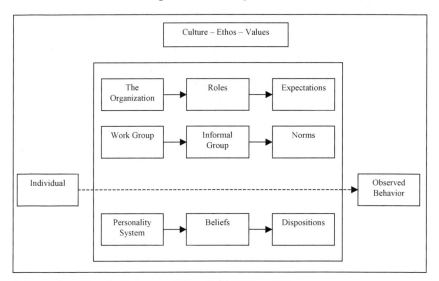

*Adapted from Getzels, Lipham, and Campbell, 1968, p. 102.

Proportionate Contribution of Idiographic versus Nomothetic

How much the environment influences individual behavior and how much the personality affects individual behavior varies with the type of organization. A prison, for example, is much more constraining of behavior than is a college. A bank permits less idiosyncratic behavior than does a research institute. Further, even in the same *type* of organization, variations are possible. Thus, not all colleges place the same demands, formal and informal, on individuals. Community college faculty members, for example, are often permitted less latitude than are faculty at research universities, in terms of both what the rules prescribe and what the culture imposes. We can express this relationship between the nomothetic and idiographic presses graphically, as in Figure 4.7.

An optimum balance between the two presses depends on the goals of the organization and the characteristics of the environment. That is, certain types of organizations tend to be more nomothetically dominated, while others are idiographically determined—the first when environments are relatively stable, the second when they are more turbulent. In other words, stable organizations encourage the development of established structures and roles,

FIGURE 4.7
**Strength of Nomothetic and Idiographic Influences on Behavior
in Different Types of Organizations**

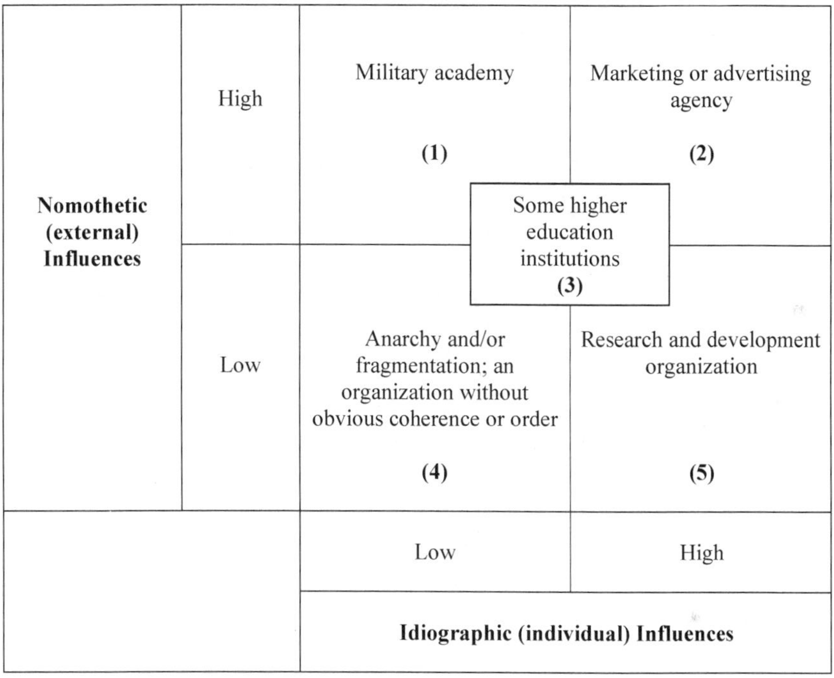

Nomothetic (external) Influences	High	Military academy **(1)**	Marketing or advertising agency **(2)**
		Some higher education institutions **(3)**	
	Low	Anarchy and/or fragmentation; an organization without obvious coherence or order **(4)**	Research and development organization **(5)**
		Low	High
		Idiographic (individual) Influences	

In cell #1, there will be high organizational pressure and few opportunities to express individual personality.

In cell #2, there will be strong organizational pressures brought on by external competition, while at the same time there will be freedom for individual creativity and initiative.

In cell #3, there will be a moderate amount of both organizational and individual pressure, resulting in some ambiguity that is often difficult to manage.

In cell #4, regulated behavior and standard operating procedures are absent and are replaced by disconnected individual efforts, which are neither legitimated nor supported by the organization as a whole.

In cell #5, there will be much freedom to express oneself with few constraints from the organization.

while unsettled organizations require more continuing input from organizational members.

The "Fit" Between and Among System Components

Thus far, we have examined the elements of general and social systems but have not described their interaction fully. As noted, systems theory is silent about the specifics of relationships among components. Nevertheless, some organizational analysts suggest that optimum functioning of any system, at either the organizational or individual level, depends on a "fit" between and among system components. At the organizational level, Nadler and Tushman (1977) provide a useful diagnostic model for comprehending the various elements in a system and examining the "fit" among them. Figure 4.8 is an adaptation of their model.

Note in this model that the organization as a system is surrounded by a boundary within which are included two human systems—individuals and groups—and two organizational systems—individual tasks and roles and the total complex of roles set in a structure. These four systems engage in a dynamic interaction that transforms inputs into outputs. In colleges and universities, inputs from the environment include faculty, students, and external funding, among others. Within the institution, faculty and administrators

FIGURE 4.8
Organizational Fits*

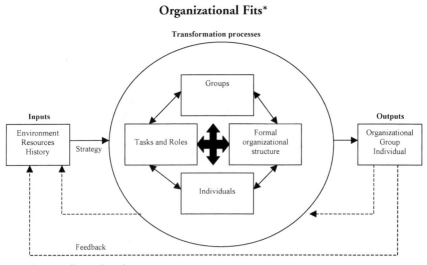

*Based on Nadler and Tushman, 1977.

perform their roles within the constraints of a structure, usually bureaucratically designed, and of a group and organizational culture that develops over time. Outputs consist of educated students, new knowledge, and service. A feedback loop senses the receptivity of the environment to these outputs and signals to the organization to maintain its current configuration and activities or to change them.

The fit hypothesis suggests that not only must all the elements in the system be synchronized (in dynamic equilibrium), but that bivariate relationships (i.e., between pairs) must be matched—or, in the words of Nadler and Tushman, consistent (see also, Van de Ven & Drazin, 1985). For example, faculty members' need for autonomy must be matched with an organizational design that allows them to enact roles without excessive intervention or constraint. Similarly, most organizations try to recruit individuals whose personalities allow them to fit into the organizational system, and organizational systems are often designed to accommodate the prevailing personalities of the typical workers. In a college or university, faculty personalities often predispose them to need considerable autonomy, and the institutions are structured, in part, to accommodate that need. On occasion, there are misfits, in which case adjustments must be made on one or both sides. Sometimes, however, the "give" can be from only one side, depending on the type of individual or organization, their histories, and strength of individual personality and current organizational leadership.

Note that the fit hypothesis also governs cross-boundary relationships. For example, as we will discover in chapter 6, the degree of flexibility of the organizational design must be consistent with the characteristics of the environment outside the boundaries of the organization. In fact, when the fit hypothesis is applied to *all* components, inside and out, it describes an ideal situation that can never quite be fully realized. There is always a dynamic tension between the organization's need to adapt to changing environmental conditions and at the same time to be relatively stable with systematic and efficient relations among internal components of the organization. Hence, a compromise in the maximization of internal and cross-boundary fits is always necessary.

A similar fit model can be created for the system at the individual level (see Figure 4.9). Here, too, the individual as a system is surrounded by a boundary. Inputs to the individual system have both nomothetic and idiographic characteristics. Every faculty and staff member, for example, brings to the workplace experience, memory, ability, intelligence, and other individual factors. The institution also provides inputs, including the prescribed roles to be played, the design of the organization, and the influence of formal and informal groups. Within the individual, system components include general

FIGURE 4.9
Systems Theory and the Individual

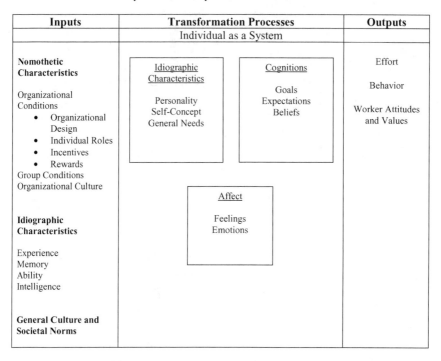

needs, self-concept, and personality characteristics as well as cognitive and affective states. The outputs of the individual system are effort, behavior, and worker attitudes and values.

Extensions of Systems Theory: Alternative Paradigms

General systems theory suggests that if we can identify important forces both within and outside the organization, we can explain organizational behavior. Similarly, social systems theory holds that if we can identify nomothetic (external) and idiographic (internal) influences, we can explain individual behavior in a social system. Alternative paradigms, however, call into question assumptions regarding the predictability of systems. Cohen and March (1974), for example, conceptualized colleges and universities as "organized anarchies" that are characterized by problematic goals, unclear technologies, and fluid participation.

Goals of colleges and universities are problematic because they are difficult to define, operationalize, and measure. Consider the goal of providing a high-quality general education experience to all students. Definitions of what constitutes "general education" are likely to differ based on faculty members' preferences for various subject matter content. Education itself is an abstract outcome, unlike corporate profits, which are clear indicators of success. Even if organizational members could agree on the definition and indicators of high-quality general education, they might still disagree about the best way to measure the outcomes (e.g., standardized test scores or assessments of compiled portfolios of student work).

Transformation processes of colleges and universities—that is, the technologies through which inputs are converted into outputs—are not well understood or easily predictable. A faculty member, for example, could use the same pedagogical approach in two classrooms and obtain dramatically different results. In the research domain, scientific breakthroughs may be more likely to occur when previous practices are ignored, and scientists are able to deviate significantly from what previous studies have shown to be true (Kuhn, 1962, 1970). What constitutes success in teaching, research, and service, therefore, may be so idiosyncratic and localized that it is nearly impossible to draw specific generalizations to improve practice.

Finally, governance and decision-making processes are characterized by fluid participation. Due to variations in work schedules among faculty and administrators, it is difficult to bring together the same group of people to make decisions. Participation in committee meetings is often sporadic; there are few occasions, therefore, when the same group of people makes decisions on related issues. A high degree of variability in decision-making participants makes the outcomes difficult to predict.

Organized anarchy highlights the unpredictability of complex internal organizational systems. Similarly, chaos theory notes the challenges of being able to make accurate predictions about the external environments in which systems are embedded (Lorenz, 1993). Chaotic environments are nonlinear, which means that the future will not necessarily represent an extension of the past. Under these conditions, organizational leaders are not to able use historical or present-day data to predict the future state of the environment (e.g., enrollment projections, state funding patterns).

Organized anarchy and chaos theory do not negate the importance of systems theory. In fact, both perspectives can be viewed as important extensions of systems theory. If systems are characterized by problematic goals, unclear technologies, and fluid participation, then leaders need to be cautious about their ability to predict system outcomes accurately. Leaders need to be aware that individuals tend to react not only to the "real" demands of the system but also to their socially constructed understandings of that system. Learning to lead in the context of multiple social constructions of reality is critical to ensuring effective outcomes in organized anarchies. Moreover, in a chaotic postmodern environment, organizations likely need to support a diverse range of flexible organizational designs to allow for continuous change and promote greater responsiveness to complex external forces. Leaders need to be adept at balancing imperatives for change, along with "the ability to recreate order and pattern, at least temporarily, despite continuous compensation for internal and external shocks to the system" (Cutright, 2001, pp. 5–6). We address these challenges more extensively in subsequent chapters on external environments (chapter 5) and organizational designs (chapter 6).

Summary

General systems theory and social systems theory give us some broad conceptual tools for understanding organizations such as colleges and universities. When problems occur at the organizational system level, we can use the descriptive terms of general systems theory to identify possible domains to address those problems. Similarly, when an individual's behavior becomes apparently dysfunctional either for the individual or the organization, we can look to social systems theory explanations by examining behavior in terms of the influences of the idiographic and nomothetic domains. In the following chapters, we begin to expand and deepen our understanding of both organizations and individuals as systems.

Review Questions

1. Parental complaints about the content of a course illustrate the importance of which of the following concepts in general systems theory?
   a. Black box
   b. Equifinality
   c. Signal inputs
   d. Structure

2. An announcement by a state board of education of a planned reduction in aid to a specific institution is an example of:
   a. Maintenance inputs
   b. Dynamic equilibrium
   c. Entropy
   d. Signal inputs

3. Using social systems theory, the behavior of a student can be understood in terms of:
   a. The student and the college
   b. The student's personality and curriculum
   c. The student's needs and instructors' expectations in courses
   d. All of the above

4. The dean criticizes a faculty member for the faculty member's failure to submit book requests to the bookstore by the deadline. The dean's action is best explained by social systems theory in terms of:
   a. The dean's role
   b. The dean's needs
   c. Faculty member's ineptness
   d. A and B
   e. A and C

5. Which of the following is *not* part of a college's transformation process?
   a. Its informal organization
   b. Resources obtained from the federal government
   c. Organizational arrangements
   d. Faculty tasks

6. According to Nadler and Tushman's "fit" hypothesis, which of the following must be linked to provide more effective outputs?
   a. Enrollment targets (e.g., numbers of first-time, transfer, and part-time students) and course offerings
   b. Governance structures and faculty expectations for participation in decision making
   c. Faculty research teams and configurations of labs and office space
   d. All of the above

Case Discussion Questions

Consider the Mammoth State University case presented at the beginning of this chapter.

1. Analyze the alcohol-related incident in terms of **general systems theory**. Identify the elements in the university's environment that contributed to this incident. Is the university an overbounded or underbounded system? Which boundary relationships may need to change to prevent similar incidents in the future?

2. Consider how the vice president for student affairs responded to the bar owner's comments. How might the university and the neighborhood bars change how they interface with each other?

3. Consider how the president responded to the comments from the mayor's representative. What was the president's assessment of the relationships among the internal subsystems of the university? How might the structure of the university as an organizational system need to change to restore equilibrium?

4. Analyze the students' behaviors using **social systems theory**. How can their behavior be explained in terms of an interaction between the organizational system and individual personalities? Consider both nomothetic and idiographic dimensions of the problem. For the nomothetic dimension (the external side), consider how the university communicates its expectations for the role of student. Also consider the norms and values of student culture in large universities. For the idiographic dimension (the individual side), consider needs for self-esteem and acceptance.

References

Abrahamson, E. (1997). The emergence and prevalence of employee management rhetorics: The effects of long waves, labor unions, and turnover, 1875 to 1992. *Academy of Management Journal, 40*(3), 491–553.

Alderfer, C. P. (1976). Boundary relations and organizational diagnosis. In H. Meltzer and F. R. Wickert (Eds.), *Humanizing organizational behavior* (pp. 109–133). Springfield, IL: Thomas.

Allport, G. W. (1937). *Personality: A psychological interpretation.* New York: Henry Holt.

Argyris, C. (1990). *Overcoming organizational defenses: Facilitating organizational learning.* Needham Heights, MA: Allyn & Bacon.

Bailey, K. D. (1994). *Sociology and the new systems theory.* Albany, NY: State University of New York Press.

Bailey, K. D. (2005). Beyond system internals: Expanding the scope of living systems theory. *Systems Research and Behavioral Science, 22*(6), 497–508.

Berrien, F. K. (1968). *General and social systems.* New Brunswick, NJ: Rutgers University Press.

Berrien, F. K. (1980). Homeostasis in groups. In G. Chen, J. M. Jamieson, L. L. Schkade, and C. H. Smith (Eds.), *The general theory of systems applied to management and organization* (vol. 1, pp. 115–127). Seaside, CA: Intersystems.

Bertalanffy, L. von. (1968). *General systems theory.* New York: Braziller.

Bess, J. (1988). *Collegiality and bureaucracy in the modern university.* New York: Teachers College Press, Columbia University.

Birnbaum, R. (1988). *How colleges work: The cybernetics of academic organization and leadership.* San Francisco: Jossey-Bass.

Bogart, D. H. (1980). Feedback, feedforward, and feedwithin: Strategic information in systems. *Behavioral Science, 25*(4), 237–249.

Boulding, K. (1953). *The organizational revolution.* New York: Harper.

Boulding, K. (1956). General systems theory—The skeleton of science. *Management Science, 2,* 197–208.

Boyer, E. (1990). *Scholarship reconsidered: Priorities of the professoriate.* Princeton, NJ: Carnegie Foundation for the Advancement of Teaching.

Buckley, W. (1967). *Sociology and modern systems theory.* Englewood Cliffs, NJ: Prentice-Hall.

Burrell, G., & Morgan, G. (1979). *Sociological paradigms and organizational analysis.* London: Heinemann.

Burton, R. M. (2004). *Strategic organizational diagnosis and design: The dynamics of fit.* Boston: Kluwer.

Churchman, C. W. (1968). *The systems approach.* New York: Delacorte Press.

Cohen M., & March, J. (1974). *Leadership and ambiguity: The American college presidency.* New York: McGraw-Hill.

Conway, M. E. (1988). Organizations, professional autonomy, and roles. In M. E. Hardy & M. E. Conway (Eds.), *Role theory: Perspectives for health professionals* (2nd ed., pp. 111–132). Norwalk, CT: Appleton & Lange.

Corea, S. (2005). Refocusing systems analysis of organizations through a semiotic lens: Interpretive framework and method. *Systemic Practice and Action Research, 18*(4), 339–364.

Crosson, P. (1984). State postsecondary education—Policy systems. *The Review of Higher Education, 7*(2), 125–142.

Cutright, M. (Ed.). (2001). *Chaos theory and higher education: Leadership, planning, and policy.* New York: Peter Lang.

Del Favero, M. (2003). Faculty-administrator relationships as integral to high-performing governance systems: New frameworks for study. *American Behavioral Scientist, 46*(7), 902–922.

Donaldson, L. (2001). *The contingency theory of organizations.* Thousand Oaks, CA: Sage Publications.

Fombrun, C., & Shanley, M. (1990). What's in a name? Reputation building and corporate strategy. *Academy of Management Journal, 33*(2), 233–258.

Galliers, R., Mingers, J., & Jackson, M. (1997). Organization theory and systems thinking: The benefits of partnership. *Organization, 4*(2), 269–278.

Getzels, J. W., & Guba, E. G. (1957). Social behavior and the administrative process. *School Review, 65,* 423–441.

Getzels, J. W., Lipham, J. M., & Campbell, R. F. (1968). *Educational administration as a social process: Theory, research, practice.* New York: Harper & Row.

Gioia, D., & Thomas, J. (1996). Identity, image, and issue interpretation: Sensemaking during strategic change in academia. *Administrative Science Quarterly, 41*(3), 370–403.

Gresov, C., & Drazin, R. (1997). Equifinality: Functional equivalence in organizational design. *Academy of Management Review, 22*(2), 403–428.

Hall, A. D., & Fagen, R. E. (1980). Definition of system. In G. Chen, J. Jamieson, L. Schkade, and C. H. Smith, (Eds.). *The general theory of systems applied to management and organization* (vol. 1, pp. 73–85). Seaside, CA: Intersystems.

Hills, R. J. (1968). *Toward a science of organization.* Eugene, OR: Center for the Advanced Study of Educational Administration, University of Oregon.

Hoy, W., & Miskel, C. (2005). *Educational administration: Theory, research, and practice* (7th ed.). New York: McGraw-Hill.

Katz, D., & Kahn, R. (1978). *The social psychology of organizations* (2nd ed.). New York: Wiley.

Klir, G. J. (1969). *An approach to general systems theory.* New York: Van Nostrand Reinhold Company.

Kuhn, A. (1975). Boundaries, kinds of systems, and kinds of interactions. In A. J. Melcher (Ed.), *General systems and organization theory: Methodological aspects* (pp. 39–46). Kent, OH: Kent State University, Center for Business and Economic Research.

Kuhn, T. (1962). *The structure of scientific revolutions* (1st ed.). Chicago: University of Chicago Press.

Kuhn, T. (1970). *The structure of scientific revolutions* (2nd ed.). Chicago: University of Chicago Press.

Lawrence, P., & Lorsch, J. (1969). *Organization and environment: Managing differentiation and integration.* Homewood, IL: Richard D. Irwin.

Lorenz, E. (1993). *The essence of chaos.* Seattle: University of Washington Press.

Luhmann, N. (1995). *Social systems* (J. Bednarz Jr., Trans.). Stanford, CA: Stanford University Press.

Luhmann, N. (2006). System as difference. *Organization, 13*(1), 37–57.

Lynton, E. (1995). *Making the case for professional service.* Washington, DC: American Association for Higher Education.

Lyotard, J. F. (1984). *The postmodern condition: A report on knowledge* (G. Bennington and B. Massumi, Trans.). Minneapolis: University of Minnesota Press.

March, J., & Olsen, J. (1976). *Ambiguity and choice in organizations.* Bergen, Norway: Universitetsforlaget.

Milliken, F. J. (1990). Perceiving and interpreting environmental change: An examination of college administrators' interpretation of changing demographics. *Academy of Management Journal, 33*(1), 42–63.

Monane, J. (1967). *A sociology of human systems.* New York: Appleton-Century Crofts.

Nadler, D. A., & Tushman, M. L. (1977). A diagnostic model for organizational behavior. In J. R. Hackman, E. E. Lawler III, & L. W. Porter (Eds.), *Perspectives on behavior in organizations* (pp. 85–98). New York: McGraw-Hill.

Ogren, C. (2005). *The American state normal school.* New York: Palgrave Macmillan.

Olsen, M. E. (1968). *The process of social organization.* New York: Holt, Rinehart and Winston.

O'Reilly, C. A. III, Chatman, J., & Caldwell, D. (1991). People and organizational culture: A profile comparison approach to assessing person-organization fit. *Academy of Management Journal, 34*(3), 487–516.

Parsons, T. (1951). *The social system*. New York: The Free Press.

Parsons, T., & Shils, E. A. (Eds.). (1951). *Toward a general theory of action*. Cambridge, MA: Harvard University Press.

Peterson, M. (1998). *Improvement to emergence: An organization-environment research agenda for a postsecondary knowledge industry*. Stanford, CA: National Center for Postsecondary Improvement.

Rifkin, J. (with Ted Howard) (1980). *Entropy: A new world view*. New York: Viking Press.

Roe, A., & Siegelman, M. (1964). *The origin of interests*. Washington, DC: American Personnel and Guidance Association.

Schuster, J. (2003). The faculty makeover: What does it mean for students? *New Directions for Higher Education, 123*. San Francisco: Jossey-Bass.

Scott, W. R. (1998). *Organizations: Rational, natural, and open systems* (4th ed.). Englewood Cliffs, NJ: Prentice-Hall.

Senge, P. (1990, Fall). The leader's new work: Building learning organizations. *Sloan Management Review*, 7–23.

Smart, J. M., & Spalding, W. B. (1970, January). Concepts of system and higher education. *The Educational Forum, 34*(2), 167–175.

Trice, H., & Beyer, J. (1993). *The cultures of work organizations*. Englewood Cliffs, NJ: Prentice Hall.

Van de Ven, A. H., & Drazin, R. (1985). The concept of fit in contingency theory. *Research in Organizational Behavior, 7*, 333–365.

Weimer-Jehie, W. (2006). Cross-impact balances: A system-theoretical approach to cross-impact analysis. *Technological Forecasting and Social Change, 73*(4), 334–361.

Young, O. R. (1980). A survey of general systems theory. In G. Chen, J. Jamieson, L. Schkade, and C. H. Smith (Eds.), *The general theory of systems applied to management and organization* (vol. 1, pp. 87–106). Seaside, CA: Intersystems.

5

ORGANIZATIONAL ENVIRONMENTS

CONTENTS

The authors are most grateful for the critical comments on an early draft of this chapter by James Hearn, Vanderbilt University. The final version, of course, is our own and may or may not reflect the perspective of the reviewer.

Preview

- In recent years, members of the environment for higher education have appeared increasingly skeptical and critical, with dissatisfaction expressed by many stakeholders—especially students, their parents, prospective employers, state officials, and the corporate sector.
- Recent research focuses on understanding, explaining, and planning the interactions between institutions and their environments, in particular, the opportunities and constraints within both the environment and the institution that permit or restrict proactive behavior by the institution.
- Institutions are surrounded by a variety of influencers. General sources of impact are social, cultural, political, legal, economic, technological, and physical conditions in the environment. Proximate sources include suppliers, customers, competitors, labor unions, regulatory agencies, and special interest groups.
- Three paradigms exist for understanding and diagnosing the environment, the institution, and the interactions between them. These paradigms are positivism, social constructionism, and postmodernism.
- Positivist researchers seek to understand both internal conditions and the objective environment as completely and accurately as possible.
- Though positivist theories overlap somewhat, they appear to vary along a continuum that portrays the organization on the one hand as a passive respondent totally constrained by the environment (especially dependent on how the competition behaves); to conceiving of the organization in an active, more balanced relationship with other organizations (behaving reciprocally with them); or, finally, to an understanding of the organization as capable of influencing the environment (and hence itself) in important ways.
- The following theories can be placed along the continuum described above: population ecology theory, institutional theory, random transformation models, contingency theory, and resource dependence theory.
- Researchers have also recognized the degree to which organizational environments are viewed as a product of the perspectives and conceptualizations of one or more inside observers. This is the social constructionist paradigm applied to environments.
- A specific application of the social construction paradigm is the neoinstitutional perspective.
- Chaos theory rejects the determinism of traditional positivist theories, but it also suggests that chaos is real (not just interpreted or invented in people's minds). Chaos theory calls into question whether organizations can make good long-term predictions about their environments.

—————————— CASE CONTEXT ——————————

Wellington State University

Wellington State University (WSU), situated in a mid-size metropolitan area, began its operation as a state teachers' college in the 1880s. Since its redesignation as a state university in 1959, WSU has maintained nearly steady enrollment of approximately 9,000 students. WSU retained its emphasis on teacher education, but subsequently developed high-enrollment programs in business management and the fine arts. Programs in the sciences primarily supported the teacher education program (e.g., preparing future chemistry teachers), but were not particularly cutting edge.

After decades of stability, enrollment began to slump during the mid-1990s, due in part to a decline in the attractiveness of the teaching profession, but also due to more demanding admissions requirements imposed by the state board of higher education. Meanwhile, enrollments in nearby community colleges were booming.

WSU conducted an environmental analysis and found that it was losing teacher education students to a nearby private women's college, which had a strong national reputation in teacher education and had recently become coeducational. The influx of male students, enticed by large financial aid packages, appeared to be drawn at the expense of WSU's enrollment base.

In addition to the continuing decline in teacher education enrollments, a parallel reduction in enrollments was occurring in the business management program. Some faculty complained that the university was losing students to new online MBA programs that the other public universities in the state system were offering. Others on campus suggested that the business department was out of touch with the real needs of modern businesses.

The economy of the region was also changing. The business base was becoming more high-tech, and compared to other universities in the state system, WSU was bringing in fewer research grants and had relatively weak programs in science and technology.

Despite enrollment declines, on the other hand, student retention and graduation rates remained strong. Recent assessments documented high levels of student satisfaction, and faculty and staff morale remained high.

WSU relies on relatively few adjunct faculty; only 25% of the faculty are adjunct (lower than the nearly 50% national average), and faculty participation in governance committees is strong. But a recent accreditation report raised concerns about sufficiency of resources, including libraries, technology, and endowment. The resource situation is unlikely to improve any time soon, given that the state government has decreased its appropriations for public higher education by 20% over the past three years.

The WSU trustees perceive significant financial challenges. They have advocated program expansion, particularly for online programs, viewing this as a needed revenue stream. Meanwhile, a new governor is calling on higher education institutions to be major partners in her plans to spur economic development. The trustees and the president are trying to figure out what to make of that. "If our focus is teacher education, then are we even a player in the governor's economic development plan?" one trustee asked.

Introduction

In recent years, the members of the environment for higher education have appeared increasingly skeptical and sometimes critical, with dissatisfaction expressed by many stakeholders—especially students, their parents, prospective employers, state officials, and the corporate sector. As external constraints on institutional authority have become much stronger, higher education leaders have come under considerable pressure to make their institutions more accountable for performance (Alexander, 2000; Ratcliff, Lubinescu, & Gaffney, 2001; Toma & Kezar, 1999). Statewide boards and regional accreditation associations have become increasingly insistent that institutions assess student learning outcomes, standardize teaching loads, and lower costs. State and federal governments now mandate a range of data reporting requirements, which have spawned complex institutional research functions to calculate statistical data such as student-faculty ratios, graduation rates, campus crime incidents, and many others. State and local governments, as well as private businesses, expect higher education to address workforce development needs. These external pressures have permeated virtually all facets of academic and nonacademic work in colleges and universities, resulting in many new roles, activities, and responsibilities for administrators, staff, and faculty. In turn, these have frequently required redesign of departmental, college, and larger unit assignments and reporting relationships (Gumport, 2000; Tierney, 1998).

As systems theory notes, the environments surrounding institutions of higher education are essential in providing the variety of resources required for institutional sustenance—inputs (such as students); "tools" for transforming inputs (e.g., faculty and staff); information about changes in the economy and the national and international culture; and comparative data about other institutions. Institutional leaders are continually challenged to gather relevant information and use it to address the expectations and demands of many external stakeholders.

Early research on the conceptual foundations of organization-environment relations was represented by two quite different approaches (Davis & Powell, 1992). One group studied the focal organization (e.g., the college or university) and its perspectives on and strategies toward the environment. The other attempted to describe the multiple dimensions with which the environments themselves could be characterized (Emery & Trist, 1965). Recent research now focuses on understanding, explaining, and planning the *interactions* between organizations and their environments. In particular, the research attempts to identify opportunities and constraints within both the environment and the organization that permit or restrict proactive behavior by the organization.

This chapter presents a framework for environmental analysis that incorporates recent theoretical conceptualizations of organization-environment relations. First, systems theory is used to delineate the scope and impact of the external environment. Next, positivist theories of organization-environment relations are examined. These are arrayed on a continuum, ranging from theories that depict the environment as highly deterministic—permitting institutions few opportunities to use the environment to their advantage—to theories that suggest that organizations have extensive choices in the types of relationships that they establish with their environments. Social construction and postmodern perspectives are then offered as alternative conceptualizations of the complex relationship between organizations and environments. Finally, the chapter suggests how college and university leaders can use a multitheory, three-paradigm framework to assess their environments more validly to embed their institutions more effectively in their environments.

Systems Theory and Organizational Environments

The environment is critical in providing a variety of resource inputs to organizations, including material, financial resources, information, and personnel, among others. Environments, on the other hand, are also consumers of organizational outputs such as academic degrees and other educational services. Thus, institutions and environments are reciprocally interdependent.

Recall that chapter 4 presented a systems model of organizations that included inputs from and outputs to the environment. In systems theory, the interaction of an organization with its environment is continuous. In fact, the nature and extent of interactions across semipermeable organizational boundaries is what it means for a system to be open or closed.

The study of academic organizations, therefore, must include a detailed examination of the relationships between general and specific characteristics of the environment, the organization, and the boundary between them. Marketing managers in a college, for example, must be able to understand the nature of the student body, the competition for those students from other institutions of higher education, and the institution's relationship with feeder high schools, among other factors. Moreover, they must be able to appreciate the complex relationships among those external entities as well as the dynamic interactions between their institutions and the outside world.

College and university leaders need a conceptual framework to categorize and better understand the external forces that affect their organizations. Analyses of external environments can begin with an assessment of two conceptual dimensions. The first—the **general environment**—consists of broad forces that affect all organizations. The second—the **proximate environment**—includes specific external actors that affect a particular organization.

The General Environment

The general environment includes social, cultural, political, legal, and economic trends; technological advances; information; and the physical environment that surrounds the organization (Katz & Kahn, 1978).

Social trends relate to social class structure, demographics, and mobility patterns. Many colleges in the United States, for example, are responding to the educational needs of newly arrived immigrants who may have limited proficiency in English. **Cultural trends** involve behavioral and attitudinal expectations of society. Some examples include an increasing desire for nonhierarchical leadership and a growing awareness of the value of diversity among organizational members. Colleges and universities affiliated with religious denominations have an additional set of cultural expectations associated with particular belief systems.

Political trends are described in terms of the system of authority that governs the geographic region in which the organization is located. For example, the creation of a state-wide coordinating board for higher education may affect the distribution and concentration of power in the public higher education system. Similarly, changes in gubernatorial administrations may affect the level of state support for public higher education. **Legal trends** refer to specific laws and statutes that affect higher education organizations. Supreme Court rulings on affirmative action (*Gratz v. Bollinger et al.*, 2003; *Grutter v. Bollinger et al.*, 2003) and laws affecting the status of international students (Patriot Act of 2001), for example, have had significant effects on institutional admissions policies.

Economic trends affect the financial stability of institutions. Recessions can constrain state budgets and generate pressure to reduce appropriations to public higher education. Similarly, the stock market "bubble" of the mid-1990s precipitated significant growth in institutional endowments, only to "burst" a few years later. The economic sector also includes faculty and staff labor markets and the relative competitiveness of an institution's salary and benefits packages.

The general environment also includes **technological advances** that affect educational processes. Technology can be defined broadly as the processes by which an organization converts inputs into outputs (Perrow, 1986). Distance education technologies, including synchronous audio and video communications, have revolutionized the way institutions provide courses and degree programs. Similarly, new trends in pedagogy (e.g., constructivism and service learning) have changed the way faculty members interact with students.

Organizations often seek **information** from their environments to reduce uncertainty. According to uncertainty theorists, the main worry of organizations is not necessarily resource availability, but lack of predictable knowledge about how available those resources will be (House, Hanges, Javidan, Dorfman, & Gupta, 2004). For example, college budget officers in public institutions may be concerned over declining state funding, but their more pressing concern is with the lack of certainty about future funding. Knowing for sure that state funding will decline by a specific proportion permits development of a rational strategy for dealing with decline. Developing a state budget, however, is a highly political process whose outcomes are often unclear. In the absence of "hard data," it is difficult for institutions to develop strategies. Organizations, as a consequence, routinely collect data on a range of environmental indicators to keep tabs on changes that may affect them.

The **physical environment** refers to the organization's relationship to natural resources. Recycling, energy conservation, and land use may be considered when a higher education organization analyzes its effects on the physical environment.

The Proximate Environment

In addition to the overarching general environment, colleges and universities are subject to more concrete, direct influences. Hatch (1997), for example, suggests that the proximate environment "consists of suppliers, customers, competitors, unions, regulatory agencies, and special interests" (p. 65).

Suppliers provide raw materials, labor, and equipment, among other resources. They include high schools that provide first-time students to postsecondary institutions and community colleges that supply transfer students to four-year institutions. Labor markets and the graduate and professional programs that prepare future faculty, staff, and administrators are suppliers of human resources. Suppliers of financial resources include:

- direct government appropriations to public institutions;
- indirect government support to public and private institutions; for example, through student financial aid programs;
- parent and student payment of tuition and fees;
- research funds from governments, private foundations, and corporations;
- income from bond market interest and capital appreciation; and
- philanthropic donations.

Customers of institutions may include students as well as the organizations that employ college graduates (Chaffee, 1998). States, communities, and neighborhoods can also be thought of as consumers of the institution's public service and outreach. One example of this type of outreach is the agricultural extension service of land-grant universities. As another example, local neighborhoods can benefit from community health centers run by university medical schools. Here, the community at-large is viewed as a customer (Braskamp & Wergin, 1998).

Competitors include other institutions that compete for the same types of students as the focal organization. The set of competitor institutions has become increasingly large in recent years, given the expansion of for-profit colleges and corporate "universities." Competition for research dollars is also intense, as faculty and staff from multiple institutions submit competing proposals to governments and private foundations.

Unions represent approximately 25% of full-time faculty members (Clery & Lee, 2002). The percentage is higher in public two-year colleges (51.6%) and lower in private universities (3.1%). Unions represent faculty members in negotiations related to wages and working conditions. A faculty union on a particular campus may be affiliated with a national union such as the National Education Association (NEA) or the American Association of University Professors (AAUP). Campus leaders may also encounter the need to engage in collective bargaining with unions that represent clerical, technical, and other nonfaculty professional staff, such as the Service Employees International Union (SEIU) and the American Federation of State, County, and Municipal Employees (AFSCME).

Regulatory agencies directly and indirectly affect college and university policy and action. Institutions are subject to a range of regulatory constraints from local, state, and national governments, including laws regarding equal opportunity, workplace safety, and access for persons with disabilities. In addition, colleges and universities encounter more general interests in accountability, such as:

- concerns of federal and state governments regarding tuition increases;
- state governments mandating measurement of performance outcomes in public institutions; and
- regional and professional accreditation associations insisting on outcomes assessment.

Special interest groups also affect institutional decision making. These include institution-specific organizations such as alumni associations and athletics booster clubs. In addition, industry-wide lobbying organizations advocate on behalf of higher education—for example, the American Council on Education (ACE). Others advocate for particular sectors of higher education, such as the National Association of Independent Colleges and Universities (NAICU) and the American Association of Community Colleges (AACC).

Delineating general and proximate environments helps organizational leaders understand the scope and degree of impact that external forces have on a college or university. These perspectives, however, say little about how organizations react and respond to various environmental conditions. For example, given a complex proximate environment and a rapidly changing general environment, how can a college or university respond? Consideration of specific theories is necessary to analyze environments and take appropriate action. In the following discussion of positivist theories on organizational environments, we consider specific theories, some of which deal with deterministic environments, while others address situations where the organization has some degree of choice in how it develops its relationships with external entities. In contrast to the positivist perspective, social construction and postmodern alternatives for conceptualizing and analyzing organizational environments are then presented.

Positivist Theories of Organization-Environment Relations

Positivism assumes that an objective environment exists outside the boundaries of an organization. Organizational analysts seek to understand as completely and accurately as possible the internal conditions, the external environment, and the interaction between them. Both practitioners and researchers have long recognized the reciprocal interdependence of organization and environment. As a result, the history of environmental analysis is rich. Indeed, there are many ways to classify and understand elements in the external environment with different elements highlighted depending on the theoretical perspective taken. In general, the following theories have been the focus of a number of analysts:

- population ecology theory;
- institutional theory;
- random transformation models;
- contingency theory; and
- resource dependence theory.

Though the theories overlap somewhat, they appear to vary along a continuum that portrays the organization on the one hand as a passive respondent totally constrained by the environment (especially dependent on how the competition behaves) to conceiving of the organization in an active, more balanced relationship with other organizations (behaving reciprocally with them) or, finally, to an understanding of the organization as capable of influencing the environment (and hence itself) in important ways (Van de Ven, Emmett, & Koenig, 1974). Conceptually, these theories may be placed in a 2 × 2 table (Table 5.1) that describes all of the possible organization-environment relationships.

This table uses two variables: environmental determinism and perceived strategic choice. **Environmental determinism** refers to the degree of control the environment exercises over the organization. Some colleges are more tightly controlled by their environments than are others. Public colleges, for example, are constrained by state regulations, and small tuition-dependent institutions are often at the mercy of the marketplace, cutting programs when enrollment declines. In contrast, prestigious private colleges and major research universities with large endowments are relatively freer from external constraints, and therefore have a low degree of determinism.

The degree of determinism reflects a relatively fixed condition for the organization, although some theories offer frameworks for enacting new environments that permit greater flexibility. Nevertheless, the degree of determinism is typically slow to change. In contrast, perceptions of strategic choice are largely determined by the vision and perspectives of organizational leaders. **Perceived choice** refers to the extent to which organizational leaders view themselves as capable of taking consequential actions to guide the direction of the organization. Under conditions of perceived low choice, leaders believe that their "hands are tied" by forces beyond their control. Under conditions of perceived high choice, leaders feel that they can take useful

TABLE 5.1
Models of Organization-Environment Relations*

		Environmental Determinism (degree of control environment has over organization)	
		Low Determinism	**High Determinism**
Perceived Strategic Choice (organization's perceived degree of freedom to control environment)	**Perceived High Choice**	*Quadrant One* **Exploitive/Strategic Model** Strategic choice and adaptation (resource dependence theory)	*Quadrant Two* **Symbiotic Relationship Model** Symbiotic relationships, differentiation (contingency theory)
	Perceived Low Choice	*Quadrant Three* **Passive Interactants Model** Incremental, adaptation by chance (random transformation)	*Quadrant Four* **Deterministic Model** Minimal choice (population ecology theory, institutional theory)

*Adapted from Carlson, 1965; Daft and Weick, 1984; Hrebiniak and Joyce, 1985.

action in a range of circumstances, even when the environment is highly deterministic.

As we noted in chapter 1, a primary goal of using organizational theory is to broaden the range of perceived choices that leaders can use to improve organizations. Thus, in this chapter, we focus on theories and frameworks that can enable leaders to envision new possibilities and perceive a high degree of choice regarding how to structure relationships with the external environment.

The cross-tabulation of environmental determinism and perceived choice permits the identification of four alternative perspectives for understanding organization-environment relationships. We describe these four perspectives, moving from the most restrictive model to the most open.

Deterministic Model: Quadrant Four (perceived low choice, high determinism)

In this instance, external forces have a great deal of control over the organization. The organization may be quite dependent on how its competition behaves, or it may be constrained by state regulations or coordinating board mandates. Moreover, organizational members perceive that they have little choice but to follow these external dictates. Here we expect to see the organization largely conforming to whatever the environment demands.

Two theories—**population ecology** and **institutional theory**—attempt to explain these external constraints; they describe how market forces and political/social pressures can produce highly deterministic environments. Some conceptualizations of these theories are rather pessimistic regarding the ability of organizational leaders to transcend these constraints (perceived low choice), but others suggest that the application of these theories can actually point to some new directions for change (toward perceived high choice).

Passive Interactants Model: Quadrant Three (perceived low choice, low determinism)

Under these conditions, the environment does not constrain choice tightly, but organizational members perceive that they have limited ability to take action. Something holds the organization back from taking advantage of opportunities in its environment. For example, external resources may be plentiful, but the organization may be unable to seek those resources due to personnel constraints, lack of consensus about how to proceed, a culture of passivity rather than support for bold innovation, or some other limitation. Given these limitations, the organization simply "muddles through," and adapts to its environment incrementally. Muddling through, however, is contrary to the theory-based leadership strategies that are the focus of this book. The approach is, in fact, atheoretical and relies on "seat of the pants" guesswork, rather than systematic analysis. Unlike the other three quadrants, therefore, the passive interactants model does not offer specific theories of organizational environments that leaders can apply to their institutions.

Symbiotic Relationship Model: Quadrant Two (perceived high choice, high determinism)

External forces such as fierce competition or stringent regulations have significant effects on organizational behavior. However, organizational members may still perceive that they have choices regarding how to respond to those environmental pressures. In this instance, the organization and the environment develop a symbiotic relationship, where changes in the environment effect changes in the organization, but also where organizational actions have a significant effect on the environment. For example, a college may develop new amenities in its campus recreation facilities to keep pace with its competitors. But its competitors may respond by developing even more extensive services for students. The organization and its environment (in this case, its competitors) each have effects on the other.

Contingency theory defines a process of achieving a "fit" between the conditions of the environment and the design of the organization. If the environment becomes more competitive, for example, the organization can take steps to redesign its structures and practices to better fit the changing conditions.

Exploitive/Strategic Model: Quadrant One (perceived high choice, low determinism)

The environment here does not operate as a severe constraint, and organizational members believe that they can be agents of change, exercising their own discretion over organizational policy. A university, for example, may have a strong biology department that capitalizes on funding opportunities for biotech research. The institution has a competitive advantage, which it can and does exploit. **Resource dependence theory** points to a range of strategic actions that are likely to enable organizational leaders to reshape external environments in ways that advance the goals of the institution.

In the following sections, we discuss the specific theories that exemplify these perspectives in more detail, beginning with the more deterministic theories (Quadrant Four) and then moving to the theories that incorporate organizational choice (Quadrant One).

Population Ecology Theory

This deterministic theory explains the emergence of strong organizations in a way that parallels Darwin's conceptualization of the evolutionary processes in the animal kingdom. Population ecology suggests that organizations succeed on the basis of **natural selection** by the environment, which seeks and finds organizations that are needed and are likely to be successful in that environment (Hannan & Freeman, 1989). Each college and university tends to operate in an environmental **niche** that offers the resources upon which it and a group of competing institutions depend. Niches vary in their **carrying capacity**—that is, the number of institutions that can be supported in an equilibrium state. When the carrying capacity of a niche declines, only those organizations best adapted to that niche are likely to survive. The "survival of the fittest" notion is built around the idea that successful institutions have organizational designs that are maximally responsive to the surrounding environment. The environment thus "selects" those organizations to succeed.

More specifically, organizations in a particular niche are in competition with one another for long-lasting effectiveness (measured in terms of survival). To determine how or why any one institution is strong, it is necessary to examine competing institutions and their multiple environments. The niche for single-gender higher education, for example, has shrunk (Gueverra, 2001). As the demand for single-gender education declined, many women's colleges closed or became coeducational. Only the strongest institutions within that niche were able to survive and thrive as single-gender institutions. Less prestigious institutions with small endowments were confronted with a choice: continue to operate in a precarious financial state, or shift to a different market niche.

The natural selection model thus calls attention to competition in a changing environment. Population ecology theory also recognizes the complex relationships of many elements in the environment that may directly or indirectly affect the focal organization. It is necessary, therefore, to identify not just immediate one-to-one connections of organization to environment, but the whole ecology of the society—its economy, values, politics, etc.—as it affects how an organization operates.

Population ecology theorists differ over how much control they think the organization has over the process of environmental selection. Theorists have different perspectives regarding questions such as: Can an organization take steps so that its programs are a better fit for its niche? Can institutions successfully shift from one niche to another, if the carrying capacity of their current niche is declining?

Lenz and Engledow (1986) suggest that organizational leaders can engage in **opportunistic surveillance**—that is, they can assess their environmental niches and take steps to position their organizations more strongly vis-à-vis the competition. In other words, through strategic action, institutions can adapt to changes in their niche, address environmental needs more effectively than can competitor organizations, and ensure "selection" by the environment. Gueverra's (2001) case study, for example, found that two women's colleges were able to reverse enrollment decline through strategic activity. Thus, referring again to our 2 × 2 table (Table 5.2), opportunistic surveillance could allow an organization to move from perceived low choice to perceived high choice.

Other population ecology theorists (e.g., Dutton & Freedman, 1985), however, are skeptical that surveillance of the environment will result in effective long-term strategic planning. Over time, the environment dominates and ultimately undermines whatever strategic actions the organization takes. Short-run adaptations through experimenting and imitating are more effective than developing long-term strategies, according to these theorists.

Thus, researchers using population ecology theory have diverged with respect to determinism and agency. Does population ecology indicate that

TABLE 5.2
Potential Effect of Opportunistic Surveillance*

		Environmental Determinism (degree of control environment has over organization)	
		Low Determinism	High Determinism
Perceived Strategic Choice (organization's perceived degree of freedom to control environment)	Perceived High Choice	*Quadrant One* Exploitive/Strategic Model	*Quadrant Two* Symbiotic Relationship Model
	Perceived Low Choice	*Quadrant Three* Passive Interactants Model	*Quadrant Four* Deterministic Model

*Adapted from Carlson, 1965; Daft and Weick, 1984; Hrebiniak and Joyce, 1985.

organizations are at the mercy of environmental selection, or do organizational leaders have the capacity to reshape the niche and the organization to achieve greater "fit" (Astley & Van de Ven, 1983)?

Some researchers have raised important critiques regarding the assumptions of environmental selection. Survival of the fittest implies that impersonal, objective forces determine whether an organization is successful (Reed & Hughes, 1992). Instead, political power or social justice concerns may enable organizations to persist in spite of lack of fit with their niche or limited carrying capacity. Large, politically powerful organizations may persist despite failing to address needs within a particular niche. A public college with an abysmally low graduation rate may not suffer any consequences if its president and trustees are well connected to powerful legislators and state policy makers. In addition, society may choose to support an organization, even if the carrying capacity of the niche is limited (e.g., federal support for tribal colleges).

In higher education, colleges and universities increasingly are looking for niches within which they can assert their competencies and unique characteristics and establish some resource stability. Accordingly, enrollment management looms large in institutional research and planning (Peterson & Dill, 1997). Population ecology approaches are thus useful for understanding the historical circumstances that colleges and universities have encountered in the course of arriving at their current condition and for planning strategies that are appropriate for a particular niche.

To summarize, population ecology theory draws attention to competition and organizational survival. Some population ecology theorists emphasize the organization's ability to adapt to its niche, or even shift to alternative niches if deemed necessary for survival (e.g., women's colleges becoming co-educational). Other theorists suggest that there is little that organizations can do to ensure their survival; they are either a good match for the niche and will be retained, or they are not well adapted and will become extinct. According to this view, organizational efforts to adapt to changes in a niche are likely to be "too little, too late" as other organizations, given their historical strengths, will already occupy better positions within the niche. Undoubtedly, there are many occasions when organizations are able to adapt their core processes to meet environmental needs more effectively. And there are numerous examples of failed attempts to remain viable within a particular niche. Additional research is needed to understand the environmental circumstances and organizational strategies that distinguish these two outcomes.

Institutional Theory

"To be different, or to be the same . . ." is an important question for organizations that wish to position themselves strategically within competitive markets (Deephouse, 1999). The argument for trying to be different lies in recognizing that organizations may need to distinguish themselves from other, similar-appearing institutions to stand out in a competitive environment. Colleges and universities may be able to attract more students by highlighting their distinctive features and unique programs.

On the other hand, there are competing pressures for *sameness*. Organizations that conform to more recognizable, traditional, and acceptable standards avoid questions of legitimacy that may hinder their acquisition of resources and their marketability. Institutional theory suggests that organizations by accident and choice mirror the norms, values, and ideologies of the general environment in which they are embedded. Organizations that conform to external expectations tend to be deemed legitimate by society and viewed as worthy of support. Organizations that stray too far from these expectations are seen as deviant and are less likely to receive support from external constituencies. Thus, institutional theory posits a deterministic environment where organizations may have limited discretion in the types of strategic choices they make. The range of choice is limited by external pressures for conformity.

Institutional theory emphasizes the normative elements in the environment that shape organizational practices. The **institutional environment** is defined as the set of expectations that emerges from influential external agents. Colleges and universities are embedded in institutional environments where state governments, professional associations, accreditation organizations, and other external agents generate rules, regulations, and requirements for organizational performance, leading colleges and universities to adopt practices that conform to institutionalized expectations.

When organizations conform to institutionalized expectations, they are more likely to be viewed as legitimate—that is, acting in accordance with well-established and accepted patterns of behavior. Legitimate actions are likely to be rewarded by the environment with additional public support, larger numbers of applicants to academic programs, and more highly qualified faculty and staff who want to work at these institutions. Organizational behavior is thus shaped by institutionalized forces in the environment. Social and cultural values set a path for organizations, and deviations from that path may yield negative consequences.

DiMaggio and Powell (1983) describe external pressures as restrictions that can confine an organization to an "iron cage" (Max Weber's classic label) and severely limit the organization to designs and strategies that resemble other successful organizations in their field. This phenomenon is known as **isomorphism**. Organizations become isomorphic when their characteristics overlap with institutions that are perceived to be effective in their market niche. DiMaggio and Powell suggest that institutions engage in three kinds of conformity to environmental expectations: coercive, mimetic, and normative. That is, organizations can be forced to conform to explicit rules or laws (coercive), they can intentionally copy other organizations to reduce competitive uncertainty (mimetic), or they can follow standards that apply almost universally among institutions in a given industry (normative).

Coercive conformity in higher education often comes about through the accreditation process. Accreditation associations seek to ensure that all higher education institutions meet certain standards of quality. Similarly, governing boards and coordinating boards can enforce conformity across a state's public higher education system by requiring institutions to adhere to academic and admissions policies (Dill, 2001).

Mimetic conformity often arises as a result of competitive market forces. If a college installs high-speed Internet access in its residence halls, for example, then competitor colleges are likely to upgrade their Internet capabilities as well. Similarly, colleges expend significant resources to enhance intercollegiate athletics programs. College leaders have come to believe that many students and alumni expect institutions to have "big-time" college sports. If a competitor college gains exposure through athletic success, then other colleges seek to gain the same advantage. In academic departments, Riesman

(1956) characterized this process as an "academic procession" in which the less prestigious institutions are forced (unofficially) to follow the more noteworthy ones or be considered of lower quality. A common goal among college leaders, for example, is to advance "up" the Carnegie classification system, or change their institutional designation from "college" to the more prestigious "university" (Morphew, 2002). Institutions attempt to develop graduate programs, seek research grants, and raise admissions requirements to attain a more prestigious position in the academic hierarchy.

Normative conformity is reinforced by strong social and cultural expectations for certain organizational behaviors. The public, for example, expects colleges and universities to award grades, credits, and degrees. Thus, almost all institutions have a system by which students take courses, receive grades, and earn credits that culminate in a degree. Deviation from this system would likely damage the legitimacy of a college; it would risk losing its claim to providing a "real" education, and prospective students may hesitate to apply.

It should be noted that innovation and change in higher education are often achieved by institutions that can afford to risk the charge of nonconformity—that is, believing that they are trendsetters—or by institutions without positive reputations to lose. Thus, institutional theory also deals with the issue of **deviance**. Some institutions are able successfully to ignore convention and operate outside the bounds of normative expectations. Evergreen State College in Olympia, Washington, for example, provides portfolio assessment of student work, rather than awarding grades. Colorado College offers a unique one-course-at-a-time calendar, rather than the traditional semester system. Leaders can attempt to determine how far they can "stretch" their institution out of the legitimacy frameworks set up by the more well-known and powerful institutions. Remaining stuck in the middle leaves them undistinguished and unable to innovate. On the other hand, going too far beyond the recognized canons of acceptability will take them out of the market, and actors in the external environment will consider them too different from the respectable models.

Decisions about being different from or aiming for similarity with other institutions depend, in part, on assumptions made by leaders about the potential of organizations to deviate from industry or professional norms. Assumptions of a deterministic environment, for example, may leave little room for creative strategies that differ markedly from prevailing practices in other organizations. A different set of assumptions, however, suggests that organizations can take actions to shape the institutional expectations for which they are often held accountable.

More recent iterations of institutional theory (sometimes called the **neo-institutional perspective**) have explored the potential for multidirectional effects between organizations and institutionalized environments (Scott, 1998). Researchers have studied how institutionalized environments shape organizations, *and* how organizations can change the perceptions and expectations of external actors. Organizational leaders can lobby to change laws, alleviate burdensome regulations, and shape public perceptions of the mission and purpose of higher education. If organizational leaders are successful in changing the institutionalized environment, then the organization can escape the "iron cage" of environmental determinism that we described earlier. Organizational environments become less deterministic, and organizational leaders begin to perceive a higher degree of choice in the actions that they can pursue. (See Table 5.3, which describes a movement from Quadrant Four to Quadrant One.)

Random Transformation Model

The random transformation model (March & Olsen, 1976) suggests that organizational failures and successes occur largely by chance, primarily, the model's proponents say, because there is no known causal relationship between the environment and the organization. No rational explanation of a "fit" between organization and environment can explain survival over the long run. Shifts in both organization and environment according to this

TABLE 5.3
The Neoinstitutional Perspective*

		Environmental Determinism (degree of control environment has over organization)	
		Low Determinism	High Determinism
Perceived Strategic Choice (organization's perceived degree of freedom to control environment)	**Perceived High Choice**	*Quadrant One* **Exploitive/Strategic Model**	*Quadrant Two* **Symbiotic Relationship Model**
	Perceived Low Choice	*Quadrant Three* **Passive Interactants Model**	*Quadrant Four* **Deterministic Model**

*Adapted from Carlson, 1965; Daft and Weick, 1984; Hrebiniak and Joyce, 1985.

model are little more than random, and chance alone accounts for the success of an organization. Periodically, a great leader, a recession, or a catastrophe arises, but there is no predicting the timing of these events or strategies to avoid them.

We reiterate, however, that organizational theories have demonstrated that a wide range of organizational phenomena is not random. Categories of problems and patterns of behavior within and outside the organization can often be identified and can serve as a useful guide in making decisions and taking actions to improve organizational effectiveness. A foundational theory in the positivist tradition—contingency theory—can provide some guidance for making these adjustments.

Contingency Theory

The basic premise of contingency theory is that organizational effectiveness is contingent on a judicious, rational matching of organizational variables to environmental conditions. Contingency theorists attempt to identify both the environmental variables and organizational elements that can best predict which organizational designs and leadership approaches are likely to be most effective. Leaders can then restructure organizations based on which design is the best fit for their environment.

Burns and Stalker (1961) found that, for successful organizations, certain characteristics of organizational design more often than not fit with environmental conditions (see Table 5.4). For example, organizations operating in stable environments (i.e., low rate of change) tend to have clear lines of authority and distinct areas of responsibility. Burns and Stalker describe these organizations as "mechanistic." Work is highly routinized, standardized, and formalized (i.e., many rules). In a stable environment, it is feasible and more efficient to formalize many administrative roles and prescribe precisely what tasks each person is to do, since there is less likelihood that outside changes

TABLE 5.4
Burns and Stalker's Contingency Theory

Environmental Condition	Appropriate Organizational Design
Stable, low rate of change	Mechanistic
Dynamic, high rate of change	Organic

will occur rapidly and require associated internal shifts in procedures. Mechanistic organizations produce uniform, consistent outcomes with minimal waste. Efficiency is enhanced through standard operating procedures; workers do not have to "reinvent the wheel" each time they encounter a problem.

However, when organizations operate in environments characterized by high rates of change (e.g., shifts in economic conditions, enactment of new laws, swift changes in technology), a different type of organizational design is more likely to be effective. Burns and Stalker describe this design as "organic." In organic organizations, work patterns, lines of authority, and areas of responsibility blur, as different people assume leadership for different tasks based on expertise. Organic organizations are less routinized, standardized, and formalized than are mechanistic organizations. The result is flexibility and higher levels of innovation.

While the work of Burns and Stalker was innovative and useful for both theory and practice, it was limited in its capacity to predict institutional effectiveness from alternative organizational designs. Adding other independent variables would help in making more accurate predications. Robert Duncan (1972), building on the work of Burns and Stalker, added another independent environmental variable, degree of **environmental complexity**.

In Duncan's theory, environmental complexity ranges from homogeneous (simple) to heterogeneous (highly complex). Homogeneous (simple) environments are composed of elements that are very similar to one another, while heterogeneous (complex) environments are characterized by a variety of different elements.

Effective organizations seek to match their internal organizational designs with these environmental contingencies. When the environment is highly complex, organizations tend to be more effective when they have a large number of departments and subunits to deal with the complexity. In contrast, when the environment is relatively simple (with only a few external constituencies to attend to), then the organization can be effective with a simpler internal structure and fewer departments.

Consider the difference between a research university and an institution with a more finite mission such as a theological seminary or a fine arts conservatory. Research universities serve a diverse array of external constituencies. To be effective, the organizational structures of research universities must be similarly complex, with many departments and centers that specialize in addressing the needs of these constituencies. On the other hand, institutions with more limited missions have a much smaller set of external constituents, their environments are less complex, and they are able to operate effectively with fewer departments.

Hypothetically, if the conditions of the *environment* are properly related (via theory) to the *design* of the organization, then the organization will be more effective. For example, in a stable/homogeneous environment, it should be possible to set up a fairly predictable, bureaucratic organization since it will not be necessary for the college to respond quickly to environmental uncertainties. A well-structured, machine-like college, in other words, should be able to operate efficiently in this environment. But in a highly uncertain (dynamic/heterogeneous) environment, a college that sets up a rigid bureaucracy will find itself in deep difficulty, since it is less likely to discern the environment accurately (Weick, 2003) and will, therefore, be unable to adapt quickly internally as the environment changes.

Consider each of the four possible matches of environmental contingency and organizational design in Duncan's theory (Table 5.5). Organizations that operate in a stable environment with little complexity (category 1) tend to be more effective when their structures are mechanistic with a low level of departmentalization. As an example, think of a community college in a small city, where its programs are targeted specifically to a few major businesses in its service area. This institution attends to a small range of environmental stimuli. Relatively few departments, therefore, are needed to address external expectations. And as long as environmental conditions remain stable (e.g., no major recession), then a mechanistic design will produce consistent, efficient outcomes.

TABLE 5.5
Contingency Theory: Environments and Organizational Design*

		Degree of Complexity in the External Environment	
		Low complexity	High complexity
Rate of Change in the External Environment	Low rate of change (stable)	*Category 1* Mechanistic, Low Degree of Departmental Specialization	*Category 2* Mechanistic, High Degree of Departmental Specialization
	High rate of change (dynamic)	*Category 3* Organic, Low Degree of Departmental Specialization	*Category 4* Organic, High Degree of Departmental Specialization

*Based on Duncan, 1972.

In an environment where there is a low rate of change and high complexity (category 2), effective organizations tend to be mechanistic and highly departmentalized. Consider the stable environment of a comprehensive state college, which tends to serve a consistent number of students from the region. This college can operate successfully with a mechanistic design that develops routines for many key functions, such as admissions, marketing, and student services. The academic programs, however, may have become increasingly specialized, given advancements in their respective disciplines and professional fields. Here, the organization responds to complexity in the academic environment by becoming more complex itself (e.g., through the development of graduate programs and specialized tracks within majors).

In Duncan's third category, the environment is changing rapidly (dynamic), but the dimensions of the environment pertinent to the organization are limited (low complexity). Here, the most effective organizational design is predicted to be organic with few departments. Think of a small, independent college with a strong liberal arts curriculum. The environment is not particularly complex, since the college attracts students from a rather narrow range, typically high-achieving students who want a challenging general (rather than professional) education. A few general education departments (e.g., humanities, basic sciences, fine arts) would suffice to address student expectations. However, this small market niche is highly competitive, and the college may find itself in need of innovative academic offerings to attract students. An organic design would facilitate the creativity needed to maintain the college's edge over its competitors.

The fourth category pertains to a dynamic, complex environment, where an organic, highly departmentalized structure is likely to be effective. Consider a public research university where external expectations and financial resources are constantly in flux. An organic design is needed to keep pace with external change. Not only are expectations and resources shifting, they are also highly differentiated. Universities have a diverse set of expectations for teaching, research, and public service. They also rely on a diversified base of resources (e.g., legislative appropriations, tuition revenue, and return on endowment). These institutions need a large number of departments to address the multiplicity and variety of external demands.

Resource Dependence Theory

Resource dependence theory is manifested in organizations that see the possibility of effective action vis-à-vis the external environment. This perspective builds on the notion from systems theory that all organizations depend on their environments for resources. Since organizations cannot produce all of their necessary resources internally, nor can they obtain required resources at will from the environment, they are dependent on external entities (Pfeffer & Salancik, 1978).

These external entities have two sources of power over the focal organization (Froosman, 1999). First, they can determine whether the organization receives the resources it needs, and, second, they can determine how the organization uses the resources. In other words, certain resources may have "strings" attached. Many federally funded programs such as Upward Bound require that institutions provide certain student services and staff their programs in specific ways. The U.S. Department of Education decides whether institutions receive Upward Bound funding, and it determines how the institution can use the Upward Bound funds. Similarly, a wealthy donor may insist that a contribution be used to endow a faculty position in business administration even though the college may have greater needs in other departments. The donor in this case controls not only whether the college receives the resource, but how the college uses it as well.

The level of an organization's dependence on external entities varies based on how important the resource is to the focal organization (its **criticality**) and how many alternative sources of the resource are available in the environment (its **scarcity**). When a needed resource is both critical and scarce, the organization is highly dependent on the supplier of that resource.

Resource dependence theory recognizes an organization's need to do more than adapt internally to remain competitive. The organization must also establish strategic relationships with suppliers of its various resources. The active engagement of organizations with specific resource providers is a useful way of understanding organization-environment relationships. Researchers have identified several strategies that organizations can use to address their resource dependencies (Pfeffer & Salancik, 1978), including various techniques that enable the organization to develop a countervailing power base to offset controlling influences from the environment. We describe three such techniques—(1) dependency reduction, (2) external linkages, and (3) enactment of a new environment.

Dependency Reduction

Organizations can reduce their dependence on one particular supplier of resources or on a particular set of customers. By reducing dependence on one supplier, the organization minimizes its vulnerability to scarcity. For example, a public college may seek to reduce its dependence on state appropriations by building its endowment, which, in turn, will make the college less vulnerable to fluctuations in government support. The institution now has a broader array of funding sources, so the level of scarcity has declined for a critical resource. In another example, a college could expand its marketing efforts in other states to reduce dependence on its traditional set of feeder high schools. In addition, effective marketing can increase the number of applications and yield larger incoming classes, thus making any one source of students less critical.

Colleges can also diversify their set of consumers. Many institutions have continuing education divisions that offer credit and noncredit courses outside the traditional academic structure. These courses are often developed to reach new student markets. Distance learning courses also expand the institution's customer base by reducing the barrier of geographic location. By offering programs to a diverse array of students, the institution becomes less susceptible to fluctuations in any one particular segment of the market.

Dependency-reduction approaches, such as contracting with multiple suppliers or expanding the base of customers, reduce dependence on any one supplier or market segment. However, organizations run the risk of simply substituting one set of dependencies for another. For example, if a public college becomes heavily reliant on its endowment to generate revenue, then college budgets are more subject to volatility in the stock market. The college merely substitutes one form of dependence (state support) for another (return on investment). Similarly, if college marketing efforts target out-of-state high schools and neglect local high schools, then the college may lose its traditional enrollment base and become overly dependent on out-of-state students. Thus, diversification is a key to successful dependency-reduction strategies.

External Linkages

A second approach to managing resource dependence is attempting to increase the dependence of other organizations on the focal organization. In this case, the focal organization becomes more important to the outside world, thus ensuring a steadier stream of resources. An example of this in higher education is the rise in formation of university-industry partnerships that are independent of the traditional academic teaching organization (Slaughter & Leslie, 1997). These linkages ensure some continuity of funding for organized research in the university. Other examples include partnerships between K–12 school systems and higher education institutions as well as workforce development programs targeted toward the needs of specific companies. Here, local school systems and businesses come to depend on the higher education institution for their own key inputs. Their success becomes intertwined with the success of the institution, so they are more inclined to advocate on behalf of the institution for resources. Local business leaders, for example, may press state legislators for additional funding to institutions that train their workforces.

Colleges and universities can gain stability in their resource environments by entering into relationships that make other organizations more dependent on them. The potential danger in this instance is entering into too many external relationships for perhaps the wrong reasons. Most institutions are ill-equipped to exploit every possible external relationship. Institutions that jump at any opportunity to create an external partnership are subject to mission drift and loss of institutional focus (Balderston, 1995).

Another caveat to using external linkages is that the focal organization is now actually more dependent on the environment, making it potentially weaker. Organizations cede some of their autonomy when they enter mutual dependence relationships. Articulation agreements between community colleges and universities, for example, may limit the flexibility of both institutions. The community college curriculum must be aligned with general education requirements in the university, and university admissions standards become linked to faculty grading practices in the community college. However, the increased stability and predictability of student enrollments may be worthwhile. Perhaps more critical, if an organization establishes linkages with weak external entities, it obtains fewer benefits in leveraging additional resources and may in fact find that its own viability is jeopardized.

Enactment of a New External Environment

A third approach to managing resource dependence is enacting a new environment for the organization. Rather than considering the environment to be an unchangeable force, organizational leaders can work to make external conditions more hospitable. Marketing, lobbying, and coalition formation are just a few of the strategies that leaders can use to change the way the environment views the organization. College and university officials may, for example, appoint powerful community leaders to committees in the institution or ally themselves with comparable institutions to create more powerful lobbying positions.

Mergers and consortium arrangements are other examples of creating new environments. Here, the organization envelops the environment (makes the environment part of itself) to gain more control over it. For example, in the Amherst, Massachusetts, area, students in a five-college consortium can take courses at any of the institutions, thereby dampening the fluctuations in demand for courses at any one college. All of these linkages with external agents establish a continuity of inputs and a relatively greater certainty of expected resources (Table 5.6).

The theories discussed thus far in this chapter reflect a range of perspectives:

TABLE 5.6
Managing Resource Dependence

Dependency-Reduction	• diversification of suppliers • diversification of consumers
External Linkages	• partnerships and joint programs with other organizations • formal policies that link multiple organizations (e.g., articulation agreements)
Enactment of a New Environment	• marketing • lobbying • coalition formation • merger • consortium

- the organization as largely controlled by the environment (population ecology, institutional theory);
- a more passive interaction between the organization and its environment (random transformation);
- a symbiotic relationship between the organization and its environment (contingency theory); and
- the organization as relatively unconstrained by the environment (resource dependence theory).

These theories vary along dimensions of environmental determinism and agency (choice), yet each one assumes that organizations respond to an objective environment that exists outside the boundaries of the organization. Alternative social construction perspectives, however, suggest that the environment is a creation of people *inside* the organization.

Social Construction Perspectives on Environment

Social constructionists assert that characteristics of the external environment—such as the degree of complexity or the amount of uncertainty—are not tangible entities that can be revealed through objective analysis. Instead, the environment for any organization is the product of the cognitive and communicative processes enacted by the members of that organization. As organizational members share their views and interpretations of what is occurring outside the organization, they construct a composite perspective or image that represents in their minds the condition of the external world. Their subsequent actions are, in part, a response to that composite perspective. Thus, as Hatch (1997) notes, organizational members respond to an external environment that they created themselves.

According to social constructionists, environmental characteristics have less to do with objective data and are related more strongly, instead, to such factors as how narrowly or broadly the institution interprets its mission, the institution's history, and the interpretive systems that people bring with them to their organizations. Different organizational leaders, for example, may examine the same environmental data (marketing reports, enrollment projections), and one leader may identify a threat, while another would find an opportunity.

The meaning and potential impact that an environment has for the organization is the result of the (mostly unconscious) assumptions that organizational members have about reality in general and specifically (more consciously) about the environment that surrounds them. Do organizational members generally assume that the environment is hostile and competitive, or is the prevailing view one of hopeful collaboration with external partners? These types of assumptions shape perception and filter what organizational members see (or fail to see). Thus it is important to understand how organizational members gather, screen, select, and retain information about the environment.

The social construction of the external environment does not mean that organizational members have license to construct whatever environment they like. Through communication and negotiation, organizational members develop an understanding of the external environment and come to share (to a greater or lesser extent) a common interpretation of those conditions. An organization tends to have a predominant view of the external world, and individuals who interpret that world may encounter a variety of social pressures to revise their thinking. Consider, for example, an admissions recruiter who tends to view the environment as a network of similar professionals who share information and best practices. If she were to go to work for a different college, which viewed the external environment in highly competitive terms, her frame of reference would be dramatically different from the dominant social construction of reality in her workplace.

Sometimes, for various reasons, formal leaders or other organizational members distort the environment to advance their interests or those of a dominant coalition. Indeed, there are usually conflicts among organizational members about what the environment "really" looks like. An enrollment manager, for example, may want to see the college's environment as full of competition, since that may result in more importance for her. If she is powerful enough, she may be able to convince other people that she is right. If others begin to take actions based on those assumptions, then she has been successful in getting the organization to adopt her interpretation of the environment. As critical theorists note, people and subunits with the most power tend to influence the total organization's interpretation of the environment (Deetz, 1992; Mumby, 1996).

In the following sections, we examine some processes through which the environment is socially constructed. First we explore how organizational members make sense of environmental conditions—a process Weick (1995) calls **sensemaking**. We then explore how the organization can shape external perceptions through communicating a compelling institutional image.

The Importance of Sensemaking

Sensemaking involves the development of frames of reference that enable people to comprehend, explain, and interpret events in organizational life. On a practical level, we engage in sensemaking throughout our daily lives. In a job interview, for example, we usually attempt to organize a dizzying array of stimuli from multiple, sometimes conflicting sources. We read symbols and signals (some overt, others more subtle) and attempt to generate some context for moving forward and taking action. A similar process occurs when leaders attempt to identify and address organizational problems. As Donald Schön (1983) notes:

> In real-world practice, problems do not present themselves to practitioners as givens. They must be constructed from the materials of problematic situations which are puzzling, troubling, and uncertain. In order to convert a problematic situation to a problem, a practitioner must do a certain kind of work. [Practitioners] must make sense of an uncertain situation that initially makes no sense. (p. 40)

The sensemaking process is both cognitive and social. Life experiences are made sensible when people place stimuli into some type of **cognitive framework**. We can, for example, view an experience as one within a category of experiences that we encountered previously. Or we can create a new frame of reference for interpreting the experience. As Birnbaum (1988, p. xv) notes, "The most creative administrators are those who not only perceive complex patterns and relationships but also discover and invent new patterns where others find only confusion." Thus sensemaking entails both finding order and pattern in life *and* creating and inventing new ways of seeing (Weick, 1995). When leaders are able to "re-envision" problems (i.e., make new sense of a complex world), they can help others conceive of alternatives that they otherwise would not have considered. New frames of reference thus enable people to see problems differently and to envision innovative solutions.

Sensemaking is also a **social process** that involves seeking information from others, collectively assigning meaning to that information, and then taking actions based on shared understandings (Thomas, Clark, & Gioia, 1993). As a social process, sensemaking produces common frames of reference and shared images of the organization and its environment (Morgan, 1986). Members of groups and teams, for example, may discuss their previous experiences with specific tasks and projects and then construct a collective understanding of how they will proceed together with their work. Thus they develop a common frame of reference that guides their subsequent actions.

Making sense of the external environment is a primary task for many organizational members, especially for those in boundary-spanning roles who have direct connections with external constituencies. Boundary spanners are in positions where they can shape how others within the organization view the environment. They supply frames of reference that other organizational members can use to interpret the environment.

When organizations have access to a wide range of frames of reference about the environment, they are more likely to be adaptive than are organizations with more limited frames of reference (Bolman & Deal, 2003; Pondy, 1978). External collaborative partnerships with K–12 schools or local businesses, for example, can elicit new images of how the organization relates (or should be relating) to its environment. These cross-boundary interactions can help boundary spanners develop a richer vocabulary for explaining and interpreting the external world. Sensemaking, therefore, draws our attention to the importance of boundary spanners; specifically, the cognitive processes that they use in their jobs to interpret the environment as well as the social processes they use that can shape how the entire organization constructs the environment.

Sensemaking may be especially important in turbulent or chaotic environments. Weick's (1993) study of a firefighting disaster showed how sensemaking can break down under the weight of overwhelming stimuli, but it also revealed that improvisation and norms of respectful interaction can make organizations more resilient in times of external stress.

Institutional Identity and Image

Identity and image are key concepts in how social constructionists view cross-boundary relations. An organization's **identity** is what its members consider to be the central, enduring, and distinctive character of the institution (Albert & Whetten, 1985). Catholic colleges, for example, are characterized by their religious identity, and organizational members express a commitment to that identity to greater or lesser degrees. An institution's identity is closely related to how organizational members make sense of the mission of the institution in which they work. Open access missions of community colleges, for example, may be associated with an institutional identity of democratizing higher education. A clear and compelling institutional identity can create a sense of common purpose among organizational members, and "generate tremendous energy and commitment" to the organization (Hartley, 2003, p. 76).

Identity, therefore, is a concept that characterizes in part the impressions that organizational members have of the institution in which they work. **Image**, on the other hand, is a picture of how people *outside* the organization view the institution (Dutton & Dukerich, 1991). Colleges and universities make significant investments in efforts to shape the public's image of their institutions. Marketing, lobbying, fund-raising, and public relations departments attempt to influence how prospective students, legislators, donors, and the general public view a particular institution. Colleges and universities attempt to convey images of inclusiveness toward diversity, promotion of economic development, and contribution to the public good. One potential problem is that institutions may attempt to convey too many images, in which case the public receives a muddled picture of what the institution seeks to achieve.

Gioia and Thomas (1996) conducted one of the first studies of image and identity in higher education organizations. They found that image and identity are important perceptual lenses that guide the sensemaking process for higher education leaders. Gioia and Thomas studied organizational change in a large research university. An upswing in innovative, entrepreneurial behavior was attributed to a new institutional image that the senior leadership team constructed. This leadership team focused institutional dialogue on the question of what a "top 10" research university would look like. The image of a "top 10" research university resonated with the aspirations of faculty and staff; it was how they hoped external stakeholders would view their work. "This vision communicated not only aspirations for the future but also the message that the university was not yet in the elite circle, although by implication it could be and would be if the change effort were successful" (p. 380).

The hoped-for image clarified how organizational members viewed their institution—that is, the "top 10" image had an effect on the institution's identity. "The working logic was that the desired image would motivate a change in identity that would produce a desire for quality improvement" (p. 382). The new image changed how organizational members identified with the institution; it encouraged faculty and staff to view their institution as innovative and prestigious.

In Gioia and Thomas's (1996) case study, university leaders developed and communicated a new image for the institution, which resonated with faculty and staff and, in turn, altered the identity of the institution. Specifically, organizational members socially constructed a more prestigious identity based on an image of becoming a "top 10" research university. In contrast, Ravasi and Schultz (2006) explored how changes in the external environment can destabilize an institution's identity, and push organizational members to re-evaluate their conceptualizations of the organization.

Organizations may experience an **identity threat** when external conditions change rapidly and dramatically. A state governor's public announcement regarding plans to merge or close campuses is likely to be perceived as an identity threat to institutions within that state system of higher education. Identity threats may compel organizational members to reflect on the mission and purposes of their institution and ask questions such as, "What is this organization *really* about?" Organizational members also may attempt to make sense of the threat by assessing the current external image projected by the institution ("How is the organization perceived externally?"). These sensemaking processes can yield a revised identity claim that helps organizational members arrive at a clearer understanding of the institution's identity ("This *is* what the organization is really about."). The new, clarified identity gives rise to a new desired image, which the organization then projects to its external environment ("This is how we want the organization to be perceived externally.").

In response to a governor's threatened closure of campuses, faculty and staff at a small public college may revisit the college's mission and reassess how external entities perceive the college. They may realize that the prevailing perception of the institution is one of small size—a perception that had served the college well in the past. Students from surrounding communities wanted a "small college" experience with a public institution price. But the external image of small size, in the current context, may work against the college. Small may be viewed as inefficient, and small colleges thus may become a target for closure. In response, organizational members may construct a revised identity claim based on service to the region ("We serve the southeast region of the state."), thus de-emphasizing the size factor. Through strategic communications, the college may begin to communicate a new desired image to external stakeholders, including mayors and state legislators in the region who could rally support for the college. This process is displayed in Figure 5.1.

Image and identity are important concepts for understanding how external stakeholders and organizational members make sense of an institution. Image helps external stakeholders understand the manifest and latent values and priorities of an institution (e.g., is the institution serious about academics or is it a "party school"?). Institutional identity reflects the values and aspirations that organizational members have for themselves and for their institutions (for example, "I want to work at a prestigious university," or "I want to promote social change through democratizing education."). A powerful image can convey to external audiences a clear sense of the institution's mission, and a coherent identity can unify workers around a set of shared commitments that guide future action (Spender & Grinyer, 1995; Staw, 1980).

Postmodern Perspectives on Environment

Postmodern theorists claim that the positivist emphasis on prediction and control and the social constructionist focus on sensemaking and image are

FIGURE 5.1
Organizational Responses to Identity Threats*

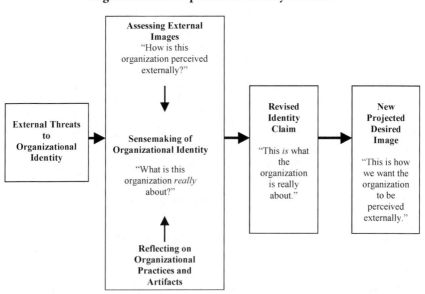

*Based on Ravasi & Schultz, 2006.

based on problematic assumptions. Prediction and control are not possible if the environment is fragmented and chaotic. Leaders who follow positivist prescriptions for controlling the external world, moreover, may exploit the environment and cause harm to natural and human resources (Shrivastava, 1995). In addition, sensemaking and image are complicated by power differences among organizational members. Organizational images tend to represent the interests of dominant actors, and sensemaking may be constrained by strong norms that privilege certain constructions of reality over others (Bloland, 2005). In this section, we explore the implications of **chaos theory** for understanding the complexities of a postmodern (fragmented, unpredictable) environment.

During the early 1960s, Edward Lorenz, a meteorologist at the Massachusetts Institute of Technology, was working on computer simulations of weather patterns. He noticed, quite by accident, that when he rounded calculations to a different number of decimal points, the outcome of the simulation was dramatically different. The implication of this finding is that systems—including weather, ecological, and human systems—can be extremely sensitive to initial conditions. A tiny change or imprecision in initial conditions can magnify at an enormous rate and produce previously unforeseen outcomes.

The sensitivity of a system to initial conditions, known as the **butterfly effect**, represents the notion that the flapping of a butterfly's wings could create tiny changes in the atmosphere that later magnify to become a tornado or hurricane (Lorenz, 1993). Conversely, if the butterfly had not flapped its wings, then the weather system might have developed much differently.

As an organizational example, a dean may routinely cancel courses due to low enrollment. Some courses may not attract sufficient numbers of students to continue to pay faculty members to teach them. From the dean's perspective, it is purely a budget decision. Unknown to the dean, however, the course that he cancelled this year and the instructor who was not rehired are exceptionally popular with a small but active group of students, who then organize protests, which proclaim that budget cuts are damaging their education. The protests attract negative media attention, which causes the provost to monitor closely every management decision made by the dean. Ultimately, the relationship between the dean and the provost becomes strained, and the provost does not renew the dean's contract. A seemingly insignificant budget decision is magnified to the point where the dean is fired.

Chaos theory suggests that events can unfold in a nonlinear fashion; in other words, the future is unlikely to follow patterns established in the past. A series of previously noncontroversial budget decisions, for example, does not guarantee that the next decision will meet with little opposition. This is not to say, however, that events are merely random occurrences. Events may appear to be random; but, in fact, they are probably part of complex patterns that can only be discerned retrospectively. Thus, organizational analysts cannot reliably identify and measure a set of initial conditions and accurately predict the future. Too many disruptive events occur between initial measurements and assessments of future outcomes. No one may have predicted, for example, that the dean's contract would not be renewed based on a course cancellation decision. Retrospectively, however, we can trace the dean's firing back to complex interactions related to student activism, institutional desire to avoid negative publicity, and a provost who resorts to stringent oversight in times of crisis.

Chaos theory also calls into question whether organizations can make good long-term predictions about their environments. If the future is unlikely to represent an extension of the past, then assumptions based on experience and historical trends may be poor guides for strategic planning. As Mintzberg (1994) notes, the fallacy of strategic planning is that it assumes that "the world is supposed to hold still while a plan is being developed and then stay on the predicted course while that plan is being implemented" (p. 110). External conditions, however, seldom remain constant long enough for accurate predictions to be made.

Turbulence in the external environment can disrupt patterns of organizational behavior. Occasionally, turbulence can be so severe that it destroys organizational patterns and, perhaps, the organization itself. But more often, the organization is able to recreate order and pattern. The presence of **attractors** keeps a chaotic system from spiraling out of control. "Attractors are those elements in a system that have drawing or organizing power" (Cutright, 2001, p. 5). Returning to the discussion of Lorenz and his computer simulations, slight deviations in the initial calculations produced very different forecasts, but his models never suggested unheard of weather phenomena, such as a sudden dramatic drop in the earth's temperature. Attractors tend to keep a system within boundaries. For example, despite significant turbulence in the higher education environment, institutions remain centered on a teaching-learning exchange between faculty and students. New modes of distance education, new forms of accountability, and new terms of faculty employment have not eliminated the basic pattern upon which these institutions are built.

In sum, chaos theory recognizes the difficulties inherent in environmental analysis and related strategic planning. Chaos theory addresses the difficulty of making long-term predictions of any system, even when initial conditions are known to an accurate degree. Often, environmental effects can be known only retrospectively, and the time horizon for strategic planning is significantly attenuated.

Summary

Here are some general themes about institution-environment relationships that have been discussed in this chapter.

1. The conception of the organization-environment relationship is critical. Whether leaders see the opportunities for action by the organization as totally controlled by the environment, in contrast to conceiving of the possibility of independent organizational action may point strategists in the direction of different techniques to assure survival and success.

2. The environment is not static. As the environment changes, the organization is often compelled to change as well (Allmendinger & Hackman, 1996). Adaptive organizations are able to change their internal structures and processes to make them a better fit with the opportunities available in the environment. The degree of fit between the organization and the environment may determine whether the organization is successful. For example, under conditions of limited resources and declining organizational autonomy, the organization that best "fits" those circumstances will be most likely to survive (**population ecology theory**).

3. It is best to conceive of the environment as containing a variety of potential influencers or stakeholders. Some of them are proximate and immediate, others one step removed (i.e., the general environment), but both sources must be taken into account. Organizational analysis needs to rely on a variety of techniques to be sure that all or most variables that potentially affect the organization are noted.

4. All of these elements are in some sort of "mix." Sometimes the mix is stable and homogeneous, sometimes dynamic and heterogeneous. **Contingency theory** provides a useful way to analyze the environment, since it provides an awareness of the potency of different organizational strategies for both internal organizational design and cross-boundary relations.

5. **Population ecology** and **institutional theory** can be used to understand macroenvironmental trends that affect the higher education system in general as well as specific institutions. Organizational leaders can use these theories to "step out" of their immediate organizational context and gain the advantage of a broader perspective.

Population ecology theory suggests the need for analyzing competitor institutions and degrees of relative fit with market niches. Institutional theory can be used to identify sources and types of external pressures (e.g., coercive, mimetic, normative). Leaders can then weigh the relative benefits of conforming to external expectations or deviating from traditional standards.

6. **Resource dependence theory** is useful for understanding the microenvironment of particular institutions. "A resource dependence analysis begins by identifying an organization's needed resources and then tracing them to their sources" (Hatch, 1997, p. 78). Through such an analysis, leaders come to understand the extent of the organization's dependence on external entities. In response, organizations can offset some of this dependence by creating countervailing power through diversification and external linkages and by introducing changes to their environments. Resource dependence theory reminds leaders that they can be active agents in the construction of their environments. They are not passive recipients of external mandates; they can rejuvenate institutions through aggressive and sagacious action in their environments. This analysis serves as a balance to population ecology and institutional theory, which suggest a greater degree of environmental determinism. The neoinstitutional perspective provides a similar check on deterministic thinking.

7. **Contingency theory** can be used to assess issues of fit between organizational components and environmental characteristics. Strategic planning, goal formation, and organizational restructuring can be informed by an analysis of congruence between current institutional functioning and emerging environmental expectations. However, it is important to keep in mind that environmental assessments are social constructions that reflect the sensemaking processes of those conducting the assessment. Organizational leaders should be mindful, therefore, of potential limitations of perspective (e.g., groupthink and potential marginalization of people from traditionally underrepresented groups).

8. **Chaos theory** suggests that other organizational theories are best used to understand environments retrospectively, rather than as lenses to predict the future. While contingency theory, resource dependence theory, population ecology, and institutional theory can be used to trace organizational outcomes back to the initial conditions that produced them, these theories are less useful in predicting how the environment will respond to a particular organizational initiative. Leaders can use theories of organization-environment relations to chart a

course of action for the organization, but chaos theory brings with it the caveat that such plans are subject to variation in initial conditions (e.g., turbulence), which can produce unforeseen, but not necessarily unheard of, outcomes for the institution.

Theories about organizational environments can help higher education leaders gain a better understanding of important **resource networks** that can put their institution on better financial footing. In addition to financial resources, these theories suggest the importance of **external linkages** to community organizations, local businesses, public schools, neighborhood associations, state legislators and policy makers, and other constituency groups. These theories also provide frameworks for understanding **competition** in the higher education marketplace—competition for students, faculty, research funding, and prestige. More generally, these theories help leaders understand how external forces affect the functioning of institutions of higher education.

The next chapter examines a variety of possible organizational responses to both the environment itself and the perceptions of key organizational members. In particular, organizational design and structural alternatives for colleges and universities are explored.

Review Questions

1. An urban university attracts a variety of students from diverse racial and socioeconomic backgrounds. The president wants to develop a service policy that takes into account this diversity. Which of the following characteristics of the immediate environment should he be most concerned with?
   a. Its stability versus turbulence
   b. The amount and specific nature of the diversity
   c. The success of other nongovernmental organizations that are engaged in educational enterprises
   d. The availability of funds to support the desired services
   e. Other, more important factors—please name them

2. A consultant for a university is asked to examine the environment and recommend a marketing strategy to recruit students. She will benefit most from which of the following approaches?
   a. Random transformation
   b. Natural selection

    c. Institutionalization

    d. Information and uncertainty

3. The dean of the school of education urges all departments to reach out to community colleges that send students to the university in an attempt to clarify and solidify transfer credit arrangements, thereby ensuring a more reliable flow of applicants. Does resource dependence theory suggest that this approach will enhance the university's stability and effectiveness or put it at greater risk?

    a. Enhance stability

    b. Make more risky

    c. Neither

    d. Some of each

4. A director of admissions at a small college observes that the pool of largely local applicants from which the college has traditionally drawn its class is becoming more difficult to identify, largely because of changes in the demography of the community in which the college is located. Which of the following staff changes, if any, would best address this ambiguity in the pool?

    a. Divide the territory so that each admissions staff person has a more specialized role.

    b. Create a staff development program so that all staff are equally qualified to manage the new diversity of applicants.

    c. Recruit new staff whose characteristics better match those of the applicant pool.

    d. Recommend to the college president that she carve out a more specialized curricular program and set of institutional objectives that will address the needs of a narrow range of applicants.

5. On the basis of her understanding of chaos theory, a college president has hired a new dean of the college of arts and sciences who agrees not to engage in long-range planning with her staff and faculty. Which of the following explanations might be attributed to the president's thinking?

    a. The institution will not be able to change significantly because its course of development was firmly and ineluctably set in place by its founders.

    b. The rate of change in the environment outside the institution is rapid and increasing, making it nearly impossible to plan rationally on a long-term basis.

c. Disorder and chaos are healthy organizational characteristics that lead to innovation.

d. Planning is more than accurate prediction; it is a state of mind that elevates linear thinking and depresses the possibility of considering functional "punctuations" in the equilibrium that may have been brought on by planning.

Case Discussion Questions

Consider the Wellington State University (WSU) case that was presented at the beginning of this chapter.

1. **Institutional theory** suggests the importance of understanding external expectations for institutions. Identify the sources and types of external pressures that WSU is encountering. How might these pressures be changing? How can the institution respond to emerging external demands?

2. **Population ecology theory** focuses on competitor institutions and the degree of fit within a particular market niche. Describe WSU's market niche. Is the niche expanding or contracting? Would it be useful for WSU to shift to a different market niche, or should the institution attempt to strengthen its position within its current niche?

3. **Resource dependence theory** notes the importance of establishing strong external linkages to attain stability in resource streams. What external linkages could WSU establish that would strengthen its resource base? (Remember that student enrollments are an important resource.)

4. **Contingency theory** highlights the need to examine the level of complexity and the rate of change in the external environment, and adjust the internal structure of the organization accordingly. How has WSU's environment become more complex? What external forces are driving a faster rate of change? How might WSU need to adjust its internal structures to address the needs of a complex, rapidly changing environment?

5. **Chaos theory** calls into question the utility of long-term planning based on assessments of the current environment. Instead of adjusting to every shift in the external environment, the role of organizational leaders is to make sense of seemingly chaotic events and provide direction for future activity. How might WSU's leaders shape a clear identity for the institution? Upon what strengths can the institution build for the future?

References

Albert, S., & Whetten, D. (1985). Organizational identity. In L. Cummings & B. Staw (Eds.), *Research in Organizational Behavior, 7*, 263–295. Greenwich, CT: JAI Press.

Alexander, F. K. (2000). The changing face of accountability: Monitoring and assessing institutional performance in higher education. *Journal of Higher Education, 71*(4), 411–431.

Allmendinger, J., & Hackman, J.R. (1996). Organizations in changing environments: The case of East German symphony orchestras. *Administrative Science Quarterly, 41*(3), 337–369.

Astley, W. G., & Van de Ven, A. H. (1983). Central perspectives and debates in organization theory. *Administrative Science Quarterly, 28*, 245–273.

Balderston, F. (1995). *Managing today's university: Strategies for viability, change, and excellence* (2nd ed.). San Francisco: Jossey-Bass.

Birnbaum, R. (1988). *How colleges work: The cybernetics of academic organization and leadership*. San Francisco: Jossey-Bass.

Bloland, H. (2005). Whatever happened to postmodernism in higher education?: No requiem in the new millennium. *Journal of Higher Education, 76*(2), 121–150.

Bolman, L., & Deal, T. (2003). *Reframing organizations: Artistry, choice, and leadership* (3rd ed.). San Francisco: Jossey-Bass.

Braskamp, L., & Wergin, J. (1998). Forming new social partnerships. In W. Tierney (Ed.), *The responsive university: Restructuring for high performance* (pp. 62–91). Baltimore, MD: Johns Hopkins University Press.

Burns, T., & Stalker, G. (1961). *The management of innovation*. London: Tavistock.

Carlson, O. (1965). *Adoption of educational innovations*. Eugene, OR: Center for the Advanced Study of Educational Administration, University of Oregon.

Chaffee, E. E. (1998). Listening to the people we serve. In W. Tierney (Ed.), *The responsive university: Restructuring for high performance* (pp. 13–37). Baltimore, MD: Johns Hopkins University Press.

Clery, S., & Lee, J. (2002). Faculty salaries: Recent trends. *The NEA 2002 Almanac of Higher Education* (pp. 11–20). Washington, DC: National Education Association.

Cutright, M. (Ed.). (2001). *Chaos theory and higher education: Leadership, planning, and policy*. New York: Peter Lang Publishing.

Daft, R. L., & Weick, K. E. (1984). Toward a model of organizations as interpretation systems. *Academy of Management Review, 9*(2), 284–295.

Davis, G. F., & Powell, W. W. (1992). Organization-environment relations. In M. D. Dunnette and L. M. Hough (Eds.), *Handbook of industrial and organizational psychology* (2nd ed., vol. 3, pp. 315–375). Palo Alto, CA: Consulting Psychologists Press.

Deephouse, D. (1999). To be different, or to be the same? It's a question (and theory) of strategic balance. *Strategic Management Journal, 20*, 147–166.

Deetz, S. (1992). *Democracy in an age of corporate colonization: Developments in communication and the politics of everyday life*. Albany: State University of New York Press.

Dill, D. (2001). The regulation of public research universities: Changes in academic competition and implications for university autonomy and accountability. *Higher Education Policy, 14*(1), 21–35.

DiMaggio, P. J., & Powell, W. W. (1983). The iron cage revisited: Institutional isomorphism and collective rationality in organizational fields. *American Sociological Review, 48*, 147–160.

Duncan, R. B. (1972). Characteristics of organizational environments and perceived environmental uncertainty. *Administrative Science Quarterly, 17*, 313–327.

Dutton, J., & Dukerich, J. (1991). Keeping an eye on the mirror: The role of image and identity in organizational adaptation. *Academy of Management Journal, 34*, 517–554.

Dutton, J., & Freedman, R. (1985). External environment and internal strategies: Calculating, experimenting, and imitating in organizations. In R. Lamb & P. Shrivastava (Eds.), *Advances in Strategic Management, 3*, 39–67.

Emery, F. E., & Trist, E. L. (1965). The causal texture of organizational environments. *Human Relations, 18*, 21–32.

Froosman, J. (1999). Stakeholder influence strategies. *Academy of Management Review, 24*(2), 191–205.

Gioia, D., & Thomas, J. (1996). Identity, image, and issue interpretation: Sensemaking during strategic change in academia. *Administrative Science Quarterly, 41*(3), 370–403.

Gratz v. Bollinger et al. (2003). No. 02–516. 539 U.S.

Grutter v. Bollinger et al. (2003). No. 02–241. 539 U.S.

Gueverra, J. (2001). Women's colleges in Massachusetts: Responses to enrollment declines. *Review of Higher Education, 24*(4), 351–368.

Gumport, P. (2000). Academic restructuring: Organizational change and institutional imperatives. *Higher Education, 39*, 67–91.

Hannan, M., & Freeman, J. (1989). *Organizational ecology.* Cambridge, MA: Harvard University Press.

Hartley, M. (2003). "There is no way without a because": Revitalization of purpose at three liberal arts colleges. *Review of Higher Education, 27*(1), 75–102.

Hatch, M. (1997). *Organization theory: Modern, symbolic, and postmodern perspectives.* New York: Oxford University Press.

House, R. J., Hanges, P., Javidan, M., Dorfman, P., & Gupta, V. (Eds.) (2004). *Culture, leadership, and organizations: The GLOBE study of 62 societies.* Thousand Oaks, CA: Sage.

Hrebiniak, L. G. & Joyce, W. F. (1985). Organizational adaptation: Strategic choice and environmental determinism. *Administrative Science Quarterly. 30*, 336–349.

Katz, D., & Kahn, R. L. (1978). *The social psychology of organizations.* New York: Wiley.

Lenz, R. T., & Engledow, J. L. (1986). Environmental analysis: The applicability of current theory. *Strategic Management Journal, 7*, 329–346.

Lorenz, E. (1993). *The essence of chaos.* Seattle: University of Washington Press.

March, J. G., & Olsen, J. P. (1976). *Ambiguity and choice in organizations.* Bergen, Norway: Universitetsforlaget.

Mintzberg, H. (1994, January–February). The fall and rise of strategic planning. *Harvard Business Review, 72*, 107–114.

Morgan, G. (1986). *Images of organization.* Newbury Park, CA: Sage.

Morphew, C. (2002). A rose by any other name: Which colleges became universities. *Review of Higher Education, 25*(2), 207–223.

Mumby, D. (1996). Feminism, postmodernism, and organizational communication studies: A critical reading. *Management Communication Quarterly, 9*(3), 259–295.

Patriot Act of 2001. HR 3162. Public Law 107–56.

Perrow, C. (1986). *Complex organizations: A critical essay* (3rd ed.). New York: McGraw-Hill.

Peterson, M., & Dill, D. (1997). Understanding the competitive environment of the postsecondary knowledge industry. In M. Peterson, D. Dill, L. Mets, & Associates (Eds.), *Planning and management for a changing environment: A handbook on redesigning postsecondary institutions* (pp. 3–29). San Francisco: Jossey-Bass.

Pfeffer, J., & Salancik, G. (1978). *The external control of organizations: A resource dependence perspective.* New York: Harper & Row.

Pondy, L. (1978). Leadership is a language game. In M. McCall, Jr., & M. Lombardo (Eds.), *Leadership: Where else can we go?* (pp. 87–99). Durham, NC: Duke University Press.

Ratcliff, J., Lubinescu, E., & Gaffney, M. (Eds.). (2001). *How accreditation influences assessment.* San Francisco: Jossey-Bass.

Ravasi, D., & Schultz, M. (2006). Responding to organizational identity threats: Exploring the role of organizational culture. *Academy of Management Journal, 49*(3), 433–458.

Reed, M., & Hughes, M. (1992). *Rethinking organization: New directions in organization theory and analysis.* Newbury Park, CA: Sage.

Riesman, D. (1956). *Constraint and variety in American education.* Lincoln, NE: University of Nebraska Press.

Schön, D. (1983). *The reflective practitioner.* New York: Basic Books.

Scott, W. R. (1998). *Organizations: Rational, natural, and open systems* (4th ed.). Upper Saddle River, NJ: Prentice Hall.

Shrivastava, P. (1995). Ecocentric management for a risk society. *Academy of Management Review, 20*, 118–137.

Slaughter, S., & Leslie, L. (1997). *Academic capitalism.* Baltimore, MD: Johns Hopkins University Press.

Spender, J.-C., & Grinyer, P. (1995). Organizational renewal: Top management's role in a loosely coupled system. *Human Relations, 48*(8), 909–926.

Staw, B. (1980). Rationality and justification in organizational life. In L. Cummings & B. Staw (Eds.), *Research in organizational behavior* (vol. 2, pp. 45–80). Greenwich, CT: JAI Press.

Thomas, J., Clark, S., & Gioia, D. (1993). Strategic sensemaking and organizational performance: Linkages among scanning, interpretation, action, and outcomes. *Academy of Management Journal, 36*, 239–270.

Tierney, W. (Ed.). (1998). *The responsive university: Restructuring for high performance.* Baltimore: Johns Hopkins University Press.

Toma, J. D., & Kezar, A. J. (1999, Spring). Reconceptualizing the collegiate ideal. *New Directions for Higher Education, 105*. San Francisco: Jossey-Bass.

Van de Ven, A. H., Emmett, D. C., & Koenig, R., Jr. (1974). Frameworks for inter-organizational analysis. *Organization and Administrative Sciences, 5*, 113–129.

Weick, K. (1993). The collapse of sensemaking in organizations: The Mann Gulch disaster. *Administrative Science Quarterly, 38*, 628–652.

Weick, K. (1995). *Sensemaking in organizations*. Thousand Oaks, CA: Sage.

Weick, K. (2003). Contradictions in a community of scholars: The cohesion-accuracy tradeoff. In J. L. Bess (Ed.), *College and university organization: Insights from the behavioral sciences* (pp. 15–29). Amherst, MA: I & I Occasional Press.

6

CONCEPTUAL MODELS OF ORGANIZATIONAL DESIGN

CONTENTS

The authors are most grateful for the critical comments on an early draft of this chapter by Ellen Earle Chaffee, Valley City State University. The final version, of course, is our own and may or may not reflect the perspective of the reviewer.

Preview

- Demands for greater accountability, shifts in the locus of decision making, the transformation of the marketplace, and academic innovation have engendered new interest in the organizational designs of colleges and universities.
- Organizational design relates to the internal configuration of organizations and considers the allocation of tasks to people and departments, the reporting relationships among people and departments, and the communication and coordination patterns that characterize the organization.
- Positivist theories of organizational design focus on formal systems of communication, division of labor, coordination, control, authority, and responsibility.
- A key challenge of organizational design is to find ways to coordinate the work of differentiated units without impinging on the work of highly trained specialists.
- Contingency theory identifies five independent variables that are likely to predict the most effective organizational design for a particular set of circumstances. These variables include the organization's environment, technology, goals, culture, and size.

--- CASE CONTEXT ---

Organizational Design Issues at Southern Gulf University

Southern Gulf University (SGU) occupies a prime piece of oceanfront property where the scent of saltwater can be detected all across campus. For many years, SGU thrived on its laid-back reputation, where faculty and students were as likely to discuss a novel over a beer at the local seafood shack as they were to discuss it in the classroom. Lacking big-time college athletics, SGU relied on its location and excellent faculty to attract serious-minded yet outdoorsy and adventurous students.

The relaxed academic setting was offset somewhat by an efficient—some would say rigid—administrative structure. The president was a former military officer, and the provost, Rebecca Carlson, had been a medical doctor before shifting careers into university administration. Both had been in their positions for less than four years. Most of the administrative units that reported to them were tightly controlled; the staff in these units made few errors, but they were not terribly innovative. Getting it right was viewed as much more important than doing it quickly or better. As an example, most units had not upgraded their data management software in nearly a decade. To a certain extent, the faculty governance committees mirrored this pattern. Proposals for new courses and programs were reviewed painstakingly for every detail.

SGU faculty and administrators, however, were encountering a rapidly changing external environment. Legislators in the state capital were looking to spur economic development through competitive grants to universities and corporations. Some of the entrepreneurial faculty at SGU took advantage of these opportunities and capitalized on the financial resources that the state government made available to them.

The new grants were used in part to "buy out" faculty from their teaching responsibilities so they would have more time to devote to research projects. However, disparities in teaching loads grew—with some faculty teaching six or more courses per year and other faculty barely teaching at all. Resentment between the "haves" and the "have-nots" was beginning to boil over in several faculty meetings across campus. Provost Carlson, however, was surprised to learn of these problems for the first time in SGU's accreditation self-study report.

The provost had decided to spend a quiet Saturday morning in her office reviewing the initial draft of the self-study report. She knew that several members of the committee charged with writing the report had an "axe to grind" with her office, but she was startled by the structural problems identified in the report.

One area of concern was the conflict between the Office of Graduate Studies and the research faculty in the graduate programs. The Graduate Studies dean called for a uniform teaching load for all faculty members teaching graduate courses. Faculty in the research-oriented departments, however, balked at increasing their teaching loads and asked to be exempt from many teaching and advising duties.

A second concern was the process for approving new courses and programs. The faculty committees charged with this task were notoriously slow and had delayed the university's development of evening and online courses. Concurrently, the Division of Continuing Education had been developing new academic programs outside the traditional governance system, and many of these programs were generating significant revenue for the university. However, since the programs were developed outside the faculty governance structure, they were not necessarily consistent with the priorities of the academic departments. Sociology faculty members, in particular, were concerned that a new online continuing education program in criminal justice would siphon students away from the sociology major.

The third concern in the report pertained to the growing number of research partnerships with the corporate world, each with its own set of operating procedures and strictures regarding intellectual property rights. Research administration had become increasingly complex, and the small staff in the Office of Research was frequently overwhelmed. Faculty were requesting more guidance regarding publication and intellectual property issues for their scientific discoveries, but the Office of Research could barely maintain its accounting functions. Staff interactions with faculty were primarily bureaucratic and focused on enforcing rules, rather than on addressing faculty members' questions and concerns.

The self-study report called for a dramatic restructuring of graduate education, continuing education, and research administration. The draft report did not offer specific recommendations for reform, but it was evident that organizational design issues were interfering with the academic mission of the institution.

Introduction

Recent trends in higher education, including greater demands for accountability, dramatic changes in the marketplace, and new innovations in teaching and learning, have engendered growing interest in organizational design. In recent years, for example, external expectations for colleges and universities have become much stronger, and institutional leaders have come under considerable pressure to reduce costs and make their institutions more accountable for performance. Pressures for efficiency and responsiveness have had significant effects on the organizational designs of colleges and universities, often leading to higher levels of centralization, formalization, and uniformity (Gumport, 2000). Decisions previously made at lower administrative levels and/or by faculty members are now being pushed toward upper levels in the administrative hierarchy. Time for analysis, reflection, and consultation is often sacrificed in favor of speed and efficiency.

An additional source of external pressure is the changing nature of higher education markets—particularly markets for students and for research support. The student market has become increasingly divided into segments that differ by age, enrollment plans (full or part time), and educational goals (e.g., seeking a degree, planning to transfer, or looking for only a specific course). Competition within these segments is often intense, given the wide range of educational providers that are now accessible either in person or online. Intense competition also characterizes the pursuit of research funding. Expectations for research productivity are no longer confined to elite universities; faculty in nearly every sector of higher education are devoting significant energy to their research agendas (Schuster & Finkelstein, 2006). As larger numbers of faculty seek research support, the availability of such funding has declined, especially from federal and state government sources. To be successful in these competitive markets, colleges and universities need organizational designs that are flexible and amenable to change. As Nadler, Gerstein, and Shaw (1992) note, "How a firm organizes its efforts can be a source of tremendous competitive advantage, particularly in times where premiums are placed on flexibility, adaptation, and the management of change" (p. 3).

Pressures for change, however, are not entirely external. Faculty members are adopting new pedagogies and instructional technologies; others are exploring interdisciplinary research. Still others are involved in the profit-making sector where their research is used in commercial ventures. Innovations such as these raise important questions about how the work of colleges and universities should be organized.

A Brief Definition of Organizational Design

The word *design* in the title of this chapter connotes both a consciously planned arrangement and an aesthetic sensitivity. Organizations must arrange their structural components in ways that allow them to achieve institutional goals and objectives efficiently. Often these patterns also embody artistic elements such as balance, harmony, grace, texture, contrast, perspective, dissonance, conflict, and resolution.

Definitions of organizational design vary widely in what they comprise. Some authors include in the topic the entire gamut of organizational variables. For example, Galbraith, Downey, and Kates (2002) say that organizational design "is the deliberate process of configuring structures, processes, reward systems, and people, practices and policies to create an effective organization capable of achieving the business strategy" (p. 2). Since a number of these topics are discussed fully in other chapters in this book, we choose here a narrower definition that concentrates especially on the elements in the *internal structure* of an organization. Using the human body as a metaphor, one can think of structure as the framework of bones and the muscles and ligaments that hold them together. Daft (1983, p. 202) suggests that organizational structure includes:

1. The **allocation of tasks and responsibilities** to individuals and departments within the organization

2. The designation of formal **reporting relationships**, including number of levels in the hierarchy, and span of control of managers and supervisors
3. The grouping together of individuals into **departments** and the grouping of departments into the total organization
4. The design of systems to ensure effective **communication, coordination**, and **integration** of effort in both vertical and horizontal directions

Thus, the focus of this chapter is on the internal characteristics of organizations and their impact on the effectiveness of the organization and the individuals who work in it. We look inside the "black box" of systems theory (see chapter 4) and, using other theories, try to understand more fully how the organization as a system operates internally.

Description and Overview of This Chapter

This chapter and the next explore the design of colleges and universities in terms of how different possibilities may be related to the effectiveness of the academic and administrative workforce. We examine first a critical concern in organizational design—addressing the tension between differentiation and integration. Second, we consider how organizations have responded to this basic challenge. In the next sections of the chapter, we describe the basic variables that affect the design of colleges and universities. These independent variables include the external environment, technology, goals, organizational culture, and size.

The following chapter (chapter 7) describes a continuum of organizational design types. There we take up in detail such topics as bureaucracy, matrix organizations, and structureless "virtual" organizations. Following this, we discuss two social construction theories—**loose coupling** and **structuration**—that offer different ideas for designing organizations. Chapter 7 concludes with an overview of postmodern critiques of bureaucratic structure and a discussion of alternative postmodern organizational designs.

A Brief Review of a Typical College or University Design

It is important at the outset to reiterate in this discussion of the design of colleges and universities that there are multiple, overlapping subdesigns whose responsibilities and whose modes of integration are often not spelled out completely (Mintzberg, 1983a, 1983b). Virtually all colleges and universities have an administrative structure designed in traditional hierarchical format, with faculty arrayed as **line workers** at the bottom of the hierarchy. However, the commonly observed relative powerlessness of workers at the lowest levels in an organizational hierarchy is, in this case, offset by a complementary substructure just for faculty that usually includes a **faculty senate** and its committees. This faculty governance structure borrows heavily from principles of direct or representative democracy. It has sole responsibility for a number of academic issues, but it shares responsibility with the administrative structure for others. The responsibilities of and relationships between these two entities are inherently somewhat ambiguous, and important institutional policy decisions often must be negotiated.

The coexistence of academic and administrative decision-making structures results in complicated and sometimes slow-moving decision-making processes where it is difficult to arrange efficient "fits" among the parts of the system—linkages in which communication and collaboration can take place and where incentives to do so can be maintained. Further, the decentralized nature of large universities and the allegiances of faculty to outside academic professional organizations in their disciplines engender centrifugal forces that create problems of goal setting, planning, and strategy formation for the institution as a whole.

Differentiation and Integration: Basic Issues in Organizational Design

Certainly, one of the most fundamental problems that all organizations face is how to divide the work to be done, and then make sure that the units remain coordinated in their efforts. Organizational design, then, is concerned with how to "package" the work to be done into manageable units and then how to link the newly separated units through a pattern of communication and authority, accompanied by incentives to collaborate (Barnard, 1938; Lawrence & Lorsch, 1969).

The allocation of tasks to specific units produces differentiation within the organization. **Differentiation** refers to the degree of departmental specialization in an organization. A college with many divisions and departments performing unique functions is highly differentiated. On the other hand, a college with a limited number of units with such distinctively different roles has a low level of differentiation. In the latter case, larger departments perform multiple functions.

Integration involves the linking and coordination of departmental functions and of the roles and behaviors of unit members. A college's general education program, for example, may require considerable integration among academic departments in different disciplines serving undergraduate students, while its more specialized graduate programs may have less need for integration.

Differentiation is readily evident in most college and university organizational charts. Higher education organizations are typically differentiated by function. For example, academic affairs (teaching and research are sometimes differentiated further), student affairs, and administration and finance are often organized into distinct units. The academic function is further divided into colleges, schools, divisions, and departments based on the programs in which faculty are engaged (e.g., law school differentiated from school of education). Academic divisions and departments may be differentiated further into various degree programs and research units.

Differentiation among academic affairs, student affairs, and administration and finance may be justified on the basis of efficient allocation of tasks to those with the greatest expertise in that particular decision domain. Differentiation allows faculty members, for example, to concentrate on curriculum and teaching, student affairs staff to focus on the holistic development of students, and administrators to address institution-wide issues, including budgets, accountability, and overall mission achievement. However, differentiation often leads to units functioning as independent "silos" with little interaction among them (Benjamin & Carroll, 1998). Research has shown that once organizational members are separated into smaller units, they tend to **suboptimize**; that is, they identify with and work toward the goals of their own unit rather than the goals of the organization as a whole. The independent units may lose touch with each other and with the institutional mission. As a typical example, faculty responsible for teaching usually interact infrequently if at all with those involved in assisting students in extracurricular activities.

Recently, however, higher education researchers and administrators have begun to focus on issues of integration—for example, facilitating connections between academic affairs and student affairs (Kezar, 2003). The integration of organizational units relies on vertical and horizontal coordination. **Vertical coordination** links higher and lower organizational units and occurs primarily through authority, rules, planning, and budget controls. **Horizontal coordination** attempts to assure adequate linkages among units at the same level and is established through meetings, task forces, and persons serving in liaison roles. A provost's leadership council, for example, may bring together all of the academic deans at an institution.

Horizontal coordination modes can be arrayed on a continuum describing the possible mechanisms of coordination. As Figure 6.1 shows, "the coordinating mechanisms form a continuum, with direct supervision the most

FIGURE 6.1
Coordinating Mechanisms (and Examples) on a Continuum
of Horizontal Decentralization*

Direct Supervision	Standardization of Processes	Standardization of Outputs	Standardization of Skills	Mutual Adjustment
• manager oversees the work	• procedural manuals, union contracts	• graduation require- ments for all academic programs	• minimum education levels required for various jobs	• collaboration, research teams

Horizontally Centralized ⟵——————————————⟶ **Horizontally Decentralized**

*Based on Mintzberg, 1983a, p. 108.

horizontally centralizing and mutual adjustment the least, and with the three forms of standardization—first work processes, then outputs, finally skills—falling in between" (Mintzberg, 1983a, p. 108).

The type of coordinating mechanisms used should fit the goals, structural configuration, and culture of the organization. Mintzberg (1983a, p. 153) suggests a number of "matches" among these variables (Table 6.1).

While unchecked differentiation may have negative organizational consequences, excessive integration may be perceived as constraining and limiting, especially for highly educated faculty and staff who prefer a great deal of autonomy in their work. The challenge, then, is to find ways to coordinate differentiated units efficiently without impinging on the autonomy of specialists. How organizations have responded to this basic challenge is the focus of the remainder of this chapter.

Alternative Modes of Designing an Organization: Mechanistic and Organic

There are many ways to differentiate tasks and people into departments, and there are many ways to integrate the work of the differentiated units. Different modes of differentiation and integration have engendered a wide variety of organizational designs. Most of the different kinds of organizational designs can be organized parsimoniously along a continuum of characteristics whose ends are labeled **organic** and **mechanistic** (see Figure 6.2).

TABLE 6.1
Matching Structural Configurations and Coordinating Mechanisms

Structural Configuration	Prime Coordinating Mechanism
Simple Structure: few top-level administrators, almost no middle management, limited specialization among workers	Direct supervision
Machine Bureaucracy: hierarchical chain of command, high degree of centralization, formal rules guide behavior	Standardization of work processes
Divisionalized Form: a large organization is divided into relatively autonomous divisions; each division has its own personnel, facilities, and budget	Standardization of outputs
Professional Bureaucracy: decentralized, relatively flat administrative structure	Standardization of skills
Adhocracy: flexible structure with frequent changes in task and authority relationships	Mutual adjustment

First, Daft and Noe (2001) define an optimum organic organizational design as: "One that is free flowing and adaptable, has few rules and regulations, encourages teamwork that crosses functional and hierarchical boundaries, and decentralizes authority and responsibility to lower level employees. Job responsibilities are broadly defined and spans of control are generally wide" (pp. 529–530).

A mechanistic structure according to Daft and Noe is characterized by "rigidly defined tasks, many rules and regulations (high formalization), little

FIGURE 6.2
Organizational Design Continuum

Mechanistic	**Organic**
closely defined tasks, many rules, centralized	loosely defined tasks, few rules, decentralized

teamwork, and centralized authority. There is a clear chain of command and narrower spans of control" (p. 530).

We turn now to a discussion of how colleges and universities can be organized by looking intensively at the variables that help determine the type of design (relatively organic or more mechanistic) that will emerge under different organizational conditions. In particular, we consider independent variables such as environment, technology, goals, organizational culture, and size. And, we review how yet another variable—interdependence— intervenes between the independent variables and the dependent variable— organizational design.

Actually, two types of dependent variables need to be taken into account in conceptualizing organizational design. The first comprises the **departmental structural form and the mode of control**. The second is composed of the resultants of particular structures and control modes. These resultants are presented in this chapter as **first-level outcomes** (innovation, motivation, job satisfaction, culture, workplace climate) and **second-level outcomes** (organizational effectiveness). Figure 6.3 provides a graphic depiction of the causal flow in organizational design.

The five independent variables (environment, technology, goals, culture, and size) are conceptualized as having both direct and indirect effects on organizational design. The indirect effect is realized through *structural interdependence*. An independent variable such as size, for example, could have an

FIGURE 6.3
Effects of Independent and Intervening Variables on Organizational Design

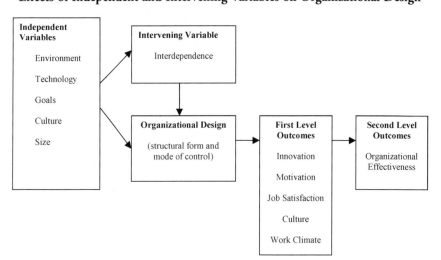

effect on the degree of interdependence among departments in a college. The effect of size on interdependence could, in turn, have a "ripple effect" on organizational design. That is, changes in size could lead to changes in interdependence, which then produce changes in design. In the next section of this chapter, we examine each of the five independent variables and their potential direct and indirect effects on organizational design.

Determinants of Organizational Design

To ensure organizational effectiveness, organizational design must take into account a variety of conditions at the individual, group, and system levels. Is there a "best" way to organize? No, as we learned from the concept of **equifinality** in systems theory (chapter 4), there are many different ways to design an organization, and the diversity and uniqueness of colleges and universities suggest a rich variety of workable schemes. On the other hand, not all organizational designs in colleges and universities are equally efficient or effective. Researchers fortunately have begun to identify some general principles that direct us to forms of organizational design that seem to lead to more efficient and effective outcomes and to more employee satisfaction and positive workplace climates.

Consideration of five major contingencies is necessary for understanding and deciding on the optimum design for a particular organization: (1) the external environment with which it must deal, (2) the technologies it uses, (3) its goals, (4) its culture, and (5) its size. The contingency hypothesis in general is that the more the organization accounts properly for these variables in its organizational design, the more efficient and effective it will be (Mintzberg, 1983a). As Burrell and Morgan (1979) note,

> Contingency theory postulates that the effectiveness of the organization in coping with the demands of its environment is contingent upon the *elements* [emphasis in the original] of the various subsystems which comprise the organization being designed in accordance with the demands of the environment (or, more accurately, sub-environments) with which they interact; this implies that the elements of different subsystems must be congruent in terms of the characteristics along each of the basic dimensions by which they are defined. (p. 176)

College and university leaders must, consequently, be continually aware of the nature of these contingencies in their planning and policy making.

First, we provide a brief overview of each of these independent variables, just to provide a general impression for them, after which we discuss each more fully.

1. **Environment**. What happens outside the boundaries of the college or university? Is the environment stable or unstable—for example, a changing or consistent applicant market; variations or continuity in budgets each year; changing or level economic circumstances? Further, is it homogeneous or heterogeneous? Are most of the students similar, or are there many differences among them? Are competing institutions alike or dissimilar?

   Morrison and Wilson (1997) suggest that the environment comprises three components: market (including customers and clients such as students, parents, elected officials, employers, and professional associations); industry (the competitive academic institutions); and macro-environment (social, technological, economic, scientific, and other factors that affect colleges and universities). Different parts of the organization are involved with all of these factors at different times.

2. **Technology/tasks**. An organization's technology is defined as the process by which inputs are converted into outputs (Perrow, 1986). In higher education organizations, technology questions include: Are the transformation tasks (teaching, research, public service) routine, or do they require fresh decisions for each task? Is there a repertoire of easily acceptable technologies for the various tasks, or must new preparation be done each time? Do the technologies of the different products and services overlap, or, do they require separate subunits and specialized personnel?

   As part of the technology, the control structure that characterizes the industry or field has an effect on the organization's design. Some fields have a loose control structure with little direct oversight over employees; others use tighter control and more supervision. Higher education, as an industry, has traditionally employed a mixture of loose and tight control structures. The former provides faculty with high levels of personal discretion over their work; the latter predominates in administrative functions where control tends to be more hierarchical. The resulting overall *academic* organizational design tends to be flat with low levels of formalization and standardization within departments (Birnbaum, 1988). Trends toward accountability and standardized assessment, however, may result in policies favoring greater direct oversight over the transformation processes and additional scrutiny of faculty and staff productivity (Colbeck, 2002).

3. **Goals**. What product or service does the organization espouse and (in reality) produce? What is the desired and acceptable quality of the

output? Goals identify what the organization signifies for organizational members, consumers, and clients. They set a tone for the way that the organization is designed.

4. **Culture.** While we explore the idea of organizational culture extensively in chapter 11, here we suggest that it is essentially the emotional "feel" of the organization. For example, is it bureaucratic or collegial? Is it close-knit with cooperative norms or impersonal and self-serving? To some extent, culture is determined by other variables, such as size and type of institution (e.g., community college, small liberal arts college, research university), but culture itself has an impact on organizational design. If there is a high degree of trust (a culture variable) among organizational members, for example, then there is less need for direct supervision. This is translated into an organizational design that is quite different from an organization characterized by distrust.

5. **Size.** Size can be measured in many ways, but the variable usually includes such quantitative phenomena as number of employees, budget, and student enrollment. Generally, larger organizations are quite different from smaller ones in their organizational design (Blau & Schoenherr, 1971; Gooding & Wagner, 1985; Pugh, 1981). In *Big School, Small School*, Barker and Gump (1964) examined the effects of small school size on high school students' behaviors. For example, when there were not enough students for a baseball game, each student learned how to play many positions, and the rules (and roles) were flexible. In a small entrepreneurial company or in a research unit in a university, there are different kinds of roles as well, and those roles are diffuse and played out flexibly. Hence, depending on the size of the unit, a different organizational design may be appropriate.

To summarize, the design of an organization follows from all of these independent variables. Next, we examine these variables in more detail, using some of the literature that has produced conceptualizations and frameworks that can be used effectively in the design of colleges and universities.

External Environment: First Independent Variable

Again, one principle of effectiveness of organizations (and, consequently, of good organizational design) is matching the design with characteristics of the environment. Hypothetically, the better the match between environmental characteristics and organizational design, the more effective the organization will be.

Organizations cannot afford to be maladaptive to the clients and constituencies they serve. What happens outside an organization has important implications for what happens inside. This is seemingly obvious, but far too often, college leaders pay close attention to some aspects of the environment—for example, courting potential donors—but do not recognize other characteristics (e.g., demographics or economic trends) that would direct them to a redesign of the organizational structure. If the aim, for example, is to produce knowledgeable individuals as graduates of the institution at the least cost, it is possible to create some "ideal" organizational structure that purports to accomplish that end. Classes could be held in huge lecture halls for all students. But in doing so, some conditions outside the system (such as the diverse learning needs of incoming students) are ignored, and the ideal "efficient" structure might not work. Some students need remedial courses and others more advanced work. Such variation in student input characteristics vitiates the validity of the assumption of homogeneity of inputs in the environment on which a large lecture class is based. Thus, taking the environment into account in designing the organization is crucial to overall effectiveness.

Hypothetically, if the organizational design is properly related to the conditions in the environment, then the organization tends to be effective. In contrast, lack of fit between organizational design and external conditions is likely to lead to ineffective outcomes. Thus, if a college or university is found (or thought) to be ineffective, it is possible to trace the explanation to the mismatching of organizational design to the characteristics of the environment. Structural changes that bring the organization's design into better alignment with the environment will likely improve overall organizational performance.

Daft (1995), for example, notes that organizational designs should account for the degree of environmental uncertainty the organization encounters. If the environment is highly uncertain (e.g., very complex and unstable), then organic structures with high levels of decentralization and teamwork will be more effective. In contrast, when the environment is simple and stable, mechanistic structures with clear roles and authority relationships will produce higher levels of effectiveness. Thus, Daft argues that the appropriate organizational design is contingent on the degree of environmental uncertainty (see Table 6.2).

Technology: Second Independent Variable

Scott (1998; citing Hulin & Roznowski, 1985, p. 47) notes that technology "refers to the physical combined with the intellectual or knowledge processes by which materials in some form are transformed into outputs." Bedeian

TABLE 6.2
Contingent Relationships Between Organizational Design and Environmental Uncertainty*

Amount of Environmental Change			
	Low (stable environment)	*Low Uncertainty* • Mechanistic structure; formal, centralized • Few departments • No integrating roles • Little imitation • Oriented toward current operations	*Low Moderate Uncertainty* • Mechanistic structure; formal, centralized • Many departments, some boundary spanning • Few integrating roles • Some imitation • Some planning
	High (unstable environment)	*Low Moderate Uncertainty* • Organic structure; teamwork, participatory, decentralized • Few departments, much boundary spanning • Quick to imitate • Oriented toward planning	*High Uncertainty* • Organic structure; teamwork, participatory, decentralized • Many departments, differentiated; extensive boundary spanning • Extensive imitation • Extensive planning and forecasting
		Simple	Complex
		Environmental Complexity	

*Based on Daft, 1995, p. 92.

and Zammuto (1991, p. 192) provide a related definition: "The techniques or processes used to transform labor, knowledge, capital, and raw materials into finished goods or services."

Most organizations have what is called a **core technology**—the primary function the organization performs that defines the production processes in which it engages. Core technologies use varying degrees of standardization in transforming organizational inputs—for example, the transformation of students' cognitive capabilities when they enter the institution. Sometimes we know a great deal about how to transform something—say, make a chair out of the wood of a tree. For other technologies, however, we may know very little that can be generalized—for instance, how to create a customized product for a client, or a new song, or an educated person. The core technologies of higher education—associated with the transformation processes for teaching, research, and public service—are often exceptionally difficult to standardize (Cohen & March, 1974; Cutright, 2001).

Technology as a term has been applied to three levels of work organizations: system, group, and individual. That is, as noted above, most organizations as a whole have an overall core technology that to a large extent determines their organizational designs. The underlying technology of teaching often relies on communication in face-to-face faculty/student interactions. In fact, this technology dictates the design of many colleges and universities. Departmentalization follows largely from the alleged necessities of keeping together in specialized departments faculty who have been trained in common subject matter specializations. In addition, technologies are used at smaller unit levels such as the classroom (e.g., seminar classrooms versus lecture halls). And, finally, each faculty member develops a unique technology or pedagogy.

The idea that technology rigidly controls the design of an organization—for example, its structure, modes of communication, patterns of work flow—is sometimes called the **technological imperative** (Ellul, 1980). At the organizational level of analysis, the foundational research by Joan Woodward (1965, 1970) in England is particularly informative in understanding how the technological imperative operates. In a study of 100 British manufacturing firms, she found three categories of technology:

1. **small batch and unit production**—here, work entails much special-order, customized production;
2. **large batch and mass production**—in this case, the processes are mostly assembly line in design (i.e., long production lines with a variety of parts assembled later); and

3. **continuous process production**—where no assembly is needed, and the process is largely automated.

Woodward found that the organizational designs for each of these types was significantly different in terms of levels in the hierarchy and number of employees supervised (i.e., span of control). Mass production organizations, for example, were characterized by higher degrees of centralization and large spans of control. Small-batch organizations were more decentralized with smaller spans of control. Equally important, the more successful firms had designs quite different from those of the unsuccessful, thus reinforcing the idea that proper design is contingent on the use of the proper technology. Mass production organizations were more effective when matched with a mechanistic design, while small-batch organizations achieved better performance with more flexible organic designs.

To understand the organizational technology of a college, we can ask: Into which of the three categories above does an institution fall? And does the associated technology properly match the goals and objectives of the institution? For example, does a college use a small-batch model because it believes that each student should receive a customized education? And does the internal organizational design match that belief and technology? Given small-batch technology, a decentralized organic design is likely to yield the most effective outcomes for this college.

Other theorists (particularly researchers in England at the Aston School) developed the Woodward model further. In the United States, Charles Perrow (1970) advanced the theory by developing a model in which two variables can be used to characterize technology. The two variables are:

1. the degree to which the **inputs** entering the organization are stable and predictable, and
2. the degree to which the **procedures** for processing the raw material are known.

That is, the most effective organizational design varies, depending on (1) how much variance there is in the inputs taken from outside the organization's boundaries, and (2) how easily the transformation procedures or techniques can be determined. Table 6.3 illustrates the juxtaposition of the two variables and the resultant types of organizations that fit these conditions.

When inputs are homogeneous and when procedures can be standardized, then **routine technologies** such as large lecture classes are effective. In contrast, one-on-one tutorials may be necessary when students are heterogeneous in their learning needs, even if the content area is fairly standardized.

TABLE 6.3
Classification of Technology*

		Input Variety	
		Few Exceptions (homogeneous)	**Many Exceptions** (heterogeneous)
Procedures and Tasks	**Not well understood, difficult to standardize**	Craft Technology (e.g., dissertation advisement)	Nonroutine Technology (e.g., stem cell research)
	Well understood, possible to standardize	Routine Technology (e.g., large lecture class)	Engineering Technology (e.g., one-on-one tutorial)

*Adapted from Perrow, 1967.

Perrow describes this process as an **engineering** technology. Customized **craft technologies**, however, are more effective when students' needs are fairly uniform but the procedures for assisting them are difficult to standardize (e.g., dissertation advisement). Finally, when inputs are heterogeneous and when procedures are not well known or are evolving, then **nonroutine technologies** are used—as is the case in many research laboratories.

For each of these types of organizations to operate effectively, the organizational design must be appropriate to the technology. If the technology is *routine*, for example, relatively little individual decision making is required. Organizational members deal with limited amounts of data, and most processes can be standardized. Coordination is achieved through rules, policies, and procedures (Pfeffer, 1978, pp. 45–50). Mechanistic bureaucracy is, therefore, likely to emerge as the most effective organizational design. If the technology is *nonroutine*, on the other hand, with many exceptions in the inputs and with few known methods for transforming them, then a more organic organizational design is necessary—for example, an aggregation of loosely connected professionals (Brown & Eisenhardt, 1997).

We can apply this model to colleges and universities, and ask whether the inputs entering each institution are stable and homogeneous and whether we know what to do with the inputs once they have arrived. For colleges, one of the inputs is students. On the basis of the above theory, what prescriptions can be made about the type of organizational design that will best fit the technological contingency—craft, nonroutine, routine, or engineering? The same question can be asked about research. Which of the four categories would be an effective organizational design for research?

The answers to each of these questions may be quite different. Indeed, how the technologies for teaching and research can be reconciled in an institution's organizational design is an important question. Most four-year colleges and universities prefer to ask faculty to perform both roles and to aggregate them in academic departments whose outputs are both educated students *and* sophisticated research. An alternative would be to group teaching specialists and research specialists separately, as is often done in many countries around the world. For community colleges, which are less concerned with research, the organizational design question is somewhat less complicated.

We can summarize to this point. We are getting closer to answering the question, of which organizational designs may work best (although several may work equally well). Thus far, we have shown that environment and technology are important. Each leads to a decision about how to group people to allow the work to be done efficiently and effectively. In uncertain environments, organizations with loosely structured designs have been shown to be more successful. Further, when technologies are unclear and the inputs vary greatly, organizations whose workers have greater autonomy seem to be more effective. Now we turn to the third contributor to the organizational design decision.

Goals: Third Independent Variable

An organizational goal is both a target and a limitation. It is the official representation of the desired "state of the system" for the future, and it sets priorities for organizational members on the tasks on which they work. Organizations sometimes chart their progress toward achievement of goals through **benchmarking**—marking, in operational terms, the organization's outcomes over time, compared with peer organizations (Barak & Kniker, 2002).

Many organizations, including colleges and universities, establish missions that convey not only a sense of their aims and values, but the allegedly unique character or quality that is embodied in all of their programs and services as well. Goals that are formally stated by the organization may not, however, reflect the real or operative goals (Perrow, 1961; Steers, 1977) that drive organizational activity. A college or university may espouse a goal of "educating every student to the best of his or her ability," but in actuality direct most of its resources to educating students with prior high-level academic achievements.

Both official and operative goals have a profound effect on the structure of the organization and the processes by which the organization carries out the tasks needed to produce a product or service. Decisions about what to produce (e.g., what kinds of degrees to offer, what kinds of research to conduct) and how to produce it are based to varying extents on goals.

Clear goals with short-term time perspectives lend themselves to mechanistic organizational designs, while ambiguous goals, whose achievement takes place over long periods and which are difficult to measure, are usually matched with more organic designs. The goal of a 90% passage rate on a professional licensure exam, for example, is clear and measurable. To achieve this goal, the academic department may organize itself in a mechanistic way with many formal rules and procedures for teaching to ensure that students are prepared for the test. On the other hand, if the goal is to provide high-quality liberal arts education, it is less clear how this goal can be measured. Interested parties may have a variety of ideas about how "liberal arts" is defined and about what "high quality" means. In this case, the academic department may use an organic organizational form, which provides greater autonomy and flexibility. A broad range of activities may be seen as addressing the goal.

Culture: Fourth Independent Variable

The design of an organization is also influenced by its own norms and values (Schein, 1992). Organizational culture reflects propensities for different types of behavior. Some cultures are collaborative, and workplace cooperation is highly valued. In other organizations, the culture reinforces individual accomplishments and pits members against each other in competition for limited rewards.

Several cultural variables should be considered in relation to organizational design. A trusting culture, for instance, requires fewer controls than does one that is distrustful (Tierney, 2006). Flexible, organic designs may be appropriate under conditions of high trust, while mechanistic designs with more extensive oversight may be necessary when organizational members do not trust each other.

The strength of collegiality in a college or university culture will also determine to some degree the types of organizational designs that will be effective (Bess, 1988). Organic, decentralized designs, for example, provide opportunities for faculty and staff to participate in informal decision-making venues. In this case, the design of the organization is consistent with faculty and staff members' emphasis on the value of collegiality.

As a further example, some institutions describe themselves as learning-centered colleges, where student success and pedagogical innovation are highly valued (O'Banion, 1997). In these institutions, the focus shifts from what faculty prefer to teach to what students need to further their learning.

Organizational design decisions attempt to maximize opportunities for student learning. In some cases, these decisions will lead to more organic designs that facilitate interdisciplinary collaboration and experimentation with new pedagogical approaches. In other instances, more mechanistic structures may be necessary—for example, a requirement that all programs provide evening courses that are accessible for students who work full time.

Size: Fifth Independent Variable

Recall from systems theory (chapter 4) that with increasing size comes more specialization, more division of labor, more complexity, and hence, more need for coordination. So organizational designs must take into account the conditions of larger or smaller size (Pfeffer, 1982). Integration problems are more pronounced in large, highly differentiated organizations, and linkages across separated units tend to be managed through more mechanistic methods. Bureaucratic rules and regulations are created to systematize relationships across units, since relying on interpersonal interaction is too uncertain. If linkages across units are maintained solely through interpersonal interactions, then knowledge of the linkage remains secluded in the memories of individuals. If those individuals cannot be reached (e.g., they are on vacation), or if they retire or take a job at another institution, then people in the organization will have difficulty in getting the information they need. Rules, in contrast, codify and disperse knowledge throughout the organization. This enhances efficiency, since workers no longer must invent a new rule each time they encounter a novel situation (Hoy & Sweetland, 2000).

Rules establish a permanent record of procedures that can be accessed by organizational members, including new employees. As noted earlier, in small organizations, roles tend to be more diffuse, and many members are authorized to play different roles as circumstances dictate. Because institutions of higher education often are decentralized into many different departments, even large institutions sometimes appear to be designed like small ones and seem to acquire a culture that follows from small size. A small graduate program that admits only a few students each year could feel like a small community, even if it exists within a large, complex university. Generally, however, formalization and routinization ensure continuity of practices. Students, for example, may be required to pass basic mathematics courses before they can enroll in upper division physics courses.

Interdependence: The Intervening Variable

Interdependence refers to the flow of work and the connections—both physical and psychological—that are required between organizational members and/or departments (Pfeffer, 1978). As inputs (e.g., students or research knowledge) flow from one part of an organization to another, they must conform to agreed-upon specifications. Otherwise, the input to the receiving department may be out of the range of its acceptable standards and hence may not be able to be transformed with the technology available in the receiving department. Students passed from a prerequisite course without the necessary knowledge, for example, may not be able to do the work in the advanced course.

Organizational members in different departments must also be connected, at least by a willingness to cooperate and at best by a desire to do so (Barnard, 1938). This psychological sense of interdependence can be accomplished in a number of ways, including job rotation (rarely practiced in higher education) and the inculcation of a loyalty to the institution as a whole rather than to the individual department.

Several kinds of interdependence have been documented (Thompson, 1967; Victor & Blackburn, 1987). James Thompson proposed three critical alternatives: pooled interdependence, sequential interdependence, and reciprocal interdependence. **Pooled interdependence** occurs when units are independent of one another, but the failure of one means the failure of all. Assume, for example, that a college wants to produce a "liberally educated graduate." If students are taught in three fields—social science, natural science, and humanities—and one of the fields fails to do its work, then the goal of the institution will *not* be accomplished, even if the other two departments are successful.

Note that relatively little coordination is necessary across departments that are in a pooled interdependence relationship. The goal is achieved if the contributing independent departments do their jobs. There is an assumption, of course, that as each department contributes its part to the whole, there are highly predictable changes in the student to permit entrance into more advanced courses. As undergraduate students progress through their college years, of course, they diverge in their interests and talents, especially as they begin their concentrations within academic majors. Here, pooled interdependence becomes easier for faculty in the student's major to manage, as students take more courses within their own departments, and more accurate predictions of students' needs can be made than could be done when the students were spread out over a larger number of departments.

The second form of interdependence, **sequential interdependence**, is most frequently associated with an assembly line type of organization, sometimes called "long-linked technology," where the procedures must be articulated very clearly for the line to work properly. The departments in an organization whose design is predominantly sequential are in a line—

serially—and are dependent on one another sequentially. The outputs from one are the inputs to another.

For example, enrollment data from the registrar's office become the computing center's inputs; the latter's outputs are reports to staff in the residential life office who need to know how many students need on-campus housing. These departments are in sequential interdependence. Note that tighter coordination is needed here. Making accurate decisions depends, in this case, on units being responsive to each other's needs. It is usually accomplished through careful scheduling of operations and the imposition of overseeing supervisors in a multilevel hierarchy. Almost invariably, this is more costly than other forms of linkages across subunits because of the added costs of supervisory personnel.

Reciprocal interdependence is the third form. Here, the outputs of one department become the inputs to another—and the converse.

> Intensive technology requiring reciprocal interdependence is most dramatically illustrated by a general hospital. At any moment an emergency admission patient may require some combination of dietary, X-ray, laboratory, and housekeeping or hotel services, together with the various medical specialties, pharmaceutical services, occupational therapies, social work services, and spiritual or religious services. Which of these is/are needed and when, can be determined only from evidence about the state of mind of the patient. (Thompson, 1967, cited in Bedeian & Zammuto, 1991, pp. 199–200)

An example from higher education is a registrar's office that seeks data about expected enrollments in various courses from the academic departments and gives back information to them in the form of room assignments (large lecture halls for some classes, small seminar rooms for others). Note that much coordination is needed here. It relies mostly on "horizontal mutual adjustment" (Mintzberg, 1983a) as workers keep in close touch with one another to assure that uncertainties about the transformation process are kept as low as possible.

It is instructive to inquire about the interdependence among departments in universities whose missions include teaching, research, and service. How much of the work is pooled? How much is sequential? How much is reciprocal?

Higher education seems largely pooled for research. Faculty members may work alone on their research, and if each of the individual faculty members is successful, then the university as a whole accomplishes its mission. Research practices differ, however, by field. Indeed, as of late, research in the social sciences and hard sciences is becoming increasingly collaborative.

Interdisciplinary research, for example, may be characterized by reciprocal interdependence, where the work of one specialist becomes the input for another, and vice versa (Lattuca, 2002).

Teaching appears to require reciprocal interdependence, as faculty need to collaborate on linking the content and aims of their courses. College curriculum committees attempt to link courses, but they leave to individual faculty members the problems of managing interdependence. In fact, faculty members, for the most part, do not accept this responsibility. Instead, students are expected to bridge the gaps among disciplines as they put together their general education. That is, the student alone must make the connection between, say, the meaning of "uncertainty" in physics and in philosophy.

So, as noted in each of the sections above, environment, technology, goals, culture, and size have effects on the nature of the interdependence that workers have with one another as they transform inputs, as well as a direct impact on the design of the organization. Interdependence is an *intervening* variable in the sense that it alone is not usually an independent contributor to organizational design but is the result of the five other independent variables—environment, technology, goals, culture, and size. Assumptions and decisions about each of these five variables dictate how the relationships among the departments are structured (interdependence), which, in turn, affects the organization's overall design.

Frequently, tensions or power struggles emerge between the decentralized units (schools and departments) striving to be autonomous and adaptive to their distinctive, perhaps unique, local environments, and a central administration seeking to address system-wide needs for internal efficiency in accordance with budgetary limitations. An important caution in discussing the dependent variable of organizational design in colleges and universities, therefore, is to take into account the level of the organization being considered. Environments, technology, goals, culture, and size may not be the same for the institution as a whole as it is for its many decentralized departments. It may be difficult, therefore, to impose a uniform design for the entire organization. If environments, technology, goals, culture, and size differ among the various subunits of an organization, then a range of structural arrangements may be needed within a single institution.

Summary

As noted at the outset, organizational design is composed of a structure comprising components, a relationship among those components, and a mode of control. The design of organizations follows from at least five important variables: environment, technology, goals, culture, and size. These variables have an impact on the patterns of interdependency among the parts of the organization, which in turn affects the overall design of the organization. For example, when environments are simple and stable, sequential interdependencies can be more firmly established. When environments are turbulent and uncertain, decentralized, organic systems are more appropriate, since professional expertise can be used more readily.

In higher education, environments for different kinds of colleges and universities are immersed in varied contexts, depending on location, mission, economic constraints, and competing institutions. The technologies used in colleges and universities vary depending on some assumptions about the nature of the inputs to the organization—students and knowledge—and about the processes that are available for transforming those inputs. Higher education institutions pursue goals that are difficult to define and measure (e.g., producing socially responsible graduates) and goals that are concrete and quantifiable (e.g., graduation rates and amount of research funding). Different types of goals require different organizational designs—more organic designs for abstract goals, more mechanistic designs for quantifiable ones. Colleges also vary in culture. Some have informal atmospheres that fit well with organic designs, others are more formal and tightly controlled, which is consistent with mechanistic design principles. And, of course, institutions of higher learning vary in size. Large organizations tend to be more mechanistic than small ones; however, departments within large institutions can develop organic structures that give these units the feeling of a smaller organization.

In institutions where the mission dictates that fewer functions are to be performed (e.g., just teaching in community colleges), the design may be easier to plan and make workable than in institutions that have many missions (e.g., research universities). The teaching and research missions may require different organizational designs, given differences in technology, goals, and associated cultures. Hence, some of the inefficiencies in higher education may stem from a failure to build organizational designs that meet the potentially conflicting needs of the various components within institutions.

Review Questions

1. Administrators in a large community college have divided the courses offered in both daytime and evening into credit and noncredit divisions. This differentiation of function requires a corresponding integration.
   a. True
   b. False

2. Given the current market for students in higher education, which of the following will have the most influence on institutional effectiveness?
   a. Environment
   b. Technology
   c. Goals
   d. Culture
   e. Size

3. A long-standing liberal arts college serving a stable suburban area will find that its organization will be more efficient if it:
   a. Carefully defines the curriculum to be offered over a four-year period
   b. Allows many annual deviations in the curriculum
   c. Both of the above

4. If students in a large state university are "batch processed," the core technology in Perrow's theory that will be most efficient for teaching is:
   a. Craft
   b. Routine
   c. Nonroutine
   d. Engineering

5. In a college where relationships among faculty and administrators have traditionally been collegial, which of the following organizational designs is likely to be most effective:
   a. Mechanistic, bureaucratic
   b. Organic, loosely coupled
   c. Not enough information to predict

6. The achievement of a high-quality liberal arts education can best be accomplished through which of the following kinds of interdependence among the academic departments?
   a. Pooled
   b. Sequential
   c. Reciprocal

Case Discussion Questions

Consider again the Southern Gulf University (SGU) case presented at the beginning of this chapter.

1. Daft (1995) suggests that the effectiveness of a particular organizational design is contingent on the amount of **environmental uncertainty** (refer to Table 6.2). Based on the increasing level of

uncertainty in Southern Gulf University's environment, is its current organizational design likely to be effective over the long term? If not, what changes in design would you suggest to the provost?

2. SGU's faculty are now engaged in extensive off-campus research collaborations. Their funding sources and external partners are numerous and varied, and their research procedures are complex and longitudinal. SGU's Office of Research, however, continues to operate as a small bureaucracy designed to deal with routine tasks such as accounting and financial reports. Describe the "mismatch" of **technologies** between the research faculty and the Office of Research. If the Office of Research wants to be an authentic partner with the faculty in their research endeavors, what kinds of organizational design changes may be necessary?

3. The course and program approval process at SGU reflects sequential **interdependence**, where the outputs of one committee (a departmental curriculum committee) become the inputs to another committee (university-wide faculty senate) and so on until the proposal is approved. The Division of Continuing Education, however, operates outside of that system and does not vet its proposals through faculty governance. The program duplications that result reflect a coordination problem for the university. What type of interdependence (pooled, sequential, or reciprocal) could be established between faculty governance committees and the Division of Continuing Education? Which type of interdependence could keep SGU responsive to external markets, while ensuring that faculty members are able to review the programs sufficiently?

References

Barak, R., & Kniker, C. (2002). Benchmarking by state higher education boards. *New Directions for Higher Education, 118* (pp. 93–102). San Francisco: Jossey-Bass.

Barker, R. G., & Gump, P. V. (1964). *Big school, small school.* Stanford, CA: Stanford University Press.

Barnard, C. (1938). *The functions of the executive.* Cambridge, MA: Harvard University Press.

Bedeian, A. G., & Zammuto, R. F. (1991). *Organizations: Theory and design.* Chicago: Dryden Press.

Benjamin, R., & Carroll, S. (1998). The implications of the changed environment for governance in higher education. In W. Tierney (Ed.), *The responsive university: Restructuring for high performance* (pp. 92–119). Baltimore, MD: Johns Hopkins University Press.

Bess, J. L. (1988). *Collegiality and bureaucracy in the modern university.* New York: Teachers College Press.

Birnbaum, R. (1988). *How colleges work: The cybernetics of academic organization and leadership.* San Francisco: Jossey-Bass.

Blau, P. N., & Schoenherr, R. A. (1971). *The structure of organizations.* New York: Basic Books.

Brown, S., & Eisenhardt, K. (1997). The art of continuous change: Linking complexity theory and time-paced evolution in relentlessly shifting organizations. *Administrative Science Quarterly, 42,* 1–34.

Burrell, G., & Morgan, G. (1979). *Sociological paradigms and organizational analysis: Elements of the sociology of corporate life.* London: Heinemann.

Cohen, M. D., & March, J. G. (1974). *Leadership and ambiguity: The American college president.* New York: McGraw-Hill.

Colbeck, C. (2002). State policies to improve undergraduate teaching. *Journal of Higher Education, 73,* 425.

Cutright, M. (Ed.) (2001). *Chaos theory and higher education: Leadership, planning, and policy.* New York: Peter Lang.

Daft, R. L. (1983). *Organization theory and design* (1st ed.). Minneapolis: West Publishing.

Daft, R. L. (1995). *Organization theory and design* (5th ed.). Minneapolis: West Publishing.

Daft, R. L., & Noe, R. A. (2001). *Organizational behavior.* Fort Worth, TX: Harcourt College Publishers.

Ellul, J. (1980). *Système techicien (English). The technological system* (J. Neugroschel, Trans.). New York: Continuum.

Galbraith, J., Downey, D., & Kates, A. (2002). *Designing dynamic organizations: A hands-on guide for leaders at all levels.* New York: AMACOM.

Gooding, R. Z., & Wagner, J. A., III. (1985). A meta-analytic review of the relationship between size and performance: The productivity and efficiency of organizations and their subunits. *Administrative Science Quarterly, 30*(4), 462–481.

Gumport, P. (2000). Academic restructuring: Organizational change and institutional imperatives. *Higher Education, 39,* 67–91.

Hoy, W. K., & Sweetland, S. (2000). Bureaucracies that work: Enabling, not coercive. *Journal of School Leadership, 10,* 525–541.

Hulin, C. L., & Roznowksi, M. (1985). Organizational technologies: Effects on organizations' characteristics and individuals' responses. In L. L. Cummings & B. M. Staw (Eds.), *Research in organizational behavior, 7* (pp. 39–85). Greenwich, CT: JAI Press.

Kezar, A. (2003). Enhancing innovative partnerships: Creating a change model for academic and student affairs collaboration. *Innovative Higher Education, 28*(2), 137–156.

Lattuca, L. (2002). Learning interdisciplinarity. *Journal of Higher Education, 73*(6), 711–739.

Lawrence, P. R., & Lorsch, J. W. (1969). *Organization and environment.* Homewood, IL: Irwin.

Mintzberg, H. (1983a). *Structure in fives: Designing effective organizations.* Englewood Cliffs, NJ: Prentice-Hall.

Mintzberg, H. (1983b). *Power in and around organizations.* Englewood Cliffs, NJ: Prentice-Hall.

Morrison, J. L. & Wilson, I. (1997). Analyzing environments and developing scenarios for uncertain times. In M. W. Peterson, D. D. Dill, and L. A. Mets (Eds.), *Planning and management for a changing environment: A handbook on redesigning postsecondary institutions.* San Francisco: Jossey-Bass.

Nadler, D., Gerstein, M., & Shaw, R. (1992). *Organizational architecture: Designs for changing organizations.* San Francisco: Jossey-Bass.

O'Banion, T. (1997). *A learning college for the 21st century.* Phoenix, AZ: Oryx Press.

Perrow, C. (1961). An analysis of goals in complex organizations. *American Sociological Review, 26*(6), 854–866.

Perrow, C. (1967). A framework for the comparative analysis of organizations. *American Sociological Review, 32*(2), 194–208.

Perrow, C. (1970). *Organizational analysis: A sociological view.* Belmont, CA: Wadsworth Publishing Company.

Perrow, C. (1986). *Complex organizations: A critical essay* (3rd ed.). New York: McGraw Hill.

Pfeffer, J. (1978). *Organizational design.* Arlington Heights, IL: AHM Publishing Corporation.

Pfeffer, J. (1982). *Organizations and organization theory.* Boston: Pitman.

Pugh, D. S. (1981). The Aston program of research: Retrospect and prospect. In A. H. Van de Ven & W. F. Joyce (Eds.), *Perspectives on organizational design and behavior* (pp. 135–166). New York: John Wiley.

Schein, E. (1992). *Organizational culture and leadership* (2nd ed.). San Francisco: Jossey-Bass.

Schuster, J., & Finkelstein, M. (2006). *The American faculty: The restructuring of academic work and careers.* Baltimore, MD: Johns Hopkins University.

Scott, W. R. (1998). *Organizations: Rational, natural, and open systems* (4th ed.). Upper Saddle River, NJ: Prentice Hall.

Steers, R. M. (1977). *Organizational effectiveness: A behavioral view.* Santa Monica, CA: Goodyear.

Thompson, J. D. (1967). *Organizations in action.* New York: McGraw Hill.

Tierney, W. (2006). *Trust and the public good: Examining the cultural conditions of academic work.* New York: Peter Lang Publishing.

Victor, B., & Blackburn, R. S. (1987). Interdependence: An alternative conceptualization. *Academy of Management Review, 12,* 486–498.

Woodward, J. (1965). *Industrial organization: Theory and practice.* London: Oxford University Press.

Woodward, J. (1970). *Industrial organization: Behaviour and control.* London: Oxford University Press.

7

BUREAUCRATIC FORMS AND THEIR LIMITATIONS

CONTENTS

The authors are most grateful for the critical comments on an early draft of this chapter by Robert Hendrickson, Pennsylvania State University. The final version, of course, is our own and may or may not reflect the perspective of the reviewer.

Preview

- Organizations are commonly designed according to bureaucratic principles. Characteristics of bureaucracies include division of labor, standardization, formalization, impersonal relationships, promotion based on technical competence, and a well-defined hierarchy.
- Bureaucratic organizational designs assume one or more of the following forms: functional, product, client/customer, time/place, and matrix.
- Function-based organizational forms promote skill specialization and reduce duplication of services, but they also emphasize narrow ranges of skills, focus on short time horizons, and obscure accountability for overall outcomes.
- Product-based organizational forms foster an orientation toward overall outcomes and toward the needs of unique market segments. They also allow for diversification and expansion of skills training, but sacrifice economies of scale.
- Matrix organizational forms can adapt quickly to changing external environments, but they generate role conflict for organizational members, given divided loyalties and multiple supervisors.
- Loose coupling theory explains how people, units, and events can be responsive (accountable) to each other, yet retain their structural separateness (autonomy).
- Structuration theory suggests that social systems (e.g., administrative task forces, academic departments) appropriate rules and resources from their environments. These rules and resources "structure" the activities of the social system.
- Postmodern theories suggest the utility of de-differentiation—that is, the organization seeks to reduce the level of structural differentiation in order to minimize coordination costs.
- Feminist theory proposes an alternative to bureaucratic organizational design: a "web of inclusion," which builds from the center out, rather than from the top down.

——————————— CASE CONTEXT ———————————

Restructuring at High Plains University

High Plains University is a private master's institution with a history of frequent turnover among top-level administrators. The "revolving door" at the top of the institution has dampened the level of commitment that faculty and staff at all levels feel toward the institution. There is a palpable sense of defeatism, as many organizational members have resigned themselves to the fact that the institution is merely a "stepping stone" to bigger and better things elsewhere. It was in the context of these dampened spirits that Paul Strong was appointed to the position of vice president for administration.

High Plains University is relatively small with an enrollment of 4,000 students. Nearly every nonacademic function (e.g., admissions, maintenance, purchasing) reports to the vice president for administration. Vice President Strong reorganized these administrative functions three times in his first two years in office, but none of the reorganizations was deemed successful.

The first reorganization sought to create a more efficient administrative structure, and to clarify who was accountable for which outcomes. Separate offices for undergraduate and graduate admissions were combined into one unit. Alumni relations shifted from the public relations department to the office for institutional advancement. Care for the athletic fields became a responsibility of the facilities and maintenance department, rather than the athletic department.

This reorganization yielded cost savings, but it also engendered strong opposition by some staff. Graduate admissions staff felt that their concerns were ignored by the more numerous undergraduate admissions officers, and they raised concerns that the university was neglecting graduate programs. The alumni relations director was continually at odds with the fund-raising staff, whom he thought were too heavy-handed in their interactions with potential donors. Even the football coach complained that he did not like the way the maintenance staff cut the grass on the practice field.

After strong resistance by staff, Vice President Strong reorganized on the basis of teamwork. He believed that many of the conflicts and disagreements would be alleviated through more frequent communication and collaboration. Staff members from the registrar's and admissions offices, for example, were placed on enrollment management teams, public relations staff and marketing personnel were grouped into communications teams, and so on. These teams, however, failed to achieve the benefits of collaboration; instead, the results were confusion (who is supposed to do which tasks?) and obstruction ("that's not my job").

Acknowledging the failure of team-based restructuring, Vice President Strong disbanded the teams and returned to groupings by functional specialization. However, the move was greeted by staff apathy and by anger from those employees who had made a strong commitment to their teams. Moreover, poor performance continued to pervade many of the administrative functions of the college. A student satisfaction survey revealed a

range of complaints and concerns. The student billing office and the registrar, for example, used different data management software; sometimes
the college continued to bill students who were no longer enrolled, and
sometimes the registrar prohibited a student from registering for lack of
payment, when, in fact, the student had already paid his or her tuition in
full. Students also encountered inconsistencies between printed materials
and information posted on administrative web sites (e.g., conflicting deadlines for adding or dropping a course).

Neither functional specialization nor teamwork yielded the expected
outcomes, and the overall sense of accountability in the college remained
low. There was a great deal of duplication in certain functions, yet there
were significant gaps in other areas. Frustrated with the outcomes, Vice
President Strong admitted to a colleague that he is at a loss about how to
proceed.

Introduction

I n the previous chapter, we considered some of the basic components
of organizational design. The chapter introduced the independent and
intervening variables that need to be considered in designing an effective
organization. In this chapter, we take a close look at the most common kind
of organizational design—bureaucracy. Virtually all colleges and universities
have been organized at least partly along bureaucratic lines, so it is important
to understand their advantages and disadvantages.

Bureaucratic organizations tend to be extremely efficient (though not in
all circumstances). Why are they so? One answer lies with the thinking of a
giant in the field, Max Weber (1864–1920), whose theories we sketch out
below.

Bureaucratic Structure

Weber was a social scientist who studied the effects of alternative organizational structures on performance. In his early observations, Weber was im-
pressed by differences he found in the Prussian and German armies in the
19th century. The Prussian army, he discovered, seemed to be dominated by:

- tradition (class and status)—for example, brother-in-law generals,
  poker player friends as chief of staff;
- charismatic authority—that is, loyalty to individual commanders,
  rather than to the army as a whole;

- promotions based on personal relations or money rather than on competence in military matters;
- few written rules that guided either control or action; and
- personal and arbitrary strategies made up on the spur of the moment without coordination with others.

The German army, on the other hand, was characterized by order through legal authority and well-established sets of rules and regulations that applied to all personnel.

Weber (1924, 1946) synthesized the organizational characteristics of the German army into what has become known as the bureaucratic model. These characteristics are noted in Table 7.1 below.

Weber's ideas were based on his presumption of the importance of rationality, impersonality, and objectivity in decision making and in the application of rules. His basic hypothesis was that given environmental contingencies that support them, the more the characteristics of bureaucracy are present in an organization, the more effective and efficient that organization will be. It is important to stress, however, that bureaucracy is not *invariably* the most efficient form of organizational design. There are occasions when formal bureaucracies may not be appropriate—for example, conditions of an unstable or unpredictable external environment and/or complex technology when rapid, impromptu interactions are necessary. Imagine a research and development (R&D) team in which each member has unique skills, and the project outcome depends on shifting roles, collaboration, and mutual respect. In these kinds of organizations, bureaucratic structures would

TABLE 7.1
Elements in the Weberian Conceptualization of Bureaucracy

1. **Division of labor** into specialized tasks
2. **Procedural specification**—routinization, standardization
3. **Rules**—operations and activities governed by written rules
4. **Impersonality**—rational and universalistic application of rules
5. **Selection and promotion based on objective criteria** and technical competence *within* constraints of seniority
6. **Hierarchy of authority**—levels of status and authority that extended to official duties only
7. **Fixed ranges for salaries and pensions**
8. **Assured and visible career track**
9. **Technical training of officials**
10. **Appointment by merit**

diminish the autonomy, creativity, and spontaneous experimentation necessary for success. So, to be valid, the Weberian hypothesis must be modified somewhat to add a requisite condition: *given* a stable, predictable environment and routine production technology, the more the characteristics of bureaucracy are present, the more effective the organization will be.

We can even make this hypothesis more specific with respect to each of the separate bureaucratic characteristics. For example, given appropriate environmental and technological conditions, the higher the level of specialization (or any other characteristic of bureaucracies), the more effective the organization will be.

In fact, bureaucracies have both positive functions and dysfunctions. For example, the relationship between degree of specialization and productivity is usually curvilinear. Up to a point, specialization results in greater efficiency, but after that point, human "diseconomies" result. These include boredom, fatigue, and stress (Robbins, 1997a).

In the following sections, five bureaucratic characteristics with particular relevance for higher education organizations are considered in some detail: division of labor, procedural specification, impersonal interactions, promotion and selection of personnel, and hierarchy.

Division of Labor

Weber realized that work can be accomplished more effectively when personnel are allowed to specialize in a particular task or function. Hence, to be efficient, bureaucracies must find ways to divide labor by functional specialization. Specialization can be defined as "the degree to which organizational tasks are subdivided into separate jobs" (Daft, 1989, p. 18). Weber argued that bureaucracies consist primarily of aggregations of specialists—an image consistent with the departmentalized structures and highly specialized personnel employed in colleges and universities.

Quite a bit of research has gone into determining the degree to which organizations are specialized, and the extent to which specialization is efficient. The more specialization, the more lateral coordination (oversight and control) is needed across the specialized tasks and personnel. Depending on size and the nature of the interdependence among specialized units, coordination is accomplished through two "strategies of control, a personal centralized one and a decentralized bureaucratic one" (Galbraith, 1977, p. 40). "When organizations are small, decisions are centralized at the top and personally communicated to the implementers. Large organizations decentralize decisions but control choices through rules, procedures, and performance measurements created by specialists" (pp. 40–41).

The problem of coordination is complicated, however, by the creation and exchange of information. When departments are sequentially or recipro-cally interdependent (see chapter 6), a great deal of information must be generated for the fit between them to be smooth. Hence, to be efficient, organizations must seek ways to maintain or reduce the amount of informa-tion to be processed during the coordination effort. Rules and procedures accomplish this, as does the employment of professional workers who can be relied on to use their own discretion in making decisions (Thompson, 1965).

Examples of the division of labor in colleges and universities are well known. For faculty, the division of labor is not by function, as it is for the administration, but by academic subject matter. The degree of specialization for faculty is, however, somewhat problematic. For example, one might con-sider how much specialization there should be among faculty in their in-structional roles. Should the subject matter areas be divided up into even more subdivisions than at present, with each of the smaller segments being taught by a more specialized faculty member? Large universities are fre-quently highly specialized in their teaching and research areas, but too high a degree of specialization by subject matter may produce a fragmented un-dergraduate experience, especially if integration across the specialized curric-ular areas is neglected. Consider also whether the noncognitive or affective objectives of teaching in colleges and universities should be split into smaller pieces (Bess, 1982). For example, to take one highly improbable extreme, teaching the value of tolerance could be assigned to a "professor of tolerance" and teaching good dietary habits to a "professor of diets." Most institutions appear generally to endorse a much broader division of labor by assigning cognitive development to academic departments (where subject matters are broken down further) and noncognitive development to student affairs units. Whether this organizational design is the most effective method for addressing institutional goals of developing students holistically, however, is an important question.

Procedural Specification

Bureaucracies typically publish their policies and procedures in written man-uals to which employees have ready access. Different organizations can choose to specify procedures in different ways, and the differences may be characterized in terms of routinization, standardization, and formalization.

Routinization refers to the regularization of procedures—to the schedul-ing and managing of events with regular patterns. Sets of rules prescribe uni-versalistically how all organizational members should deal with frequently occurring problems that must be addressed in the course of the workday.

Standardization is the practice by which organizations "reduce the infi-nite number of things in the world, potential and actual—to a moderate number of well-defined varieties" (March & Simon, 1959, p. 159). Instead of requiring organizational members to make judgments about each situation or problem, standard categories are created, and tightly written job descriptions and procedures are prescribed for each one. Routinization and standardization remove the need for individuals to exercise discretion over every decision, especially when all the information needed to make the decision is not immediately available (March & Olsen, 1989). They limit decision making to more circumscribed domains where the consequences can be predicted more accurately. They seek to make the irregular regular.

Formalization is the degree to which the organization attempts to specify the behaviors of its members through formal rules and procedures (Pugh & Hickson, 1976). Formalization makes the informal more formal. Often it is the extent to which rules, procedures, instructions and communications are written down, rather than informally known and understood (Price, 1997).

Varying manifestations of formalization range from those that are coercive to those that are enabling (Adler & Borys, 1996). **Coercive formalization** uses enforcement mechanisms that require strict adherence to formal rules and regulations. The goal is to force organizational members to comply with the wishes of top management. In contrast, **enabling formalization** assumes that deviations from formal rules can be helpful to the organization by virtue of the learning opportunities they create. Rules and procedures do not need to prescribe exact behavioral specifications. Instead, they can be "a flexible set of guidelines or best practices that enable one to deal more effectively with the surprises that occur" (Hoy & Miskel, 2005, p. 103). To illustrate a comparison of the two types of formalization, under coercive formalization, rules that residence hall assistants must follow are accompanied by clear negative sanctions for noncompliance, while under enabling formalization, residence hall assistants are given leeway to bend the rules if situations seem to call for it.

Rules also serve the latent function of reducing friction and minimizing conflict among organizational members (Gouldner, 1954). They act as a **buffer** among coworkers and between supervisors and employees. By using an official rule to justify behavior, a supervisor can remove the inference that personality or personal feelings may have influenced his or her judgments of others. When a dean refuses to give a faculty member an additional travel allowance, for example, the justification can be that the rules permit only a certain amount to be spent each year. As a result, the faculty member is unlikely to view the dean's decision as a personal affront; the dean is simply following the rules. Furthermore, explicit demonstrations of unequal power are usually felt as personal insults. College norms typically honor equality and human dignity, at least as ideals. Direct orders, personally delivered, even when justified by authority, are often resented. Rules help avoid this blatant demonstration of power and status inequality.

Another function of rules is **indulgency** or **strategic leniency** (Blau & Meyer, 1971). Supervisors can use the granting of favors that violate rules as bargaining chips to elicit desired behaviors among subordinates. A supervisor may, for example, waive a deadline for an employee who has typically performed well. The supervisor expects her leniency to be reciprocated by continued high performance. Leniency, however, may lead to perceptions of preferential treatment and charges of discrimination. Use of these tools of leadership and motivation, consequently, must take into account the culture of the organization, especially the modes of communication among organizational members.

Organizational members may find rules and regulations oppressive and seemingly unnecessary. Indeed, from the perspective of organizational efficiency, rules sometimes result in merely *satisfactory* rather than *optimum* achievement of organizational goals. Organizational members may tend to follow rules even when other options would better serve the organization's purposes. Indeed, just "following the rules" themselves may displace or replace the operational goals of the organization (March & Simon, 1959). This excessive legalism among organizational members in bureaucracies tends to take time, cost money, and distract from more desirable, immediately productive activities (Thompson, 1965).

Impersonal Interactions

Interpersonal interactions in bureaucracies are characterized by

1. Limited involvement with others
2. Interactions among office employees strictly limited to business
3. Universalistic judgments most common; no special considerations given to certain people for different reasons
4. A system of rules covers the rights and duties of employees

Weber recognized that impersonal relationships actually *protected* subordinates from arbitrary and capricious actions on the part of supervisors, since each person was to be treated with equality. A college dean in a bureaucracy, for example, would be required by formal rule to treat all faculty members equally, thus restricting, yet protecting each. Each faculty member, for example, would understand that rules for course load assignments prevent a desirable, if arbitrary, reduction in an individual's load by the dean, but they also prevent the dean from giving excessive course load assignments to a faculty member. Note how this positive function of bureaucracies is sometimes overlooked.

Promotion and Selection Based on Technical Competence

In the Weberian or "ideal" bureaucracy, workers are chosen to move up the hierarchy on the basis of their seniority and merit—that is, knowledge and skills that are important to the organization. The paths to upward mobility in a bureaucracy are well known to organizational members, and they see their organization as providing an opportunity for career advancement.

In colleges and universities, the paths to upper-level positions differ in the faculty and administrative sectors. In the faculty sector, there are usually just three or four levels—instructor, assistant professor, associate professor, and professor. Except in some limited areas, these roles are not in a hierarchical relationship. Moreover, the usual tasks to be performed by occupants of each level of the faculty career path are essentially the same. Faculty at all levels teach, do research, and provide service. To be sure, only senior faculty may be asked to serve on promotion and tenure or merit evaluation committees, but performance in these roles is not usually seen as a path toward upward mobility. Nor is task authority any greater for senior faculty once they have tenure; associate and full professors perform virtually the same functions and exercise decision-making authority over collective issues largely through egalitarian means. The faculty career path is seen, therefore, not so much as an opportunity for different roles and greater responsibility and authority, but for job security, higher status, and additional salary.

In recent years, however, alternative clinical and nontenure-track faculty career routes have been introduced more extensively into higher education, which has engendered to some extent more hierarchical relationships. Full-time faculty have status, power, and authority that part-time and adjunct faculty do not. Adjunct and part-time faculty lack job security through tenure and typically earn lower salaries than do full-time, tenured faculty. Persons in adjunct career positions, moreover, have little opportunity for change in title or status.

The career route for administrative personnel, on the other hand, is more traditionally bureaucratic, with many more levels through which individuals can move to gain more responsibility, authority, status, and salary. Individuals are promoted on the basis of longevity (the length of their employment) and, within the longevity categories, on their recognized greater merit—that is, skill and achievements. Hence, organizational members respect supervisors not only because of the office they hold, but because the incumbent in the office is judged to have earned his or her place through the exercise of superior competence.

Well-Defined Hierarchy of Authority

Weber notes that in earlier times, hierarchical roles usually derived from magic and superstition. Rights of command and duties of obedience ascribed to these roles stemmed from belief in the unusual, often allegedly magical or supernatural powers of some individual (e.g., the divine right of kings, which suggests that the monarch has "God-given" authority to rule). Weber called this kind of authority *charismatic*.

In addition to charisma, authority, according to Weber, can be *traditional*—obedience to a person who occupies a position vested by tradition with authority. Organizational traditions may support deference, for example, to long-serving employees who are seen as embodying the collective wisdom and institutional memory of the college. Professors who hold endowed chairs, as another example, may exert greater authority in college governance than do other faculty members on the basis of their esteemed positions.

Weber also describes *rational-legal* authority—that is, obedience to formal offices in an organization. In colleges and universities, administrators usually possess rational-legal authority defined by a **hierarchy of offices**. According to Thompson (1965), "a hierarchy is a system of roles—the roles of subordination and superordination arranged in a chain so that role 1 is subordinate to role 2; and until a role is reached that is subordinate to no other role, except perhaps to a group of people such as a board of directors or an electorate" (p. 58).

Hierarchies usually involve **line** and **staff** personnel. Line personnel perform functions that directly affect the transformation process. Faculty members are line personnel insofar as they are in direct contact with students. As researchers, they may be line (doing the research themselves) or staff (supervising others). Staff personnel perform support roles for the line functions in the administration of a college or university. Staff functions include financial aid, maintenance, legal services, and purchasing, among others. Whether personnel in student affairs divisions (e.g., student activities, residential life) constitute line or staff depends on the philosophy of the institution.

Efficient hierarchies usually require a **scalar chain of command**—that is, an unambiguous, unbroken, vertical chain from top management to the bottom of the hierarchy so that managers are not bypassed (e.g., a dean of housing bypassing the vice president for student affairs and going directly to the president). Related to this notion is the idea of **unity of command**. Hierarchies work best when organizational members receive direction from only one supervisor. Later we discuss an alternative organizational design (a matrix design) where this principle may not be practiced and where there is no detriment to the effectiveness of the system.

Many organizations recognize the inflexibility of a chain of command and the formal lines of communication and authority that are established. In higher education, furthermore, both a political and a professional mode of decision making are overlaid on the administrative hierarchy rendering the "official" hierarchy subject to checks and balances that vitiate the concepts of scalar chain of command and unity of command (Bess, 1988). So, for example, in matters of promotion and tenure of faculty, the authority of both the faculty and the administration *jointly* is involved in the decisions. In different types of institutions, the balance of power may lie on the side of the faculty (e.g., in large, research universities) or with the administration (perhaps in some community colleges).

Another aspect of hierarchies has to do with **span of control**, which refers to the number of workers who fall under the control of a supervisor. Span of control—the number of workers—is often a function of the technology of the organization and the leadership preferences of those in power. Some organizations have many levels in the hierarchy: they are "tall," and the span of control is narrow (people supervise a relatively small number of workers). In other organizations, the hierarchy has fewer levels and is "flat"; in these instances, the span of control is wider.

One advantage of a tall hierarchy and a narrow span of control is the greater time available for supervisors to assist the organizational members who report to them. On the other hand, because more supervisors are necessary, administrative costs are higher. Moreover, since there are more levels in the hierarchy, decision making may be delayed or communications distorted.

Supervisors in a flat hierarchy with a broad span of control are not able to provide constant, close oversight to the many people who report to them. The latent effect of this policy is to decentralize decision making to the lowest level of expertise—desirable even in bureaucracies. Some chief executives in bureaucracies favor a broad span of control as a philosophy of management. They realize that a wider span of control can benefit both employee initiative and commitment to the organization by encouraging more participation in decision making.

In many colleges and universities, where autonomous, self-directed faculty members are performing the line activity, the span of control over academic matters tends to be broad. Faculty members have professional authority over their work, which is not usually subject to hierarchical oversight. The tradition of academic freedom supports this principle and thus allows a flat, broad span of control. In the more administrative domains, where closer supervision over organizational members is sometimes seen as necessary, a narrower span of control and a taller hierarchy are found.

It is important to remember that bureaucracy is an *ideal* form that makes sense for certain contexts or contingencies. An organization can be analyzed to ascertain (1) whether it should be bureaucratic, and (2) if so, where it may fail to achieve all of the ideal characteristics that Weber believed bureaucracies should have. As Blau and Meyer (1987) note:

> Weber's writings on bureaucracy present what he termed an "ideal type." This is a methodological construct, a device used by Weber to generalize about the bureaucratic form of organization. It does not represent an average of all existing bureaucracies (or other social structures) but a pure type, derived by abstracting the most characteristic bureaucratic aspects of all known organizations. Since perfect bureaucratization is never fully realized, no existing organization precisely fits the ideal type. (p. 25)

Weber's theorizing provided a range of variables to describe organizational designs, which can include varying degrees of specialization, standardization, and formalization. Organizations can have many levels of hierarchy (i.e., they can be tall), which is often associated with centralized decision making, or they can have fewer levels (i.e., they can be flatter), which may permit more decentralization.

Centralization, Decentralization, and Participation

Patterns of centralization and decentralization shape how people participate in an organization. When structures are centralized, organizational members may not participate directly in decision making. A supervisor, director, or elected representative may participate on their behalf. When structures are decentralized, participation is often more direct.

Helsabeck (1973) provides a schema that succinctly lays out the range of participation possibilities. By juxtaposing the range of participation and the degree of centralization, Helsabeck arrays four quadrants in which virtually all kinds of organizations can be portrayed. Moreover, Helsabeck identifies four kinds of typical decisions necessary for all subsystems at any level in the organization: **authority allocation, resource allocation, resource acquisition,** and **production.** For different institutions, each of these decision types can be located in one of the four quadrants within the matrix. In other words, it is possible to plot where colleges and universities have charged their organizational members with responsibility for different types of decisions. By graphing these four kinds of decisions, we can visualize the patterns of centralization and decentralization within an organization and, by extension, characterize the extent and type of participation by organizational members.

Figure 7.1 depicts a situation where one hypothetical institution has distributed the four kinds of decisions at both the institution-wide and subunit levels. We can illustrate each decision type with an example. Decisions about constructing new facilities such as academic buildings and residence halls are classified as institution-wide resource allocation decisions (type 2), which in this institution are highly centralized and made by only a few people at the top of the hierarchy (e.g., by the president and one or two vice presidents). In contrast, approvals for new academic programs—an institution-wide production decision (type 4)—are centralized in this institution and made by many participants (e.g., a college-wide curriculum committee with representatives from each academic department).

Other types of resource allocation decisions in this institution are decentralized to the unit level (i.e., not mandated by the top of the hierarchy) but

FIGURE 7.1
Typical Decisions Plotted by Amount of Participation and Degree of Centricity for a Hypothetical Higher Education Institution*

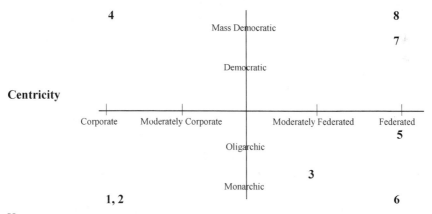

Key:
1. Institution-wide authority allocation decisions
2. Institution-wide resource allocation decisions
3. Institution-wide resource acquisition decisions
4. Institution-wide production decisions
5. Unit-level authority allocation decisions
6. Unit-level resource allocation decisions
7. Unit-level resource acquisition decisions
8. Unit-level production decisions

* Adapted from Helsabeck, 1973, p. 6.

are made by only one or two people. For example, decisions about allocating office space to faculty—a unit-level resource allocation decision (type 6)— are decentralized in this institution to each academic department, where the department chair alone makes decisions about office assignments. In contrast, unit-level production decisions (type 8) in this institution are decentralized but are made by many unit-level participants, rather than by the department chair alone. All faculty members in a department, for example, participate in creating the teaching schedule for each semester.

Further, a decision about whether to give the faculty senate final authority to determine new personnel policies is an example of an institution-wide authority allocation decision (type 1), which in this institution is centralized and made by those at the top of the hierarchy, perhaps by the president alone. Institution-wide resource acquisition decisions (type 3), in contrast, are moderately decentralized in this institution, but are made with relatively low participation. Fund-raising responsibilities, for example, are decentralized to the deans of the various schools within the institution.

Decisions about who is selected to serve as a department chair are unit-level authority allocation decisions (type 5). In this institution, those decisions are decentralized with a moderate degree of participation (e.g., only tenured faculty are eligible to vote for department chair). Finally, decisions about seeking research grants are unit-level resource acquisition decisions (type 7), which in this institution are decentralized, with a relatively high degree of participation (e.g., by faculty research teams within each academic department).

These four types of decisions—authority allocation, resource allocation, resource acquisition, and production—are representative of those addressed in virtually every organization at institution-wide and subunit levels. One can imagine additional types of decisions that can be plotted on the figure to clarify the distribution of authority in those particular areas and to suggest new configurations of decision-making participation. Such diagnostic procedures help in the design of efficient and effective organizations.

This analysis also reveals that colleges and universities centralize some decisions and decentralize others. Moreover, centralized and decentralized decisions can be made hierarchically or with much participation. Specifically, centralized decisions can be made by those at the top of the hierarchy or by a representative body such as a faculty senate. Decentralized decisions may be determined by the heads of the decentralized units (e.g., department chairs) or by the members of the units themselves.

Common Bureaucratic Forms

With more than 4,300 higher education institutions in the United States, it might be expected that there are many organizational differences in how the work of higher education gets done. Indeed, a wide variety of individual roles and collections of roles in departments can be found, all with varying degrees of both hierarchical and lateral connections.

In this section, we discuss a number of ways that organizations typically divide their labor force, including division by function performed, by product or service, by client, by time, by place, or by matrix. Usually, combinations of these forms of division of labor are found, with "hybrid structures" that take advantage of the benefits of multiple forms of organization (Galbraith, Downey, & Kates, 2002).

Functional Forms

Most organizations are divided into different **functions** that must be performed in order to transform inputs into finished products. For example, most organizations (including colleges and universities) have some form of departments that focus on marketing (admissions), production (teaching and research), and purchasing, among others. For each of these functions, there is a distinctive set of activities and tasks.

This functional division of labor is the most common means of dealing with the flow of inputs across different departments in a sequence (by analogy, an assembly line). That is, each department "adds value" by performing its specialized function as the inputs pass through. Thus, in higher education, students flow through the different academic departments, which adds value (knowledge and skills) that the students can use in later pursuits. A functional form of organization looks like the familiar organization chart in Figure 7.2.

Function-based departments consist of organizational members who perform the same or similar tasks. Grouping them together leads to greater efficiency because control over processes and the quality of the output can be the responsibility of a single supervisor, who can address the narrowly specialized issues and problems of the department. In fact, when workers are performing the same tasks, there is less need for supervision and coordination *within* the unit, since the commonality of knowledge and skills can be readily shared informally among the organizational members themselves. There is also less distortion of communication, less ambiguity, and less conflict. Functional departments must, however, be linked according to their sequential interdependencies. That is, when one functional department's *input* depends on the *output* of another department, there is usually (though not always) a formal organizational tie and an associated responsible person or persons to assure smooth coordination between the two (e.g., a liaison between departments).

Thus, if the product needs to be delivered in a given sequence (e.g., curricula in mathematics first, then the physical sciences) organizations are more

FIGURE 7.2
Example of a Functional Form of Organization

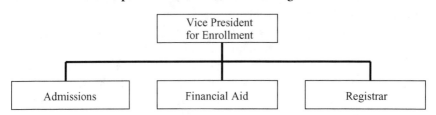

For a sequential operation, the flow of inputs moves laterally across departments.

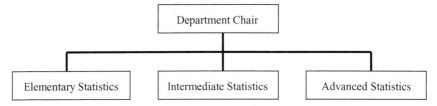

efficient when they are set up in functional forms. In the form of a hypothesis: The more the technology requires sequential interdependence (versus other types), the more efficient a functional (versus product or matrix) form of organization will be.

Note that while departmental efficiency is enhanced through organization by function, problems of integration are then created for the organization as a whole. As noted above, if departmental interdependence is sequential, a level of supervision must be introduced to coordinate work *between* departments.

Beyond efficiencies of supervision, there are various advantages and disadvantages of a functional form of organization, particularly in the management of human resources (Hellriegel, Slocum, & Woodman, 1995). The advantages (adapted from Duncan, 1979) are that they:

1. Promote skill specialization
2. Reduce duplication of scarce resources
3. Enhance career advancement for specialists within large departments
4. Facilitate communication of knowledge and procedures
5. Aid supervisors in sharing expertise with subordinates
6. Expose specialists to others within the same specialty
7. Provide economies of scale

There are disadvantages, however. Functional forms also:

1. Emphasize a narrow range of routine tasks, which encourages short time horizons
2. Foster parochial, suboptimizing perspectives by managers that limit their capacities for top management positions
3. Reduce knowledge of other departments and communication and cooperation between them
4. Multiply interdepartmental dependencies, which can make coordination and scheduling difficult
5. Elevate decision making to senior managers
6. Obscure accountability for overall outcomes

In spite of the apparent logic of the conclusions about organizing by function, current organizational design research is exploring whether functional forms are effective in every case. Instead, **teams** of different kinds of experts completing a set of specialized tasks may be better than many whole departments of different kinds of specialists (Hackman, 1990). Rather than having separate functional departments for admissions, orientation, and institutional research, for example, the organization can create an enrollment management team composed of experts from each functional area. These **cross-functional** units may be more effective than homogeneous departments when the tasks themselves are complex and closely linked (sequentially or reciprocally interdependent). If workers performing different tasks are in the *same* unit, then they can work out issues informally and interpersonally, instead of interdepartmentally.

Some organizations are more effective if they do not overspecialize in functional departments but organize instead with departments that have a mix of tasks. A trade-off is usually most efficient—some functionally organized departments, some heterogeneous. It is important to recognize that conflicts always exist and adjustments are always necessary as organizations shift back and forth among different forms of organizational design.

Product Forms

Functional forms usually evolve into product forms as divisions grow large enough to need their own self-contained and self-controlled functional subdivisions. Imagine a purchasing department for a small college. Initially, the purchasing department can manage all of the buying for the whole institution. As the institution gets bigger, however, the various subunits develop their own buying needs, which require specialized knowledge by purchasing agents. These subunits in large organizations then form their own purchasing departments.

So, for example, a college of business may find itself with needs for different purchasing protocols from a school of continuing education. Or a new law school added to a university may find itself wishing to control its own purchases. At this point, the organization may believe that it is more efficient to decentralize the purchasing function to the local unit level. Hence, each unit (college or school) then has its own purchasing agent. And perhaps also its own accountant, its own marketing staff, and its own security personnel, among others.

This kind of organization is called a **product form** of organization and is sketched out in Figure 7.3. Note that each unit has its *own* functional form of organization. Product forms of organization have many advantages. They:

1. Foster an orientation toward overall outcomes and toward different and unique segments of the market.
2. Allow diversification and expansion of skills and training.
3. Permit design or redesign of products from end to end.
4. Ensure accountability by departmental managers, and promote delegation of authority and responsibility.

FIGURE 7.3
Product Form of Organization

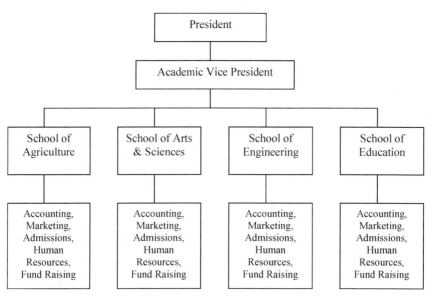

5. Heighten departmental cohesion and involvement in work.

But, there are disadvantages as well. Product forms of organization:

1. May use skills and resources inefficiently (e.g., duplication of specialists across multiple departments)
2. Make it difficult for specialists to seek career advancement placements out of their departments
3. Impede specialists' exposure to others within the same specialties
4. Put multiple role demands on people, which, in turn, creates stress
5. Sacrifice economies of scale (adapted from Duncan, 1979)

Client or Customer Forms

In addition to functional and product forms, there are several other possible modes of organization. Sometimes it is more effective to organize around types of clients served. For example, instead of a department of English, a department of biology, and a department of applied psychology in a function-based form of organization, imagine a department of developmental education, an honors college, or an accelerated baccalaureate program for working adults. Each of these units is aimed at a specific clientele and comprises many of the subdivisions identified earlier in both functional and product type organizations.

Client forms of organization have several advantages. By fostering cross-boundary sensitivity to changing market conditions, they allow and enhance a primary focus on specialized markets. In contrast to functional forms, which concentrate on process efficiency, and product types, which emphasize product quality, client forms of organization attempt to maximize client satisfaction.

Time or Place Forms

Another form is organization by place or time—for example, the "European division" or the "evening division." Again, each of these is broken down into functional and/or product divisions. Place- and time-based forms of organization have the advantages of providing opportunities for employees and clients to identify with the special characteristics of the work context. Faculty and students in an "evening division," for example, may identify strongly with the unique mission of that division to provide access for adults who work full time.

Matrix Forms

This design mode is used when conditions suggest that neither functional nor product forms serve the organization as well as required, and when there is a need for the organization to be rapidly and continually adaptive to short-run product design and production. Matrix designs originated in the needs of the aerospace field, where the armed forces demanded production of many different products by the same firm, with each new product requiring temporary inputs from many process specialists, especially in the design phase (Davis & Lawrence, 1977; Hanna, 1988). Today, matrix designs are fairly common (see, for example, Ruizendaal, 2006).

In a matrix design, specialized personnel are lent to a temporary unit created to procure a particular product or service (Byrne, 1993). The loaned personnel are therefore members of both a "project team" and the department from which they have been borrowed. Hence, each member owes allegiance to two distinct authorities—the temporary project manager and the specialized department manager. Each member's performance is evaluated by each manager.

An illustration of a matrix form for higher education appears in Figure 7.4. Faculty members in the academic departments can be lent out to different academic programs or special research projects.

FIGURE 7.4
Example of a Matrix Form of Organization*

		Programs and Projects				
		Nursing Program	Engineering Program	Nuclear Physics Program	Criminal Justice Program	Survey Research Center
Academic Departments	Sociology					
	Philosophy					
	Physics					
	English					
	Statistics					

*Based on Robbins, 1997b.

As might be imagined, problems of conflicting role demands and divided loyalties require considerable sensitivity and coordination (Kolodny, 1981). Matrix forms have other disadvantages as well. The multiple lines of authority require more upper-level administrative attention. Indeed, the power positioning between specialized loaning departments and borrowing projects makes for an uneasy organizational uncertainty, where political skills may be used. Organizational members also may experience more role ambiguity, stress, and anxiety, leading on occasion to lower effectiveness.

On the other hand, matrix forms have many advantages (Hellriegel, Slocum, & Woodman, 1995). They make specialized knowledge available for multiple projects or client-centered departments. Thus, a faculty member in a statistics department can be lent to any number of projects or other undergraduate departments or to a specialized research center. Further, because matrix organizations use human resources as needed, lending departments can "store" specialists to be available without cumbersome administrative reorganization or periodic, demoralizing layoffs.

Matrix organizations require communication among different departments and projects to improve the linkages across the system and to induce a more organization-wide orientation and focus. In addition, by maintaining the flexibility of staffing, matrix organizations can adapt more readily to changing conditions in the environment. An organization can respond to an announcement by the federal government of a request for proposals (RFP), for example, with fewer bureaucratic drawbacks if matrix forms and the possibilities of short-term assignments of personnel are already in place.

The development of a matrix structure requires a shift, however, from traditional academic structures, which are organized by function or product. To implement a matrix design, institutions would need to initiate more joint faculty appointments and design new ways to account for faculty activity across multiple departments and colleges. Michigan State University, for example, supports joint appointments between the colleges of agriculture and veterinary medicine, and basic science departments are linked to both the college of medicine and the colleges that had traditionally housed these departments. One result of this matrix design "is an enhanced ability to build a web of relationships for addressing unforeseen issues that arise" (Wegner, 2002, p. 8).

In fact, no organization is organized exclusively by function, product, or matrix; they are always hybrids or mixtures of all three. Organizational design is usually a decision that generally conforms not only to considerations of organizational efficiency but also to needs for power and control. Each kind of organizational design gives different persons or categories of persons more or less control over others (Ouchi & Maguire, 1975). For example, in a functional design, power accrues to the function most critical to total organizational output. In a product form of design, on the other hand, more power is found in the product division that is most successful in contributing to total organizational output.

Organizations continually make decisions about when and how to design by product versus function versus matrix or by client or time or place. They must weigh the advantages and disadvantages at each particular time.

Social Construction of Organizational Structure

Enacting Structure

The previous discussion of bureaucratic organizational design makes the epistemological assumption that structural arrangements in organizations are orderly, relatively permanent arrangements of roles, responsibilities, and authority relationships that are real and can be known and understood by organizational members. In contrast, the social constructionist paradigm offers a more fluid conceptualization where structures are created and recreated continually through daily interactions in the organization.

Karl Weick (1969) was among the first to argue that structures are "enacted" through the actions of organizational members. **Enactment** refers to the idea that "when people act, they bring events and structures into existence and set them into motion. People who act in organizations often produce structures, constraints, and opportunities that were not there before they took action" (Weick, 1988, p. 306). Thus, whereas positivists view structure as something tangible that an organization *possesses* (signified by boxes in an organizational chart), enactment theory claims that structure is something that an organization *does* (Orton & Weick, 1990) as it continually evolves.

Consistent with the principles of social construction, enacted structures are both cognitive and social. Structure exists in the minds of organizational members; it is a cognitive map that preserves a record of previous actions, sorts and arranges perceptions of current experience, and produces expectations for the future (Weick, 1988). In an organizational context, these cognitive maps do not remain isolated within the individual mind. Instead, cognitive structures (mental maps) become social structures through communication.

More specifically, people talk with other organizational members (and sometimes with external clients) about actions they have observed or in which they have taken part. They begin to develop an interpretive framework that assigns meaning, significance, and consequences to those actions

(Weick, 1988). These interpretive frameworks, when shared by multiple organization members, begin to structure their subsequent actions and interactions. The shared frameworks set the parameters for organizational behavior. How often people work together, how much effort they put forth on such projects, how much priority they assign to tasks—all of these structural considerations are shaped by the shared mental models prevalent in the organization. Human interpretations, rather than objective structural arrangements, reveal how organizations operate. The amount of differentiation in an organization, for example, may have less to do with the departmental structure displayed on the organizational chart, and more to do with the unique relationships that organizational members establish with their colleagues within and outside their work units.

The following sections examine two theories that provide additional insights into the social construction of organizational structure: loose coupling (one type of enacted structure) and structuration theory.

Loose Coupling Theory

Loose coupling refers to a system in which the components have weak or indirect linkages, but the components remain responsive to each other (Weick, 1976). The "couplings" or connections between the different parts of the system are not well specified, but instead of drifting toward suboptimization, the subunits seek to interact and work collaboratively.

As we noted regarding enactment, loose coupling also has both cognitive and social dimensions. Loose coupling emerges, in part, due to cognitive limitations such as information processing constraints, faulty memories, and short attention spans. Because of cognitive limitations, people "notice different parts of their surroundings, will tune out different parts at different times, and will process different parts at different speeds. As a result of the idiosyncratic worlds formed under these conditions, people will find it difficult to coordinate their actions and will share few variables or weak variables, all of which leads to loose coupling" (Orton & Weick, 1990, p. 206).

In previous sections on bureaucratic structure, coordination difficulties were viewed as problems to be fixed. In loose coupling theory, however, coordination gaps enable people and units to be responsive to each other without relying on formal authority or prescribed role behaviors. A loosely coupled organization does not specify all of the connections among people and departments. Instead, it leaves room for people to figure out for themselves how to fill the interstices in the organizational chart. Organizational members are given the latitude to enact structure, rather than having it imposed on them.

In the absence of prescribed coordination mechanisms, loosely coupled units are relatively autonomous of each other, but they are not completely separate. The units are still bound together as part of the same system. What binds them together, however, is *not* the formal organizational structure. As Spender and Grinyer (1995) noted, loose coupling "implies some source of organizational cohesion other than administrative structure, since it is the structure itself that is loosened" (p. 910). Instead, the source of cohesion and connectedness in a loosely coupled system is **collective action**. This is the social dimension of loose coupling.

Collective action shapes collective cognition. Loosely coupled structures are created when the cognitive worlds of multiple individuals begin to overlap (Bormann, 1996). Mental images begin to overlap when people communicate extensively and share common experiences. Consider the potential effects of an all-day staff retreat. Brainstorming, visioning, and planning activities create shared experiences and form patterns of continuing mutual influence and interaction.

When people in different units begin to share common frames of reference, there is no need for extensive oversight or formal coordination. Instead, organizational members act on their own volition in ways that are consistent with their shared cognitive frameworks (Staw, 1980). Faculty members in different departments, for example, may teach in similar ways even though they may never coordinate their syllabi. Instead, a common frame of reference and set of shared commitments guides their behaviors. There is no need to impose uniform procedures on these faculty; they are already operating in a coordinated fashion (Dee, 2004).

Loosely coupled systems are held together not through managerial control, but through the interactions and sentiments that organizational members construct together. The role of formal leaders in a loosely coupled system is to serve "not as the source of innovation, but as the creator of an energizing context" (Spender & Grinyer, 1995, p. 921). Leaders can encourage collaboration, build a trusting workplace climate, and address the inevitable conflicts that emerge when units and people—formerly divided by *different* cognitive maps—begin to work together. As a practical example, college leaders cannot expect that formal structures and reward incentives will guarantee successful collaboration between academic affairs and student affairs units. Members of these units have very different professional backgrounds and orientations toward work. They will need time to build trust and opportunities to engage in pilot projects or other limited-scale actions where the consequences of failure are not so high as to deter participation. Then, if successful, these "small wins" (Weick & Westley, 1996) can generate ongoing motivation and desire to maintain connections across distinct units.

Loosely coupled units are responsive to each other, but each unit retains its distinctive identity and autonomy. As Orton and Weick (1990) note, however, there are other forms of coupling. When autonomous units are not responsive to each other, then the system is **decoupled**. Consider, for example, student affairs and academic affairs units that never engage in any joint programming or planning. In effect, they are operating as separate systems; their efforts are decoupled from each other. In contrast, **tightly coupled** structures enforce responsiveness, but constrain the autonomy of the sub-units. If the student affairs unit were merged with the academic affairs unit, it is likely that academic affairs administrators would have more power in determining the future strategy of the merged unit; here, the student affairs unit loses its autonomy and becomes tightly coupled to academic affairs' directives. These forms of coupling are displayed in Table 7.2.

Some have criticized higher education organizations for being too loosely coupled and have advocated tighter coupling. Balderston (1995), for example, argued that loose coupling can lead to overexpansion and mission drift. But these conditions are actually associated more closely with decoupling, where units are not responsive to each other and suboptimization prevails. Similarly, Lutz (1982) criticized loose coupling as contributing to slow decision making and lack of responsiveness to change in the external environment. But again, these conditions are associated more closely with tightly coupled systems. Tight coupling may cause an institution to "freeze" in uncertain times (Birnbaum, 1988; Pfeffer & Salancik, 1978), as organizational members wait for formal leaders to sort out the uncertainty and tell them what to do.

It is important to keep in mind, however, that loose coupling is not a universal good. Units may be responsive to each other, but their collective actions may actually be harmful to the organization and perhaps to constituents in the external environment (Shrivastava, 1995). Loose coupling can explain both productive collaboration as well as the collective exploitation of

TABLE 7.2
Forms of Coupling*

Type of Coupling	Degree of Autonomy	Extent of Responsiveness
Loose coupling	Autonomous units	Responsiveness across units
Decoupling	Autonomous units	Lack of responsiveness
Tight coupling	Lack of autonomy	Responsiveness enforced, controlled

*Based on Orton and Weick, 1990.

others. Ethical considerations, therefore, play a large role in determining the appropriate outcomes of organizational structures.

In addition, organizations contain many forms of coupling (tight, loose, and decoupled) simultaneously. Recall that the social construction paradigm suggests that multiple realities will be constructed within any organization. These multiple realities cannot be controlled by organizational leaders, but as Spender and Kessler (1995) noted, leaders can create venues for communication and encourage experimentation across subunits. These actions provide opportunities for organizational members to construct the couplings that they deem appropriate given the specific local conditions in which they are working. Leaders can also provide opportunities for professional development and skill enhancement so that these interactions are informed by strong collective expertise.

Structuration Theory

Structuration theory provides yet another way of thinking about organizational design. Like loose coupling theory, it suggests that individuals and groups are active agents who create the structures with which they work (Giddens, 1984). Organizational behaviors, in this case, determine structure; however, behaviors are constrained by structures created previously. This phenomenon is known as the **duality of structure**—that is, people are active agents who create structure, but they are also constrained by the structures that have been enacted previously.

Organizational members enact structures through their daily interactions, but these interactions occur within a structural context that people have created over time. Thus, structural change is possible, since structures are created anew in each interaction, but existing structures as mental maps represent constraints on thinking and acting differently (Hatch, 1997). For example, if previous patterns of interaction have enacted a mechanistic, hierarchical structure, then current and future patterns of interaction are mediated through that existing structure. Therefore, if organizational leaders want to change the structure to become more organic and nonhierarchical, they must change the behavioral patterns that created and maintained the existing structure in the first place.

Interaction patterns within organizations, therefore, are central to structuration theory. The theory suggests that a social system (e.g., an administrative team, an academic department) is defined by the relational and communication patterns that emerge within the group and between the group and other social systems. **Structures**, in this theory, are the rules and resources that group members use to sustain the social system. **Rules** are the decision modalities adopted by the group (e.g., consensus decision making, collaborative problem analysis). **Resources** are the knowledge frameworks and legitimization modalities (e.g., status, ethics, and power) used in group interaction. **Structuration** is the process by which social systems are produced and continually redefined through members' use of structures (i.e., rules and resources).

Each social system creates and continually enacts its own structural mix of rules and resources. Although structures appear to be created anew by each group, Poole, Seibold, and McPhee (1996) assert that groups often appropriate structures from other social systems or from society at large. **Appropriation** involves adopting structural features from the environment and "developing a situated version of them" (p. 122). Higher education governance systems, for example, have appropriated norms (rules) of participatory democracy from the U.S. political system (which, in turn, were drawn in part from earlier democratic systems, such as ancient Greece). Similarly, quality assurance through regional accreditation associations, rather than through a national ministry of education, reflects appropriation of federalized power relations (resources), which favor decentralization of authority and minimal oversight.

Structuration theory suggests that organizational structures can be quite stable, when interaction patterns become routine or a matter of habit. Structures can also be dynamic, because they depend on the daily reproduction of interaction patterns. If interaction patterns are disrupted, then the structure becomes open to change. Therefore, if administrators want to restructure a college, their success will depend not only on selecting an appropriate organizational design, but also on the extent to which people change their daily patterns of interaction.

Thus, structuration theory explains both structural stability and the ways in which structures change over time. When organizational members appropriate rules and resources consistently, structural reproduction is similar over time, and the social system appears stable. The deliberative, consensus-based system of shared governance, for example, has remained fairly consistent since the 1966 Statement on Government of the American Association of University Professors. On the other hand, "reproduction does not necessarily imply replication" (Poole, Seibold, & McPhee, 1996, p. 123). As certain features of the social system's context are modified, structures may change gradually or be eliminated. Recent pressures for accountability, for example, may be changing the mix of rules and resources appropriated for institutional governance.

Structuration is not always, nor even often, a conscious activity. It is unlikely, for example, that faculty and administrators creating a new governance structure decide to appropriate certain features from the broader political system in the United States as a whole. Groups and individuals tend to appropriate that which is familiar to them as well as structures with which they have experience. Consider, for example, the tendency for administrators who are new to a campus to appropriate rules and resources similar to those they used in their previous places of employment.

Unreflective appropriation of rules and resources, however, can lead to stagnant groups and organizations. A "we've always done it this way, so why change" mentality may set in. Alternatively, higher education leaders can be mindful of how departments, units, and groups appropriate rules and resources. When existing rules and resources are identified, they can be used as levers for change. Ortiz and Gonzales (2000), for example, described how a high school principal and a college president constructed a new dialogue around Latino student eligibility for university admissions. They created venues for interaction among students, parents, teachers, counselors, and college admissions staff, and these interactions generated new rules and resources for guiding change.

Viewing organizations from a structuration perspective offers organizational analysts a way of conceiving of structure that is distinctively different from the positivist perspective. Structuration theory highlights the agency of organizational members and provides more opportunities for imaginative and unique approaches to each organization's problems. On the other hand, the structuration perspective is limited in that it does not provide a framework for predicting organizational outcomes. In other words, structuration theory may help us understand the creative processes associated with building structures to carry out work, but it does not provide independent variables that can help us predict or control the outcomes (dependent variables).

Postmodern Views on Organizational Design

Contemporary realities of global markets, international competition, rapid development and obsolescence of technologies, and political demands for institutional responsiveness and accountability suggest a need to re-examine traditional organizational designs. As Bolman and Deal (2003) note, "Dramatic changes in technology and the business environment have rendered old structures obsolete at an unprecedented rate, spawning a new interest in organizational design. Pressures of globalization, competition, technology, customer expectations, and workforce dynamics have prompted organizations worldwide to rethink and redesign structural patterns" (p. 47). Thus, many theorists and practitioners are searching for alternative forms of organizational design.

Postmodern theorists have figured prominently in critiques of traditional organizational designs (Bergquist, 1993; Brown, 1995; Dickens & Fontana, 1994; Reed & Hughes, 1992). These critiques are often leveled at bureaucratic and mechanistic designs, which have been characterized as rigid and inflexible. These designs tend to centralize power and resources and provide little autonomy for organizational members. As a result, innovative activity may decline, and organizational members may begin to feel psychologically distant from their work. Other postmodern critics cite problems with **goal displacement**. Recall that the *methods* organizational members use to achieve a goal (e.g., adherence to well-specified rules and work roles) may become more important than the goal itself. In this case, both organizational members and customers/clients are challenged to cut through "red tape" to get things done.

An alternative to bureaucratic designs is the **network organization**, which reflects the fragmentation that postmodern theorists claim characterizes organizational life. In a network organization, departments and units within a single organization are replaced with partnerships among several organizations. Instead of a single organization producing products or services, several network partners collaborate, with each network partner assuming responsibility for one part of the production process. Community colleges and four-year institutions, for example, may develop network structures for developmental education. Community college faculty may provide remedial instruction, and the four-year college may provide residential housing and academic advising. In this way, different institutions provide pieces of the overall program or service.

Taken to an extreme, the network outsources all major functions—that is, it becomes what some have called a **virtual organization** in which the network becomes nothing more than a loose confederation of organizations.

In network organizations (compared to bureaucracies), "controls are typically not imposed on the network by a central authority but are negotiated by the network partners" (Kartseva, Gordijn, & Tan, 2006, p. 57). Network organizations are also more likely to be responsive to rapid technological changes or environmental turbulence, but they do have their downsides. Network partners may exploit each other, some partners may monopolize information or resources, and weaker members of the network may be forced into concessions on key issues. Thus, it is important for network organizations to be built on more than economic efficiency; a set of values and beliefs should unite the network partners as well.

The postmodern paradigm also provides a different way of thinking about integration and differentiation. Due to high levels of specialization and departmentalization, complex organizations such as colleges and universities are highly differentiated. This creates a need for integration. Organizations need to connect disparate strands of activity to achieve their overall missions. Long-standing traditions of top-down leadership suggest that it is the job of top management to develop organizational designs that link people together (e.g., through functional, product, or matrix designs). According to the postmodernists, however, this presents a problem. Integration is achieved through hierarchical relationships, which reinforce the dominance of existing power structures and the interests of top management.

In contrast, some postmodernists have suggested that organizations can reverse the conditions that created the need for integration in the first place. They can engage in **de-differentiation** (Clegg, 1990; Mercier & McGowan, 1996). Rather than achieving integration structurally through organizational design, integration becomes the job of each person and each group in the organization. Self-managed teams are an example of a de-differentiated structure. In these teams, there are no formal mechanisms for integration and no vertical lines of authority. Integration is achieved through aggregating individual talents. It is interesting to consider the possible applications of de-differentiation to colleges and universities. Think of a learning community where a small group of faculty takes collective responsibility for providing education to a particular cohort of students. Consider a self-managed enrollment management team, rather than bureaucratic linkages among admissions, financial aid, and institutional research.

Feminist theorists have also critiqued bureaucratic organizational designs—specifically, in their analyses, through the lens of gender. They argue that an emphasis on authority, rules, and regulations reinforces patriarchal domination. These theorists envision an alternative organizational design where power is dispersed, face-to-face relationships are used instead of impersonal rules, and skills and information are shared instead of parceled out by top management on a "need to know" basis.

Helgesen (1995) proposed an alternative to hierarchical, bureaucratic designs: a **web of inclusion**, which builds from the center out rather than from the top down. The image is an organically connected web, rather than the traditional pyramid of organizational charts. The spindles of the web represent a multifaceted communication network that links everyone (regardless of job title) to the center. If we think of an organizational leader as the center of a web, then we can begin to envision leadership that is accessible and includes all levels of personnel in decision making. Here, organizational power is deconstructed and replaced by a network of personal authority.

When leaders seek to shift from hierarchical authority to personal authority, they must consider several issues. First, it is important to recognize that this is a difficult shift for many leaders to make. As Hoy and Miskel (2001, p. 93) noted, "The temptation of most leaders is to retreat behind a shield of authority in an attempt to depersonalize relationships." Relying on personal authority means that leaders must learn to challenge their own assumptions and relax their rigid notions about rules and roles.

Some may argue that self-definition of roles and self-determination of organizational design is a recipe for chaos. Who would make sure that the works gets done? What if people performing similar jobs refused to work together? What if people just went off and did their own thing without checking in with anyone (Cutright, 2001; Eve, Horsfall, & Lee, 1997)? Indeed, the transition to a postmodern organization may be difficult, inefficient, and potentially disastrous, but if certain organizational conditions are present, the postmodern organizational form can be innovative and liberating for those who work in it.

Postmodern organizational designs require a high degree of trust among organizational members. People must trust each other's competence, rather than rely on direct supervision to ensure that the work gets done. The postmodern organization also depends on authentic communication; organizational members must do the hard work necessary to understand the viewpoints of others and to question their own beliefs and values. People must be psychologically engaged to be open with each other, confront differences honestly, and construct roles that empower people to express their talents in innovative ways.

Summary

In this chapter, we discussed the elements of bureaucratic structure, paying particular attention to division of labor, procedural specification, interpersonal interactions, selection and promotion of personnel, and hierarchy. Bureaucratic structures are ubiquitous because they are efficient when well designed and led (especially humanistically). Their utility, however, is also contingent on the need for bureaucracy itself. If other forms of organizational design are needed, then the imposition of bureaucracy can be both inefficient and personally dissatisfying to organizational members. In this chapter, we noted that bureaucracies can be organized in several different ways—for example, by function performed, by product or service, or through a matrix design, among others.

Whereas the positivist, bureaucratic approach focuses on coordination and relatively fixed arrangements of roles and responsibilities, the social constructionist paradigm offers a more fluid conceptualization where structures are enacted through interactions among organizational members. We then examined two theories of enacted structure: loose coupling and structuration. Finally, we offered network organizations and de-differentiation as postmodern perspectives on organizational structure. In the next chapter, we focus on the roles of individuals working within the structures of organizations.

Review Questions

1. Which of the following is *not* a characteristic of the Weberian conception of bureaucracy?
   a. Division of labor into specialized tasks
   b. Job rotation
   c. Hierarchy of authority
   d. Well-known career route

2. Bureaucratic rules governing the number of credits students are required to take in their major can be functional because:
   a. Faculty advisors are not required to make independent judgments
   b. The power that faculty have over students is displaced to the rules themselves rather then manifested personally
   c. Less time and effort needs to be devoted to monitoring actual credits taken by students
   d. All of the above
   e. None of the above

3. College and university bureaucracies try to adhere to the concept of "unity of command" so that:
   a. Organizational members become used to the military connotations of "command"
   b. Supervisors learn how to give orders
   c. Organizational members are not given conflicting instructions from more than one supervisor
   d. Faculty are not permitted excessive autonomy in their work

4. Organizing academic departments by discipline is an example of which of the following bureaucratic forms?
   a. Function
   b. Product
   c. Client/Customer

    d. Time/Place

    e. Matrix

5. A community college that offers daytime and evening classes can be said to have a bureaucratic organization structured by which of the following principles?

    a. Function

    b. Product

    c. Client/Customer

    d. Time/Place

    e. Matrix

6. A large university that receives a three-year grant to conduct research on a biological innovation will need to staff the grant. It will probably use a matrix form of organization so that:

    a. Many supervisors will have input into the faculty working on the grant

    b. More stability in the research unit can be established

    c. Faculty loyalty to the project will be enhanced

    d. Specialized regular university faculty can be brought together for a limited time

    e. More than one of the above

7. Which of the following statements describes a loosely coupled college structure?

    a. The law school is not responsive to the president's call to increase faculty diversity.

    b. The chemistry department responds to the college's general education initiative by developing new field-based courses that are related to faculty members' research interests.

    c. The school of education is compelled by order of the president to undergo an accreditation review.

    d. The psychology department seeks a large number of grants without the approval or knowledge of university administrators.

8. The dean of a law school reorganized her office to improve services to students and faculty. However, the resulting matrix structure continued to perform poorly. How would structuration theory account for this ineffective reorganization?

    a. The dean did not select an appropriate bureaucratic design; the design was a poor fit for the organizational conditions.

    b. The dean incorrectly determined that the school needed a dynamic structure, when a stable one would have been more effective.

    c. Staff members continued to reconstruct the same patterns of behavior, and the social organization of the work groups did not change, even though the structural design was altered.

    d. Structure is irrelevant to organizational performance.

9. A social constructionist would likely claim that organizational design is:
    a. Constructed entirely within the cognition of managers
    b. A mechanism to regulate work flow and assess performance against standardized benchmarks
    c. An organizational response to external control
    d. Produced and reproduced through communications and interactions that are shaped by the organization's history, mission, and culture

10. Postmodern perspectives on organizational design:
    a. Criticize control-centered structures that reinforce the interests of top managers
    b. Emphasize structures that promote open communication and trust
    c. Favor structures that encourage the development of personal relationships, rather than relying on impersonal authority
    d. All of the above

Case Discussion Questions

Consider again the High Plains University case presented at the beginning of this chapter.

1. Vice President Strong reorganized all administrative areas by function, and then changed course to implement cross-functional teams, before returning to organization by functional specialization. Why did these reorganizations fail to achieve the intended result? What problems are likely to present themselves when an organization overspecializes in functional departments? What problems are likely to emerge when an organization makes a rapid shift to team structures (consider structuration theory and postmodern perspectives on structure and authority)?

2. The social construction perspective suggests that successful organizational restructuring depends not only on selecting an appropriate organizational design, but also on the extent to which people change their daily patterns of interaction. How might Vice President Strong

attempt to change the daily interaction patterns of administrative staff? Through what communication venues can such changes be effected?

3. Consider how loose coupling could be applied at High Plains University to attain the benefits of coordination among functions *and* specialization within functions. How could loose coupling, for example, enable the registrar's office to be responsive to the admissions office without making one office subordinate to the other? What steps are necessary to encourage loose coupling among administrative units?

4. Consider the defeatism and low level of commitment among administrative staff at High Plains University. Can a postmodern organizational design (e.g., web of inclusion, de-differentiation) address some of these concerns? If so, what steps are necessary to implement this type of structure?

References

Adler, P. S., & Borys, B. (1996). Two types of bureaucracy: Enabling and coercive. *Administrative Science Quarterly*, 41(1), 61–69.

Balderston, F. (1995). *Managing today's university: Strategies for viability, change, and excellence* (2nd ed.). San Francisco: Jossey-Bass.

Bergquist, W. (1993). *The postmodern organization: Mastering the art of irreversible change.* San Francisco: Jossey-Bass.

Bess, J. L. (1982). *University organization: A matrix analysis of the academic professions.* New York: Human Sciences Press.

Bess, J. L. (1988). *Collegiality and bureaucracy in the modern university.* New York: Teachers College Press.

Birnbaum, R. (1988). *How colleges work: The cybernetics of academic organization and leadership.* San Francisco: Jossey-Bass.

Blau, P. M., & Meyer, M. W. (1971). *Bureaucracy in modern society* (2nd ed.). New York: Random House.

Blau, P. M., & Meyer, M. W. (1987). *Bureaucracy in modern society* (3rd ed.). New York: Random House.

Bolman, L., & Deal, T. (2003). *Reframing organizations: Artistry, choice, and leadership* (3rd ed.). San Francisco: Jossey-Bass.

Bormann, E. (1996). Symbolic convergence theory and communication in group decision making. In R. Hirokawa & M. Poole (Eds.), *Communication and group decision making* (2nd ed., pp. 81–113). Thousand Oaks, CA: Sage.

Brown, R. H. (Ed.). (1995). *Postmodern representations: Truth, power, and mimesis in the human sciences and public culture.* Urbana: University of Illinois Press.

Byrne, J. A. (1993). The horizontal corporation. *Business Week*, December 20, 76–81.

Clegg, S. (1990). *Modern organizations: Organization studies in the postmodern world.* London: Sage.

Cutright, M. (Ed.). (2001). *Chaos theory and higher education: Leadership, planning, and policy.* New York: Peter Lang.

Daft, R. L. (1989). *Organization theory and design* (3rd ed.). Minneapolis: West Publishing.

Davis, S. M., & Lawrence, P. R. (1977). *Matrix.* Reading, MA: Addison-Wesley.

Dee, J. (2004). Turnover intent in an urban community college: Strategies for faculty retention. *Community College Journal of Research and Practice, 28*(7), 593–607.

Dickens, D. R., & Fontana, A. (Eds.) (1994). *Postmodernism and social inquiry.* New York: Guilford Press.

Duncan, R. (1979). What is the right organization structure? Decision tree analysis provides the answer. *Organizational Dynamics, 7*(3), 59–80.

Eve, R. A., Horsfall, S., & Lee, M. E. (Eds.). (1997). *Chaos, complexity, and sociology: Myths, models, and theories.* Thousand Oaks, CA: Sage.

Galbraith, J. R. (1977). *Organization design.* Reading, MA: Addison-Wesley.

Galbraith, J. R., Downey, D., & Kates, A. (2002). *Designing dynamic organizations: A hands-on guide for leaders at all levels.* New York: AMACOM.

Giddens, A. (1984). *The constitution of society.* Berkeley, CA: University of California Press.

Gouldner, A. (1954). *Patterns of industrial bureaucracy.* New York: The Free Press.

Hackman, J. R. (Ed.). (1990). *Groups that work (and those that don't): Creating conditions for effective teamwork.* San Francisco: Jossey-Bass.

Hanna, D. P. (1988). *Designing organizations for high performance.* Reading, MA: Addison-Wesley.

Hatch, M. (1997). *Organization theory: Modern, symbolic, and postmodern perspectives.* New York: Oxford University Press.

Helgesen, S. (1995). *The web of inclusion: A new architecture for building great organizations.* New York: Currency/Doubleday.

Hellriegel, D., Slocum, J. W., Jr., & Woodman, R. W. (1995). *Organizational behavior* (7th ed.). Minneapolis, MN: West Publishing.

Helsabeck, R. E. (1973). *The compound system: A conceptual framework for effective decision-making in colleges.* Berkeley, CA: Center for Research and Development in Higher Education.

Hoy, W., & Miskel, C. (2001). *Educational administration: Theory, research, and practice* (6th ed.). New York: McGraw-Hill.

Hoy, W., & Miskel, C. (2005). *Educational administration: Theory, research, and practice* (7th ed.). New York: McGraw-Hill.

Kartseva, V., Gordijn, J., & Tan, Y-H. (2006). Toward a modeling tool for designing control mechanisms for network organizations. *International Journal of Electronic Commerce, 10*(2), 57–84.

Kolodny, H. F. (1981, March/April). Managing in a matrix. *Business Horizons,* 17–35.

Lutz, F. (1982). Tightening up loose coupling in organizations of higher education. *Administrative Science Quarterly, 27,* 653–669.

March, J. G., & Olsen, J. P. (1989). *Rediscovering institutions: The organizational basis of politics*. New York: The Free Press.

March, J. G., & Simon, H. A. (1959). *Organizations*. New York: John Wiley & Sons.

Mercier, J., & McGowan, R. (1996). The greening of organizations. *Administration and Society, 27*(4), 459–482.

Ortiz, F., & Gonzales, R. (2000). Latino high school students' pursuit of higher education. *Aztlan, 25*(1), 67–107.

Orton, J. D., & Weick, K. (1990). Loosely coupled systems: A reconceptualization. *Academy of Management Review, 15*, 203–223.

Ouchi, W. G., & Maguire, M. A. (1975). Organizational control: Two functions. *Administrative Science Quarterly, 20*(4), 559–569.

Pfeffer, J., & Salancik, G. (1978). *The external control of organizations: A resource dependence perspective*. New York: Harper & Row.

Poole, M. S., Seibold, D., & McPhee, R. (1996). The structuration of group decisions. In R. Hirokawa & M. S. Poole (Eds.), *Communication and group decision making* (2nd ed., pp. 114–146). Thousand Oaks, CA: Sage.

Price, J. L. (1997). Handbook of organizational measurement. *International Journal of Manpower, 18*(4/5/6), 305–558.

Pugh, D. S., & Hickson, D. J. (1976). *Organizational structure in its context: The Aston program*. Lexington, MA: D. C. Heath.

Reed, M., & Hughes, M. (Eds.). (1992). *Rethinking organization: New directions in organization theory and analysis*. London: Sage.

Robbins, S. P. (1997a). *Essentials of organizational behavior* (5th ed.). Upper Saddle River, NJ: Prentice Hall.

Robbins, S. P. (1997b). *Managing today*. Upper Saddle River, NJ: Prentice Hall.

Ruizendaal, G. (2006, January 21). The matrix master, *Economist, 378*(8461), 1–3.

Shrivastava, P. (1995). Ecocentric management for a risk society. *Academy of Management Review, 20*, 118–137.

Spender, J.-C., & Grinyer, P. (1995). Organizational renewal: Top management's role in a loosely coupled system. *Human Relations, 48*(8), 909–926.

Spender, J.-C., & Kessler, E. (1995). Managing the uncertainties of innovation: Extending Thompson (1967). *Human Relations, 48*(1), 35–56.

Staw, B. (1980). Rationality and justification in organizational life. In L. Cummings & B. Staw (Eds.), *Research in organizational behavior* (vol. 2, pp. 45–80). Greenwich, CT: JAI Press.

Thompson, V. A. (1965). *Modern organization: A general theory*. New York: Alfred A. Knopf.

Weber, M. (1924). *The theory of social and economic organizations* (A. M. Henderson & T. Parsons, Trans. and Ed., 1947). New York: Free Press.

Weber, M. (1946). *From Max Weber: Essays in sociology* (H. H. Gerth & C. W. Mills, Trans. and Ed.). New York: Oxford University Press.

Wegner, G. (2002). *Michigan State University. Strategy without deep pockets: Enhancing institutional capacity from within*. Philadelphia: University of Pennsylvania, Knight Higher Education Collaborative.

Weick, K. (1969). *The social psychology of organizing* (1st ed.). Reading, MA: Addison-Wesley.

Weick, K. (1976). Educational organizations as loosely coupled systems. *Administrative Science Quarterly, 21*, 1–19.

Weick, K. (1988). Enacted sensemaking in crisis situations. *Journal of Management Studies, 25*(4), 305–317.

Weick, K., & Westley, F. (1996). Organizational learning: Affirming an oxymoron. In S. Clegg, C. Hardy, & W. Nord (Eds.), *Handbook of organization studies* (pp. 440–458). Thousand Oaks, CA: Sage.

8

ORGANIZATIONAL ROLES

CONTENTS

The authors are most grateful for the critical comments on an early draft of this chapter by Ronald Heck, University of Hawaii. The final version, of course, is our own and may or may not reflect the perspective of the reviewer.

Preview

- Ambiguity and misinterpretation of roles are prime sources of problems in the internal organization of colleges and universities.
- Roles in formal organizations have a variety of positive functions. First, they set limits on employee behavior by prescribing and proscribing what is legitimate. Second, roles standardize individual behavior of workers performing similar jobs, thus assuring predictability of uniform outcomes across different workers. Third, roles stabilize expectations of performance so that output is uniform over time. Fourth, roles circumscribe responsibilities. Last, roles establish contractual relationships, which carry positive and negative sanctions.
- Roles are organizationally defined positions that are connected with one another in some presumably systematic and rational way, particularly in larger organizations that have become bureaucratic.
- Roles derive their meaning from other roles in the system, and in this sense they are complementary.
- A role episode is a sequence of activities in an organization by which roles are made manifest. It is the way members of organizations find out what their jobs are.
- A number of key interacting and contributing parts explain how roles are developed, transmitted, received, and responded to. These include:
  1. organizational factors and the corresponding formal job descriptions;
  2. role senders, who interpret the organizational jobs and transmit them—with varying degrees of accuracy and clarity;
  3. the focal persons or role incumbents, who receive the transmissions—again, with varying degrees of accuracy; and
  4. the response of the focal person, considered both psychologically and behaviorally.
- A number of intervening variables also affect both how the role is sent and how it is received. Among these are personal attributes of the role sender and of the role receiver and interpersonal relations that develop between sender and receiver.
- Role socialization refers to the process by which a new member of an organization learns about the formal goals and the procedures for attaining them that are associated with the job as well as the values, norms, and expected informal interaction patterns.
- A latent role is a role that emerges as a result of functions performed by either the individual or the organization that are not specified in the job description.
- Role conflict is a state of cognition or affect of a role incumbent characterized by incongruity or incompatibility of expected behaviors communicated by the incumbent's role senders.
- Role conflict has a number of effects. The greater the role conflict, the

greater the job-related anxiety and the greater the dissatisfaction with relations with fellow workers
- Role ambiguity refers to uncertainty concerning expected role performance. There are two kinds of role ambiguity: perceptual and objective. The
first suggests that ambiguity lies in the mind of the individual—in the perception and conception of the received role; the second points to the quality of the communication sent.
- Role ambiguity has been found through research to be related to personal
tension, anxiety, depression, and resentment. Further, the greater the role
ambiguity, the lower the productivity of the group, the perceived productivity of the group, involvement in the group, and job satisfaction.

————————————— CASE CONTEXT —————————————

Service Learning at Superior College

Superior College, a private liberal arts institution, is located in a major metropolitan area. The green lawns and manicured landscaping of the campus are in sharp contrast to the asphalt and concrete of the city center.
But rather than seclude itself from the surrounding neighborhood, Superior
College is an active partner with the community. It is no surprise, then, that
service learning is viewed as an important component of student life at
Superior.

Service learning is an experiential form of education in which students
are active participants in organized activities that meet the needs of a
community, and where faculty members typically provide structured time
for students to reflect on their service experiences. For many years, service learning at Superior College was viewed as an extracurricular activity.
The director of service learning reported to the vice president for student
affairs. When a new president was appointed, however, he articulated a
vision of service learning as an important pedagogical tool for faculty and
encouraged its formal incorporation into the curriculum.

The new president reorganized the administrative structure so that Di-
neka Butler, the director of service learning, reports to both the vice president for student affairs and the vice president for academic affairs. (See
abbreviated organization chart in Figure 8.1.) The president hoped that the
new arrangement would foster greater collaboration and would increase
the likelihood that faculty would implement service-learning components
in their courses.

The new organizational structure, however, brought about a number of obstacles and challenges, especially for the director of service learning. For one thing, the vice president for student affairs continued to hold an extracurricular view of service learning. He had solidified a range of connections with the community organizations that hosted students in their service-learning activities. These included homeless shelters, environmental agencies, and after-school reading programs in elementary schools. He was rightfully proud of these connections and continued to urge Director Butler to spend more time out in the community.

The vice president for academic affairs, on the other hand, strongly endorsed and promulgated the view that faculty should adopt service learning as a pedagogical practice. She argued that service is an important learning mechanism for students and, therefore, an appropriate pedagogical tool for faculty. She urged Director Butler to spend more time in the academic departments, talking with faculty about the benefits and best practices of service learning. The vice president for academic affairs wanted stronger connections with faculty, but provided no advice or guidelines on how to build those connections. The college president reiterated both of these institutional objectives in public speeches where he praised the college's connections to the community and identified faculty adoption of service learning as a key initiative in the college's new strategic plan.

Director Butler finds that she is now asked both to spend more time

FIGURE 8.1
Abbreviated Organization Chart

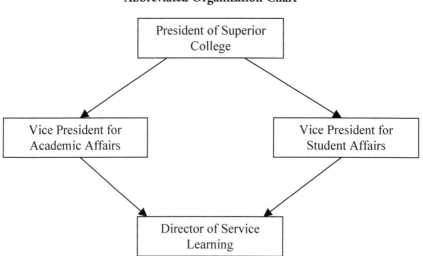

out in the community *and* attend a large number of academic department meetings. But she has a small staff (in fact, just one part-time secretary and a work-study student) and a limited budget.

As a former community organizer with a master's degree in social work, Director Butler is quite skillful in working with nonprofit agencies and in advising students regarding their placements in service organizations. She has also participated in a range of professional development activities to enhance her knowledge of student development theories. Her experience in working with faculty, however, is limited, and her previous efforts to reach out to faculty seemed to fall on deaf ears. Faculty members appeared distant and disengaged from her service-learning work. She wondered how she could possibly make connections with this group of faculty who are so very different in their professional backgrounds.

Director Butler began to lose confidence in her ability to accomplish the tasks assigned to her. Indeed, her performance deteriorated. Her relationship with the vice president for student affairs, previously very collegial, had become strained, because she no longer could attend to all of the external connections that the vice president had established.

She now hesitates to make decisions on her own, because she feels that she has to check with the academic vice president on all issues related to faculty. The academic vice president typically has very little time to meet with her, so projects continue to get delayed. A competent, skillful employee now feels adrift. For the first time, she contemplates leaving the college for another job.

Introduction

Most organizational members in colleges and universities occupy positions of responsibility in which they are expected to play a variety of roles. While we have a general sense of the daily activities of a faculty member, a dean of students, a financial aid officer, or a trustee, these roles are often defined differently in different types of institutions (e.g., community colleges and research universities) as well as in specific settings (e.g., University of California at Berkeley and New York University). Outside observers and those in positions of authority are often left with only vague notions of what behaviors can be expected by a role incumbent. Indeed, the role incumbents themselves are frequently uncertain about their responsibilities. Thompson, McNamara, and Hoyle (1997) report that role conflict and role ambiguity are prime sources of job dissatisfaction and communication problems in educational organizations, which, in turn, lead to performances that fail to meet personal and organizational expectations (see also, Greene & Organ, 1973).

Ambiguity and misinterpretation of expected role behavior is one of the prime sources of problems in the internal organization of colleges and universities. Inefficiencies in operations arise in part from misunderstandings of what the different roles entail and from miscommunication or uncoordinated communication among members at all levels in the organization. Middle managers in higher education—academic department chairs, for example—often have rather undefined roles that result in various kinds of ambiguity—as perceived by others as well as by the managers themselves (Gmelch & Parkay, 1999; Montez, Wolverton, & Gmelch, 2003). They also have multiple constituencies to whom they must simultaneously pay attention, giving rise to feelings of conflict in obligations to each constituency. Such conflicts often cause problems in individual task execution, personal anxiety, and overall organizational effectiveness and efficiency (Bedeian & Armenakis, 1981; Miles & Perreault, 1982; Whetten, 1978).

While the concept of "role" has been implicit in studies of administrative and faculty roles, rewards, and socialization (Austin, 2002; Blackburn & Lawrence, 1995; Boyer, 1990; Colbeck, 1998; Lindholm, 2003; Tierney & Bensimon, 1996), practically no theory-building research on role systems in higher education has appeared in recent years. Robust conceptual frameworks are needed to advance our understanding of complex roles and role relationships in colleges and universities. Examining the dimensions of roles in organizations in general, and exploring their effects on workers and their units in higher education, can lead to more sophisticated understanding and better planning. Our approach in this chapter is partly to unpack the components of roles and examine their uses in organizations in order to better understand the concept itself.

In this chapter, we explore the opportunities of and constraints on individual behavior in organizations as influenced by the system of formal roles in the organization in which the individuals work. We examine the system of roles in higher education organizations and the ways that faculty, staff, and administrators communicate and shape those roles. How, for example, does a college create a pattern of expectations for its student development staff so that they find direction for performing their tasks? How do faculty members learn and understand what is formally expected of them in their jobs? And how do organizational members modify, amplify, supplement, and create the formal roles that they accept as employees?

Organizational Benefits and Detriments of Precise Role Definition

Precise role definition has both organizational benefits and detriments that parallel the ways that rules are established and used in organizations (Gouldner, 1954). Both formal roles and written rules are intrinsic parts of a bureaucratic control system (Mintzberg, 1983b). Roles in formal organizations have a variety of positive functions. First, they **set limits** on employee behavior by prescribing and proscribing what is legitimate. Thus, in some types of organizations, coworkers learn not to tread on another's responsibilities and to attend primarily to their own. In other kinds of organizations, such as colleges and universities (or parts of them), roles are often intentionally ambiguous, as an overlap or duplication of roles is seen to be effective in the long run—for example, overlap in the decision-making roles of faculty and administration (Cohen, March, & Olsen, 1976).

Second, roles **standardize behavior** of organizational members performing similar jobs, thus assuring predictability of uniform outcomes across different people—for example, that data-entry personnel in the university's computer center all perform similarly. On the other hand, some roles are only broadly defined. Because most faculty roles are only marginally standardized, the behaviors involved in teaching, for example, are only moderately predictable, even if one knows who the faculty member is.

Third, roles **stabilize expectations** of performance so that output is more uniform over time. Those who receive output from organizational members whose roles are highly interdependent with their own must believe that they can depend on consistent quality standards. A first semester teacher of statistics, for example, must play the role well enough to permit colleagues who teach statistics in the second semester to make reasonably accurate predictions of the achievements and learning abilities of students entering that class.

Fourth, roles **circumscribe responsibilities**. The effect of this is to permit workers to defend themselves against accusations of poor performance where the tasks fall outside of their formal role definition. They can say, "That's his job, not mine." Last, roles establish **contractual relationships**, which carry positive and negative sanctions. A person in a social system who voluntarily elects to play a role (e.g., accepts employment) is required to perform that role or be subject to dismissal (Katz & Kahn, 1978). Thus, roles and their acceptances make manifest and legitimize authority relationships in organizations.

While assigned roles have many positive consequences for organizations, they sometimes can be detrimental, particularly when defined with excessive precision (Kelloway & Day, 2005). As noted above, the benefits of roles are that they can sanction (positively and negatively) conformity, connect different tasks, and hold people accountable. On the other hand, the fact that roles circumscribe behavior inhibits worker flexibility and adaptability. An assistant dean of students, for example, who is told *exactly* what to do will not be inclined to deviate from the role no matter what his or her student charges may need.

Precisely specified roles also set upper limit productivity norms, thus subtly encouraging workers to perform only up to the minimum acceptable standards listed in formal job descriptions, rather than to the maximum of their capacities. Looser role specification, on the other hand, permits many employees with expertise to participate in decision making, even if the realm of the decision is not part of their formal role responsibilities (Follett, 1942).

Next, we examine the two prevailing positivist orientations toward organizational roles—as functional positions and as expected behaviors. We begin with a brief history of role theory in organizational studies and then examine the theoretical foundations of the functional and behavioral perspectives.

Role Theory in Organizations

Role theory examines the dimensions of roles by exploring their effects on organizational members and on the organization as a whole. The literature on role theory has grown substantially in recent years. Robert Merton and Talcott Parsons made pioneering contributions to the theory in the period after World War I, followed in 1958 by the landmark study of Gross, Mason, and McEachern who attempted to develop a set of role concepts that were usable in a number of different social sciences. The seminal works of Biddle and Thomas (1966) and Sarbin and Allen (1968), and the innovative study of organizational role stress by Kahn, Wolfe, Quinn, and Snoek (1964), dramatically opened up the field. In 1970, the first empirically based and extensively adopted scales to measure role stress were developed by Rizzo, House, and Lirtzman. And Kemery, Bedeian, Mossholder, and Touliatos (1985) were among the first to look intensively at the outcomes of role stress in organizations.

There are two general categories for defining roles (Hardy, 1987; Welbourne, Johnson, & Erez, 1998). One is that role refers to a functional position in a network of interlocking responsibilities. This conception sees role in terms of the requirements of the organization for certain outcomes that serve as inputs to other roles. In other words, what **function** does performance of this role serve in the overall role structure of the unit or organization?

In this version of the theory, the focus is on organizational roles in general without being specific about what *behaviors* are associated with them (Mintzberg, 1979, 1983a). The question is, "How does a particular role contribute to the overall mission or objective of the organization?" For example, the role of a fiscal officer could be stated as assuring that the college's financial matters are executed responsibly, while the role of a dean of students is to carry out the institution's obligations for affective growth of students outside of the classroom.

A second approach in role theory, however, is to describe roles in terms of **behaviors expected**, rather than the functional effects of the roles, as described above. Of concern in this approach are interactions between the organization and the individual, as the organization places demands and expectations on its members. As Katz and Kahn (1978) note, "Roles describe specific forms of behavior associated with given positions; they develop originally from task requirements" (p. 43). From the tasks required to be done, a role or set of roles emerges for one or more people. Roles in this behavioral sense are formal positions that are defined in terms of expected rights and duties. For example, what behaviors does the job description for a resident assistant require? How does this set of responsibilities fit into the network of other roles in the organizational structure of a residential housing unit?

In the following sections, we discuss more extensively the functional and behavioral perspectives on organizational roles.

Roles as Functional Positions in Bureaucracies

Roles, as functional positions, are organizationally defined positions connected with one another in some presumably systematic and rational way, particularly in larger organizations that have become bureaucratic (Merton, 1957). Formal roles are defined *by the organization* and are *not* determined in any way by individual feelings. As Katz and Kahn (1978) note, bureaucratic organizations are the clearest development of a pattern of interlocking roles in the sense that "roles are employed without the encumbrances of socially inherited status or personality contamination" (p. 45). In other words, formal roles deal only with organizationally specified functional requirements, not with the personality or feelings of the role incumbent.

In role theory, an organization consists of individuals who occupy positions, called **offices**, that are interrelated and connected through mutual expectations. An office is "a particular point in organizational space," explain Katz and Kahn (1978, p. 188). Further, they suggest, "Office is essentially a relational concept, defining each position in terms of its relationship to others and to the system as a whole. Associated with each office is a set of activities or expected behaviors" (p. 188). In other words, offices are connected to one another reciprocally and to the organization as a whole. For example, faculty are connected to each other and to academic deans (as are the deans to them), and all are connected to the organizational system. These roles make sense only when we see how they are related to each other. No one role standing alone is interpretable.

Roles derive their meaning from other roles in the system, and in this sense are complementary. It is difficult, if not impossible, for example, to define either the role of student or that of teacher without specifying the relationship of teacher to student. That is, we understand what it means to be a faculty member only if we can see the relationship between the roles of faculty member and the roles of students. We cannot say that a teacher teaches without understanding that there is a student who learns. This interdependency of role relationships can be traced back to the work of Ralph Linton (1936).

In bureaucracies, roles are tightly connected through formal authority relationships (Evan, 1993). In more organic systems, however, roles tend to be more loosely and informally related.

The role structure in organizations is commonly differentiated further into three hierarchical levels: technical, managerial, and institutional (Parsons, 1960). The **technical level** comprises organizational members who engage in the central transformation tasks of the organization—such as faculty members. The **managerial level** includes people who perform supervisory functions and who integrate input and output activities with members of the technical level. Deans fall into this category. Faculty members may also perform these functions as they carry out their research roles (e.g., a faculty member overseeing a team of research assistants). Organizational members at the **institutional level** (e.g., the president and board of trustees of a college) spend most of their time promoting the organization to its external constituencies and seeking support for its activities. Typically, members operating at the institutional level tend to interact with high-status persons and powerful, prestigious external organizations. As Evan (1993) observes:

> Members of an organization, particularly at managerial and institutional levels in the hierarchy, tend to become involved in highly complex rolesets in their intraorganizational as well as extraorganizational roles. If their status-sets are relatively prestigious, they are motivated to engage in a great range of interactions in their various statuses that often, directly or indirectly, enhance their organizational role performance and in turn contribute to the organization's level of effectiveness. (p. 271)

Conflict between and among these three levels is a frequent occurrence, particularly in terms of deadlines, information requirements, and core values

(Floyd & Lane, 2000). For example, trustees, presidents, deans, and faculty commonly have different perceptions about the need for change and hence come into conflict about desirable organizational strategies.

Role as Expected Behavior

At the outset, we noted that the first conception of roles was in terms of functional outcomes expected by the institution. Having just outlined that approach above, we now turn to the second mode of thinking about roles—**role behavior**, which has its locus in individual decisions, rather than in functional positions in a bureaucracy. Behavior of individuals, quite clearly, is a key to organizational effectiveness and efficiency. Hence, if we can define and describe role behavior more precisely, then we are better able to work backward to the likely influences on that behavior, especially when it is deemed effective or ineffective. Knowing the reasons why people behave in roles gives us some leverage in intervening properly in the management of the role system.

Role behavior has a number of definitions, including: (1) "the recurring actions of an individual, appropriately interrelated with the repetitive activities of others to yield a predictable outcome" (Katz & Kahn, 1978, p. 189), and (2) the response of a focal person to the complex set of information and influences received. To use either definition, we must first identify the boundaries of the relevant system in which the role behavior takes place and then observe the *recurring* events of the focal individual of concern. These events will lead to the *sources* of the behavior—namely, the set of expectations emanating from various offices in the organization that are related to the role of the focal individual.

Modes of Inquiry: How to Study Role Behavior

What follows is a model that explains how roles are developed, transmitted, received, and responded to in an organization. The model includes four factors: (1) **role senders**, who create and/or interpret roles and corresponding formal job descriptions, and then transmit them to others with varying degrees of accuracy and clarity; (2) **sent expectations**, which include both the role sender's behavioral expectations for the focal person and the potential rewards and sanctions regarding compliance; (3) the **received role**—again, with varying degrees of accuracy and clarity; and (4) the **response of the focal person**, considered both psychologically and behaviorally. A number of intervening variables also affect how roles are sent, received, and carried out. These include **organizational factors**, **personal attributes** of the role sender and of the role receiver, and the **interpersonal relationships** that develop between the role sender and the role receiver. The model is depicted graphically in Figure 8.2.

The relationships among the variables lean heavily on **role episode** analysis developed originally by Kahn, Wolfe, Quinn, and Snoek (1964) and later elaborated by Katz and Kahn (1978). Below we present a modification and elaboration of the basic model.

The Role Episode

The underlying principle of the model is the concept of the role episode—a sequence of activities in an organization by which roles are made manifest. The sequence may involve assembling a product, delivering a service, or making a decision. Role episodes display role relationships within organizations and reveal sources of differences in role expectations and related behaviors. The role episode model, therefore, is especially useful in diagnosing organizational problems. By breaking down the modes by which roles are created and transmitted, one can identify each of the potential sources of misunderstanding.

Role Senders

Role senders are people in positions of authority who have the responsibility and power to define the official role, prescribe and make public its responsibilities, and communicate its practical meaning to the focal person—for example, in a written job description. The total number of role senders for a particular organization member comprises his or her **role set**. In a typical organization, the role set comprises those in the work flow structure who have some hierarchical relationship (above, laterally, or below) with the focal person as well as others who do not have a formal relationship with the focal person but do have expectations for his or her behavior. Thus, role senders for people working in administrative offices (e.g., admissions, registrar, financial aid) may include their supervisors, their peers, and those who report to them. On the academic side of the institution, there is usually some ambiguity about who constitutes the role senders for faculty, since their individual role sets are different and diffuse, often including persons outside the organization, such as research colleagues at other institutions.

It may be useful to identify the complete role set for a particular organizational member, since doing so helps point to potential **conflicting expectations** among role senders and, hence, role conflict for the individual. The case example offered at the beginning of this chapter illustrates the potential for conflict when those in the role set (in this case, the vice president for student affairs and the vice president for academic affairs) are sending different types of role expectations to the focal person (here, the director of service

FIGURE 8.2

Role Origins, Role Transmission, Role Reception, and Role Behavior*

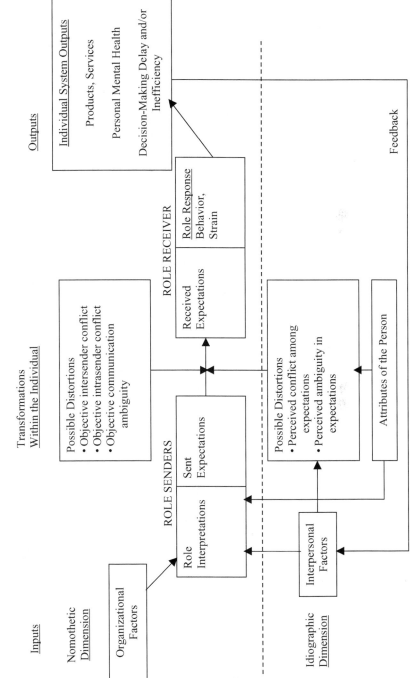

*Adapted from Katz and Kahn, 1978, p. 196.

learning). In addition, an analysis of the role set may reveal **gaps** in the sent roles that may leave work undone. For example, leaders may believe on occasion that organizational members are not responding to instructions, when in actuality, leaders in the role set have not communicated their expectations clearly. As Katz and Kahn (1978) note,

> All members of a person's role-set depend on that person's performance in some fashion; they are rewarded by it, judged in terms of it, or require it to perform their own tasks. Because they have a stake in that person's performance, they develop beliefs and attitudes about what he or she should and should not do as part of the role. Such prescriptions and proscriptions held by members of a role-set are designated *role expectations* [emphasis in the original]; in the aggregate they define the role, the behaviors expected of the person who holds it. (p. 190)

Sent Expectations

The concept of sent expectations has two components: the role sender's behavioral expectations for the focal person, and the consequences (rewards, sanctions) that the role sender will impose for subsequent actions by the focal person. The first part of sent expectations consists of prescriptions and proscriptions held by members of a role set about the expected behavior of a focal person. Many of these are preferences with respect to specific acts—that is, things the focal person should do or avoid doing. For example, deans may expect faculty to hand in their grade reports no later than three working days after the final examination. Or students are expected to register nonuniversity guests when entering the residence halls.

Sent expectations may also refer to personal characteristics or style— ideas about what a person should do, think, or believe. For example, "Here at X Community College, we think faculty should wear business attire in class." A military college might develop other formal expectations of proper dress for faculty and students. Another institution might expect students not to be openly emotional about personal beliefs (e.g., pressures against student activism).

The second dimension of role expectations consists of evaluative standards or sanctions applied to the behavior of any person who occupies a given organizational office or position—that is, what will happen if the role incumbent succeeds or fails. Institutional expectations for good teaching, for example, can be evaluated through student surveys in each course and/or through direct classroom observations. Role senders (in this case, department chairs and deans) can communicate to faculty members that positive course evaluations and classroom observations will lead to a higher salary or a promotion. In contrast, poor course evaluations and problematic observations could lead to reductions in valued rewards such as travel funds and sabbaticals.

In sum, what an organizational member is expected to do and what happens if he or she does or does not are *both* part of sent expectations. This dichotomization is useful conceptually, since the role sender may be quite clear about expectations, but may not have considered the consequences of noncompliance, or even the rewards for extraordinary performance. Yet, failure to communicate both expectations and rewards/sanctions may be a source of institutional problems.

The Sent Role

The sent role consists of communications stemming from the role sender's expectations, and is sent by members of the role set in an attempt to influence the focal person. Four variables can be used to describe the communications associated with the sent role: sign, magnitude, specificity, and range. Each of these variables can take on different values—that is, they can vary in direction and/or strength.

Sign indicates whether the sent message is prescriptive or proscriptive, positive or negative. It tells what can or cannot be done. For example: "Students must achieve a grade of at least a 'C' to proceed to the next course"—contrasted with "Students may not take more than nine credits." The first is positive and prescriptive; the second, negative and proscriptive. Organizational researchers often examine signs to better understand the more subtle norms and values that guide behavior in the organization.

Magnitude reveals the strength of the influence attempt. Here are two examples of this concept: "Staying late to complete work is a *very* important part of this organization," or "Most people here *usually* stay late." Another example is, "All faculty members *always* keep office hours," compared with "Faculty members are *usually* expected to make themselves available to students at convenient times." In both cases, the first example conveys more strength regarding expected behaviors.

Specificity is the extent to which expected behaviors are concrete and detailed versus general and ambiguous. For example: "Employees will be on time" is less specific than "Employees will report at 8:00 a.m."

Range refers to the conditions under which compliance is expected. Does everyone who occupies the role have to comply, or are only some people required to? This term is different from specificity, since it relates not to the particulars of the work but to the characteristics of the person who does the work. For example: "This rule applies to all employees" versus "Faculty members are exempt."

Next, we turn to the receiving side of the role episode scheme. In Figure

8.2, attention is on the focal person—that is, any individual whose role or office is under consideration.

The Received Role

While the sent role is the organization's communication to the individual, the received role is the focal person's perceptions and cognitions of what was sent (Katz & Kahn, 1978). The *received* role has an immediate influence on the individual's behavior and provides a source of motivation for role performance. The sent role arouses some motivational force, sometimes positive, sometimes negative. For example, a worker who perceives an order to be illegitimate might resist.

Note that the received role also includes self-motivation. Intrinsic satisfactions emanate from the role and serve as stimuli to continued commitment to role performance. A financial aid officer, for example, may receive a role assisting low-income students with grant and loan applications. This received role may trigger intrinsic satisfactions from the work itself, and these satisfactions may keep the financial aid officer strongly committed to his or her role. Each person is thus a role "self-sender." Part of the received role comes from the focal person's own internal motivations and beliefs.

Intervening Variables

Three intervening variables—organizational factors, characteristics of focal persons, and interpersonal relationships within the organization—affect or interface with the ways roles are sent and received.

Organizational Factors

Organizational factors determine, in part, how roles are communicated and understood. The following three factors are critical: size, position in the organization, and type of organization (Kahn, Wolfe, Quinn, & Snoek, 1964).

Size. How big the organization is determines in part the amount of role differentiation—the extent to which the required organizational activities are divided into specialized roles (Katz & Kahn, 1978). Recall from systems theory that as the organization grows, it becomes more differentiated—that is, more and different roles are created. Further, the more role differentiation, the more role specificity: as organizations break down tasks into finer and finer roles, the more precisely prescribed those roles become. For those working in large universities, more role differentiation and more role specificity are seen. In smaller colleges, more loosely defined roles can be found, with many people performing a wide range of tasks.

In large organizations with highly prescribed roles, there is more role conflict and resulting role strain (tension). One might ask why this would be so. If large size also means more specific roles, might not role players experience *less* ambiguity about what their responsibilities are? The answer comes from the concept of entropy that we considered in chapter 4 on systems theory. As roles become more and more narrowly defined, it becomes less clear to whom complex multitask projects should be assigned. "Is this my job or yours?" (It is probably both.) Yet another finding about organizational size is that the larger the organization, the less consensus there is across the organization about role expectations.

In addition, large organizations have more administrative and coordinating roles than do small organizations. However, even though the total number of administrative roles is large, the *proportion* of administrative roles to line roles (i.e., the administrative component of the organization) is lower in large organizations than in small organizations (Blau, 1994). That is, as organizations grow, more supervision is needed to connect the differentiated parts, but the number of line positions (e.g., faculty members, counselors) grows faster than the number of administrative posts. Thus, in very large organizations (such as universities), there will be many supervisors, but the "administrative component" or administrative burden as a proportion of total costs will decline, thus, technically, making the institution more efficient.

Position in the organization. The second organizational factor is position, which refers to vertical role location in the hierarchy as well as proximity to the boundary of the organization. Research on this subject is considerable (see, for example, Adams, 1976; Ancona & Caldwell, 1992; Friedman & Podolny, 1992; Miles & Perreault, 1982; Rangarajan, Chonko, Jones, & Roberts, 2004; Singh, 1998; Whetten, 1978). These studies have shown that frequency and strength of role conflict vary, depending on where the role is in the organization. People who occupy roles deep in the organization (i.e., closer to the core processes) experience less role conflict than do those in roles that involve cross-boundary interactions (Kahn et al., 1964). In higher education, a number of roles involve cross boundary activities—for example, the college president, faculty with research grants, and admissions recruiters. The reason for the greater conflict experienced by these persons has to do with the number of role senders in their role sets. Having to interact simultaneously with and respond to both internal and external role senders can create role conflict (Schuler, 1977).

Position in the organizational hierarchy also makes a difference in the experience of the role. Middle managers experience more role conflict than do either higher-ranking or lower-ranking organization members. Department chairs, for example, who occupy mid-level leadership positions, have multiple role senders from both above *and* below. In attempting to adjudicate between these two sets of claimants, mid-level leaders frequently find themselves in role conflict situations. Research has shown, however, that individuals who adopt positive behavioral styles often develop more effective responses to role conflict (Tidd & Friedman, 2002).

Type of organization is a third organizational factor. The more professional versus bureaucratic the organization, the more diffuse the role specification, because professional norms discourage close specification of role behaviors. Professionals demand more discretion and autonomy in their roles and, hence, resist precise role specification.

Managerial attitudes and organizational culture are additional conditions affecting roles. The more humanistic versus calculative the values of the culture (Etzioni, 1961), the less role specificity in organizations. In the former case, there is more tolerance of individual differences and more willingness to adjust role expectations according to idiosyncratic characteristics of the role incumbent.

Personal Factors: Attributes of the Person

Considering once again the role episode diagram (Figure 8.2), note that, in addition to organizational factors, there are two more sets of variables that modify the sent role—attributes of the person and interpersonal factors (Graen, 1976; Graen, Orris, & Johnson, 1973). We address the personal attributes first.

Individuals occupying organizational roles invariably have idiosyncratic personalities, and these, in turn, influence how roles are defined by those in role-sending positions. In other words, role senders consider the attributes of the people to whom they send roles and modify the sent role based on their understanding of the characteristics of the focal person (Katz & Kahn, 1978). For example, academic deans tend to deal differently with different department chairs. The dean may communicate precise role expectations for a chair who lacks confidence in his or her ability to do the job, and the same dean may allow an experienced chair to largely self-define the role.

Not only do role senders change the sent role, however. The focal person (in this example, the department chair) is likely to interpret the sent role in ways that confirm his or her desires and hopes. It has been found, for example, that the flexibility or rigidity of an individual is related to interpretations of role expectations (Kahn et al., 1964). Rigid focal persons tend not to recognize role conflicts as conflicts, while flexible persons can cope more readily with perceived conflicts (Raffel, 1999). Because of these potential distortions on both ends—sender and focal person—it is important to recognize how and why roles may not seem to be understood and why role behavior may not seem to meet expectations.

The above should not be construed as meaning that personality is a part of the role. As outlined earlier, once the organization determines the role, it is official. The personality of the individual is not considered in the evaluation of performance in the role. This impartial interpretation of role performance is different from recognizing that the definition of the role can be negotiated in the early stages of employment.

Interpersonal Factors

Interpersonal factors constitute a third set of variables that modifies the sent role. As people in organizations work together, they develop distinctive relationships—unique ways of interacting. Sometimes organizational members develop great trust in one another; sometimes the opposite happens. Sometimes they have a mutual understanding about underlying philosophies and ways of behaving; other times, they may be in fundamental disagreement. The nature of this emergent relationship affects both how the role is sent and how it is received. In addition, norms of acceptable group behavior almost always constrain role behavior in some way. Work groups, for example, may send roles to new members that communicate the desired pace of role behaviors (e.g., "Don't work too quickly and make the rest of the group look bad") and the expected quality of role outcomes (e.g., "Don't make mistakes that reflect poorly on the team").

Response of the Focal Person

Note that the role episode diagram (Figure 8.2) moves from left to right. In the interests of promoting organizational efficiency, in most instances, the desired outcome is for role behavior to conform to role expectations. In other words, the hope is that organization members will receive and understand the sent role and perform it according to specification. Of course, some deviation from expectation is necessary for innovation to take place; however, role episode analysis is concerned with efficient execution of roles that have already been specified by the organization—not the emergence of new roles.

So under what conditions does role behavior, in fact, conform to role expectations? Each of the components or concepts in the theory (e.g., role expectations, sent role) is related in some way to the modification of role behavior (the dependent variable) to assure compliance with role expectation. We can pose a general hypothesis: "The closer the received role is to the sent role, the closer role behavior will be to role expectations." For example, if a department chair asks a faculty member to do "X," and he communicates the role correctly, and the faculty member receives it correctly, the faculty member is more likely to achieve the chair's expectation.

Social Construction Conceptualizations of Roles

There is some degree of controversy in the literature over whether the Katz and Kahn model described above portrays organizational members as too passive, and whether the model is biased toward reinforcing the status quo. Graen (1976), for example, believes that to characterize role behavior in this way is to suggest that organizational members are relatively passive *role takers*, with little *role-making* influence. An alternative to the positivist approach views role structure as emergent and enacted, thus highlighting the agency of individuals to construct their own roles in relation to others.

Graen and Scandura (1987; see also, Roos & Starke, 1981) have elaborated an alternative social constructionist model, which they call a theory of **dyadic organizing**. Although the emphasis in their model is on two-person relationships, the theory generally holds for all role behavior. The theory suggests that there are three phases in the adoption of a role. The first is quite similar to Katz and Kahn's role-*taking* approach. During this first phase, new role incumbents attempt to learn what role senders expect of them. The second phase, however, involves a series of negotiations, usually more informal, as focal persons negotiate and attempt to persuade role senders to accept the focal person's interpretation of the role. Other researchers have referred to this process as **role enactment** (Starbuck, 1976). Some early writers on role theory—symbolic interactionists such as Znaniecki (1967)—suggested that people work out their roles as they imagine how others prefer their behavior to be.

In the third and final stage, called **role routinization**, the relationships between the parties are stabilized, and, over time, the energy expended on role negotiation ceases. Then the focal person concentrates on role performance for extended periods. The first two phases are thus more dynamic, the third, more static. For organizations that operate in a turbulent environment, however, stabilization of roles may never be achieved—an inevitable source of some degree of worker ambiguity, conflict, and anxiety, but a potential source for creativity, innovation, and professional vitality as well.

Graen and Scandura's (1987) theory of dyadic organizing helps us understand the complex, evolving roles of the higher education workplace. The role negotiation phase, in particular, provides insight into how new role incumbents become socialized to their roles. **Role socialization** refers to the process by which a new member of an organization learns about the formal goals and procedures that are associated with the job as well as the values, norms, and expected informal interaction patterns (Merton, 1957; Van Maanen, 1976).

Typically, newly employed organizational members initially see their roles as part of a "fuzzy" system and only later achieve a firmer sense of their role responsibilities (Montgomery, 2000). Through their interactions with others, new employees learn what is expected of them. Social constructionists extend this view and suggest that role socialization is a "mutually adaptive process between the organization and the individual" (Tierney & Rhoads, 1994, p. 6). Roles are not merely transmitted from a role sender to a role receiver; people have an opportunity to shape the way they enact their role in an organization. Socialization, in this conceptualization, is a fluid process that is not restricted to one-way influence—that is, unidirectional effects from role senders to role receivers. Instead, socialization can be viewed as a complex interaction of mutually shaping effects, where both organizational leaders and new organizational members shape expectations for role performance.

To be sure, organizational members are obligated to address formalized role expectations. Faculty must turn in grades, institutional advancement officers must raise funds, and admissions recruiters must attract new students to the institution. But during the role negotiation phase, according to social constructionists, organizational members have the ability to shape their roles in ways that are consistent with their own expectations for work. For example, faculty members in a university can attempt to shape their roles to emphasize teaching or research productivity more strongly. A library director can reshape the role so that it encompasses leadership for new media and information technologies. A new director of housing can expand the role from being an organizer of student activities and an enforcer of student discipline, to also serving as an educator in a residential learning community.

Of course, the role negotiation phase may be fraught with peril. A faculty member seeking to emphasize her teaching role may underestimate the extent to which the decision on her promotion and tenure will be determined by her research productivity. A library director seeking to extend his reach into new media and information technology may generate conflict with a chief information officer who expects to call the shots regarding technology decisions. And an early-career housing director seeking to develop a residential learning community may be taking on more than she is prepared to handle if she does not have a strong background in pedagogy and learning theory.

However, as social constructionists note, organizational expectations for role performance are often fluid (at least to some degree), and organizational members can shape and reshape the roles that they enact. For example, as new members enter an organization, the expectations for role performance often change. Rice, Sorcinelli, and Austin (2000) have documented how a new generation of faculty has reshaped the academy's thinking about teaching and research roles. New faculty members have demonstrated emerging commitments to service learning, civic engagement, and community-focused research agendas. Institutional expectations for faculty role performance, in turn, have shifted in many institutions to include recognition of these new commitments (O'Meara, 2005).

Social constructionist perspectives emphasize the dynamic processes of role negotiation where expectations for role performance are created and shaped through ongoing interactions among organizational members. Roles are viewed as the product of social interaction, and new organizational members have an opportunity to change the expectations typically associated with various roles. However, as postmodern and feminist scholars have noted, not all employees have the same amount of leverage in the role negotiation process. Women and people of color may be at a particular disadvantage in some organizations.

Postmodern and Feminist Perspectives on Roles

Tierney and Rhoads (1994) argue that organizational role expectations often need to change to meet the values and expectations that newcomers bring to the organization. Some organizations, however, are rigid and unyielding to new ideas about roles and role performance. Feminist scholars suggest that roles sent by organizational leaders may reflect a controlling, patriarchal view toward employees (Ferguson, 1994; Martin, 1990). In paternalistic organizations, role communication is formalized and hierarchical, and role performance is evaluated in terms of compliance with directives issued by higher-level leaders.

In a patriarchal organization, people who seek greater variation from traditional role expectations may encounter negative consequences if they pursue courses of action that deviate too significantly from the status quo. Faculty of color, for example, may experience institutional pressures to perform additional advising and service roles, even though tenure and promotion guidelines clearly express a priority for research (Baez, 2000; Turner & Myers, 2000). Similarly, Tierney and Bensimon (1996) found that women faculty may be pressured into doing "smile work" and "mom work":

> Smile work takes many different forms, but basically it is a culturally imposed strategy women use to fit into departments with a tradition of male dominance. Sometimes these are departments in which the faculty have not internalized the need to be more diverse and have hired women and/

or minorities because of external pressures to comply with affirmative action goals. Typically, they tend to think of equal opportunity as "adding women" without reconsidering socialization practices in order to be more welcoming. Male-dominated cultures encourage feminine stereotypical behaviors that make women appear "unobjectionable," congenial and cheerful rather than strident and unpredictable. (p. 83)

In addition to pressures to be congenial and cheerful, women faculty may encounter expectations for them to assume a maternal role. "Mom work" involves women faculty assuming the role of nurturer. Students may expect women faculty to address their emotional needs. Women faculty in Tierney and Bensimon's (1996) study found that students, as role senders, expected them to be forgiving if they were late with an assignment and supportive if they were having a difficult time adjusting to college. "Mom work" also extended to the academic department, where women faculty were often engaged in "more than a fair share of a department's domestic-type work" (p. 87), including the teaching of introductory seminars, which require a great deal of student contact time. Conformity to these sent roles contributes to an ongoing cycle of exploitation where women are sent roles that are less valued by the organization.

Baez (2000) suggests that marginalized organizational members can redress power imbalances through acts of resistance that attempt to redefine organizational roles. In his research, Baez found that faculty of color engaged in community-focused service activities despite their knowledge that the service role was not highly valued in promotion and tenure decisions at their institution.

> In other words, they knew that their institution required conformity with prevailing notions of merit, but they felt also that their work forced their colleagues to rethink (if not accept) its importance in creating social change . . . Race-related service, and the agency that supports it, therefore, might set the stage for the contestation of institutional structures and roles, and the notions of merit ensured by them. (pp. 382–383)

The faculty members in this study took actions that required role senders—such as department chairs and colleagues on promotion and tenure committees—to change their thinking about role expectations and to value a wider range of activities in assessing faculty performance.

To break a cycle of oppression, organizational leaders can heed voices of resistance. Rather than punish employees for noncompliance, leaders can reexamine the gendered and racial assumptions of sent roles. Moreover, it is

critical to consider who is sending roles. Do white males have a disproportionately large influence on sent roles? Some observers (Johnsrud, 1993; Tierney & Bensimon, 1996) suggest that having a critical mass of women and
people of color in leadership positions contributes instead to the creation of
an affirming workplace climate for all employees.

Role Conflict

To this point we have identified the components in a role episode analysis,
which reflects the basic assumptions of the positivist paradigm and its emphasis on the prediction and control of organizational behavior. We have
also explored social constructionist and postmodern alternatives to conceptualizing organizational roles. Now, we can use these frameworks as lenses for
understanding how and why organizational problems associated with role
conflicts arise and what their effects are on both the organization and the
individual (Beehr & Glazer, 2005). The literature on role conflict is extensive
(see especially Jackson & Schuler, 1985; Tubre, Sifferman, & Collins, 1996).
What follows is an overview only.

First, a definition of role conflict is necessary. Role conflict is "the degree
of incongruity or incompatibility of expectations communicated to a focal
person by his/her role senders" (Gross, Mason, & McEachern, 1958, p. 248;
see also Kumar, 1997; Miles & Perreault, 1982). Usually, these incongruities
or incompatibilities can be traced to two sources: inadequate time and logical
or ethical incompatibilities (Naylor, Pritchard, & Ilgen, 1980). Role conflicts
exist in the sent role and/or the received role—that is, the sent role can contain the seeds of conflict in expected behavior. Or, the focal person may perceive the received role as having some incompatibility (regardless of whether
it does exist).

Rizzo, House, and Lirtzman (1970) conceptualized four different kinds
of role conflict, which are depicted graphically in Figure 8.3. They are described below in somewhat revised form—divided into external and internal
conditions that cause the individual to be at least temporarily unable to make
a decision.

Person-role conflict is the extent to which role expectations received
from role senders are perceived to be inconsistent with role expectations generated internally by the focal person's own values and "self-sent" to that person's cognitive state. For example, a university fund raiser may be required
to ask for money from people whom the fund raiser believes cannot afford
it or for projects which the fund raiser does not believe are worthy.

Intersender conflict is the extent to which role expectations sent by at

FIGURE 8.3
Nomothetic and Idiographic Origins of Role Conflict

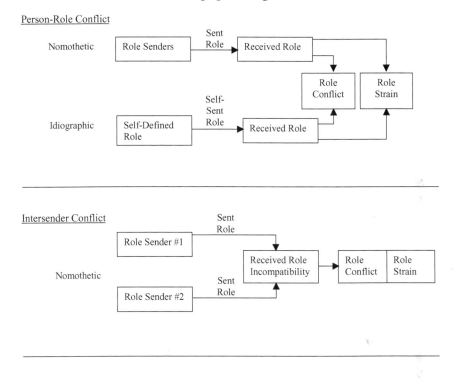

least two role senders seem to demand behavior that is contradictory, mutually exclusive, or incompatible. Students may expect a faculty member to
perform in one way (e.g., giving time and attention to teaching), while the
faculty member's colleagues may demand other kinds of performances, such
as research publications. In addition to the time limitations for performing
both roles, they demand different skills. Teaching requires casting knowledge
in pedagogically sound language, while research necessitates using concepts
suited to theory articulation and development. Faculty members may believe
that the combination of teaching and research expectations is incompatible
with the skills and preferences they have developed; hence, the two roles are
perceived as being in conflict.

Intrasender conflict is the extent to which a focal person perceives two
or more sent role expectations from one role sender that are impossible to
fulfill simultaneously. For example, a dean wants her faculty to be supportive
and nonjudgmental with students, while the faculty simultaneously adminis-
ter punishments for violations of rules.

FIGURE 8.3
Continued

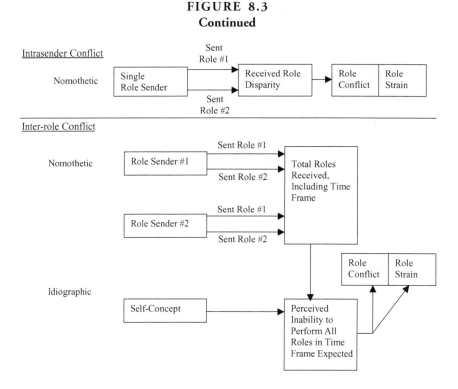

Inter-role conflict (often called role overload) is the extent to which the various role expectations communicated to a role incumbent appear to exceed the available time and resources to meet the role expectations. Consider again the case presented at the beginning of this chapter. The vice president for student affairs expects the service-learning director to spend significant time working with community groups, but the vice president for academic affairs wants her to meet more often with faculty in the academic departments. Given limited time and resources, the director will experience inter-role conflict.

A significant amount of research on role conflict shows detrimental effects for individuals and organizations. Daly and Dee (2006) found that role conflict contributed to diminished job satisfaction and lower levels of organizational commitment among faculty members. Other research suggests that role conflict contributes to higher levels of dissatisfaction in interpersonal interactions with colleagues and diminished work group performance (Liddell & Slocum, 1976). Schuler (1975, 1977) discovered that the relationship between role conflict and satisfaction was negative throughout organizational hierarchical levels (high, medium, and low), but that role conflict had less of an impact on satisfaction among top executives.

Role conflict can produce high levels of role strain and stress for organizational members. In cases of inter-role conflict (role overload), role strain can be reduced by merging or blending two roles that previously competed for an employee's attention. The blending of formerly competing roles is possible when we consider the potential for role negotiation suggested by social constructionists. If organizational members can shape and reshape roles, then there is potential for creative blending and role reformation. Colbeck (1998), for example, found that faculty members can "expand available time and energy by engaging in behaviors that simultaneously satisfy expectations for both research and teaching roles" (p. 650). Faculty can integrate research and teaching when they write textbooks based on their teaching, when they involve students in their research, and when their research examines pedagogical issues in the classroom (e.g., how to improve the teaching of organic chemistry). Similarly, a department chair may integrate curriculum development and grant-seeking roles by developing a funding proposal to create new courses in an emerging field of study. Of course, some organizations have rigidly defined roles that preclude the opportunity to aggregate many disparate activities into one role. In some instances, collective bargaining agreements may prescribe precisely who will perform a role and for what length of time.

Role Ambiguity

Role ambiguity refers to uncertainty concerning expected role performance. As with the concept of role conflict, the literature on role ambiguity is abundant. (See, for example, Breaugh & Colihan, 1994; Huxham & Vangen, 2000; King & King, 1990; Sawyer, 1992.) Research shows that role ambiguity has a detrimental effect on job satisfaction and, to a lesser extent, a negative effect on job performance (Abramis, 1994).

Role ambiguity can be classified as perceptual or objective. **Perceptual role ambiguity** suggests that the ambiguity lies in the mind of the individual—in the perception and conception of the received role. **Objective role ambiguity** points to the quality of the communication—the nature of the sent role. These two types of role ambiguity arise from the interaction of the sent role and the received role as indicated in Figure 8.4.

Perceptual role ambiguity stems from the lack of clarity *within the individual* about the responsibilities, task specifications, and expectations of the work. Even if the sent role is clear, there may still be perceptual role ambiguity. A new faculty member, for example, may receive clear guidelines for

FIGURE 8.4
Sources of Perceptual and Objective Role Ambiguity

		Received Role	
		Understood	**Not Understood**
Sent Role	**Clear**	No Ambiguity	Perceptual Role Ambiguity
	Garbled or Contradictory	False Perceived Clarity	Objective Role Ambiguity

teaching an introductory undergraduate course, but if the faculty member has had little training in pedagogy, the sent role may still be perceived as ambiguous.

Objective role ambiguity, in contrast, originates in messages from the role sender. A director of enrollment management, for example, may not communicate clearly what is expected of each admissions officer. As a result, the admissions staff receive an ambiguous role and may be uncertain about how to meet the director's expectations. An additional possible outcome is that the admissions officers believe that they actually understand the garbled role sent by the director. In this case, they operate with a false sense of clarity, which may yield actions that do not meet the director's intended expectations.

It is important to recognize that a *balance* between role clarity and ambiguity is often most effective. Total role clarity may be intrusive and nonfunctional (Ivancevi & Donnelly, 1974), and some degree of ambiguity may be useful for stimulating innovative practice. Role ambiguity may reflect situations where not all roles and connections among roles can, or should, be specified by the organization. This scenario could facilitate loose coupling among roles, which provides latitude for organizational members to enact their roles free from the constraints of an organizationally defined sent role. Loosely coupled systems may lead to more rapid development of new roles in the organization, more flexible connections among roles across the organization, and more adaptive role responses to changing external conditions (Orton & Weick, 1990). Wise leaders, then, recognize the trade-off between clarity and ambiguity for both employee productivity and satisfaction (Hurrell, Nelson, & Simmons, 1998).

Supplementary Role Concepts

Manifest-Latent

A number of other concepts are frequently used in organizational role diagnosis. One important supplementary concept refers to organizational roles that emerge unintentionally and remain sub rosa—that is, they are not part of the *formally* recognized role behaviors created to address official organizational goals. The role episode diagram (Figure 8.2), for example, does not include either the unintended functions played by the organization as a whole or the unintended functions played by individual workers playing certain roles. Understanding these latent functions often reveals the ways in which they have important influences on the performance of official roles. For example, it is sometimes alleged that some faculty interactions with students are more likely to satisfy the faculty member's own psychological needs (e.g., for ego enhancement) than they satisfy the educational needs of the students. More positive latent functions involve the adoption of behaviors by organization members that are *not* officially part of their duties, yet perform critical functions for those who receive the services (such as a faculty member helping a student complete a financial aid application). It is important, therefore, to identify these sometimes hidden roles. We can characterize them in two ways.

The **manifest role** is the apparent or overt role. For example, one of the roles of a teacher is to transmit information. A **latent role** emerges as a result of functions performed by either the individual or the organization but are not specified in the job description. For example, the faculty member as "role model" is a latent role. As such, it is rarely identified as a *formal* role requirement in a job description.

Two of the best-known latent roles are the faculty roles of **cosmopolitan** and **local**. These notions were originated by Alvin Gouldner in the late 1950s (Gouldner, 1957, 1958). Cosmopolitan workers are "those low on loyalty to the employing organization, high on commitment to specialized role skills, and likely to use an outer reference group" (Hoy & Miskel, 1991, p. 147). Research faculty, for example, often find their allegiances more closely allied with external organizations where their skills may be more recognized and rewarded than within the college or university. Locals, on the other hand, are "high on loyalty to the employing organization, low on commitment to specialized role skills, and likely to use an inner reference group" (p. 147). Locally oriented faculty members, then, are more likely to be engaged in activities on campus such as governance committees, athletic events, and fine arts performances.

These two concepts are especially useful in understanding the differences among colleges and universities with different missions. Many research universities employ a large number of cosmopolitan faculty—faculty whose primary orientation is not toward service to their institutions (except indirectly) but toward colleagues in the professional, disciplinary community at-large. These roles are latent because when faculty members are hired, they are not *formally* asked to be locals or cosmopolitans. Usually, a mix of locals and cosmopolitans evolves to serve the various needs of the institution. Unfortunately, there are status differences among occupants of the different roles, with cosmopolitans who have achieved national recognition for their work considered more valuable and important to the institution. Institutional reward systems seem to follow this pattern.

Diffuseness-Specificity

A second important supplementary concept in role theory concerns the diffuseness or specificity of the role description that is communicated by the role sender to the role receiver (Parsons, 1951). As noted at the outset, roles are set in a context of reciprocal relationships. Some relationships between office holders connote a specific range of responsibilities and obligations—for example, math teacher and student, landlord and tenant, doctor and patient. In some role relationships, however, the nature of the reciprocity is diffuse—unspecified and left to the discretion of the focal persons. For example, the roles of friend, political leader, spouse, and parent are not prescribed concretely, but emerge as relationships develop.

When the role is diffuse, the actors may (with the implicit permission of the organization) choose different parts of the role to be relevant to the relationship. Sometimes a role with the same name may be specific in one context but diffuse in another. One can imagine, for example, that the relationship between a dean and a faculty member in a small college may be different in diffuseness/specificity from the same relationship by these role incumbents in a large university.

Universalism-Particularism

A third key supplementary concept in role theory is **universalism-particularism**. These terms refer to the degree of influence that personal and interpersonal factors have on the communication between role sender and focal person. In contrast to diffuseness-specificity, which addresses the dyadic relationship between the parties, universalism-particularism concerns the relationship between one role incumbent and the *entire category* of persons occupying the other role.

A role is played out *universalistically* if the role incumbent holds all persons occupying another role to the same standards and expectations. A role is played out *particularistically* when the role incumbent takes into account unique characteristics of the particular other in the relationship and behaves accordingly. For example, the role of faculty member to student can be universalistic—that is, treat every student equally, regardless of special circumstances (e.g., a disadvantaged background). Or it can be particularistic, taking into account unusual circumstances.

In most organizations, organizational and/or subgroup norms influence how roles will be acted out. Hence, to better understand interpersonal relations in organizations, both formal rules and the norms that reinforce universalism or particularism must be accounted for. To be critical of a person's alleged failure to carry out a role to the letter of the law, for example, demands an appreciation of the extent to which universalistic or particularistic evaluation criteria are being supported in the organization.

Note that a role can be specific or diffuse at the same time that it is universalistic or particularistic. For instance, an organization can be quite specific in defining the role (e.g., carefully written job descriptions), but how the role is defined further can be determined by the preference of the role sender based on either universalistic or particularistic predispositions. The director of a university personnel department may have set specific responsibilities for her administrative assistant. If the director is particularistic in orientation, she may modify her role expectations depending on the characteristics of the person serving as her administrative assistant. Or, conversely, the director may disseminate open (diffuse) job descriptions, but expect everyone in that job to be treated in exactly the same way—universalistically.

Quality-Performance Orientation

The last supplementary concept in role theory is quality-performance orientation, which refers to the degree of emphasis on status versus achievement in an organization's role relationships. In some organizations, role relationships are influenced by personal characteristics that may not be relevant to the task to be performed—for example, a person's age, gender, seniority, title, race, or membership in some high-status group. This **quality orientation** assumes that personal qualities are surrogate measures of real competencies. For example, older employees may be assumed to be more competent than younger employees (or vice versa). Having a degree from a prestigious college may connote competence, regardless of one's actual achievements. In other organizations, however, role relationships are based primarily on achievement. Thus a **performance orientation** refers to a role relationship that is based almost exclusively on the achievements of the role incumbent.

Summary

It is often difficult to perceive the truly operative role constraints on people in educational organizations, partly because latent roles are hidden, yet potentially powerful. Role analysis in higher education, moreover, is complicated by the ambiguity and overlap of the several authority structures that govern faculty, administrative, and student systems (Birnbaum, 1988; Blau, 1994). The subtle inputs of role senders across these systems make it difficult for senders to articulate and role incumbents to discern.

However, by identifying the main ingredients that comprise a role, we can pinpoint more precisely what may cause a discrepancy between what the organization desires and expects and what the role incumbent understands and does. The role episode model presented in this chapter can serve as a platform for analyzing roles and role behaviors in higher education organizations. College and university leaders can use the model to understand and improve role communication and assist faculty and staff in the process of enacting roles that fulfill both individual and organizational needs.

Besides the impact of role uncertainty on the organization, there is a corollary impact on the person performing the role. He or she suffers both psychologically and in performance effectiveness when roles are excessively ambiguous or when they are overly specified. The person's psyche and performance also will suffer when he or she must attempt to work through excessive conflicts in the role.

Colleges and universities continue to perform many of the same functions in society as they have historically, but they have added a large number of new ones as well. The complexities of a changing world, however, have forced institutions of higher education to examine closely how best to organize themselves to accomplish their ends. Roles that were played effectively in the past need to be re-examined to determine whether they fit into the demands of external and internal constituencies. In addition to the requirement that roles make institutions more efficient, moreover, roles need to be designed so that they provide satisfaction and fulfillment for their incumbents.

In this chapter, we attempted to provide a coherent picture of how roles may be conceived in organizations. While administrative leaders cannot be expected to review all of the dimensions of roles, they can and should consider carefully as many of the variables that affect roles and role relationships as possible. By so doing, both the organization and the role incumbent will be better able to achieve their goals.

Review Questions

1. A person's role is determined by:
   a. The expectations of the organization

   b. The expectations of the person's role senders
   c. The sent role
   d. All of the above

2. Greater role conflict tends to be associated with all but which one of the following?
   a. Unsatisfactory departmental relations
   b. Slower and less accurate departmental performance
   c. Less rapid promotion rates for individual faculty
   d. Lower commitment to the department

3. A lower-ranking member of a university administration is told by a vice president that university rules require all employees to address their supervisors by their official titles, but the employee believes that informal, egalitarian work relationships are both more effective and ethical. In complying, the employee will probably experience:
   a. Intersender role conflict
   b. Intrasender role conflict
   c. Person-role conflict
   d. Role overload (inter-role conflict)

4. A college that is governed largely by rules and regulations without regard to idiosyncratic preferences of individuals can be said to have a role system that is:
   a. Universalistic
   b. Particularistic

5. A college with a system of diffuse roles can best explain which of the following?
   a. A student who becomes good friends with a teacher
   b. A school bookkeeper whose job performance conforms closely with job expectations
   c. A dean whose style of leadership is to send many memoranda
   d. The relationship between a member of the personnel department and a faculty member during their first encounter with one another

6. Which of the following affects the nature of the formal role sent to all of the faculty members in a college?
   a. Person-role conflict
   b. The size and shape of the hierarchy of authority
   c. The relationship that evolves between the role sender and the focal person

    d. The emotional maturity of the focal person
    e. All of the above

7. The dean of the college of arts and sciences in a major research university finds that the institutional incentives available to her to motivate faculty are inadequate. This could be because most of her faculty have a latent role orientation that is:
    a. Cosmopolitan
    b. Local

8. The chair of the psychology department suggests to a new faculty member that she needs to publish at least three articles a year to gain tenure. The faculty member's students, however, plead with her to extend her office hours. The faculty member is equally committed to teaching and research. She is experiencing which of the following kinds of role conflict?
    a. Person-role
    b. Intersender
    c. Intrasender
    d. Role overload (inter-role)

Case Discussion Questions

Consider the Superior College case that was presented at the beginning of this chapter.

1. What were the sources of role conflict for the director of service learning? What have the consequences been of role conflict for her job performance and satisfaction?
2. To what extent is the director's situation attributable to the organizational design in which she now works? (Recall the challenges associated with matrix organizations that we discussed in chapter 7.)
3. What structural remedies could college leaders implement to improve the director's situation? Keep in mind that any new structural arrangement is likely to have its own set of strengths and weaknesses, which should be compared to the advantages and disadvantages of the current structure.

References

Abramis, D. J. (1994). Work role ambiguity, job-satisfaction, and job-performance: Meta-analyses and review. *Psychological Reports, 75*(3), 1411–1433.

Adams, J. S. (1976). The structure and dynamics of behavior in organizational boundary roles. In M. D. Dunnette (Ed.), *Handbook of industrial and organizational psychology* (pp. 1175–1199). Chicago: Rand McNally.

Ancona, D. G., & Caldwell, D. F. (1992). Bridging the boundary: External activity and performance in organizational teams. *Administrative Science Quarterly, 37*(4), 634–665.

Austin, A. (2002). Preparing the next generation of faculty: Graduate school as socialization to the academic career. *Journal of Higher Education, 73*(1), 94–122.

Baez, B. (2000). Race-related service and faculty of color: Conceptualizing critical agency in academe. *Higher Education, 39*, 363–391.

Bedeian, A. G., & Armenakis, A. A. (1981). A path analytic study of the consequences of role conflict and ambiguity. *Academy of Management Journal, 24*, 417–424.

Beehr, T. A., & Glazer, S. (2005). Organizational role stress. In J. Barling, E. K. Kelloway, & M. R. Frone (Eds.), *Handbook of work stress* (pp. 7–34). Thousand Oaks, CA: Sage.

Biddle, B., & Thomas, E. (Eds.). (1966). *Role theory: Concepts and research.* New York: John Wiley & Sons.

Birnbaum, R. (1988). *How colleges work: The cybernetics of academic organization and leadership.* San Francisco: Jossey-Bass.

Blackburn, R. T., & Lawrence, J. H. (1995). *Faculty at work: Motivation, expectation, satisfaction.* Baltimore, MD: Johns Hopkins University Press.

Blau, P. M. (1994). *The organization of academic work* (2nd ed.). New Brunswick, NJ: Transaction Publishing.

Boyer, E. (1990). *Scholarship reconsidered: Priorities of the professoriate.* Princeton, NJ: Carnegie Foundation for the Advancement of Teaching.

Breaugh, J. A., & Colihan, J. P. (1994). Measuring facets of job ambiguity: Construct validity evidence. *Journal of Applied Psychology, 79*, 191–202.

Cohen, M. D., March, J. G., & Olsen, J. P. (1976). People, problems, solutions, and the ambiguity of relevance. In J. G. March and J. P. Olsen, *Ambiguity and choice in organizations* (pp. 24–37). Bergen, Norway: Universitetsforlaget.

Colbeck, C. (1998). Merging in a seamless blend: How faculty integrate teaching and research. *Journal of Higher Education, 69*(6), 647–671.

Daly, C., & Dee, J. (2006). Greener pastures: Faculty turnover intent in urban public universities. *Journal of Higher Education, 77*(5), 776–803.

Etzioni, A. (1961). *A comparative analysis of complex organizations.* New York: The Free Press.

Evan, W. M. (1993). *Organizational theory, research and design.* New York: Macmillan Publishing.

Ferguson, K. (1994). On bringing more theory, more voices, and more politics to the study of organization. *Organization, 1*, 81–99.

Floyd, S. W., & Lane, P. J. (2000). Strategizing throughout the organization: Managing role conflict in strategic renewal. *Academy of Management Review, 25*(1), 154–177.

Follett, M. P. (1942). *Dynamic administration*. New York: Harper.

Friedman, R. A., & Podolny, J. (1992). Differentiation of boundary spanning roles: Labor negotiations and implications for role conflict. *Administrative Science Quarterly, 37*(1), 28–47.

Gmelch, W., & Parkay, F. (1999). *Becoming a department chair: Negotiating the transition from scholar to administrator*. Paper presented at the annual meeting of the American Educational Research Association, Montreal.

Gouldner, A. (1954). *Patterns of industrial bureaucracy*. Glencoe, IL: Free Press.

Gouldner, A. (1957). Cosmopolitans and locals: Toward an analysis of latent social roles—I. *Administrative Science Quarterly, 2*, 281–306.

Gouldner, A. (1958). Cosmopolitans and locals: Toward an analysis of latent social roles—II. *Administrative Science Quarterly, 3*, 444–480.

Graen, G. (1976). Role-making processes within complex organizations. In M.D. Dunnette (Ed.), *Handbook of industrial and organizational psychology* (pp. 1201–1245). Chicago: Rand McNally College Publishing Company.

Graen, G., Orris, J., & Johnson, T. (1973). Role assimilation in a complex organization. *Journal of Vocational Behavior, 3*, 395–420.

Graen, G. B., & Scandura, T. A. (1987). Toward a psychology of dyadic organizing. *Research in Organizational Behavior, 9*, 175–208.

Greene, C. N., & Organ, D. W. (1973). An evaluation of causal models linking the received role with job satisfaction. *Administrative Science Quarterly, 18*(1), 95–103.

Gross, N. C., Mason, W. S., & McEachern, A. W. (1958). *Explorations in role analysis*. New York: John Wiley & Sons.

Hardy, M. E. (1987). *Role theory*. New York: Appleton-Century-Croft.

Hoy, W., & Miskel, C. (1991). *Educational administration: Theory, research, and practice* (4th ed.). New York: McGraw-Hill.

Hurrell, J. J., Nelson, D. L., & Simmons, B. L. (1998). Measuring job stressors and strains: Where have we been, where are we, and where do we need to go? *Journal of Occupational Health Psychology, 3*, 368–389.

Huxham, C., & Vangen S. (2000). Ambiguity, complexity, and dynamics of the members of collaborations. *Human Relations, 53*(6), 771–806.

Ivancevi, J. M., & Donnelly, J. H. (1974). Study of role clarity and the need for clarity for three occupational groups. *Academy of Management Journal, 17*(1), 28–36.

Jackson, S. W., & Schuler, R. S. (1985). A meta-analysis and conceptual critique of research on role ambiguity and role conflict. *Organizational Behavior and Human Decision Processes, 36*, 66–78.

Johnsrud, L. (1993). Women and minority faculty experiences: Defining and responding to diverse realities. *New Directions for Teaching and Learning, 53*, 3–16.

Kahn, R. L., Wolfe, D. M., Quinn, R. P., & Snoek, J. D. (1964). *Organizational stress: Studies in role conflict and ambiguity*. Malabar, FL: Krieger Publishing.

Katz, D., & Kahn, R. (1978). *The social psychology of organizations* (2nd ed.). New York: John Wiley & Sons.

Kelloway, E. K., & Day, A. L. (2005). Building healthy workplaces: What we know so far. *Canadian Journal of Behavioural Science, 34*(4), 223–235.

Kemery, E. R., Bedeian, A. G., Mossholder, K. W., & Touliatos, J. (1985). Outcomes of role stress: A multisample constructive replication. *Academy of Management Journal, 28*(2), 363–375.

King, L. A., & King, D. W. (1990). Role conflict and role ambiguity: A critical assessment of construct validity. *Psychological Bulletin, 107*, 48–64.

Kumar, E. S. (1997). Development of a measure of role conflict. *International Journal of Conflict Management, 8*(3), 187–215.

Liddell, W. W., & Slocum, J. W. (1976). Effects of individual-role compatibility upon group performance: Extension of Schultz's FIRO theory. *Academy of Management Journal, 19*(3), 413–426.

Lindholm, J. (2003). Perceived organizational fit: Nurturing the minds, hearts, and personal ambitions of university faculty. *Review of Higher Education, 27*(1), 125–149.

Linton, R. (1936). *The study of man.* New York: Appleton-Century.

Martin, J. (1990). Deconstructing organizational taboos: Suppression of gender conflict in organizations. *Organizational Science, 1*, 339–359.

Merton, R. (1957). *Social theory and social structure* (rev. ed.). Glencoe, IL: The Free Press.

Miles, R. H., & Perreault, W. D., Jr. (1982). Organizational role conflict: Its antecedents and consequences. In D. Katz, R. L. Kahn, & J. S. Adams (Eds.), *The study of organizations* (pp. 136–156). San Francisco: Jossey-Bass.

Mintzberg, H. (1979). *The structuring of organizations.* Englewood Cliffs, NJ: Prentice-Hall.

Mintzberg, H. (1983a). *Structure in fives: Designing effective organizations.* Englewood Cliffs, NJ: Prentice-Hall.

Mintzberg, H. (1983b). *Power in and around the organization.* Englewood Cliffs, NJ: Prentice-Hall.

Montez, J., Wolverton, M., & Gmelch, W. (2003). The roles and challenges of deans. *Review of Higher Education, 26*(2), 241–266.

Montgomery, J. D. (2000). The self as a fuzzy set of roles, role theory as a fuzzy system. *Sociological Methodology, 30*(17), 261–314.

Naylor, J. C., Pritchard, R. D., & Ilgen, D. (1980). *A theory of behavior in organizations.* New York: Academic Press.

O'Meara, K. (2005). Encouraging multiple forms of scholarship in faculty reward systems: Does it make a difference? *Research in Higher Education, 46*(5), 479–510.

Orton, J., & Weick, K. (1990). Loosely coupled systems: A reconceptualization. *Academy of Management Review, 15*(2), 203–223.

Parsons, T. (1951). *The social system.* Glencoe, IL: The Free Press.

Parsons, T. (1960). *Structure and process in modern societies.* Glencoe, IL: The Free Press.

Raffel, S. (1999). Revisiting role theory: Roles and the problem of self. *Sociology Research Online, 4*(2), Y119–Y134.

Rangarajan, D., Chonko, L. B., Jones, E., & Roberts, J. A. (2004). Organizational variables, sales force perceptions of readiness for change, learning, and performance among boundary-spanning teams: A conceptual framework and propositions for research. *Industrial Marketing Management, 33*(4), 289–305.

Rice, R. E., Sorcinelli, M. D., & Austin, A. E. (2000). *Heeding new voices: Academic careers for a new generation.* New Pathways Working Paper Series, Inquiry #7. Washington, DC: American Association for Higher Education.

Rizzo, J. R., House, R. J., & Lirtzman, S. I. (1970). Role conflict and ambiguity in complex organizations. *Administrative Science Quarterly, 15,* 150–163.

Roos, L. L., & Starke, F. A. (1981). Organizational roles. In P. C. Nystrom & W. H. Starbuck (Eds.), *Handbook of organizational design* (vol. 1, pp. 290–308). New York: Oxford University Press.

Sarbin, T. R., & Allen, V. L. (1968). Role theory. In G. Lindzey and E. Aronson (Eds.) *The handbook of social psychology* (vol. 1, pp. 223–258). Reading, MA: Addison-Wesley.

Sawyer, J. E. (1992). Goal and process clarity: Specification of multiple constructs of role ambiguity and a structural equation model of their antecedents and consequences. *Journal of Applied Psychology, 77,* 130–142.

Schuler, R. S. (1975). Role perceptions, satisfaction, and performance: A partial reconciliation. *Journal of Applied Psychology, 60,* 683–687.

Schuler, R. S. (1977). Role perceptions, satisfaction, and performance moderated by organizational level and participation in decision-making. *Academy of Management Journal, 20*(1), 159–165.

Singh, J. (1998). Striking a balance in boundary-spanning positions: An investigation of some unconventional influences of role stressors and job characteristics on job outcomes of sales people. *Journal of Marketing, 62*(3), 69–86.

Starbuck, W. (1976). Organizations and their environments. In M. D. Dunnette (Ed.), *Handbook of industrial and organizational psychology* (pp. 1069–1123). Chicago: Rand McNally.

Thompson, D. P., McNamara, J. F., & Hoyle, J. R. (1997). Job satisfaction in educational organizations: A synthesis of research findings. *Educational Administration Quarterly, 33*(1), 7–37.

Tidd, S. T., & Friedman, R. A. (2002). Conflict style and coping with role conflict: An extension of the uncertainty model of work stress. *International Journal of Conflict Management, 13*(3), 236–257.

Tierney, W., & Bensimon, E. (1996). *Promotion and tenure: Community and socialization in academe.* Albany, NY: State University of New York Press.

Tierney, W., & Rhoads, R. (1994). *Faculty socialization as cultural process: A mirror of institutional commitment.* ASHE-ERIC Higher Education Report No. 93–6. Washington, DC: The George Washington University.

Tubre, T. C., Sifferman, J. J., & Collins, J. M. (1996, November 4). *Jackson and Schuler (1985) revisited: A meta-analytic review of the relationship between role stress and job performance.* Unpublished paper, Texas A & M University.

Turner, C. S., & Myers, S. L. (2000). *Faculty of color in academe: Bittersweet success.* Des Moines, IA: Longwood Division, Allyn and Bacon.

Van Maanen, J. (1976). Breaking in: Socialization to work. In R. Dubin (Ed.), *Handbook of work, organization, and society* (pp. 67–130). Chicago: Rand McNally College Publishing.

Welbourne, T., Johnson, D., & Erez, A. (1998). The role-based performance scale: Validity analysis of a theory-based measure. *Academy of Management Journal, 41*(5), 540–555.

Whetten, D. A. (1978). Coping with incompatible expectations: An integrated view of role conflict. *Administrative Science Quarterly, 23*(2), 254–271.

Znaniecki, F. (1967). *The laws of social psychology.* New York: Russell & Russell.

9

MOTIVATION IN THE HIGHER EDUCATION WORKPLACE

CONTENTS

The authors are most grateful for the critical comments on an early draft of this chapter by Charles Walker, St. Bonaventure University. The final version, of course, is our own and may or may not reflect the perspective of the reviewer.

Preview

- Motivating organizational members in colleges and universities has recently been receiving increasing attention as institutions seek to maximize output in the face of reduced budgets.
- Motivation theories applied to organizations have traditionally been classified into need theories and process theories, but new approaches have been introduced in recent years.
- Abraham Maslow offered one need theory, widely cited today, which suggests a hierarchy of prepotent needs guides behavior.
- Individuals vary in their needs for achievement; hence, managers must carefully calculate the kinds of incentives that will best accommodate the differences among organizational members.
- Human beings can be both satisfied and dissatisfied at the same time. The elements in the work environment that lead to satisfaction are substantively different from those that contribute to dissatisfaction.
- While some theories of motivation suggest that need satisfaction proceeds upward through a hierarchy, with each satisfied need "releasing" the next higher need, other theorists suggest that when there are few opportunities for the higher need to be satisfied, individuals regress to lower need satisfaction priorities.
- Not all human behavior is driven by unconscious needs or drives. Indeed, in considering how much effort to expend at work, organizational members often take into account their perceived ability to perform a task, the likelihood of a reward following from successful completion of the task, and the desirability of the reward.
- Organizational members almost invariably set goals for themselves that are based on the difficulty of the work and their sense of self-efficacy and on how they perceive others doing similar work.
- Workers become less motivated when they believe that the rewards for the work they are doing are less than the rewards received by colleagues for doing the same or similar work or when they sense that colleagues are expending less energy to obtain the same rewards.
- In addition to needs, psychological states are also potential motivators. These states are determined by an array of job characteristics. Each job has a strong or weak motivating potential, depending on how the work is designed.

———————————————— CASE CONTEXT ————————————————

Motivation in the Sierra State University Library

Sierra State University, a large public Hispanic-serving institution (HSI), had experienced significant enrollment growth over the previous two decades. Under the state's formula funding system—based in large part on enrollment—revenues to Sierra State had been increasing. A severe economic recession and a change in power in the governor's office, however, generated a series of budget cuts. The new governor campaigned on improving K–12 education and could not politically afford to slash that sector of the budget, so the public higher education sector, including Sierra State, received a disproportionately large cut in state funding. These cuts were beginning to affect the core units of the university, including the library.

Dan Rodriguez, the library director at Sierra State, removed his glasses and rubbed his eyes. He had spent a long evening reviewing the annual reports produced by the library department heads, and he came to a realization that morale was dangerously low. The library had experienced three consecutive years of budget cuts, and the diminished resources were taking a toll on the staff.

To cut costs, the number of circulation and reserves staff was cut by 30% through attrition and early retirements. The remaining staff members were compelled to assume additional responsibilities with few prospects for promotion or pay raises. Initially, the staff expressed a willingness to "pitch in" and work extra hours to address the needs of students and faculty. However, after nearly three years of retrenchment, staff members were beginning to demonstrate signs of dissatisfaction and demoralization. Rates of absenteeism were creeping up, and the quality of work had begun to decline.

In another bleak report, the head of the collections department summarized a litany of faculty complaints regarding the paucity of books and journals in their respective fields of study. Not only were funds limited for collection development, but due to personnel reductions, collections staff were no longer afforded time to meet with academic departments regarding their curricular and research needs. "We feel like glorified acquisitions clerks," reported one collections staff member. "We could make significant contributions by helping the academic departments think about their collections needs, but we are told that we should spend our time elsewhere." Moreover, collections staff have not been provided with any professional development funds for the previous three years. The head of the collections department reported that she lost two talented staff members to other universities that offered them better prospects for professional development and advancement. There were also rumors that the head of collections herself would leave the university. Apparently, she had expressed displeasure that her salary and benefits were lower than those of the head of library information technology (IT).

The IT staff, however, had their own set of concerns. They felt that other units in the library treated them with resentment. Information technology was a relatively new addition to the library, and other units openly expressed concern that resources were being siphoned off to support IT. As a result, the IT staff reported a chilly work climate. Library staff in other units did not socialize with IT staff, and the heads of the other library departments often neglected to inform the IT staff of library-wide social events. The IT director reported that her staff felt no sense of belonging to the library; they felt as if they were "outsiders."

Introduction

Higher education leaders must address the needs of a wide variety of organizational members at different levels of skill and maturity and with diverse roles and responsibilities. Understanding and accounting for these needs helps leaders identify strategies that not only may improve the effectiveness and efficiency of college and university organizations, but also enhance the quality of life for organizational members.

Research has demonstrated a significant relationship between the strength of individual motivation and the quality and quantity of organizational outputs (Harter & Schmidt, 2000; Harter, Schmidt, & Hayes, 2002). A central challenge for leaders at every level in institutions of higher education, therefore, is to find ways to enhance and sustain the motivation of staff and faculty members to pursue both organizational and individual goals under varying circumstances.

External stakeholders also have concerns about work motivation in colleges and universities. As one example, external stakeholders may question the policy of granting tenure to faculty, with its virtual guarantee of lifetime employment, on the grounds that it is alleged to protect "dead wood" faculty who are no longer producing at the highest level.

Motivation Defined

The idea of motivation stems in part from the Latin word for movement—*movere*. It is an intangible force that impels an individual to act in certain ways with varying modes, strength, and duration (Atkinson, 1964; Goddard,

Hoy, & Hoy, 2004). Motivation thus produces effort. Usually, the higher the motivation, the greater the effort. In addition, when people are motivated, they tend to persist longer in their efforts.

Others suggest that motivation refers to the sensation of a "gap," the filling of which is emotionally satisfying. The force may be conscious or unconscious, general or specific to a situation (usually both). It can be generated or stimulated by conditions outside the individual (extrinsic motivation) or by internal factors (intrinsic motivation). **Extrinsic motivation** is based on rewards that may be expected from external sources (e.g., pay, promotion, recognition) and on anticipated sanctions that can dissuade people from engaging in certain behaviors. In contrast, **intrinsic motivation** is based on expected cognitive and noncognitive rewards and satisfactions from performing the activity itself without reference to external incentives. The external and internal stimuli frequently interact and collectively result in psychological (cognitive or affective) states and/or physical movements that lead to major or minor transformations in the individual. In other words, combinations and permutations of both internal and external phenomena combine to propel human action (Mone & Kelly, 1994).

In this chapter, we explore a number of ways of understanding what motivates human beings in general and individuals specifically. In the discussion of each of the motivation theories considered in this chapter, we identify both internal and external stimuli and the results of their interaction on individual behavior.

Motivation Applied to Behavior in Organizations

How much does motivation affect levels of performance? Research shows that if a person wants to stay employed and is willing to do the required *minimum* effort, more motivation can increase performance by only about 9%. (The correlation between motivation and performance has been calculated to be about .30 [Kast & Rosenzweig, 1979, p. 251]). It appears obvious that much more than motivation alone accounts for achievement on the job. Other factors, such as ability, quality of equipment used, and the inputs of other people, must be taken into account. This is especially true with tasks that involve other organizational members (i.e., interdependence through sequential or reciprocal linkages).

While it might seem that an increase in performance of only 9% would be a relatively minor improvement, two factors argue for the importance of understanding motivation. One is that the expenditure of maximum effort by workers has important repercussions on other variables. For example, improved performance may have a positive effect on organizational morale and may reduce levels of absenteeism and turnover. The other factor is that a 9%

gain in performance may make the difference between high-quality and low-quality output. It is just that "extra effort" that yields excellent rather than just acceptable results.

Free Will

It is important to make explicit at the outset a set of assumptions about theories of motivation and human nature—broad and conceptual ideas about the range of possibilities for understanding individuals' interactions with their environments. In our discussion, we consider whether an individual is truly "free" to be an active agent determining his or her own destiny. One view, a "constraint" perspective, suggests that the environment outside of individuals severely limits their ability to make decisions that contravene social and cultural dictates. The constraint perspective also suggests that another set of limits lies *within* the individual. For example, innate, subconscious needs may constitute such powerful drives that conscious resistance is not possible. In both cases, freedom to determine one's own actions does not appear to be possible. The first constraint says that individuals generally must follow the expectations of other persons and groups in their environments or they lose out in the competitive search for sustained supportive inputs (e.g., salary, promotions, professional advancement). The second constraint says that individuals must accommodate their behavior to their essential inner identity and psychological core or suffer a disruption of their internal balance (e.g., stress, dissatisfaction, depression).

Such theories of motivation, however, are quite deterministic. They suggest that either basic innate drives direct people toward certain behaviors, or the environment prescribes a set of behaviors that people are compelled to carry out. In response, cognitive psychologists have introduced notions of competence, intrinsic motivation, self-determination, and optimal experience in studies of individual motivation. **Agency** theorists have opened up the arena for discussions of how people engage in consequential actions that deviate from the status quo. These approaches argue that people have at least some **free will** and can take action on their own behalf through a conscious appraisal of the benefits to both their psyches and their social situations. For example, Deci and Ryan (1985) note:

> Motivation theories are built on a set of assumptions about the nature of people and about the factors that give impetus to action. These assumptions, and the theories that follow from them, can be viewed as falling along a descriptive continuum ranging from the mechanistic to the organismic. *Mechanistic* theories tend to view the human organism as passive, that is, as being pushed around by the interaction of physiological drives

and environmental stimuli, whereas *organismic* [emphasis in the original] theories tend to view the organism as active, that is, as being volitional and initiating behaviors. According to the latter perspective, organisms have intrinsic needs and physiological drives, and these intrinsic needs provide energy for the organisms to act on (rather than simply to be reactive to) the environment and to manage aspects of their drives and emotions. The active-organism view treats stimuli not as causes of behavior, but as affordances or opportunities that the organism can utilize in satisfying its needs. (pp. 3–4)

Our perspective in this chapter is consistent with the organismic perspective. In organizational settings, people are typically able to exercise some degree of active choice; they are not simply cogs in a machine. Even in a bureaucracy, organizational members can actively shape their work context (Blau, 1955). Thus, most theories of work motivation assume that organizational members are, to some extent, acting on intrinsic needs and drives that provide energy for behavior, or they are acting on cognitive perceptions of the work environment and making somewhat calculated decisions regarding where to invest their energies. In the following sections, we examine two categories of motivation theory:

1. **need theories** (sometimes characterized as theories of arousal), which emphasize inner forces that impel behavior
2. **process theories,** which recognize the role of cognition in motivation and focus more on the interaction of external and internal forces

Need Theories

Psychologists generally agree that individual needs are a force emanating from inside a person and that they create a tension when they are not met through some type of action. The particular need orients the person toward certain actions, impels a level of effort, and sustains the efforts generated. Four key theories or schools of thought in the need theory category are applicable to higher education: (1) Maslow's hierarchy of needs, (2) McClelland's need for achievement theory, (3) Herzberg's two-factor theory, and (4) Alderfer's reconceptualization of Maslow's need theory.

Maslow's Hierarchy of Needs

Abraham Maslow, whose need theory we examine first, was a giant in the early days of motivation theory development, and his theory is widely cited today, largely because it is intuitively convincing. There has been relatively little empirical confirmation or validation of the theory, however, and, indeed, some disconfirmation (Wahba & Bridwell, 1976). Yet, it is useful to explore how Maslow's hypotheses may help explain behavior in colleges and universities.

Central to Maslow's theory are the notions that:

1. Each person is a "wanting animal."
2. Each person is rarely completely satisfied except for short periods. As soon as one desire is satisfied, another is activated.
3. "[H]uman needs are organized into a hierarchy of relative prepotency" (Maslow, 1943, p. 375).

In other words, the satisfaction of each need forms the foundation for the emergence of the next, more prepotent need. Thus, "gratification becomes as important a concept as deprivation in motivation theory, for it releases the organism from the domination of" lower needs (p. 375).

In Maslow's theory, a gratified need "releases" the individual from the domination of more basic, even physiological, needs, allowing for the arousal of those of a higher order, such as those connected with social goals. As we look at faculty, staff, and administrator motivation in colleges and universities, it is useful to identify the need levels that are salient and those that have been frustrated, since from an organizational perspective, more effective behavior will be forthcoming when workers are offered opportunities to address higher-order needs.

To see how the hierarchy organizes human needs, it is necessary to have a more extended definition of the basic needs in Maslow's theory. They appear below (and in Figure 9.1), abbreviated from Maslow's richer description:

Physiological needs are basic human physical needs, such as for food, clothing, sleep, and shelter. Most of these needs usually are not the direct concern of college and university management as it is assumed that these needs have been largely fulfilled outside of work settings. Most workers in colleges and universities do not come to their jobs hungry and cold. However, the life circumstances of the institution's lowest-paid workers, such as cafeteria workers and cleaning staff, induce some, though unfortunately not all, institutions to take actions (e.g., living wage initiatives) that address the unmet basic physiological needs of employees.

Safety needs are for continuity from day to day and for protection against danger and threat. They represent a "preference for some kind of undisputed routine or rhythm . . . a predictable, orderly world" (Maslow, 1970, p. 86), especially one that is relatively free of arbitrary unanticipated deprivation. In a peacetime society, most individuals can enjoy a high degree

FIGURE 9.1
Maslow's Hierarchy of Needs

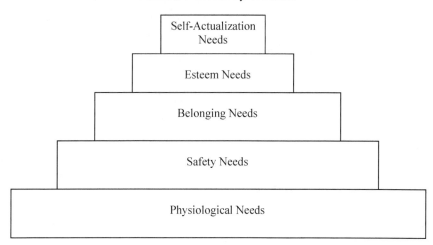

of freedom from fear of physical harm. In work situations, however, where arbitrary or capricious behavior, intentional or unintentional, is part of management practice, organizational members may find their work lives full of uncertainty (e.g., concern about whether their jobs will be eliminated).

Belonging and social needs are those needs that people have for social relationships, acceptance by peers and supervisors, and opportunities to give and receive friendship and love. Organizational leaders may underestimate the importance of the work setting to address these needs.

Esteem needs comprise two sets of needs in Maslow's scheme—self-esteem and esteem from others. He says: "There are, first, the desire for strength, for achievement, for adequacy, for mastery and competence, for confidence in the face of the world, and for independence and freedom. Second, we have what we may call the desire for reputation or prestige (defining it as respect or esteem from other people), status, dominance, recognition, attention, importance or appreciation" (Maslow, 1970, p. 90).

Self-actualization needs refer to the desire to achieve one's full potential. Satisfaction of these needs results in independent, autonomous, self-sufficient, self-accepting, and realistically perceptive individuals. Self-actualized people are also more spontaneous and creative. Satisfaction is dependent largely on a person's own resources rather than on other people. Organizations can, however, contribute to satisfying these needs by providing challenging opportunities for psychological growth, creativity, and personal satisfaction.

Maslow recognized that these are not all of a man's[1] needs, though they are the most basic. He also postulated that there are impulses to satisfy curiosity, to know, to explain, and to understand. This set of cognitive needs forms another hierarchy, but in Maslow's conceptualization, it is subordinate to the hierarchy of basic needs. That is, the basic needs must be met first, before people can satisfy their cognitive needs. This also applies to needs for order, symmetry, closure, structure, and aesthetic experiences—each of which is subordinate to the hierarchy of basic needs. For comparison, consider another list of basic needs provided by Michael Maccoby (1988) in Table 9.1.

Certain characteristics separate Maslow's basic need hierarchy into **higher and lower needs**. For example, individuals choose the stronger lower need when two needs are frustrated. Second, the higher needs develop more fully later in life. Third, the higher the need, the longer the gratification can be postponed without destruction of the person's psychological well-being.

In later writings, Maslow came to think of higher and lower needs in terms of growth and deficiency. The lower needs are essentially "empty holes" that must be filled up to maintain the individual's health. These, then, are deficits, or **deficiency needs**. **Growth needs**, on the other hand, describe the lifelong dynamic processes leading ultimately to self-actualization. A faculty member, for example, who is motivated largely to satisfy her lower-order needs is thus deficiency motivated, while another faculty member who has had her safety, belonging, and respect needs at least partially satisfied, exhibits behavior that is growth motivated.

TABLE 9.1
Eight Value Drives in the Workplace*

Value Drives	*Examples*
Survival	sustenance, nutrition
Relatedness	attachment, care
Pleasure	comfort, sex
Information	sensory stimulation, knowledge
Mastery	competence, control
Play	exploration, fantasy
Dignity	respect, self-esteem
Meaning	universal, cultural, individual

*Source: Maccoby, 1988.

1. Maslow used the male personal pronoun and has been accused of being sexist in his understanding of human motivation. We use "man" here to reflect his theory, but see the criticism of Glazer (1997) and the alternative theories of motivation voiced by Gilligan (1982) and Belenky, Clinchy, Goldberger, & Tarule (1986).

As noted above, in the Maslow schema, the satisfaction of lower needs is a prerequisite to the activation of the higher needs. The hierarchy, however, is not fixed invariably for all people. Some are able to sublimate some of the lower needs; others, through continual environmental deadening of their ambition and hope, have been conditioned to lower their levels of aspiration and are satisfied mostly by the lower needs—that is, they never release the energies of their higher needs. However, the lower needs do not have to be satisfied completely for the higher needs to emerge.

In fact, most people's basic needs are partially satisfied and partially unsatisfied at the same time. A more realistic description of the hierarchy would be in terms of decreasing percentages of satisfaction as an individual moves up the **hierarchy of prepotency**. Further, the emergence of a new need after satisfaction of a lower-order need is not sudden and disconnected, but rather a gradual emergence by slow degrees (Maslow, 1970).

Do satisfied organizational members work harder or more creatively? Or does satisfaction diminish the drive for continued or new satisfactions? It depends on which needs are satisfied. If the organization provides conditions that satisfy lower-level needs, but not those that address upper-level needs, then workers are unlikely to see the organization as worth working hard for. In terms of effective and efficient organizational functioning, several underlying, but unstated, hypotheses in Maslow's hierarchical framework are as follows. First, there is an intimate connection between human fulfillment and a fully functioning organization. Second, workers whose deficiency needs are satisfied are freed to be more creative and, in addressing their growth needs, are more likely to work hard.

Important policy and management implications can be drawn from these conclusions (Maslow & Kaplan, 1998). Understanding human motivation can contribute at the macro level to more efficient organizational design and at the individual level to greater effort and more satisfaction. Using Maslow, we can reason that since motivation is derived from the strength of needs, if we can identify the need level at which a person is operating, we can better look to the sources of that motivation. In a college or university, if we see a faculty member who persistently complains about inadequate heat, poor lighting, and difficult working conditions—that is, about safety needs—it is probably unfair to judge his or her unsatisfactory work solely as a personal failure, because the worker may have been forced by organizational conditions to operate at the safety level, never being able psychologically to rise to higher levels.

Need for Achievement

The second of the need theories to be discussed is the theory of **need for achievement** of McClelland (1971) and others (McClelland & Burnham,

1976; Sagie & Elizur, 1996). High levels of need for achievement are characterized by:

1. a strong desire to assume personal responsibility for finding solutions to problems,
2. a tendency to set moderately difficult achievement goals and take calculated risks,
3. a strong desire for concrete feedback on task performance, and
4. a single-minded preoccupation with task and task accomplishment.

Low need for achievement, on the other hand, is typically characterized by a preference for low risk levels and shared responsibility on tasks (Steers & Black, 1994).

Achievement motivation is stored in the mind, rather than openly manifested. Often people are not aware of their feelings about achievement. Indeed, organizational leaders may be able to help individuals become more achievement motivated via counseling in the workplace. Self-motivated high achievers prefer challenges and like to set their own goals. They also typically prefer moderate challenges over others that may lead to failure. Immediate feedback is important to sustaining the motivation of workers with high need for achievement. Note the contrast with Maslow, who suggested that the higher the need level that is motivating a person, the longer gratification (e.g., positive feedback) can be delayed.

Managers seeking to improve the performance of organizational members by enriching jobs with more challenge, variety, and responsibility must recognize that these incentives may work only for people who already demonstrate high levels of need for achievement. Further, organizational leaders should seek the optimum amount of challenge for members with different levels of motivation (Csikszentmihalyi, 1990).

Needs and Satisfaction: Two-Factor Theory

Whereas Maslow's and McClelland's need theories concentrated on direct assessments of need/drive strength, other research on motivation in organizations yielded quite a different theory. Herzberg (1968) and his colleagues used a "critical incident method" to assess motivation.[2] They asked workers to describe incidents that were essentially satisfying or resulted in marked improvement in their satisfactions. They then asked the same workers to report other incidents that resulted in a decrease in satisfaction. The incidents

---

2. Many critics of Herzberg's theory believe that the method itself may have biased the results. Other research methods have often failed to confirm the two factors; see House and Wigdor (1967) and Phillipchuk and Whittaker (1996).

were then content analyzed (i.e., scrutinized for common responses). Herzberg, Mausner, and Snyderman (1959) found that the kinds of incidents identified in response to the second prompt differed markedly from those in response to the first. The reported incidents that were said to have led to satisfaction were related to achievement, recognition, the work itself, responsibility, and advancement. Herzberg called these **motivators** (also known as intrinsic factors).

On the other hand, incidents reported by workers that were related to their *dissatisfactions* were interpersonal relations with subordinates or supervisors, technical supervision (e.g., by a dean or department head), administrative policies (e.g., working on Saturdays), working conditions (e.g., too hot), and personal life (health). Herzberg and colleagues called these **hygienes** (also known as extrinsic factors). The origin of this term is intriguing; it is a medical metaphor. "Although hygiene is very important in preventing serious infection, hygiene alone typically does not produce a cure just as hygiene factors alone cannot produce high levels of satisfaction" (Hoy & Miskel, 2005, p. 132).

The conclusion of Herzberg, Mausner, and Snyderman: the elements in the work environment that satisfy a person are not the same as those that dissatisfy a person (Figure 9.2). Rather than one continuum that runs from highly satisfied to highly dissatisfied, there are actually two continua: one for recording the strength of motivators (satisfaction continuum) and one for assessing the value of hygiene factors (dissatisfaction continuum).

FIGURE 9.2
Herzberg's Two-Factor Theory*

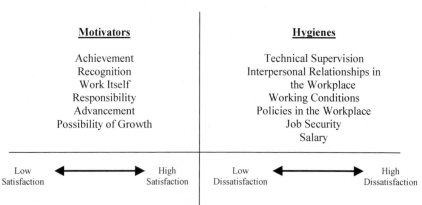

*Adapted from Herzberg, Mausner, and Snyderman, 1959.

The leadership and policy implications that follow from these findings are important. If institutions of higher education focus on providing conditions in the work environment that fall into the second category (hygienes), then the *most* benefit that can result is the *prevention* of worker dissatisfaction. It is not possible to engender satisfaction with these elements.

As a practical example, let us consider student affairs professionals. According to two-factor theory, such organizational members will not be satisfied with their work no matter how well they get along with supervisors, no matter how clear their roles are specified, and no matter how comfortable their offices. Provision of these conditions will probably remove dissatisfaction, but it will not motivate these workers. Instead, satisfaction and motivation can be enhanced when student affairs professionals receive recognition for their work with students, when they are given responsibility for high-profile projects, and when the work itself is enjoyable and stimulating. Similarly, investments in professional development activities are likely to simulate personal growth and strengthen satisfaction.

Similarities Between Maslow and Herzberg

It appears that Herzberg's satisfiers are similar to Maslow's esteem and self-actualization needs, while the dissatisfiers are comparable to Maslow's lower-order needs. In other words, Herzberg's motivators are roughly comparable to Maslow's growth needs, and his hygienes are more comparable to Maslow's deficiency needs. Herzberg, however, posited no necessary *hierarchy* of needs. Two-factor theory does not suggest that dissatisfaction must be addressed before satisfaction. For Herzberg, a person can be *both satisfied and dissatisfied at the same time*. This finding is critical to understanding the different sources of job satisfaction and dissatisfaction.

Ambients

A great deal of empirical research on two-factor theory has been reported in the literature. Some of it suggests that certain factors in the worker's environment may contribute to *both* the removal of dissatisfactions *and* to the improvement of satisfactions. These aspects of the environment, called **ambients** (Hackman, 1992), are mentioned equally as often as satisfiers and dissatisfiers. Salary, growth possibility, risk opportunity, relationships with coworkers, and status are examples of such stimuli. The reason for this ambiguity of motivational status—hygiene or motivator—is that different people place different values on different aspects of the work situation, particularly as their personal life circumstances change. A person at an early career stage may value salary differently from someone who is sending children to college. In this case, the person with significant financial obligations may view salary as both a hygiene factor and a motivator.

Satisfaction, Motivation, and Performance

We now examine an important hypothesis in two-factor theory—namely, the more satisfied a worker is, the more effort he or she will exert and, therefore, the better off the organization will be. This theory hypothesizes that people experience a "high" or "pleasure" from a satisfying experience. Like a drug "fix," it is a satisfaction fix. They then need to continue the habit. Hypothetically, the greater the satisfaction, the greater the motivation. But a competing hypothesis may also be true, namely: the more satisfaction, the *less* a person feels inclined to work. Some may say, for example, "My output is good enough, and I have sufficient rewards; I don't need any more." As the old saying goes, contented cows work only up to a point and no more. This is still an open question in organizational theory. Most empirical evidence suggests that more satisfaction produces only minimal amounts of additional effort. Studies have found only small correlation coefficients: $+.14$ (Vroom, 1964) and $+.17$ (Ostroff, 1992).

There is, however, a difference between the motivation to *produce* and the motivation to *participate* in an organization (March & Simon, 1958). Satisfied workers may, after all, stay longer in their organizations (Rosser, 2004), even if they do not produce more. In the long run, this longevity will decrease the costs of recruiting and training new employees.

ERG Theory

A major revision of Maslow's theory has been developed by Clayton Alderfer (1972), who claims that there are only three (not five) basic sets of needs: (E) existence—physiological, physical, safety, working conditions; (R) relatedness—interpersonal relationships with coworkers, friends, and family; and (G) growth—freedom for personal development, self-esteem, and self-actualization. Alderfer, like Maslow, found empirical evidence that satisfaction of *lower-order* needs led to a diminution in their strength. People then begin to work on the next highest level need. Unlike Maslow, who suggested that satisfied needs diminish in their motivating power, Alderfer found that the lack of satisfaction of *higher-order* needs often led to a *return* to a concern for the satisfaction of lower-level needs—in other words, to a resumption of strength of the lower need. He called this the **frustration-regression** hypothesis. For example, if faculty members' growth needs are frustrated by lack of professional development opportunities, then needs for relatedness (i.e., good relations with colleagues) become more important to these faculty members. Conceivably, however, the increased emphasis on social relationships could divert attention from producing high-quality work.

Alderfer discovered that a frustrated higher-level need may not continue to be a motivator despite satisfaction of lower needs; the higher-level need may be extinguished. Alderfer puts a limit on how long a person will continue to stand for the frustration of a higher need. For him, despite the satisfaction of a lower need, if the next-highest-level need continues to be frustrated, at some point it will *not* serve as a motivator, no matter how well lower needs have been satisfied. For example, a faculty member may give up on prospects for attaining a high level of professional growth after years of frustration. Table 9.2 displays the relationships among frustrated needs, need strength, and need satisfaction.

Different implications for leadership follow from the adoption of Maslow, Herzberg, or Alderfer. If we believe Maslow, it is necessary to provide means for satisfying deficiency needs so that organizational members can be motivated at higher levels. If a leader sees an unmotivated person, then he or she would attempt to understand where *lower* needs are not being satisfied. For example, a manager may need to attend to a new employee's need for belonging, so that higher-order needs such as esteem and self-actualization can be fulfilled later. Following Alderfer, the lack of motivation could be attributed to this same absence of support for lower-level need satisfaction, but also to conditions that cause frustration of upper-level needs. Colleges and universities are challenged to provide ongoing professional development opportunities for all stages of the career, so that mid- and late-career faculty and staff do not become frustrated in their attempts to attain a high level of professional growth. Finally, if Herzberg's two-factor theory is used, hygienic needs are unrelated to motivators. The cause of an unmotivated worker, therefore, lies only in the absence of conditions providing for motivation. As such, organizational leaders should provide opportunities for achievement, recognition, meaningful work, responsibility, and advancement.

TABLE 9.2
ERG Model*

Needs	Level of Frustration	Level of Strength	Level of Satisfaction
Growth	Frustration of Growth Needs	Importance of Growth Needs	Satisfaction of Growth Needs
Relatedness	Frustration of Relatedness Needs	Importance of Relatedness Needs	Satisfaction of Relatedness Needs
Existence	Frustration of Existence Needs	Importance of Existence Needs	Satisfaction of Existence Needs

*Based on Landy, 1989.

As organizational members in colleges and universities perform their work tasks, they move up and down the hierarchies of need and may experience both satisfaction and dissatisfaction in their jobs. The critical value of these theories, no matter which one is used, is that they force a careful focus on needs and identify the potential sources of satisfaction or frustration of those needs. Understanding behavior in organizations is difficult, but the availability of alternative perspectives on human needs gives the careful observer a number of tools for explanation.

Process Theories

We now turn to process theories, which assume that human motivation involves to some extent the cognitive processes of which human beings are aware, rather than unconscious universalistic sets of needs. They introduce, in addition, modes of considering the more idiosyncratic needs of individuals. Finally, process theories address more concretely than do need theories the ways in which internal needs and cognitions interact with external circumstances. In this set of theories, we examine expectancy theory, goal theory, equity theory, and job characteristics theory.

Expectancy Theory

Expectancy theory suggests that cognition and rationality play important motivating roles in inducing high or low levels of work involvement. If workers *consciously* recognize a reward as both possible and important, they are more likely to work hard toward receiving it (although their effort also depends on the probability of receiving the reward *and* the importance attached to the reward). Empirical studies (Van Eerde & Thierry, 1996) overwhelmingly show that the best performers in organizations tend to connect their own strong job performance, and the probability of receiving rewards that they value, whether those rewards are intrinsic, extrinsic, or a combination.

Earlier proponents of expectancy theory adopted some of the work of Kurt Lewin and Edward Tolman in the 1930s. The origins of the modern theory were developed by Victor Vroom (1964) and later modified by Lyman Porter and Edward Lawler (1968), among others. The theory proposes that there are essentially three cognitive motivators that lead to outcomes such as high or low effort, amount of absenteeism, and quality of work. These variables are: *expectancy*, *instrumentality*, and *valence*. The amount of effort or energy expended by an organizational member can be reasonably predicted from these factors.

Expectancy, the first independent variable, is the organizational member's assessment of the probability that his or her effort will lead to successful performance. (Expectancy is also a function at least in part of a person's feelings of self-efficacy, which have personal historical antecedents; see Bandura, 1977, and Goddard, Hoy, & Hoy, 2004.) The importance of the expectation for a good outcome is a critical feature of the theory. Organizational members make informal judgments about the likelihood that they will be able to do the required work satisfactorily (e.g., complete a project or prepare a budget). Without a great deal of thought, people assign a probability (from 0.0 to 1.0) to their chance for success. For example, a faculty member may expect that if he devotes time to do the research to get a paper in publishable form, there is an 80% chance (.8 probability) that he will be able to write a publishable paper.

Instrumentality, the second independent variable, is the organizational member's assessment of the probability that if the work is done well, rewards or other outcomes are likely to follow. These rewards can take two forms. *Intrinsic rewards* are system inputs generated internally by the individual. For example, good feelings often emerge from competencies exercised well. An enrollment manager may feel good when she sees that a projected target class comes in close to expectation. *Extrinsic rewards* are system inputs generated from beyond the borders of the system (the individual). For example, the potential for a raise, promotion, or recognition can serve as an extrinsic reward that motivates behaviors desired by the organization. Note that some extrinsic rewards may not be received immediately. For example, a promotion or extra compensation can lead to immediate feelings of satisfaction and self-efficacy (Bandura, 1977; Stajkovic & Luthans, 2002) or to yet another promotion or compensation at a later time. Professional workers, such as faculty in higher education, however, tend to find that doing the work itself provides intrinsic satisfactions that often are important in providing a great deal of the needed motivation to work hard and creatively—though, to be sure, professional recognition—an extrinsic satisfaction—is also a motivational factor. Instrumentality, therefore, is concerned with the linkage that a worker sees between performance and the outcomes and rewards likely to be received—both those that are immediate and tangible and those that are intrinsic and/or further in the future.

Valence, the third independent variable, represents the organizational member's appraisal of the attractiveness of the rewards. That is, to what degree does the employee value the reward that is likely to be made available by management (extrinsic reward) or by the work itself (intrinsic reward)? For example, even though an increase in salary may be forthcoming, if an organizational member is independently wealthy, salary increments will not mean much to him or her and are less likely to act as a motivator. Or a person may be aware that successful performance will result in more responsibility, but he may not want more responsibility because of the additional time it will require away from his family. Finally, an organizational member may desire respect from colleagues more than time off or more salary when these rewards are offered.

The equation below demonstrates how the four factors work together:

$$\text{Motivation (effort)} = f \,(\text{Expectancy} \times \text{Sum of}$$
$$[\text{Instrumentalities} \times \text{Valences}])$$

That is, the degree of motivation is a function of a worker's assessment of the probability that he or she will succeed at the task (expectancy) multiplied by the sum of his or her judgments about the organization's record in rewarding good performance (instrumentality). Each of the instrumentalities is also multiplied by the value that the organizational member places on each of those rewards. (The mathematics is not important for our purposes here, but the theory's hypothesized relationships are.)

To illustrate, how much effort (motivation) a computer center supervisor puts into the preparation of a report depends on a number of factors, including personality dispositions (such as need for achievement). It is also a function of her appraisal of the likelihood that she can be successful through her efforts. If she does not believe she can complete the work competently, according to expectancy theory, she will put less effort into it. The effort put into the work is also a function of what she recalls about the results of similar efforts in the past. For example, has the completion of such reports in the past resulted in higher levels of administration support in the form of salary increases and/or promotion? Finally, effort is also a function of whether the supervisor cares about any of the available rewards. If she is really a closet novelist at work at the university just to support herself, none of those rewards may mean much, even if they are perceived to be forthcoming. Hence, they will not motivate her to exert much effort. Table 9.3 illustrates these relationships.

Note that this motivational model does not address questions of quantity or quality of actual performance; it deals only with effort expended. The nature of the final output, however, is a product of more than just effort. It includes variables such as abilities and talents, role clarity, role acceptance, and job conditions (Campbell & Pritchard, 1976).

Goal Theory

In addition to largely unconscious needs and drives, a number of theorists have come to believe that individuals can be active agents in their own behalf

TABLE 9.3
The Expectancy Model

Effort	Expectancy	Instrumentality	Positive Valence of Rewards (examples)
Calculate next year's faculty salary levels Complete the salary report Send to the printer	Perceived probability of successful performance	Perceived probability of receiving a reward for good work	*Intrinsic* Self-confidence Self-esteem Personal happiness *Extrinsic* Increased salary Promotion Approval of peers

on the basis of consciously formulated goals. A goal is "a future state that an individual is striving to attain" (Hoy & Miskel, 2005, p. 137). Goals can guide behavior and define what an individual considers to be acceptable performance. The conscious act of setting a goal also influences how much effort is put into achieving it. Research on the impact of goals and goal setting has demonstrated their influence on motivation (Bargh, 1990; DeShon & Gillespie, 2005).

These and other findings have resulted in the emergence of an important body of motivation theory focusing on goals (Klein, 1991). The theory, most notably put forth by Edwin Locke and Gary Latham (1990), assumes that human beings act purposefully and that their behavior is governed and sustained by goals and intentions. The theory relies on the idea of self-efficacy—the belief of the person in his or her ability to perform a task—similar to the concept of "expectancy" in expectancy theory, discussed above. Motivation follows from a belief in self-efficacy more than on the external rewards that may follow from good performance.

According to this theory, organizational members are motivated to a greater or lesser extent according to the comparisons that they make between the amount of effort and skill the achievement of the goal would require and their assessment of their capacity to meet those requirements. Whether they continue to strive for the goal depends on this comparison. If this comparison reveals that the worker does not possess sufficient capacity to achieve the goal, then the worker will be unlikely to pursue it and, instead, will reevaluate his or her goals and talents.

Higher motivation follows, according to this theory, depending on the following independent variables (see Figure 9.3). The first, *perceived difficulty of the goal*, refers to the organizational member's perception of the magnitude and dimensions of the task to be performed. Clearly, too formidable a task will be demoralizing, while motivation for too easy a task will be inconsistent or low. The second variable is *goal clarity*. For routine, repetitive tasks, clear goals are motivating. In more professional settings such as higher education, however, goals that are too precise may be perceived as limited or unambitious. The third independent variable is the organizational member's sense of *self-efficacy*. A record of achievement of goals of a similar nature will generate a positive self-image and will contribute to a person's motivation to continue to work toward the goal.

The dependent variables in goal theory include focus, effort expended, and persistence at the task. These variables provide a more analytic breakdown of the dependent variable than appeared in expectancy theory—effort or motivation. Here, the dependent variable is disaggregated into three distinct parts.

The relationship between the independent variables (the expectancy box in Figure 9.3) and the dependent variables (the motivation/effort box) is moderated, however, by a number of other variables. That is, other contingencies enter into the equation that may change the impact of the independent variables on the dependent variables. In goal theory, there are four key moderating variables—ability, commitment, feedback, and task complexity. The most important is commitment—the determination to reach the goal. This, in turn, has been shown in empirical research, to be a function of such

FIGURE 9.3
Goal Theory of Motivation*

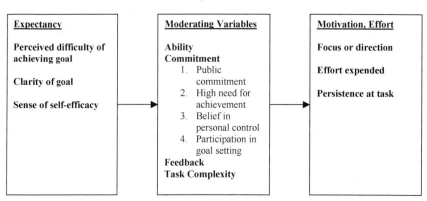

*Based on Locke and Latham, 1990.

things as public statements of commitment, high need for achievement, belief in one's control over the means for achieving the goal, and participation in setting the goal.

These 10 variables in goal theory can be set in hypothetical form. Consider, for example, an admissions director seeking to bring in a high-quality class at targeted levels. Generally, the closer the perceived goal difficulty to optimum levels, the greater the effort. Interfering with these simple relationships, however, are the moderators. So, for example, if the director is *not* committed to the goal, even if it is clear, his effort will not be forthcoming. Even more telling is the following: given circumstances where the director has low ability, the more difficult he perceives the goal to be, the less persistent his expenditure of effort.

Management by objectives (MBO) is a spin-off of goal theory. It is used in direct supervisory relationships where recognition is given to the importance of goals, goal setting, and the clarification by managers of the paths to goal achievement in the motivation of employees.

Equity Theory

Equity theory is set in the larger context of early social comparison theory (Festinger, 1954; Goodman, 1977) and later revisionist approaches (Huseman, Hatfield, & Miles, 1987). In all organizations, including colleges and universities, members continually assess the personal return they receive for the investment they put into the organization. According to J. Stacy Adams (1965), the extent to which people feel that they are being treated in a fair and equitable manner profoundly affects their motivation. When people feel that they are being dealt with inequitably or unfairly, equity theory predicts that they will act to restore their feelings of equity. Since this sometimes means a reduction of effort, it is important for administrators to understand how equity is perceived. Table 9.4 presents the determinants of perceived equity in Adams's theory.

Organizational members can perceive themselves to be in one of two conditions—equity or inequity. Equity exists when the focal person perceives that his or her rate of outcomes to inputs is equal to the ratio of outcomes to inputs of a comparison other. The following relationship obtains:

Focal Person—FP		Comparison Other—CO
Outcomes		Outcomes
—————	=	—————
Inputs		Inputs

TABLE 9.4
Variables in Equity Theory*

Inputs	All things that an individual brings and/or contributes to his or her job (including education, training, experience, time, and effort, among others)
Outcomes	All things that an individual receives or obtains as a result of performing the job (including pay, promotions, praise, recognition, friendship, and feelings of personal accomplishment, among others)
Comparison Other	Another person, real or imagined, in the person's current or past work group

*Based on Adams, 1965.

Substituting number equivalents, we might find:

$$\frac{\text{Outcomes}}{\text{Inputs}} \qquad \overset{\text{FP}}{\frac{5}{5}} = \overset{\text{CO}}{\frac{6}{6}}$$

In this case, the comparison other is receiving more rewards (outcomes) than the focal person, but the comparison other is also contributing more inputs; therefore, the focal person will view the additional increment for the comparison other as fair. Inequity exists, however, when the ratios are not in balance. Here are two examples,

$$\frac{\text{Outcomes}}{\text{Inputs}} \qquad \overset{\text{FP}}{\frac{6}{6}} \ne \overset{\text{CO}}{\frac{6}{4}} \qquad \overset{\text{FP}}{\frac{3}{2}} \ne \overset{\text{CO}}{\frac{3}{1}}$$

In the first example, both workers received the same outcome (6), even though the focal person contributed more inputs (6 versus 4). In the second example, both workers received the same outcome (3), even though the focal person contributed twice as much (2 versus 1). Both scenarios will be perceived as inequitable by the focal person.

It is important to note that there are *two* underlying comparison processes. The first is between the organizational member's own outcomes and inputs. For example, does she perceive that the effort she is investing in her job is greater in value than the rewards she receives from the organization? "Am I getting what I deserve?" The second is the comparison of the organizational member's perceived ratio to her perception of another worker's ratio. She asks herself, is my effort-to-reward ratio the same or different from another person in a comparable job? Is the other person, in fact, getting more back than I am, although he is putting in the same amount of effort? Note that inequity can occur when the ratio is higher as well as lower. For example, a worker can experience guilt if the perception is that his outcomes exceed his inputs to a greater extent than others in comparable positions.

The relevance of these calculations to understanding worker motivation comes from the effects of the perception of equity or inequity. Adams hypothesizes that people are uncomfortable in situations of inequity and will strive to restore equity. Some of these tactics are functional for the organization; others are not. A reduction in work effort to relieve the discomfort is, needless to say, not desirable from an organizational perspective. Nor are the following methods for restoring equity:

1. Altering input—the worker can perform at lower quality
2. Altering outcome—the worker can bargain for more outcomes—for example, an increase in pay
3. Cognitively distorting the inputs or outcomes—the worker can use his or her imagination to attribute less effort to self and/or more to others; or more rewards for self and less for others—for example, "I am really not working that hard."
4. Changing or trying to change the inputs or outcomes of the other— the worker can try to persuade the other to change behavior—asking, for example, "Why do you work so hard?"
5. Changing the comparison other—shifting to someone else so that the discomfort of inequity is lessened
6. Leaving the field; exiting the organization

When do workers use each of these methods? Adams is not clear, but he proposes the following hypotheses. Generally, the individual will

1. Attempt to maximize highly valued outcomes—for example, money, praise, autonomy.
2. Not try to change inputs that are costly to change or require much effort.
3. Not try to distort the situation if inputs are central to self-concept; for example, if I think I am a good teacher, I am not likely to change that self-image, either by distortion or by a change in effort just to restore equity.
4. Be more likely to distort the ratio of the other than his or her own— for example, "He is not really getting that much praise."

5. Exit the organization only when inequity is sizable and when other means to address the inequity will not work.

Note that some people are more sensitive to equity issues than are others, depending on how "other-directed" the individual is. Professional athletes, for example, tend to be highly conscious of equity ratios (consider the salary negotiations in professional sports). Further, it is important to note that equity itself may be a hygiene factor in Herzberg's two-factor theory. That is, perceived inequity may serve largely to dissatisfy, but its restoration may not result in higher motivation. For the latter to take place, motivators, in Herzberg's terminology, may be necessary. Finally, organizational culture, too, affects how people deal with restoration of equity. In cultures where uncertainty avoidance norms are high, workers tend to use distortion rather than behavioral change to rectify an inequity (Kilbourne & O'Leary-Kelly, 1994).

In higher education organizations, merit pay systems in private colleges and universities, compared to stepped-pay systems in public institutions, tend to increase the likelihood of perceived inequity among faculty, often because of the absence of public disclosure of individual salaries (see, for example, Bloom, 1999). On the other hand, some would argue that merit pay induces more motivation, at least for the more successful workers, although this may be true only in some industries. For example, money may not be a strong motivator for faculty (Bess, 1978/79).

Job Characteristics Theory

In a number of ways, job characteristics theory combines or at least modifies elements of both need and process theories. It provides a more sophisticated conceptualization of inner drives, and it concretizes the external aspects of the work situation that may enter into an organizational member's consciousness (as in expectancy theory). This theory of motivation has significantly more pragmatic utility than do some of the others in that it directs attention more concretely to features in the work environment that impinge on motivation, and that organizational leaders can modify to enhance motivation.

Job characteristics theory was developed by J. Richard Hackman and Greg Oldham (1980) and modified by many (e.g., Griffin, 1990). Hackman and Oldham suggested that what is important is the strength in each individual of three **critical psychological states** that reinforce or depress different kinds of behavior. (Note the differences in these "states" from the "needs" proposed by Maslow, Alderfer, or Herzberg.) The three psychological states are:

- **Experienced meaningfulness of the work**—the extent to which the organizational member experiences the job as generally meaningful, valuable, and worthwhile.
- **Experienced responsibility for work outcomes**—the extent to which the organizational member feels personally accountable and responsible for the results of the work that he or she performs.
- **Knowledge of results**—the extent that the organizational member knows and understands from day to day how effective he or she is at work.

People experience higher levels of motivation when these three psychological states are activated by five core characteristics of the job: skill variety, task identity, task significance, autonomy, and feedback from the job itself (see Figure 9.4).

Skill variety. "The degree to which a job requires a variety of different activities in carrying out the work, which involve the use of a number of different skills and talents of the employee" (Hackman & Oldham, 1980, p. 78). The job must have an interesting and challenging variety.

Task identity. "The degree to which the job requires completion of a

FIGURE 9.4
Job Characteristics Theory*

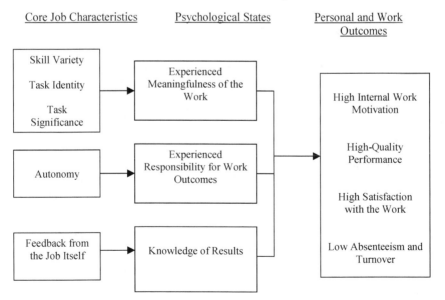

*Based on Hackman and Oldham, 1980.

'whole' and identifiable piece of work—that is, doing a job from beginning to end with a visible outcome" (Hackman & Oldham, 1980, p. 78). The work should have a distinct beginning and ending with high visibility of the transformation process.

Task significance. "The degree to which the job has a substantial impact on the lives or work of other people—whether in the immediate organization or in the external environment" (Hackman & Oldham, 1980, p. 79).

Autonomy. "The degree to which the job provides substantial freedom, independence, and discretion of the employee in scheduling the work and in determining the procedures to be used in carrying it out" (Hackman & Oldham, 1980, p. 79).

Feedback from the job itself. "The degree to which carrying out the work activities required by the job results in the employee obtaining direct and clear information about the effectiveness of his or her performance" (Hackman & Oldham, 1980, p. 80). This means internal feedback—built into the work itself rather than feedback from colleagues or supervisors. For example, student evaluations of teaching are one way that faculty receive feedback about their effectiveness in teaching.

A second form of feedback also affects the psychological states that influence work motivation. External feedback from peers, subordinates, supervisors, and clients falls into this category. Perceptions of the character or quality of this feedback are critical to motivation. Feedback that is perceived as controlling rather than "information giving" tends to reduce motivation, especially for professionals (Deci & Ryan, 2000).

The five core job characteristics are indirectly connected to the dependent variables in job characteristics theory—motivation, satisfaction, and absenteeism and turnover. The critical psychological states intervene between the job characteristics and the outcomes.

When the job characteristics are present at high levels, the psychological states will be activated, and motivation will be higher. The theory is actually slightly more precise. Three of the job characteristics—skill variety, task identity, and task significance—are more intimately related to experienced *meaningfulness*, while autonomy more directly affects experienced *responsibility*, and feedback has an impact on *knowledge of results*. If one knows something about the job characteristics, then one can predict the likely effects on motivation.

Here is how the whole theory works together. Jobs have **motivating potential** according to the strength of core job characteristics and related psychological states. The motivating potential of any job is equal to meaningfulness multiplied by responsibility multiplied by knowledge of results. To obtain the *meaningfulness* "score," add together skill variety, task identity, and task significance. A measure of autonomy can serve as the value for the *responsibility* variable, and an assessment of feedback from the job itself can be used as the value for *knowledge of results*. Figure 9.5 reflects this equation.

Each of the three psychological states is necessary to achieve a high motivating potential for a job. For example, if knowledge of results is low (due to limited feedback), then the motivating potential for the job will be reduced substantially, even if the other two psychological states (meaningfulness and responsibility for outcomes) are present at high levels.

One additional point—different organizational members are variously affected by job characteristics. For example, different individuals may have a different rank ordering of importance of the psychological states—some individuals needing more knowledge of outcomes, others having a greater need for meaningfulness. Thus, the job characteristics that are important for different workers may not be universally applicable—that is, their relative weights may vary somewhat for each individual.

While Hackman and Oldham do not directly address this dimension in detail, they do say that workers who have high "growth need strength"—a kind of achievement motivation (Atkinson & Feather, 1966)—will be more motivated in the presence of favorable job design conditions than will those with low growth need strength. For example, if a faculty member does not really care about improving his teaching (e.g., his ego enhancement may be derived from other spheres of activity), even if the university provides the conditions for improvement, it will not make much difference in his level of motivation. Thus, Hackman and Oldham incorporate parts of expectancy theory—specifically, the idea of valence—into their theory.

Finally, Hackman and Oldham are concerned with *job design* as much

FIGURE 9.5
Calculating the Motivating Potential of a Job

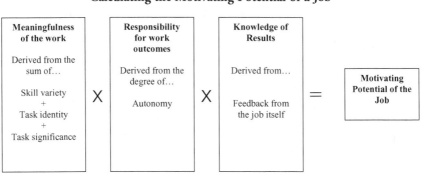

as motivation. Their theory helps us to think about how work in colleges and universities can be structured so that people have an *opportunity* to become more motivated (and, not incidentally, to exert more effort).

Social Construction and Motivation Theory

To reiterate, the traditional way of classifying theories of motivation is into two categories—need theories and process theories. The former consider motivation as stemming from a relatively stable set of innate characteristics (i.e., universally found in all human beings) and others of which are idiosyncratic (i.e., unique to each individual). Behavior, according to need theories, follows ineluctably from some essential human nature, even in a teleological sense. Process theories of motivation, on the other hand, view basic human needs and drives as malleable in the course of interaction with the environment as perceived by the individual. In this conception, both individual and environment must be taken into account in understanding motivation. Alfred Bandura (1986), however, labels theorists of both categories as "one-sided determinists" (p. 22)—that is, need theories posit that behavior is determined by inner drives, while process theories posit that the environment in large part determines behavior. In an effort to escape this characterization, some researchers attempt to present an "interactionist" perspective by suggesting that behavior is a product of the confluence of these two independent forces. Critical of this approach as well, Bandura calls it "one-sided interactionism," because it assumes that the environment and the individual are independent agents. Further, it ignores the impact of *behavior itself* on both the individual and the environment, thus changing each dynamically. As Bandura notes, "Behavior is interacting and exerting influence at the meeting [of person and environment] and is active throughout events, rather than being procreated by a union of a behaviorless person and a situation" (p. 23).

Bandura's **social cognitive theory** favors a conceptualization of interaction that is based on "triadic reciprocality," in which each of the three elements—environment, individual, and behavior—exerts influence on the others. Thus, individual motivation is uniquely shaped by the interaction of these three factors. We can consider all three interactions.

Environment-behavior. This interaction suggests that people are both *products* of their environment and *producers* of that environment. Environments (situations) are enacted through behavior. That is, we produce the environments that we respond to. An aggressive, dictatorial supervisor, for example, creates a hostile work environment. But behaviors are enacted within and constrained by the current environmental context. A collaborative work environment, for example, is constructed through cooperative behaviors across units, which, in turn, establish behavioral expectations for more cooperation in the future. If someone wanted to behave in a more individualistic way, strong norms would constrain him or her from doing so.

Behavior-individual. An individual's thoughts, feelings, and inner drives shape his or her behavior. An inner need for achievement, for example, may compel someone to apply for a promotion. But behaviors also affect individuals' psychological states, including emotions and cognitions (mental maps), which, in turn, guide *subsequent* behaviors (e.g., motivated effort). In other words, how we *feel* about our behaviors and how we *make sense* of those behaviors affect the types of actions that we will take in the future. In applying for a promotion, the applicant may have to compromise her values to work with the current management team (e.g., a believer in higher education access who is compelled to emphasize merit over need in financial aid decisions). This person may feel badly about the behaviors in which she engaged to get the job (espousing a commitment to something that is contrary to her values), and these feelings may dampen her motivation.

Individual-environment. Individual cognitions, competencies, expectations, and beliefs are developed through social processes in the work environment. Working in a community college, for example, may shape beliefs about access and expectations for equitable educational opportunities for all students. In this way, the environment shapes the individual. But individual characteristics in the aggregate can shape perceptions of the environment as well. Looking into a campus cafeteria, for example, we may see only young faces. These individual characteristics shape impressions of the environment, in this case, as one where older students may not feel welcome.

Bandura's theory suggests that individuals are active agents who construct reality through selectively encoding information from the environment, and then engage in behaviors based on those constructs. Through feedback on one's behavior, the person's own reality is shaped and reshaped by the interaction of environmental and cognitive factors. In these ways, the environment, individual characteristics, and enacted behaviors have reciprocal influences on each other, which, in turn, shape human motivation.

Feminist Theory and Motivation

Most of the literature cited above was written by men and may reflect the biases that tend to be found as a general result of ignorance of gender differences. In recent years, new perspectives on motivation, illuminated by feminist concerns, have begun to emerge in organizational theory (Calas & Smircich, 1992; Glazer, 1997; Martin, 2006). As Judith Glazer (1997) notes, because of male bias, "motivation theory offers only a partial view of human behavior" (p. 37). She observes further that research on achievement, affiliation, and power motives generally ignores the modes in which women express them, that is, not only individually but in combination with others. Indeed, Glazer argues that patterns of growth and intellectual development in women tend to engender more empathy and connectedness with others as motivational drives and impulses are played out (Mednick, 1991).

Carol Gilligan's pioneering book, *In a Different Voice* (1982), spawned numerous studies of women in organizations, including colleges and universities, and revealed the different images of relationships that women have with others—from which we can infer that the internal organizational dynamics may differ from the positivist, predictive theories described earlier in this chapter. Indeed, as Belenky et al. (1986) presciently point out, it is quite likely that male and female patterns of discourse are so different as to render "efficient" administration problematic. They suggest, for example, "The tendency for women to ground their epistemological premises in metaphors suggesting speaking and listening is at odds with the visual metaphors (such as equating knowledge with illumination, knowing with seeing, and truth with light) that scientists and philosophers most often use to express their sense of mind" (p. 18).

Ross-Smith and Kornberger (2004) similarly propose that positivist organizational theory continues to reflect conceptions of rationality that originated in the 18th-century Enlightenment, which, according to this view, are strongly associated with masculinity. Strategic planning in colleges and universities is often an example of positivism and rationality in practice, but the latent effects of masculinity in strategic planning practices may exclude other valuable insights from feminist perspectives that might inform possible institutional futures.

Studies of gender in organizational administration in higher education have raised not only practical questions of equity and efficiency, but broader organizational issues of comity, cohesion, and coherence as well. If motivation is as important in driving behavior as past researchers have claimed, then there needs to be more research on the sociological impact of gender differences. Gumport (1991), for example, argues for an examination of communities within institutions that take into account different ways of thinking about how collaboration might work. Further, as might be inferred from our discussion of paradigmatic differences and their impact on organizational structure and process—as well as how some leaders use one paradigm more than others—observers of college and university organization might well consider the ways that gender and paradigm overlap or differ.

Management and Motivation

How the theories of motivation discussed above are used in higher education organizations is in part a function of some assumptions that leaders have about basic human nature. Some leaders believe that people are basically lazy, others that they are inherently energetic, responsible, and, under the right conditions, highly motivated. These two quite different assumptions have been given the labels, **Theory X** and **Theory Y** (McGregor, 1960). If leaders believe that people are basically lazy and unmotivated (Theory X), then there is a rationale for significant leader monitoring, coercing, and punishing. That is, if it is believed people will not seek responsibility and rest on past laurels, they must be controlled. If, on the other hand, leaders believe that part of human nature is to be motivated intrinsically and to accept responsibility, then leaders can be freer to "let nature take its course" with confidence that the organization will benefit. Thus, Theory X assumptions focus on the importance of inducements and constraints to motivate workers, while Theory Y assumptions concentrate on the potential for human agency.

Summary

We have now considered many possible influences on individual motivation, including internal needs and drives (so-called need theories) as well as cognitions, psychological states, and some of the characteristics of the environment external to the individual (process theories). Both sets of theories help us understand intrinsic and extrinsic motivation. In Figure 9.6, a schematic diagram puts most of the motivation theories discussed in this chapter into perspective.

We can explore three paths to motivation in Figure 9.6. First, *individual conditions* such as personality, background, training, and experience can influence *psychological states* (meaningfulness, responsibility, knowledge of results), *needs and drives* (e.g., strong or weak need for achievement), and *acquired beliefs* (e.g., perceived equity in rewards). *Job characteristics* (e.g., skill variety, task identity, task significance) can also have an effect on psychological states. The psychological states, in turn, can have a direct effect on outcomes such as motivation.

Another route toward motivation goes through the middle of the diagram. Our needs and drives and our *goals* can affect our level of *expectancy*—that is, our view of the probability that our efforts will lead to successful performance. Similarly, our beliefs about the organization (e.g., whether we

FIGURE 9.6
Conceptual Model for Research on Motivation in Higher Education Organizations

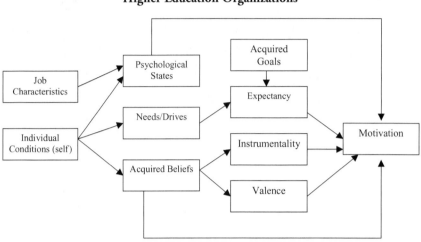

think people are treated fairly), influence our views about *instrumentality* (whether we think the organization is likely to provide rewards for good performance) and *valence* (the value that we assign to available rewards). Collectively, expectancy, instrumentality, and valence then shape an individual's level of motivation.

Finally, a third path toward motivation is direct from our acquired beliefs—for example, higher motivation if we believe that the organization is basically fair and trustworthy. This schematic diagram, albeit simplified and limited, can serve as an important heuristic device for examining the motivation of organizational members (Mitchell, 1997). It can be used to understand more thoroughly the personal and organizational variables that shape motivation.

Review Questions

1. Consider your present job in higher education. What underlying motivational "policy" do you imagine your immediate superior is attempting to execute?
   a. Need theory
   b. Equity theory
   c. Expectancy theory
   d. Goal theory

    e. Job characteristics theory

    f. Other

2. The more the organization provides circumstances that allow employees to meet and become connected to each other interpersonally, which of the following is more likely to be true (according to Maslow's perspective)?

    a. Too much work time will be spent in socializing.

    b. More work time will be freed for behavior that will heighten workers' sense of competency.

    c. There will be more support for union efforts to gain higher wages and job security.

3. According to Herzberg, which is *not* a "motivator"? An associate dean's:

    a. Satisfaction that comes from doing her work well

    b. Satisfaction with her immediate supervisor

    c. Sense of responsibility she feels about her job

    d. Perception of opportunities for moving to positions of higher responsibility

4. A new student affairs vice president arrives at a university and clarifies previously confusing university rules and regulations for workers in her division. From Herzberg's perspective, the workers are likely to experience which of the following?

    a. Greater satisfaction with work

    b. Less dissatisfaction with work

    c. Both a and b

    d. Neither a nor b

5. A new assistant professor believes that if he works hard, he will be able to teach well. Which of the following expectancy theory terms best describes this feeling?

    a. Expectancy

    b. Instrumentality

    c. Valence

    d. Motivation

    e. Reinforcement

6. In a college that strongly rewards publication and in which faculty strongly favor the particular types of rewards offered by the college, a

faculty member believes that there is very little chance that he can produce the book he would like to write. Which of the following most likely describes his state of motivation, according to expectancy theory?

a. Practically none
b. Low
c. Moderate
d. High
e. Very high

7. In equity theory, which of the following exists when the ratio of a department secretary's outcomes to inputs is equal to the ratio of the outcomes to inputs of a secretary in another department?

a. Equity
b. Inequity
c. Safety
d. Satisfaction
e. Reward

8. According to the job characteristics model, an administrative job with little or no skill variety is bound to result in very low motivation.

a. True
b. False

Case Discussion Questions

Consider the Sierra State University library case that was presented at the beginning of this chapter.

1. Rates of absenteeism and poor performance are increasing among the circulation department staff. How can Herzberg's **two-factor theory** explain the dissatisfaction and low motivation among these staff members? What remedies to the situation could the library director introduce, keeping in mind that the budget will remain relatively flat, and large salary increases or the hiring of additional staff will not be possible?

2. How can **job characteristics theory** diagnose the cause of low motivation among the collections staff who feel like "glorified acquisitions clerks"? What changes in the work roles of collections staff could elicit higher levels of motivation?

3. How can **equity theory** explain why the head of the collections department wants to leave the university?

4. The IT staff members do not feel a personal connection to their colleagues in the library, so their morale and motivation have declined. How can this condition be explained using Maslow's **need theory**? What steps could the library director take to ensure that the organization addresses the basic needs of these employees?

5. Due to budget shortfalls, the library has not invested in professional development for its staff in nearly three years. According to Alderfer's **ERG theory**, if these professional development needs are neglected for an extended period, what is the likely impact on these employees' growth needs and relatedness needs, respectively?

6. Are there any other aspects of the case that work motivation theories could illuminate for Library Director Rodriguez?

References

Adams, J. S. (1965). Inequity in social exchange. In L. Berkowitz (Ed.), *Advances in experimental social psychology* (vol. 2, pp. 267–299). New York: Academic Press.

Alderfer, C. P. (1972). *Existence, relatedness, and growth: Human needs in organizational settings.* New York: Free Press.

Atkinson, J. W. (1964). *Introduction to motivation.* Princeton, NJ: Van Nostrand.

Atkinson, J. W., & Feather, N. T. (1966). *A theory of achievement motivation.* New York: John Wiley & Sons.

Bandura, A. (1977). Self-efficacy: Toward a unifying theory of behavior change. *Psychological Review, 84,* 191–215.

Bandura, A. (1986). *Social foundations of thought and action: A social cognitive theory.* Englewood Cliffs, NJ: Prentice-Hall.

Bargh, J. A. (1990). Auto-motives, preconscious determinants of social interaction. In E. Higgins and R. M. Sorrentino (Eds.), *Handbook of motivation and cognition: Foundations of social behavior* (vol. 2, pp. 93–130). New York: Guilford Press.

Belenky, M., Clinchy, B., Goldberger, N., & Tarule, J. (1986). *Women's ways of knowing: The development of self, voice, and mind.* New York: Basic Books.

Bess, J. L. (1978/79, December/January). Money is not a motivator. *Change Magazine, 10,* 69.

Blau, P. M. (1955). *The dynamics of bureaucracy: A study of interpersonal relations in two government agencies.* Chicago: University of Chicago Press.

Bloom, M. (1999). Performance effects of pay dispersion on individuals and organizations. *Academy of Management Journal, 42*(1), 25–40.

Calas, M., & Smircich, L. (1992). Re-writing gender into organizational theorizing: Directions from feminist perspectives. In M. Reed & M. Hughes (Eds.), *Rethinking organization: New directions in organization theory and analysis* (pp. 227–253). Newbury Park, CA: Sage.

Campbell, J., & Pritchard, R. (1976). Motivation theory in industrial and organizational psychology. In M. D. Dunnette (Ed.), *Handbook of industrial and organizational psychology* (pp. 63–130). Chicago: Rand McNally.

Csikszentmihalyi, M. (1990). *Flow: The psychology of optimal experience*. New York: Harper & Row.

Deci, E., & Ryan, R. (1985). *Intrinsic motivation and self-determination in human behavior*. New York: Plenum Press.

Deci, E., & Ryan, R. (2000). The "what" and "why" of goal pursuits: Human needs and the self-determination of behavior. *Psychological Inquiry, 11*(4), 227–268.

DeShon, R. P., & Gillespie, J. Z. (2005). A motivated action theory of goal orientation. *Journal of Applied Psychology, 90*(6), 1096–1127.

Festinger, L. A. (1954). A theory of social comparison. *Human Relations, 7*, 117–140.

Gilligan, C. (1982). *In a different voice: Psychological theory and women's development*. Cambridge, MA: Harvard University Press.

Glazer, J. S. (1997). Beyond male theory: A feminist perspective on teaching motivation. In J. L. Bess (Ed.), *Teaching well and liking it: Motivating faculty to teach effectively* (pp. 37–54). Baltimore, MD: The Johns Hopkins University Press.

Goddard, R. D., Hoy, W. K., & Hoy, A. W. (2004). Collective efficacy beliefs: Theoretical developments, empirical evidence, and future directions. *Educational Researcher, 33*(3), 3–13.

Goodman, P. S. (1977). Social comparison processes in organizations. In B. M. Staw and G. R. Salancik (Eds.), *New directions in organizational behavior* (pp. 97–132). Chicago: St. Clair Press.

Griffin, R. W. (1990). Toward an integrated theory of task design. In B. M. Staw and L. L. Cummings (Eds.), *Work in organizations* (pp. 81–122). Greenwich, CT: JAI Press.

Gumport, P. J. (1991). E Pluribus Unum? Academic structure, culture, and the case of feminist scholarship. *Review of Higher Education, 15*(1), 9–29.

Hackman, J. R. (1992). Group influences on individuals. In M. E. Dunnette & L. M. Hough (Eds.), *Handbook of industrial and organizational psychology* (pp. 199–267). Palo Alto, CA: Consulting Psychologists Press.

Hackman, J. R., & Oldham, G. R. (1980). *Work redesign*. Reading, MA: Addison-Wesley.

Harter, J. K., & Schmidt, F. L. (2000). *Validation of a performance-related and actionable management tool: A meta-analysis* (Gallup Technical Report). Princeton, NJ: The Gallup Organization.

Harter, J. K., Schmidt, F. L., & Hayes, T. L. (2002). Business-unit-level relationships between employee satisfaction, employee engagement, and business outcomes: A meta-analysis. *Journal of Applied Psychology, 87*(2), 268–279.

Herzberg, F. (1968, January-February). One more time: How do you motivate employees? *Harvard Business Review*, 53–62.

Herzberg, F., Mausner, B., & Snyderman, B. (1959). *The motivation to work*. New York: John Wiley and Sons.

House, R. J., & Wigdor, L. A. (1967). Herzberg's dual-factor theory of job satisfaction and motivation: A review of the empirical evidence and a criticism. *Personnel Psychology, 20*, 369–389.

Hoy, W. K., & Miskel, C. G. (2005). *Educational administration: Theory, research, and practice* (7th ed.). New York: McGraw-Hill.

Huseman, R., Hatfield, J., & Miles, E. (1987). A new perspective on equity theory: The equity sensitivity construct. *Academy of Management Review, 12*(2), 222–234.

Kast, F., & Rosenzweig, J. (1979). *Organization and management: A systems and contingency approach* (3rd ed.). New York: McGraw-Hill.

Kilbourne, L., & O'Leary-Kelly, P. (1994). A re-evaluation of equity theory: The influence of culture. *Journal of Management Inquiry, 3*(2), 177–188.

Klein, H. J. (1991). Further evidence on the relationship between goal setting and expectancy theories. *Organizational Behavior and Human Decision Processes, 49*, 230–257.

Landy, F. (1989). *Psychology of work behavior.* Pacific Grove, CA: Brooks/Cole

Locke, E. A., & Latham, G. (1990). *A theory of goal setting and task performance.* Englewood Cliffs, NJ: Prentice-Hall.

Maccoby, M. (1988). *Why work?* New York: Simon and Schuster.

March, J. G., & Simon, H. (1958). *Organizations.* New York: John Wiley & Sons.

Martin, P. Y. (2006). Practicing gender at work: Further thoughts on reflexivity. *Gender, Work, and Organization, 13*(3), 254–276.

Maslow, A. H. (1943). A theory of motivation. *Psychological Review, 50*(4), 370–396.

Maslow, A. H. (1970). *Motivation and personality.* New York: Harper & Row.

Maslow, A. H., & Kaplan, A. R. (1998). *Maslow on management.* New York: John Wiley & Sons.

McClelland, D. C. (1971). *Motivational trends in society.* Morristown, NJ: General Learning Press.

McClelland, D. C., & Burnham, D. (1976, March-April). Power is the great motivator. *Harvard Business Review,* 100–111.

McGregor, D. (1960). *The human side of enterprise.* New York: McGraw-Hill.

Mednick, M. T. (1991). Currents and futures in American feminist psychology: State of the art revisited. *Psychology of Women Quarterly, 15*, 611–621.

Mitchell, T. E. (1997). Matching motivational strategies with organizational contexts. *Research in Organizational Behavior, 19*, 57–149.

Mone, M. A., & Kelly, D. (1994). Self-efficacy, self-esteem, and behavior in organizations. In R. H. Kilmann, I. Kilmann, and Associates (Eds.), *Managing ego energy: The transformation of personal meaning into organizational success* (pp. 103–127). San Francisco: Jossey-Bass

Ostroff, C. (1992). The relationship between satisfaction, attitudes, and performance: An organizational analysis. *Journal of Applied Psychology, 77*(6), 963–974.

Phillipchuk, J., & Whittaker, J. (1996). An inquiry into the continuing relevance of Herzberg's motivation theory. *Engineering Management, 8*, 15–20.

Porter, L., & Lawler, E. (1968). *Managerial attitudes and performance.* Homewood, IL: Dorsey.

Ross-Smith, A., & Kornberger, M. (2004). Gendered rationality? A genealogical exploration of the philosophical and sociological conceptions of rationality, masculinity, and organization. *Gender, Work, and Organization, 11*(3), 280–305.

Rosser, V. (2004). Faculty members' intentions to leave: A national study on their worklife and satisfaction. *Research in Higher Education, 45*(3), 285–309.

Sagie, A., & Elizur, D. (1996). The structure and strength of achievement motivation: A cross-cultural comparison. *Journal of Organizational Behavior, 17*(5), 431–444.

Stajkovic, A. D., & Luthans, F. (2002). Social cognitive theory and self-efficacy: Implications for motivation theory and practice. In R. M. Steers, L. W. Porter, & G. A. Bigley (Eds.), *Motivation and work behavior* (7th ed.) (pp. 126–140). New York: McGraw-Hill.

Steers, R. M., & Black, J. S. (1994). *Organizational behavior* (5th ed.). New York: Harper-Collins College Publishers.

Van Eerde, W., & Thierry, H. (1996). Vroom's expectancy models and work-related criteria: A meta-analysis. *Journal of Applied Psychology, 81*, 575–586.

Vroom, V. H. (1964). *Work and motivation.* New York: John Wiley & Sons.

Wahba, M. A., & Bridwell, L. G. (1976). Maslow reconsidered: A review of research on the need hierarchy theory. *Organizational Behavior and Human Performance, 15*, 212–240.

IO

GROUPS, TEAMS, AND HUMAN RELATIONS

CONTENTS

The authors are most grateful for the critical comments on an early draft of this chapter by Diane Dean, Illinois State University. The final version, of course, is our own and may or may not reflect the perspective of the reviewer.

Preview

- Groups are an inevitable and omnipresent organizational phenomenon.
- Organizations are fostering more worker interdependencies and collaboration.
- Many different types of groups exist within organizations, each with different characteristics.
- Membership in organizational groups can be total or marginal.
- The informal organization of work groups is a powerful determinant of formal organizational effectiveness.
- The components and characteristics of the informal organization are usually subtle and difficult to observe and influence.
- Besides their formal functions, groups serve important latent functions for organizations.
- Group members perform a variety of functional roles for the organization.
- Groups develop through recognizable stages, such as forming, storming, norming, and performing.
- Norms govern most behavior in groups, and conformity or deviance carry positive or negative sanctions.
- Certain kinds of cohesiveness in groups can materially affect group productivity.
- Groups sometimes develop a dysfunctional homogeneity of thought and action (groupthink).
- Teams are increasingly substituting for hierarchical management in many organizations.

———————————————— CASE CONTEXT ————————————————

Teaching and Learning at Davis Community College

The team of accreditation reviewers for Davis Community College had arrived on campus. They were especially interested in the innovative core curriculum that the college had developed four years ago. The curriculum was featured in a recent article in a national community college publication that described the college's creative approach to developing writing and math skills through an emphasis on critical thinking. In addition to reforming the curriculum, Davis Community College engaged in a wholesale change in its faculty development program. Faculty members created an ongoing professional development program with the goal of teaching diverse student populations more effectively, especially English-language learners. The accreditation team was curious about how this innovative program had been developed, so it scheduled interviews with members of the college's teaching and learning committee.

"This committee was unlike any other that I have served on at the college," explained Jennifer Nguyen, a dental hygiene faculty member. "Typically, when we review the curriculum, the deans round up the usual suspects from the humanities departments, and they just affirm whatever they have been doing for the past umpteen years. But not this time. It wasn't just a liberal arts thing; they brought in faculty like me, from the vocational programs."

Like most two-year institutions, Davis Community College includes both transfer and vocational preparation in its mission. Therefore, its programs (and its faculty) are structurally divided into liberal arts programs that promote transfer to four-year institutions, and vocational programs that culminate in a two-year degree and perhaps a license to practice in a specific professional area.

Five years ago, the state board of higher education began pressuring the college regarding low graduation rates and low passage rates on national licensure exams in various professional fields. "We made a very deliberate choice," reported the vice president for academic affairs. "The problem of poor retention and poor academic outcomes needed a 'team' solution. I know that it is a cliché, but we needed to think 'outside the box.' We needed new ideas."

The committee included four faculty members from liberal arts departments and three faculty members from vocational programs. "Initially, the liberal arts faculty were suspicious of us vocational folks," continued Professor Nguyen. "One of them actually asked me what I was doing there. She said, 'You don't teach in the core curriculum, so why are you here?' I said, 'Well, they are my students, too.' And we need dental hygienists who can write and compute, and think critically, so I have a vested interest in this, too."

"Actually, it was one of the vocational faculty who got us thinking about the connections between curriculum and pedagogy," explained Kevin Thornton, chair of the English department. "I remember this quite well. Right in the middle of our discussion about the writing requirements, a faculty member from dental hygiene asked, 'What good is all this, if we're still teaching the way we did 20 years ago? You could have the best curriculum in the world, but it won't do any good if we don't reach the students where they are.'"

"I must say, we didn't know how to respond to that," continued Professor Thornton. "In fact, a couple of us wanted to table that discussion. It was not part of our charge to look at teaching practices, just curriculum. And what she [Professor Nguyen] did kind of violated a norm of ours in that we usually just stick to the agenda, and we don't introduce new topics during meetings. But we talked about it some more and realized that any good response to poor grades and poor retention really needed to be about both curriculum and pedagogy."

"They resisted the idea at first," noted Professor Nguyen. "A discussion of what happens in the classroom made them uncomfortable. It was hitting too close to home—academic freedom and faculty autonomy and all that. But I have to give Kevin, the chair, some credit. He said that we needed to take some risks. He knew that this was a sensitive issue, so he gave us some time to think and some time to talk at the next meeting. He really created the context for others to share their concerns about teaching, too."

As a result of these conversations, Davis Community College created a new pedagogical resource center that offers ongoing workshops and seminars for teaching improvement. Rather than rely on outside consultants, the faculty identify in-house experts among their own ranks. Four faculty members who had engaged in innovative pedagogical practices were appointed to new positions, which the college called professorships of pedagogy. These professors provide mentoring and assistance to other faculty members across the college. They lead workshops on teaching critical thinking, empowering student voices in the classroom, and using collaborative learning techniques. The new center and the affiliated pedagogy professors sparked strong interest among the faculty in teaching improvement and led to the more widespread adoption of innovative pedagogical practices.

"I wish all of our committees were like that one," said the academic vice president. "They weren't afraid to tackle big issues. And the old divides between liberal arts faculty and vocational faculty are now much less salient than they used to be. Our professors of pedagogy are from both the liberal arts and the vocational programs. This is the entire college's curriculum, and there is broad support for making it work."

Introduction

C olleges and universities employ a wide range of specialists whose expertise frequently must be melded into collaborative work groups. Despite omnipresent complaints that there are too many committees, higher education is said to be at its best when the decision-making process includes a range of constituents. In higher education organizations, constituent involvement occurs through extended discussions among faculty, administrators, students, and external stakeholders. This collaborative aspect of colleges and universities implies that organizational effectiveness is dependent, in large part, on the performance of groups. Work groups can facilitate efficient cross-departmental interactions and improve the overall quality of organizational decisions (Hirokawa, Erbert, & Hurst, 1996). Poorly functioning groups, however, can delay decisions and blind the organization to new ways of thinking. Therefore, organizational researchers have devoted significant attention to determining why some groups work and others do not (Hackman, 1990).

In the mid-20th century, organizational leaders, even those using the Ford assembly line and bureaucratic model of efficiency, assumed that a symbolic "community" of workers could generate a meaningful sense of identification with and allegiance to the organization as a whole (Roethlisberger & Dickson, 1939). In the postindustrial 21st century, not only have work conditions changed, but so have our conceptualizations of how workers are embedded in organizations. Traditional bureaucratic models are being challenged by newer models that conceive of organizations as more fragmented (Martin, 1992). According to these views, social cohesion in the organization as a whole is less obvious and perhaps less valuable. Not only do organizational members have multiple allegiances within the organization, but they also have other loyalties and commitments outside. Lacking opportunities to identify with a larger organizational entity, workers tend to find smaller units—groups—with which to become affiliated and from which to find satisfaction. Rapid changes in the structure of work have rendered some of our traditional understandings of human relations in organizations as a whole less reliable—though by no means irrelevant (Koot, Leisink, Verweel, & Jeffcut, 2003). New conceptualizations of human relations in small groups, therefore, become especially important for understanding as they apply to colleges and universities as workplaces.

In this chapter, we consider networks of organizational members—in formal, organizationally sanctioned decision-making groups, and in the informal groups that emerge in any organization. We provide an overview of the history of the human relations movement and examine how groups form and evolve in different organizational contexts.

A Brief History of Human Relations Theory

Since the Industrial Revolution in the latter half of the 19th century, "work" has been the primary mode by which individuals have established their personal identities. Workers found these identities being defined increasingly by managers who occupied positions of power and authority in organizations. Although egregious examples of worker exploitation (e.g., long hours and unsafe working conditions) evoked both social commentary and some government remediation, with some exceptions management continued to view labor instrumentally—as "tools" for achieving managerial or organizational objectives. In the early 20th century, recognizing the apparent efficiency and effectiveness of Weberian bureaucratic organization (see chapter 7), new "scientific management" ideologies intensified management's search for ways of making workers more productive (see Fayol, 1949; Gilbreth, 1908; Taylor, 1911).

Quite apart from the morality of worker exploitation, early 20th-century management began to explore the idea that satisfied workers might actually be more productive (Haslam, 2004). Beginning in Great Britain, the field of industrial psychology slowly emerged, with sophisticated research on the factors that would improve worker productivity (Henderson, 1996). It was not until the 1920s and 1930s that another perspective on work, its meaning and its aims, came to challenge the then predominant mode (Follett, 1924; Mayo, 1933). It became known as the "human relations" school. We describe some of this thinking below in connection with discussions of the work of Mary Parker Follett, and of the Hawthorne studies at the Western Electric Company in Chicago.

Mary Parker Follett and the Human Relations Movement

Follett (1868–1933) began her career as a social worker and activist in Boston's immigrant neighborhoods. Community work shaped Follett's views about social organization and democracy, which she conceptualized as a participatory process involving the ongoing integration of differences within and among groups (Tonn, 2003). Follett's views on conflict, moreover, were revolutionary for her times. She argued that conflict was not necessarily wasteful and could in fact serve as a socially valuable mechanism for the expression of differences—and thus, for the advancement of democracy (Follett, 1924).

Follett's writings also had direct bearing on organizational administration. Her views on power, leadership, groups, and conflict were influential among business leaders in both the United States and Great Britain. One of Follett's important contributions to the field of management was her conceptualization of the "authority of the situation." She suggested that organizations are more effective when leadership resides with those who have the most expertise required by the demands of the current situation. Rather than relying on a formal authority system with officially designated leaders, group members can decide who among them has the most expertise regarding the situation that confronts them. Those with greater expertise should lead the way, regardless of their formal title or position they hold at the time. When new situations emerge, different people within the group can assume leadership roles. This conceptualization of nonhierarchical, team-based leadership presaged many later management trends. Following Follett's death in 1933, many of her ideas, however, were superseded by the work of other researchers in the human relations tradition, including a group of social psychologists from Harvard University who conducted what came to be known as the Hawthorne studies.

The Hawthorne Studies

In the late 1920s, the Hawthorne studies, conducted at a Western Electric plant outside Chicago, Illinois, produced a revolutionary and unexpected finding in social scientific behavior—the importance of the informal organization. Western Electric invited consultants from the Harvard Business School to examine whether length of the workday, rest breaks, pay rates, and lighting changes would make a difference in worker productivity. In the course of their research, the consultants discovered that some activities, interactions, and sentiments had emerged over and above what were required by management (Mayo, 1933; Roethlisberger & Dickson, 1939). These, they found, had as much or more of an effect on productivity than did the variables they set out to study.

The researchers spread through the Western Electric plant in two areas—the Relay Assembly Test Room and the Bank Wiring Room. In the Relay room, women were putting together telephone components. The researchers selected a group of them to do their work in a more controlled environment in a different part of the plant where they could be observed more easily. The researchers wanted to be able to manipulate variables such as lighting without interference from the other uncontrollable conditions in the rest of the plant.

The researchers varied the lighting from low to high. And, as expected, the productivity improved. They then increased the lighting even more. Again, performance improved. Still higher? Same result. Finally, they began gradually to lower the lighting. The effect was astounding—performance continued to improve! The researchers concluded that the group had achieved a solidarity that was not available to the workers in their undifferentiated positions on the main floor. When workers are given new status and prestige in the eyes of their peers, are given special attention by important people, and are solicited for their opinions, they feel a need to fulfill new expectations. They band together and establish group goals that supplant individual objectives.

A different phenomenon took place in Hawthorne's Bank Wiring Room, where men were soldering together telephone panels. The researchers observed that no workers completed more than two panels per day, even though the engineers claimed that two and a half should be an easily achievable standard. The researchers concluded that the workers were adhering to an unwritten **work restriction norm**. The workers had agreed among themselves what was a "fair day's work for a fair day's pay." They then held each other to their own group standard rather than that of management. This was not a case of the workers restricting output for fear that management would raise the work standard if the workers demonstrated an ability to perform at a higher level, since Western Electric's human relations policy was especially good. The workers themselves decided what was reasonable.

This is perhaps one of the most significant findings in all of the literature on organizational behavior—that control of output is *not* exclusively in the hands of management, but at least partly—and perhaps mainly—in the collective hands of workers.

Recent Developments in the Human Relations Movement

Others who have been identified with the human relations movement include Chris Argyris (1954, 1957), William F. Whyte (1943, 1948), Leonard Sayles (1966), and Sayles and George Strauss (1977). The human relations approach makes the critical assumption that there is no necessary, irreconcilable conflict between the individual and the organization (Argyris, 1954, 1957). When there is a good fit between the individual and the organization, people will expend energy on the organization's behalf at least in part because it also provides them with satisfactions from the exercise of their talents and the achievement of their personal work objectives. The human relations approach thus bases its argument on the assumption that work can be designed so that organizational members can fulfill their own needs while at the same time forwarding the objectives of the organization. One central tenet of this approach is that organizational leaders are responsible for creating organizations that develop the "whole person" (Chisholm, 1989). The following definition illustrates this position: "Human relations is a process of effective motivation of individuals in a given situation in order to achieve a balance of objectives which will yield greater human satisfaction and help accomplish company goals" (Scott, 1962, p. 43).

Cameron and Caza (2004) have reconceived this "school" somewhat and call it "positive organizational scholarship," which they say "is a new movement in organizational science that focuses on the dynamics leading to exceptional individual and organization performance such as developing human strength, producing resilience and restoration, and fostering vitality" (p. 731). The literature in this movement embraces a wide variety of old and new social science disciplines and subjects, including, for example, organizational design, compassionate responding, social networks, community building, prosocial behavior, and creativity.

The human relations movement has drawn significant attention to the importance of work groups within organizations. From the findings of the Hawthorne studies to more recent efforts to promote workplace collaboration, the work group has become a focal point for organizational analysis and leadership. We explore this phenomenon in the next section.

The Study of Groups

Most organizations are made up of groups of one kind or another—either as part of the formal structure (e.g., departments and committees) or as informal arrangements (e.g., lunch groups). Other kinds of groups—for example, teams (Sundstrom, De Meuse, & Futrell, 1990) or more recently, **self-managed teams** (Kirkman & Rosen, 1999; Manz, Keating, & Donnellon, 1990)—are receiving considerable attention in the organizational literature and in the workplace.

The complexity of work in a global, technological world suggests that rarely can one person master *all* of the required specializations of his or her work. Interdependence has become more pervasive as groups are formed to complement individual knowledge and skills. It follows, therefore, that organizations now depend much more on willing collaboration and on collective decision making than they did previously (Kezar, Carducci, & Contreras-McGavin, 2006).

If more collaborative work is forthcoming, then it is important to understand the ways that organizational members work together in small groups, and how to encourage people to work together to achieve common goals (Barnard, 1938). Small-group productivity has an important effect on overall organizational effectiveness. The relationship of group to organization as a whole is complex, as noted in Table 10.1. This is not to say that individuals are or will be less important than the group. However, when individuals work together as a unit, failing to get the commitment of all persons to collaborate may result in less than optimal group or organizational effectiveness (Cohen & Bailey, 1997). We need to understand more fully how group variables are related to individual motivation and to organizational effectiveness.

In sum, we want to understand, explain, and predict how groups will operate under different conditions. The more we know about which behaviors contribute to group effectiveness, the better able we will be to improve organizational productivity and enhance satisfaction for organizational members.

TABLE 10.1
The Relationship Between Informal and Formal Organization*

Inputs from the Formal Organization	Within Group Climate and Transformation Processes	Outputs to the Formal Organization
Role expectations	Activities	Group productivity
Technology	Interactions	Cohesiveness
Interdependence	Sentiments	Member satisfactions
Goals	Norms	
Raw material		
Member backgrounds and skills		

*This list of variables and their relationships is illustrative, but not exhaustive (see Nystrom & Starbuck, 1981).

The Definition of a Group

A group is a social system—a collection of individuals who communicate with each other most often in face-to-face interactions; though in recent times, with the advent of electronic means of communication, this last criterion may have to be abandoned. Thus, group members have to communicate directly and frequently with each other, and feel themselves to be part of a collective endeavor.

Group size has a profound effect on how members relate to one another. (A seminal overview appears in Steiner, 1972.) Groups of different sizes have different interaction patterns and different degrees of member satisfaction. Twelve members has been found to be the approximate maximum size for effective group performance, though newer, computer-assisted group process systems (e.g., "**groupware**") may permit more.

Most groups have few formal hierarchical distinctions, though informal status differences almost always exist. Groups also have social and task goals, which are sometimes explicit and formal, other times latent and assumed. The development of goals and the degree of consensus about them are important variables in the assessment of group effectiveness. Disagreements about goals among group members may result in dysfunctional conflict, personal dissatisfaction, and low motivation (Wolff, 1950). Reaching consensus, especially among group members who are in some type of interdependent relationship, is particularly difficult. It requires much time, extensive communication, and agreement on the degree of consensus that is desired rather than merely acceptable and on good leadership (Benton, 1998).

Types of Groups

It is important not to assume that all collections of people in organizations are *organizationally* relevant groups. For example, some groups are task related, while others are formed for friendship purposes. Not all of the latter are equally important to the organization (see Table 10.2 below). Task groups fall into three classes: **counteracting**, **co-acting**, and **interacting** (Fiedler & Garcia, 1987). The first type occurs when members come together to address a conflict or common concern among some or all of the members. A faculty curriculum committee seeking to resolve an overlap between courses offered in different departments illustrates this type of group. A co-acting group assembles to share issues and problems encountered by each member pursuing separate goals. Their relationship is usually pooled interdependence. Academic departments are usually co-acting groups. In department meetings, faculty members share issues and concerns that arise in their individual work. An interacting group involves persons whose work is related by virtue of their sequential or reciprocal interdependence. A research and development team whose members depend on each other for inputs and outputs is an example

TABLE 10.2
Types of Groups

Group Type	Examples
Organizational unit	Academic department, athletics department, research center/institute
Job or work team	Committee or task force (more temporary than a department)
Pressure or interest group	Employee union
Friendship or social group	Employee bowling league, employee book club
Informal group	Unofficial collection of individuals connected by common norms

of an interacting group. In short, groups can be distinguished by their conceptions of presumed or manifested conflict (counteracting), unresolved issues (co-acting), and practical needs for collaboration (interacting).

Membership in a Group

Since groups exert both subtle and overt influence over their members, the question arises of how much a person must be influenced before he or she can be considered a member of the group. One way of defining membership is by an organizational member's *participation in* the system of interlocking roles and his or her *understanding of* and agreement with: (1) the **normative prescriptions and proscriptions** for behavior in interactions between or among other members of the group, and (2) the probable positive or negative **sanctions** for conformity or nonconformity with those expectations. That is, one is a member of a group if and only if one understands and agrees with others on the behavior that is expected under different circumstances, and understands and is aware of the rewards and penalties for compliance or noncompliance. Students form and remain in groups in residential halls, for example, on the basis of mutual personal liking and agreement to follow the direction of the group or risk being ostracized by its members. By definition, then, one cannot be a member of a group if one does not "play by the rules" of the group to some degree (even if those rules are nowhere explicitly laid out). Note, however, that groups often overlap (Alderfer, 1987), so a person can be a member of several groups and may expect one group to satisfy one need and a second or third group to satisfy other needs, with varying degrees of allegiance and commitment associated with each.

Origins of Groups

Groups arise out of some formal or informal need of individuals for interaction. Organizational design may necessitate that organizational members interact to facilitate departmental interdependence. For example, since the admissions office needs to coordinate its material across schools and departments, it may form a publications committee with representation from the various academic units.

In contrast, informal groups often arise from emerging social interaction, as workers in organizations come together and work out relationships between and among them. Some interactions may be organizationally required, while others may not. Informal groups may be formed for companionship, desire for identification and belonging, understanding from friends, opportunities for initiative and creativity, help in solving work problems, and mutual protection from management (Davis, 1967; Sayles & Strauss, 1977).

George Homans (1950) discusses this process of evolving interpersonal relationships in organizations in terms of **required and emergent activities, interactions, and sentiments**. The required set stems from the need for behaviors that contribute to the output of the organization. Since it is impossible for the organization to specify all of the requirements, a related, complementary set of activities, interactions, and sentiments emerges out of the social nexus of workers joined in a common purpose. A sample set of required and emergent activities, interactions, and sentiments of faculty members is given in Table 10.3.

The organizationally required set of actions takes place within the *formal organization* structure (e.g., teaching within an academic department). In contrast, an *informal organization* emerges to address other needs for interaction. Consider, for example, a group of faculty, who use the same course management software, getting together over lunch several times each semester to discuss the latest updates in this software package. The lunch group serves as an informal organization that supplements the technology support that faculty may receive through the formal organization.

Informal Organization

The **informal organization** is a collateral or parallel organization (Zand, 1981) that arises to complement the formal or visible organization. Zand notes:

A collateral organization is distinguishable from and linked to the formal organization as follows:

TABLE 10.3
Example of Required and Emergent Activities, Interactions, and Sentiments in Higher Education

	Activities (tasks for output)	*Interactions* (with one another)	*Sentiments* (feelings toward the organization and each other)
Required	Teach 3 classes	Team teach	Tolerance of others
Emergent	Design handouts for class	Work with colleague to develop slides for computer presentation	Address the unique learning needs of each student

1. The purpose of the collateral organization is to identify and solve problems not solved by the formal (primary) organization.
2. A collateral organization creatively complements the formal organization. It allows new combinations of people, new channels of communication, and new ways of seeing old ideas.
3. A collateral organization operates in parallel or in tandem with the formal organization. Both the collateral and the formal organizations are available. A manager chooses one or the other, depending on the problem. A collateral organization does not displace the formal organization.
4. A collateral organization consists of the same people who work in the formal organization. There are no new people.
5. The outputs of the collateral organization are inputs to the formal organization. The ultimate value of a collateral organization depends on successfully linking it to the formal organization, so its outputs are used.
6. A collateral organization operates with norms (that is, expectations of how people will behave) that are different from the norms in the formal organization. The different norms facilitate new ideas and new approaches to obstacles. (p. 67)

It is extremely important that leaders understand the components of this informal system if they wish to improve group and organizational effectiveness. The phenomenon can be compared to an **iceberg**, most of whose characteristics are hidden below the surface of the water (see Figure 10.1).

The overt components are publicly observable, generally rational, and cognitively derived and oriented to operational and task considerations. Note that the overt or more easily discernible components of the organization represent most of the elements in organizational design discussed in chapter 6. Many observers believe that these more visible elements of organizations constitute virtually the whole of the organization and are, consequently, the most important to address. Note, however, that the covert, informal organization—the emergent needs, values, attitudes, emotions, and behaviors of workers—is critical to the effectiveness and efficiency of organizations and to the motivation and satisfaction of organizational members. These components, however, are generally less visible to leaders, affective and emotionally derived, and oriented to the general climate and to social/psychological and behavioral process considerations.

Benefits of Informal Organization to the Formal Organization

As Homans (1950) noted, it is not possible for organizations to specify for each individual every one of the required activities, interactions, and sentiments necessary for the organization to be effective. The collective

FIGURE 10.1
The Organizational Iceberg

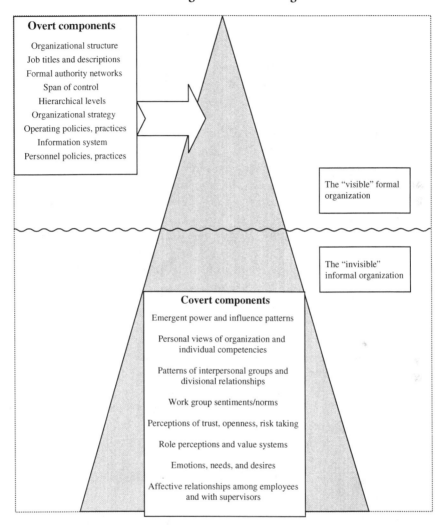

Overt components

Organizational structure
Job titles and descriptions
Formal authority networks
Span of control
Hierarchical levels
Organizational strategy
Operating policies, practices
Information system
Personnel policies, practices

The "visible" formal organization

The "invisible" informal organization

Covert components

Emergent power and influence patterns

Personal views of organization and individual competencies

Patterns of interpersonal groups and divisional relationships

Work group sentiments/norms

Perceptions of trust, openness, risk taking

Role perceptions and value systems

Emotions, needs, and desires

Affective relationships among employees and with supervisors

judgments of the informal group, therefore, may substitute for inaccurate, incomplete, or ambiguous information from organizational management (Cummings, 1981). The informal organization thus affects the formal organization—either positively by filling in unspecified gaps in formal operating procedures or negatively by subtly obstructing them.

Second, the informal organization lightens the load of the formal manager by taking up the slack in leadership. Indeed, when informal and formal goals are aligned, leaders can leave the responsibility for self-management to the informal organization and dedicate more time to more creative leadership activities.

Third, informally generated norms serve the same kind of latent "buffering" function that rules serve on the formal side of the organization. Norms prescribe behaviors that are socially acceptable and proscribe those that are not. The negative sanctions associated with violating a norm may prevent arbitrary and capricious behaviors from arising in the group, thus protecting group members from exploitation.

Norms also provide satisfactions and stability to the work group. The informal organization provides intrinsic satisfactions and motivation to perform effectively. There are simply not enough sources of reward in the formal organization to satisfy all workers. Even if resources were unlimited, many people would derive significant satisfactions from the work itself. Rewards and satisfactions such as collegiality and friendships with coworkers cannot be awarded by the formal organization (although it can provide supportive conditions). Only the informal organization can provide such benefits.

Another function of the informal organization is to reduce harmful competition among employees. The existence of group work effort norms gives members a sense of what a "reasonable" rate of productivity is for the particular work setting. Lacking this knowledge, workers may compete for management favor, potentially causing personal distress as well as organizationally dysfunctional or even subversive behavior. That is, group-sanctioned productivity standards, in addition to management standards, permit organizational members to produce at levels comparable to those of colleagues and thus provide relief from apprehensions that management expects more.

Finally, norms may generate positive, prosocial behaviors among workers (van Dyne & LePine, 1998). In an academic department, for example, norms for facilitating others' research may emerge, so, for example, faculty may offer suggestions of resources thought to be of interest to colleagues.

Group Dynamics

One of the most neglected aspects of informal organization by practicing managers is the nature of the informal status hierarchy that arises among workers. In part, the status of individual workers derives from the nature of the jobs they perform—the formal, higher-ranking jobs often, but by no means always, connoting a higher informal status. In the informal organization, assessments of talent (and other characteristics) may yield status hierarchies different from those of the formal authority ladder.

In a study of human relations in the restaurant industry, William F. Whyte (1948) conducted research that shows the effects of status differentials on worker attitudes and motivation. By observing interactions among workers in food preparation areas, he was able to note the relationships among onion peelers, carrot peelers, potato peelers, and others. He noted that when one of the workers was absent from work because of illness, and the manager reassigned the work, the workers protested vociferously. Whyte concluded that there seemed to an invisible status hierarchy among the vegetable processors. Peeling carrots, for example, ranked higher than peeling onions. Even though the two jobs were equivalent in the formal hierarchy, peeling onions is viewed as a more odious task (it makes your eyes water). Thus, the arbitrary reassignment by the manager meant demotion or promotion in the informal status that the group observed.

What is important to note here is that hidden interpersonal relationships are often difficult to discern but nevertheless constitute an integral dimension of organizational life to be addressed by leaders. In higher education at every level, informal status may not coincide with formal status. Changes in work routines often violate parts of human relationships that have evolved—the components of the iceberg below the water level—and often result in a host of unanticipated problems. This is not to suggest that the informal organizational conditions are sacrosanct and must be preserved as they are. Rather, it indicates that organizational leaders must be aware of and sensitive to them before any changes can be made in the formal system.

Another aspect of group dynamics is **communication patterns**. Researchers have found that organizational members talk to one another in groups in patterned order, reflecting both informal status and interpersonal liking. Some workers, for example, almost invariably speak immediately after others. Others tend to interrupt, still others to disagree. Careful observation of these characteristics of groups will permit more sophisticated anticipation of reactions and propitious intervention when changes are introduced.

Members of groups consciously and unconsciously make decisions about how to behave in groups. As most students know well, there is a tendency to repeat patterns begun at the start of groups—for example, sitting in the same chair at each seminar meeting throughout an entire semester. Interestingly, research reveals that there is a predictable relationship between persons who sit opposite each other at meetings. Their interactions differ from those of people sitting adjacent to one another: the opposites generally tend to disagree, while the adjacents agree more frequently. A newcomer to a meeting might well anticipate these kinds of interactions, or an organizational leader might ask proponents of opposing positions to sit next to one another.

Personal Roles in Groups

When groups have been in existence for some time, their membership must take on several important functions. These functions are usually divided into task, group-building, and maintenance roles distributed among different persons (Hellriegel, Slocum, & Woodman, 1995). Task-related roles refer to the work performance of the group. Here are some behaviors that fall into the task role category:

1. Defines problems
2. Seeks information
3. Gives information

4. Seeks opinions
5. Gives opinions
6. Tests feasibility

Group-building and maintenance-related roles refer to the requirement that the group be sustained as an efficiently working body. Persons performing this function are concerned with seeing that workers stick together and that those who do not observe group norms are punished. Corresponding behaviors are:

7. Coordinating
8. Mediating-harmonizing
9. Orienting-facilitating

10. Supporting and encouraging
11. Following

In all groups, however, some members take on self-serving roles that may not enhance group performance or lead to achievement of group goals. These roles include:

12. Blocking
13. Out-of-field remarks
14. Digressing

Depending on the particular problem at hand, leaders can identify key group role players whose contributions can be called on when propitious. If low group effectiveness is evident, the problem may be traced to either the absence of persons willing to play these essential roles or to an excess of self-serving role players (for example, numbers 12, 13, and 14 above).

Group effectiveness (or ineffectiveness) may also be traced to the belief of the group in its own efficacy (Gibson, 1999). In groups, the impact of the level of efficacy on group effectiveness is moderated by various task characteristics. The nature of the uncertainty of the task and the kinds of interdependence among group members clearly affect the degree to which confidence in the group's ability to perform well makes a difference in the performance itself. Team confidence and belief in teammates' competence has an intangible positive influence on performance—manifested most saliently in sports but no less powerfully in work groups.

Subsystems in Groups

Like any system, groups have specialized subsystems whose functions are to transform inputs effectively and efficiently. Four subsystems are operative in all groups: methodological, intellectual, emotional, and functional.

The **methodological subsystem** describes the procedures that formally guide group interactions. For example, the group may agree to operate by Robert's Rules of Order, majority rule, or unilateral decisions by the group leader. The methodological system also includes guidelines that evolve from the norms established by the group.

The **intellectual subsystem** comprises the body of content that forms a basis for consensus on language, paradigms, and assumptions that will be used in making decisions. For example, a college may establish that psychosocial development in students is a goal of equal importance to cognitive gains.

All groups also have an **emotional subsystem** that describes the ups and downs in morale. It is a collective feeling about the psychological well-being of the group. Finally, all groups have **functional task subsystems** that facilitate the transformation processes in which the group is engaged.

Each subsystem contributes to the effectiveness of the group. That is, they are independent variables that can be modified to affect the dependent variable, group effectiveness. Knowing about any one can contribute to more effective operations.

Sociometric Analysis of Groups

Sociologists and social psychologists have developed a method for scientifically determining the structure of groups. Called **block modeling**, it is an easily performed means of assessing interpersonal attitudes among members of a group. It consists of four basic procedures:

1. **Sociogram**. This is a diagram of group attraction patterns that, for example, depicts who likes whom, who chooses whom as friend.
2. **Diagram of informal interactions**. In contrast with the attitudes and feelings portrayed in a sociogram, this procedure charts who interacts with whom. It shows the frequency, direction, and initiation of various interactions.
3. **Status hierarchy within the group**. Informal status in a group is a function of closeness of behavioral conformity to the norms of the group, especially as modeled by the group leader. Measuring deviations from the behavior pattern of the group leader yields information about individual status within the group. Those who deviate

substantially from group norms are not likely to be held in high regard by the other members.

4. **"Map" of interpersonal work preference structure**. This procedure ascertains from organizational members what tasks they would like to perform and with whom they would like to work (Kilmann & McKelvey, 1975). These data are then used to aggregate people into task/affinity groups. This method takes into account the informal organization in the design of the formal organization.

Stages of Group Function and Development

Researchers have identified recognizable stages by which groups develop (Obert, 1983; Tuckman, 1965; Tuckman & Jensen, 1977). Each stage is characterized by varying modes and degrees of clarity/ambiguity, formality/informality, conflict, collaboration, and leadership styles. The stages are sequential, so identification of one stage permits anticipation of and planning for the next. The characteristics of each stage are presented in Table 10.4.

The first stage of group development (**forming**) is characterized by high levels of interpersonal politeness as members meet each other and learn about the task at hand. Group members come to agreement fairly quickly about goals and procedures (e.g., how often they plan to meet), but there is also ambiguity and uncertainty regarding group leadership and responsibilities.

In the **storming** phase, group members confront the complexities of their work and realize that they may need to revisit their interpretation of the problem they are trying to solve. Group members may have assumed that everyone was in agreement on how to proceed, but when performing their tasks together, they realize that not all of their colleagues are "on the same

TABLE 10.4
Stages of Group Development: Characteristics*

Stage	*Characteristics*
Forming	Ambiguity, politeness, uncertainty
Storming	Disagreement, alliances, questions about task and process
Norming	Guidelines established for making decisions, and resolving conflict; extensive communication
Performing	Agreement on goals, roles, and norms; creativity; self-management; self-assessment

*Based on Tuckman, 1965; Tuckman and Jensen, 1977.

page." Conflict is likely to emerge as members express differences of opinion regarding what problem they ought to be solving and how they will function together as a group. Some groups, unfortunately, never leave the storming phase. Conflict management skills and tolerance for divergent opinions are necessary to navigate from storming to norming.

The **norming** phase is characterized by an adjustment of group behavior. Norms and guidelines for making decisions and resolving conflict become clear to team members. Teamwork tasks become more fluid, as members learn how to work with each other and how to capitalize on the unique strengths that each member brings to the group. Trust grows and motivation increases as group members become more familiar with each other and more knowledgeable about the project on which they are working.

In the **performing** stage, group members function as a single unit. The group attains a high level of synergy—a work climate that enables group members to accomplish together what they could not achieve on their own. Creativity and innovation flourish. Dissent is expected and permitted, as long as it remains focused on improving group performance. At this stage of development, the group is largely self-managing. The members are competent and capable of autonomous decision making and have little need for supervision.

Tuckman (1965) argues that groups must progress through these developmental stages in order to become effective. Groups may revert to previous stages as they respond to changing circumstances (e.g., new members, new tasks), but the sequence of stages remains the same. Subsequently, other scholars have criticized Tuckman's model, arguing that group development does not necessarily progress through a series of linear stages. Gersick (1988), for example, found that group development was characterized by nonlinear patterns that vacillated between long periods of stability and radical change—a pattern known as **punctuated equilibrium**. Periodically, disruptive changes in group development were caused by the intervention of an external authority figure, the introduction of a startling new idea, or the unexpected shifting of a deadline.

The teams in Gersick's study "did not accomplish their work by progressing gradually through a universal series of stages . . . Instead, teams progressed . . . through alternating inertia and revolution in behaviors and themes through which they approached their work" (Gersick, 1988, p. 9). Teams were inert for extended periods and then made great leaps forward, only to return to an inert state until another dramatic period of activity. Gersick found that these developmental bursts were particularly associated with team members' awareness of time and deadlines. For example, among the eight teams in Gersick's study, "each group experienced its transition at the same point in its calendar—precisely halfway between its first meeting and its official deadline—despite wide variation in the amounts of time the eight teams were allotted for their projects" (p. 16).

Regardless of whether the timeline for the project was a few weeks or several months, each team experienced a significant behavioral and attitudinal transition at the midpoint of the timeline. Gersick's punctuated equilibrium model suggests that group development is characterized by long periods of inactivity interspersed with breakpoints and disruptions—rather than by an orderly developmental sequence. The implication for organizational leadership is that the midpoint of a team project represents a critical juncture that may require the infusion of additional data, information, and support for the team from others in the organization.

Group Norms

> Norms are the rules and patterns of behavior that are accepted and expected by members of a team [or group]. They help define the behaviors that members believe to be necessary to help them reach their goals. Over time, every team establishes norms and enforces them on its members. Norms often are more rigidly defined and enforced in informal groups—by peer pressure—than in formally organized teams. Such norms may further or inhibit achievement of organizational goals. (Hellriegel & Slocum, 2004, p. 211)

Group norms reflect collective expectations and guidelines for beliefs and behaviors. They represent the shared expectations for individual behavior by the group—or, more technically, they constitute the collective individual assessments of what is proper individual behavior. Norms vary in intensity, and members vary in their allegiance and adherence to them. When individuals depart from powerful group norms, they risk incurring negative **sanctions** that increase in severity the more distant the behavior is from the norm. Conformity to norms follows a bell-shaped curve, with most members clustering around the common expected behavior at the top of the bell. The informal leader of the group usually constitutes the model for the norm. Workers far away from the center are often **isolates**—only marginally part of the group. For example, if the norm in an academic department is to spend a complete day on Fridays working in the office, then faculty who decide not to do so are likely to suffer negative peer sanctions of many sorts.

On an organizational level (larger than the group), norms are sometimes referred to collectively as **organizational climate**. That is, aggregations of norms together constitute a pattern that becomes the prevailing collective "emotional weather condition" of a system (Peterson & Spencer, 1990). It includes a variety of attitudes and behaviors. Morale is also a dimension of climate. We will return to this topic in the next chapter on organizational culture.

A good manager can receive considerable assistance from the normative systems of groups. If a manager can substitute positive, collaborative norms for direct supervision, then there will be less need for constant direct oversight—an asymmetrical power condition that most organizational members find objectionable. In addition, there will be fewer needs for imposing formal rules that have other dysfunctions, as noted in the discussion of bureaucracies (e.g., excessive "red tape," decision delay, and lack of creativity; see chapter 7).

In addition to norms, it is important to consider how the **informal leader**—the nontitled, unofficial leader of the group—can advance or frustrate the efforts of formal leaders. Informal leaders by definition are organizational members whose behavior most closely conforms to group norms. By virtue of his or her modeling of normative attitudes and behaviors, the informal leader can demonstrate to others the value of following formal management directives or deviating from them.

The Development of Norms

A number of sources influence group members as they come to understand and own (to varying degrees) the beliefs and values that constitute the norms of the group (Feldman, 1984). First, there are statements by supervisors or important officials—for example, no lateness, keep office hours. While these are official rules, norms typically form around them either to reinforce or to vitiate them.

A second source of influence is critical events in group history. For example, when something goes especially well or poorly, it sets a precedent. A research team that wins a coveted grant may continue to rely on the same grant-writing techniques that were successful in this particular competition. The behaviors that were associated with success (e.g., meticulous data analysis, thorough literature reviews) become normative for the group. Conversely, certain behaviors in a team that fails to attract research funding (e.g., missing deadlines, incomplete analyses) may attract negative sanctions from team members in future grant-writing efforts.

Primacy also sets precedents. What happens first by chance tends to be perpetuated normatively. For example, seating patterns of persons around a table at a committee meeting tend to be repeated, even though no formal rules dictate them.

Finally, carryovers from other situations tend to influence the establishment of norms. If students establish relationships in one class, for instance, they tend to continue those relationships in other curricular and extracurricular experiences.

The Variety of Norms

Many different kinds of norms are operative in some strength at all times:

1. **Norms of self-presentation.** Examples of this kind of norm include how much people smile, how close or far away people stand from each other, how they dress (e.g., jeans or dark suits), how they address one another (as in sir, madam, or "hey, kid"). In most instances, language shifts according to the setting and the relative status of the interacting parties. Consider, for example, the modes of interaction among students and faculty at different types of institutions and at different levels of education (graduate versus undergraduate).

2. **Norms of prioritization.** These norms direct organizational members toward that which is most valued or most important in the organization. Faculty members in a department, for example, might come to adopt the norm that personnel matters are always first on the meeting agenda. As another example, office managers may develop routines (unofficial codifications of norms) that determine the priority to be accorded to requests for vacation times. Vacation requests may be prioritized by seniority (i.e., longtime employees are most likely to get their requests approved), by work flow (e.g., no vacations for admissions staff before application deadlines), or by some other criterion deemed important by the organization.

3. **Norms of relationship.** Some examples of this kind of norm include, "We never criticize one another in public." (Recall that norms are not written down.) Another is that one has an obligation to repay personal debts and favors. This **norm of reciprocity** (Gouldner, 1960) is the tendency to respond to the actions of others with similar actions. If we are treated with kindness and respect, then we are likely to respond in kind. Or if we encounter hostility and defensiveness, we are likely to respond in a similar fashion, thus constructing a contentious relationship.

4. **Norms governing conflict management, bargaining modes, and disagreement resolution.** This extremely important set of norms dictates the modes for organizational problem solving as well as the interpersonal relationships associated with them. Organizations whose norm is, "We don't fight in the open," are often found to have

long-standing, smoldering resentments and resistance to compliance to group expectations. Unfortunately, this phenomenon is common in organizations, since open conflict is often avoided because of its unpleasantness. It takes a highly skilled leader to bring latent conflicts out into the open and, even more important, to establish norms of conflict resolution that encourage open expression of conflict.

5. **Norms of distribution.** From these norms, people learn how the group expects to handle routine and nonroutine problems. These norms include the distribution of tasks, group functions, positions in the group hierarchy, and opinions on culturally relevant topics such as religion, government, health, work, money, and possessions. For example, with respect to tasks, the norm might be, "If it's problem type A, then X takes care of it." Or, for opinions, "Y is the person to talk to about the role of academic freedom and tenure in the academy."

6. **Norms about norms.** This final group consists of shared expectations about which norms are to be strictly enforced and which can be safely ignored. These norms often adjudicate among conflicting expectations. Suppose, for example, that there are two norms. One says that the group respects the opinions of those who have been in the organization the longest; the other says that the group values expertise. What happens when the group is dealing with an issue where younger staff members have more relevant expertise? Will the group defer to the opinions of the more senior staff, or will the views of less experienced but more knowledgeable employees prevail? Norms about what to do when these two norms are in conflict thus must also be present.

Norms do not cover every situation; they usually address only those behaviors that have some special significance for the group. Groups enforce norms that facilitate survival and achievement, protect group integrity, and keep the group safe from outside interference.

Conditions of Conformity to Norms

When norms support and reinforce organizational goal achievement, overall effectiveness is improved; therefore, it is important to know and understand the variables that contribute to conformity to norms. Group members conform to norms when group pressures are sent strongly enough to be perceived, and when the targeted individual values the group's rewards and sanctions. Weak norms, or norms that are not made manifest, will not ensure conformity. For example, if a "good teaching" norm is not communicated strongly as a departmental norm, then fewer people will conform to it.

The modes of communicating norms are also an important topic (Hackman, 1992). Two primary modes of communication use different stimuli.

Ambient stimuli—these are stimuli about group expectations that are available to all members of the group; they pervade the group and its environment. Everyone knows what is expected of all group members. An example might be dress codes.

Discretionary stimuli—in contrast to universally applied norms, these stimuli are transmitted selectively to individual group members at the discretion of their peers. These stimuli are special individual messages that convey the group's expectations about any one individual. They may be messages of approval or disapproval about one individual's behavior that may be different from another's. They may be considered norms because the remainder of the group holds them in common.

In addition, for the norm to be received, it must matter to the individual whether he or she gets the rewards or avoids the negative sanctions associated with group membership. There are two types of conformity: **compliance conformity** and **personal acceptance**. Compliance conformity derives from fear of negative sanctions, while personal acceptance conformity stems from sincere belief in the legitimacy of the norm itself. Thus, a member of the bursar's office staff may comply reluctantly with a group norm about politeness in interactions with students about loans (in order to maintain his status in the group), or he may comply because he is sincerely committed to that norm.

Sanctions for Nonconformity to Norms

Groups control the behavior of their members—how they enforce conformity to group norms—through many modes. Negative sanctions include ostracism, exclusion from social activities, refusing aid in work, reporting (tattling) to management, and sabotage. Positive modes include role modeling, verbal approval, inclusion, and personal aid. It is important to note once again that sanctions, both positive and negative, are often subtle and difficult to discern and observe. They are, nevertheless, clues to the structure and power of informal groups.

Free Riding and Social Loafing

As group size increases, members are less subject to observation and to normative pressure. Where much activity occurs in private offices, moreover, it is difficult to see how much or how hard others are working. In some organizations, a belief may arise that others are "loafing" (Price, 1993). Equity theories of motivation suggest that individuals who have this belief will reduce their effort and coast along unobserved. This proclivity for **free riding** can be overcome by communication and promulgation of individual and group efforts so that all members are aware of the others' contributions, and there is little or no loss of individuality (Diener, 1979).

This issue is especially problematic in the case of allocating rewards in merit systems (e.g., annual faculty salary evaluations) that are based on individual productivity. When rewards are divided roughly equally among members of a group (e.g., faculty in a department), regardless of their levels of productivity, a free rider problem often arises (if social norms are not strong enough to offset it). In general, stepped systems of equal annual pay raises that do not take into account individual productivity tend to promote harmony by obviating jealousies and feelings of inequity over salary differentials. On the other hand, some of the positive effects of this egalitarian method of distributing rewards are offset by especially hard-working individuals who feel that they deserve higher compensation and who resent free riding and/or those they suspect of free riding. The disruptive effects are a function of the relative importance in the group of intrinsic versus extrinsic rewards. While much of the satisfaction associated with working in higher education comes from intrinsic rewards from the work itself, the resentment of apparently inequitable external rewards accorded to free riders may intrude into the satisfactions of organizational members.

Cohesiveness and Effectiveness

The productivity of groups depends not only on individual performance but also on the willingness of members to collaborate and cooperate with other members over a relatively long period. This commitment to other members both as individuals and as members of a group is called **cohesiveness** (Seashore, 1954; Stogdill, 1972). Cohesiveness refers to pressures that group members experience to work on behalf of the group and to remain committed to it. Collectively, cohesiveness reflects members' emotional "sticking together"—a sense of caring about the well-being of all members. For any one individual, it is the perception that all or most of the members of the group are similarly committed and, hence, a recognition that failure to conform to this norm will be perceived as deviant (Hackman, 1990).

Many variables affect the degree of cohesiveness in organizations (see Wexley & Yukl, 1975). For example, when organizations increase in size, their cohesiveness seems to decrease. On the other hand, member stability and homogeneity are positively related to smaller-size groups. In groups where members must collaborate to accomplish their work, as might be expected, cohesiveness must increase. Finally, in the face of an external threat, group members often tend to "circle the wagons" and become more cohesive.

Cohesiveness is not only the by-product of other organizational variables; it has an independent impact on other key group dynamics as well. For example, the greater the cohesiveness, the greater the conformity of members to norms. Because of the group-generated pressures toward uniformity and conformity (e.g., "do it for the group"), cohesiveness generates norms of higher priority for the group than for the individual. For example, a task-based, closely knit group of faculty will insist that each faculty member keep up with his or her rate of publication, even if there is no official organizational standard.

It is important to note that there is no necessary relationship between cohesiveness and group productivity. Even if group members *are* highly conforming to group norms, group productivity may still be low if the norm calls for minimal effort. Thus, cohesiveness can be functional or dysfunctional (Etzioni, 1961; Mudrack, 1989; Sanders & Nauta, 2004; Stogdill, 1972).

Groupthink

The dysfunctions of cohesiveness are evident in "groupthink"—a concept that was brought most cogently to light by Irving Janis in 1972 and subsequently expanded (Janis, 1982; Whyte, 1989, 1998). Janis (1982) describes the phenomenon as "a mode of thinking that people engage in when they are deeply involved in a cohesive in-group, when the members' striving for unanimity overrides their motivation to realistically appraise alternative courses of action" (p. 9).

High cohesiveness, then, even when task-based, may not lead to effective performance. The thesis is that some groups become *excessively* close-knit and operate with an illusion of unanimity among group members, which may result in much rationalization and negative stereotyping of outsiders who are critical of the group's behavior.

Groupthink has a number of other negative consequences. For one, the more groupthink, the less open the group is to discrepant or unsettling information (either from inside or outside). Note how dysfunctional this can be for a research-oriented academic department, for example, which may be induced to discount information that contradicts a popular theory held in common by the group. Because a spirit of "goodwill" dominates, department members fear disrupting the social status quo.

Indeed, the group may pursue a grossly inappropriate course of action. For example, in the Bay of Pigs invasion of Cuba in 1961, President Kennedy surrounded himself with counselors and advisors in a very close-knit group.

No one wanted to deal with upsetting information that differed from what they currently believed about Cuban resistance because it would potentially disturb the good relationships the group members had with each other. The result was a failed invasion.

Recently, researchers have begun to question whether the variable "cohesiveness" is an antecedent condition of groupthink (Aldag & Fuller, 1993; Park, 1990). Empirical evidence seems to be inconclusive. As a result, another potentially more powerful explanatory concept, "perceived collective efficacy," or a common belief about the ability of the group to be successful, has been proposed. This attitude can lead to overconfidence and complacency (Lindsley, Brass, & Thomas, 1995; Sitkin, 1992). On the positive side, however, collective efficacy has been shown to be strongly related to group performance. Indeed, research has shown that there is an average correlation of .45 between collective efficacy and group performance (Stajkovic & Luthans, 1998).

The Polarization Phenomenon

When discrepant information *is* introduced to a group, however, a phenomenon known as **polarization** may take place (Fitzpatrick, 1989; Myers & Lamm, 1976). When group members are split on an issue, exposure to other positions will likely polarize the group. The dilemma for management is that cohesive work groups can be highly productive, but cohesiveness can lead to groupthink. To avoid groupthink, discrepant information must be introduced, even at the risk of making the group polarized and *less* cohesive (and, consequently, potentially less productive—at least temporarily).

A related question focuses on the relationship of cohesiveness to norms. Antimanagement norms are much more difficult to deal with when socially based cohesiveness is high. In this case, group members band together to subvert authority. On the other hand, when norms and management goals are coincident, task-based cohesiveness is a positive influence on organizational productivity. Organizational leaders can direct groups toward a stronger task orientation by organizing projects in ways that are satisfying, both individually and for the group as a whole.

Teams as Groups

"A *work team* [emphasis in the original] is a group of people with complementary skills who are committed to a common mission, performance goals, and approach for which they hold themselves mutually accountable" (Nelson & Quick, 2005, p. 178). Since the early 1980s, there has been a significant increase in interest in how teams can be made more effective in organizations, particularly in their problem-solving roles (Hackman, 1990; Parker, 1990).

Self-managed teams of 10 to 15 workers whose jobs are "enriched" by absorbing a number of management roles seem to have been quite effective (Merrell, 1979). In fact, in some organizations, teams have been given independent budgetary authority over and above that allocated to the formal hierarchy.

Borrowing from early successes with matrix designs, some organizations are finding that **cross-functional** teams—groups of specialists brought together to resolve problems or design new products—are especially effective (Ford & Randolph, 1992; Michalski & King, 1998). Membership in these teams is not bound by traditional department boundaries. The team usually meets to address a unique set of needs (e.g., organizing a multidisciplinary academic conference) and often is disbanded when the need is met. While similar to committees, cross-functional teams tend to be more immediately task oriented. Cross-functional and self-managed teams are increasingly using new information technologies that permit participation in group decision making without the necessity for members to be together physically (Hinds & Kiesler, 2002).

Social Construction, Groups, and Teams

We now turn to a consideration of the social constructionist perspective on groups and teams. This perspective, in some ways, amplifies our previous discussion of informal organization, but it also extends those views to consider interactions between formal and informal organization as well as the multiple realities that groups and teams construct within the same organization.

The informal organization is an important part of how social constructionists conceptualize organizational life. Social constructionists argue that organizations are enacted through the interactions and cognitions of organizational members. Through actions and interactions with others, people develop mental maps and frames for seeing the organization (Bolman & Deal, 2003; Senge, 1990). These frames guide behavior, aid in making sense of experiences, and serve as vehicles for constructing shared understandings and commitments for collective action (Weick, 1995). The social construction paradigm, therefore, illuminates many aspects of groups and teams in organizations, especially the informal dimensions.

Stating that the organization is a social construction, however, does not mean that all organizations are collaborative and group based. Some organizations are characterized by a dominant construction of reality that enforces passive mindsets and subservient behaviors. In other organizations, the socially constructed reality is one of firm boundaries between members rather than collaboration. In this case, the socially constructed informal organization may mirror a rigid, highly departmentalized formal structure. Nevertheless, as we noted previously, the informal organization often arises to address limitations in the formal structure; it is enacted in response to unmet needs.

Structuration theory can explain how the informal organization emerges, and how groups and teams relate to the rest of the organization (Giddens, 1984). In chapter 7, we noted that structuration theory views structure as a constellation of rules and resources that organizational members use to give form to their work together. An important element in this theory is that social systems (including organizations and the groups within them) *appropriate* rules and resources from their surrounding environments. Organizations and groups, in effect, borrow structures from the outside world and then develop a localized version of those structures for use in their own activities. In the case of groups and teams, members can appropriate structures from within the organization or adopt rules and resources from outside entities (e.g., develop a localized version of best practices identified at comparable peer institutions).

Structuration theory (Bachmann, 2001; Poole, Seibold, & McPhee, 1996) attempts to identify links between global and local issues (macro and micro concerns) by noting that:

1. Groups are embedded in larger patterns of social interaction that limit the types of structures they can appropriate. For example, group tasks, roles, and membership (e.g., appointments to administrative committees) are often determined by the larger organization. Thus, group structuration is constrained by organizational structuration.

2. Group structuration is also limited by the larger political, social, religious, and economic systems in which the organization as a whole is embedded. Curriculum committees in community colleges, for example, may not be able to appropriate structures for extensive consultation because of the need for rapid and frequent decisions to accommodate changing economic and public policy priorities.

3. Group boundaries are permeable; consequently, roles and responsibilities tend to overlap among groups in an organization, and between organizational groups and groups external to the organization. Thus, group structuration is constrained by other groups' structuration processes. The rules and resources used by a faculty senate budget committee, for example, are limited by the structures appropriated by the chief financial officer's budget team, given the overlapping governance responsibilities of these two groups.

4. The external environment not only constrains structuration, it also raises awareness about new structures that organizations and groups can appropriate. As an example, if major research universities begin to shift their resources from academic departments to interdisciplinary teams, then other institutions may begin to appropriate similar structures. Such changes would result in a reconfiguration of power among different groups in the university: more power for interdisciplinary teams and less power for academic departments.

5. The distribution of power among group members also affects the types of structures that groups appropriate. If a powerful department chair is a member of the curriculum committee, then he or she is likely to influence the rules and resources appropriated by that group disproportionately.

6. The types of structures that groups appropriate also depend on historical and situational context. A diversity committee, for example, may appropriate a subcommittee structure for Native American issues, because of the university's historical neglect of this population.

7. Finally, the professional expertise, socialization experiences, and ideologies of group members are likely to shape the structural mix appropriated by the group. Faculty members in a computer science department are likely to appropriate different structures for their department meetings from faculty in a humanities department.

Skillful appropriation of structures can play an important part in building trust and collaboration among members of a group or team. Specifically, the roles that group members appropriate can affect the development and degree of trust within the group. Team members who appropriate *functional roles* as guidelines for behavior reinforce a group dynamic where team members serve as representatives for their particular functional area—for example, student affairs, finance, enrollment management. The team, in turn, becomes structured as an arena for advocating positions and competing for scarce resources. Here, group dynamics reflect competition, rather than collaboration, among units. The appropriation of *group process roles*, in contrast, encourages collaborative thinking and cross-functional deliberation. Here, team members view themselves as analysts, problem definers, or devil's advocates, rather than as representatives of their functional area (Bensimon & Neumann, 1993).

Teams may appropriate the same authority structures that are present in their organizations. In a hierarchical organization, the people at the top of the hierarchy are likely to control the team's agenda. Alternatively, teams may appropriate different authority structures, such as leadership rotation and nonhierarchical forms of agenda setting and task allocation (Jones & George, 1998). However, if a team appropriates an authority structure that differs from its larger organization context, team members may encounter conflicting expectations between the team and the organization. Social constructionists, in this instance, highlight the need for leaders to be adept at working in organizations characterized by multiple realities, multiple authority structures, and divergent views about formal and informal structure. Unlike positivists, who view this multiplicity and ambiguity as problems to be solved, social constructionists consider these elements to be the foundation for creativity and variety in organizational life.

Postmodern Perspectives on Groups and Teams

Postmodernists offer additional alternatives for structuring groups and teams. The postmodern era is characterized by rapidly changing technologies, diverse values and lifestyles, and global modes of production and consumption (Bloland, 2005). A central unifying structure for the organization may be unrealistic (or even harmful) under such conditions. Instead, temporary teams and shifting configurations of groups and personnel may be more appropriate for accommodating the fragmentation of the postmodern era.

Martin (1992), for example, suggests that postmodern organizations have no clear center—no central authority structure that links all of the subsystems in the organization. Without a clear center, self-managed teams become even more important to overall organizational effectiveness. Self-managed teams have authority to make their own budget and personnel decisions and can accommodate a wide range of work values and employment relationships, including temporary and part-time employees.

Postmodernists and critical theorists, however, raise two important caveats regarding the use of groups and teams. First, groups and teams are not a panacea; they are not "quick fixes" for what ails the organization. Many organizations engage in periodic restructuring efforts in which they create new groups and configurations that leaders believe will be more responsive to the external environment and more capable of achieving the organization's mission. However, if the future is unlikely to be an extension of the past, as postmodernists assert, then rational plans for restructuring the organization are likely to be flawed. The organization may be restructured for a future that never materializes (or for a present that was understood only superficially). Instead of relying on frequent, large-scale restructuring, organizations can give authority to self-managed teams, whose members can use their own judgment and insight to make smaller-scale changes in practices that are adapted to the more localized environments with which they interact (Hir-schhorn, 1997).

Second, critical theorists in particular view groups and teams with a measure of skepticism. They argue that groups and teams may simply repli-cate the power disparities present in the larger organization (Deetz, 1992). Organizational leaders can assert that their organizations are collaborative, but tightly controlled groups and teams eventually make the same decisions the leaders would have made on their own. Leaders can "stack" committees with members whom they know to agree with their own positions, thus en-suring that resulting decisions are consistent with their own preferences. Groups and teams are unlikely to alter the status quo unless organizational leaders encourage members to articulate alternative views and challenge tra-ditional ways of thinking. The leaders of groups and teams, in turn, need to be skilled in managing conflict, building trust, and encouraging members to take calculated risks with innovative but untested practices.

Summary

The material in this chapter constitutes principles of organization that have critical importance to the functioning of higher education. Yet, knowledge of how groups work is constrained by the relative invisibility of the informal organization. It is much easier to point to and do something about the visible part of the organizational "iceberg," but the intimate connection between the formal and informal organization cannot be ignored (Cartwright & Lip-pitt, 1957). Organizational groups and teams have enormous influence on the quantity and quality of work and services, and this influence must be taken into account in planning and executing policy.

Hellriegel and Slocum (2004, p. 196) and Nelson and Quick (2005, p. 178) provide practical steps that groups can take to become more effective. Members of groups should:

- understand why the group exists; its members share goals and under-stand and accept the group tasks;
- abide by mutually decided guidelines or procedures for making decisions;
- communicate freely among themselves, expressing both feelings and ideas;
- not hesitate to offer help to others and to accept suggestions;
- deal with conflict within the group by focusing on ideas or methods, not personalities or people;

- engage in continuous diagnosis of individual and group processes to improve their own and the group's functioning; and
- work toward decisions based on consensus, not majority vote.

In the next chapter, we take up organizational culture—and we consider its influence on both group effectiveness and individual motivation.

Review Questions

1. Which of the following might be important initial conditions that are likely to lead to groupthink?
   a. Directive leadership
   b. High group cohesiveness
   c. Simple/static environment
   d. Methodical appraisal procedures

2. One of the ways in which groups enforce conformity to norms is
   a. Dismissal
   b. Ostracism
   c. Reduction in salary
   d. Role definition

3. With the emergence of a strong informal leader among a group of resident assistants (RAs), which of the following is likely to occur?
   a. More deviance from group norms by other RAs
   b. Less anxiety among the group of RAs
   c. Less productivity by the RAs
   d. More openness to student needs by the RAs

4. A faculty member's research productivity in terms of annual publications is a third lower than the average for the department. Another faculty member's publications exceed the average by a third. The average is also the norm. Which of the following is likely to take place?
   a. The group will quietly encourage the less productive faculty member to improve, while the more productive member will be admired by the group.
   b. The average will increase.
   c. The group will admonish both members in subtle ways.
   d. Both members will move closer to the norm.

5. A new academic vice president observes that work effort among her staff appears to be at a lower-than-optimum level. In addition to seeking explanations through analysis of organizational design, she might
   a. Examine the coincidence of the college's objectives and the norms of the staff
   b. Seek out the informal leader to determine his or her attitudes and values
   c. Both of the above
   d. None of the above

6. The dean believes that a department has established class sizes that are too small to be economically efficient. Half of the faculty in the department do not like the small classes because they have to teach more sections. The other half like the small classes because they believe they can be more effective teachers. To resolve the differences, the chair should
   a. Have each group meet separately to discuss their positions
   b. Have both groups meet together to discuss their positions
   c. Both of the above
   d. Neither of the above

Case Discussion Questions

Consider the teaching and learning committee at Davis Community College described at the beginning of this chapter.

1. A member of the committee violated a norm of the group by deviating from the prescribed agenda. She also introduced an idea that impinged on faculty autonomy, a strong norm of faculty culture. How did the group members respond? How did the committee avoid groupthink?

2. The formal organization of Davis Community College consists of structural boundaries between liberal arts faculty and vocational faculty. These structures contribute to power and status differences in the informal organization (e.g., the view that vocational faculty don't belong on curriculum committees). However, the teaching and learning committee developed a strong sense of cohesiveness. How did this emerge in spite of the structural division in the college?

3. The teaching and learning committee can be thought of as a cross-functional team. Did the cross-functional composition of the committee contribute to the development of innovative solutions?

4. Note that the academic vice president did not serve on this committee. How might his presence on the committee have changed the group dynamics? What type of leadership might have emerged within the group if he were a member?

References

Aldag, R. J., & Fuller, S. R. (1993). Beyond fiasco: A reappraisal of the groupthink phenomenon and a new model of group decision processes. *Psychological Bulletin, 113*, 533–552.

Alderfer, C. (1987). An intergroup perspective on group dynamics. In J. Lorsch (Ed.), *Handbook of organizational behavior* (pp. 190–222). Englewood Cliffs, NJ: Prentice-Hall.

Argyris, C. (1954). *Integrating the individual and the organization.* New York: John Wiley & Sons.

Argyris, C. (1957). *Personality and organization.* New York: Harper.

Bachmann, R. (2001). Trust, power, and control in trans-organizational relations. *Organization Studies, 22*(2), 337–363.

Barnard, C. (1938). *The functions of the executive.* Cambridge, MA: Harvard University Press.

Bensimon, E. M., & Neumann, A. (1993). *Redesigning collegiate leadership: Teams and teamwork in higher education.* Baltimore, MD: Johns Hopkins University Press.

Benton, D. A. (1998). *Applied human relations: An organizational and skill development approach* (6th ed.). Upper Saddle River, NJ: Prentice-Hall.

Bloland, H. (2005). Whatever happened to postmodernism in higher education? No requiem in the new millennium. *Journal of Higher Education, 76*(2), 121–150.

Bolman, L., & Deal, T. (2003). *Reframing organizations: Artistry, choice, and leadership* (3rd ed.). San Francisco: Jossey-Bass.

Cameron, K. S., & Caza, A. (2004). Introduction: Contributions to the discipline of positive organizational science. *American Behavioral Scientist, 47*(6), 731–739.

Cartwright, D., & Lippitt, R. (1957). Group dynamics and the individual. *International Journal of Group Psychotherapy, 7*, 86–102.

Chisholm, D. (1989). *Coordination without hierarchy: Informal structures in multiorganizational systems.* Berkeley, CA: University of California Press.

Cohen, S. G., & Bailey, D. E. (1997). What makes teams work: Group effectiveness research from the shop floor to the executive suite. *Journal of Management, 23*(3), 239–290.

Cummings, T. G. (1981). Designing effective work groups. In P. C. Nystrom and W. H. Starbuck (Eds.), *Handbook of organizational design: Vol. 2. Remodeling organizations and their environments* (pp. 250–271). New York: Oxford University Press.

Davis, K. (1967). Informal organizations. In K. Davis (Ed.), *Human relations at work* (pp. 212–232). New York: McGraw-Hill.

Deetz, S. (1992). *Democracy in an age of corporate colonization: Developments in communication and the politics of everyday life.* Albany, NY: State University of New York Press.

Diener, E. (1979). Deindividuation, self-awareness, and disinhibition. *Journal of Personality and Social Psychology, 37,* 1160–1171.

Etzioni, A. (1961). *A comparative analysis of complex organizations: On power, involvement, and their correlates.* New York: The Free Press.

Fayol, H. (1949). *General and industrial management.* London: Pitman.

Feldman, D. D. (1984). The development and enforcement of group norms. *Academy of Management Review, 9,* 47–53.

Fiedler, F. E., & Garcia, J. E. (1987). *New approaches to effective leadership.* New York: John Wiley & Sons.

Fitzpatrick, A. R. (1989). Social influences in standard setting: The effects of social interaction on group judgments. *Review of Educational Research, 59*(3), 315–328.

Follett, M. P. (1924). *Creative experience.* London: Longman and Green.

Ford, R. C., & Randolph, W. A. (1992). Cross functional structures: A review and integration of matrix organizations and project management. *Journal of Management, 18,* 267–294.

Gersick, C. (1988). Time and transition in work teams: Toward a new model of group development. *Academy of Management Journal, 31*(1), 9–41.

Gibson, C. B. (1999). Do they do what they believe they can? Group efficacy and group effectiveness across tasks and cultures. *Academy of Management Journal, 42*(2), 138–152.

Giddens, A. (1984). *The constitution of society.* Berkeley, CA: University of California Press.

Gilbreth, F. B. (1908). *Field systems.* New York: Myron C. Clark.

Gouldner, A. (1960). The norm of reciprocity. *American Sociological Review, 25*(2), 161–171.

Hackman, J. R. (Ed.) (1990). *Groups that work (and those that don't): Creating conditions for effective teamwork.* San Francisco: Jossey-Bass Publishers.

Hackman, J. R. (1992). Group influences on individuals. In M. E. Dunnette & L. M. Hough (Eds.), *Handbook of industrial and organizational psychology* (pp. 199–267). Palo Alto: Consulting Psychologists Press.

Haslam, S. A. (2004). *Psychology in organizations: A social identity approach* (2nd ed.). Thousand Oaks, CA: Sage.

Hellriegel, D., & Slocum, J. W., Jr. (2004). *Organizational behavior* (10th ed.). Mason, OH: Thomson-South Western.

Hellriegel, D., Slocum, J. W., Jr., & Woodman, R. W. (1995). *Organizational behavior* (7th ed.). Minneapolis: West Publishing Company.

Henderson, G. (1996). *Human relations issues in management.* Westport, CT: Quorum Books.

Hinds, P., & Kiesler, S. (2002). *Distributed work.* Cambridge, MA: MIT Press.

Hirokawa, R., Erbert, L., & Hurst, A. (1996). Communication and group decision-making effectiveness. In R. Hirokawa & M. S. Poole (Eds.), *Communication and group decision making* (2nd ed, pp. 269–300). Thousand Oaks, CA: Sage.

Hirschhorn, L. (1997). *Reworking authority: Leading and following in a postmodern organization.* Cambridge, MA: MIT Press.

Homans, G. (1950). *The human group.* New York: Harcourt, Brace, and World.

Janis, I. L. (1982). *Group think* (2nd ed.). Boston: Houghton Mifflin.

Jones, G., & George, J. (1998). The experience and evolution of trust: Implications for cooperation and teamwork. *Academy of Management Review, 23*(3), 531–546.

Kezar, A., Carducci, R., & Contreras-McGavin, M. (2006). *Rethinking the "L" word in higher education: The revolution of research on leadership.* San Francisco: Jossey-Bass.

Kilmann, R. H., & McKelvey, B. (1975). The MAPS route to better organization design. *California Management Review, 7*(3), 23–31.

Kirkman, B. L., & Rosen, B. (1999). Beyond self-management: Antecedents and consequences of team empowerment. *Academy of Management Journal, 42*, 58–74.

Koot, W., Leisink, P., Verweel, P., & Jeffcutt, P. (2003). Organizational relationships in the networking age: A concluding analysis. In W. Koot, P. Leisink, & P. Verweel (Eds.), *Organizational relationships in the networking age* (pp. 291–305). Northampton, MA: Edward Elgar Publishing.

Lindsley, D. H., Brass, D. J., & Thomas, J. B. (1995). Efficacy-performance spirals: A multi-level perspective. *Academy of Management Review, 20*, 645–678.

Manz, C. C., Keating, D. E., & Donnellon, A. (1990, Autumn). Preparing for an organizational change to employee self-managed teams: The managerial transition. *Organizational Dynamics*, 15–26.

Martin, J. (1992). *Cultures in organizations: Three perspectives.* New York: Oxford University Press.

Mayo, E. (1933). *The human problems of an industrial civilization.* New York: Macmillan.

Merrell, V. D. (1979). *Huddling: The informal way to management success.* New York: AMACOM.

Michalski, W. J., & King, D. G. (Eds.) (1998). *40 tools for cross-functional teams: Building synergy for breakthrough creativity.* Portland, OR: Productivity Press.

Mudrack, P. W. (1989). Group cohesiveness and productivity: A closer look. *Human Relations, 42*, 771–785.

Myers, D. G., & Lamm, H. (1976). Group polarization phenomenon. *Psychological Bulletin, 83*, 602–627.

Nelson, D. L., & Quick, J. C. (2005). *Understanding organizational behavior* (2nd ed.). Mason, OH: Thompson/South-Western.

Nystrom, P. C., & Starbuck, W. H. (Eds.) (1981). *Handbook of organizational design: Vol. 2. Remodeling organizations and their environments.* New York: Oxford University Press.

Obert, S. L. (1983). Developmental patterns of organizational task groups: A preliminary study. *Human Relations, 36*, 37–52.

Park, W. W. (1990). A review of research on groupthink. *Journal of Behavioral Decision Making, 3*, 229–245.

Parker, G. M. (1990). *Team players and teamwork.* San Francisco: Jossey-Bass.

Peterson, M., & Spencer, M. (1990). Understanding academic culture and climate. In W. Tierney (Ed.), *Assessing academic climates and cultures* (pp. 3–18). San Francisco: Jossey-Bass.

Poole, M. S., Seibold, D., & McPhee, R. (1996). The structuration of group decisions. In R. Hirokawa & M. S. Poole (Eds.), *Communication and group decision making* (2nd ed, pp. 114–146). Thousand Oaks, CA: Sage.

Price, K. H. (1993). Working hard to get people to loaf. *Basic and Applied Social Psychology, 14*(3), 329–344.

Roethlisberger, F. J. & Dickson, W. J. (1939). *Management and the worker.* Cambridge, MA: Harvard University Press.

Sanders, K., & Nauta, A. (2004). Social cohesiveness and absenteeism: The relationship between characteristics of employees and short-term absenteeism within an organization. *Small Group Research, 35*(6), 724–741.

Sayles, L. R. (1966). *Human behavior in organizations.* Englewood Cliffs, NJ: Prentice-Hall.

Sayles, L. R., & Strauss, G. (1977). *Managing human resources.* Englewood Cliffs, NJ: Prentice Hall.

Scott, W. G. (1962). *Human relations in management: A behavioral science approach.* Homewood, IL: Richard D. Irwin.

Seashore, S. (1954). *Group cohesiveness in the industrial group.* Ann Arbor, MI: Institute for Social Research.

Senge, P. (1990). *The fifth discipline: The art and practice of the learning organization.* New York: Currency, Doubleday.

Sitkin, S. (1992). Learning from failure: The strategy of small losses. In B. M. Staw & L. L. Cummings (Eds.), *Research in organizational behavior, 14* (pp. 231–266). Greenwich, CT: JAI Press.

Stajkovic, A. D., & Luthans, F. (1998). Self-efficacy and work-related performance: A meta-analysis. *Psychological Bulletin, 124*, 240–261.

Steiner, I. D. (1972). *Group process and productivity.* New York: Academic Press.

Stogdill, R. M. (1972). Group productivity, drive, and cohesiveness. *Organizational Behavior and Human Performance, 8*, 26–43.

Sundstrom, E., De Meuse, K. P., & Futrell, D. (1990). Work teams: Applications and effectiveness. *American Psychologist, 45*, 120–133.

Taylor, F. W. (1911). *Principles of scientific management.* New York: Harper.

Tonn, J. (2003). *Mary P. Follett: Creating democracy, transforming management.* New Haven, CT: Yale University Press.

Tuckman, B. W. (1965). Developmental sequence in small groups. *Psychological Bulletin, 6*(3), 384–399.

Tuckman, B. W., & Jensen, M. A. (1977). Stages of small group development revisited. *Group and Organizational Studies, 2*, 419–427.

van Dyne, L., & LePine, J. A. (1998). Helping and voice. Extra-role behaviors: Evidence of construct and predictive validity. *Academy of Management Journal, 41*(1), 108–119.

Weick, K. (1995). *Sensemaking in organizations.* Thousand Oaks, CA: Sage.

Wexley, K. N., & Yukl, G. A. (Eds.). (1975). *Organizational behavior and industrial psychology: Readings with commentary.* New York: Oxford University Press.

Whyte, G. (1989). Groupthink reconsidered. *Academy of Management Review, 14,* 40–56.

Whyte, G. (1998). Recasting Janis's groupthink model: The key role of collective efficacy in decision fiascoes. *Organizational Behavior and Human Decision Processes, 73*(2–3), 185–209.

Whyte, W. F. (1943). *Street corner society: The social structure of an Italian slum.* Chicago: University of Chicago Press.

Whyte, W. F. (1948). *Human relations in the restaurant industry.* New York: Arno Press.

Wolff, K. H. (Ed.) (1950). *The sociology of Georg Simmel.* New York: Free Press.

Zand, D. E. (1981). *Information, organization, and power: Effective management in the knowledge society.* New York: McGraw-Hill.

II

ORGANIZATIONAL CULTURE

CONTENTS

The authors are most grateful for the critical comments on an early draft of this chapter by Marilyn Amey, Michigan State University. The final version, of course, is our own and may or may not reflect the perspective of the reviewer.

Preview

- Culture can be defined as the philosophy, ideology, values, beliefs, expectations, attitudes, and assumptions shared by members of a social system.
- Schein (1992) suggests that culture exists at three levels: artifacts, values, and basic assumptions.
- Positivist researchers use tested theoretical constructs in the theory of culture to determine the culture of a particular institution in order to see if and how it affects organizational performance.
- Social constructionist researchers examine organizational sensemaking, which is a process that is oriented toward producing a common frame of reference and a shared vocabulary for understanding and interpreting the organization's identity, mission, goals, and performance.
- Organizational subcultures are based on different interpretations of organizational reality.
- Critical theorists raise concerns that organizational culture can oppress workers; critical theorists seek to uncover the ideology of an organization so that its assumptions can be examined.
- The postmodern paradigm identifies two important conceptualizations of culture: cultural connections as transitory and cultural identities as multiple.
- Martin (1992) developed a three-part framework for applying positivist, social constructionist, and postmodern theorizing to the study of organizational cultures. Assessments of organizational culture, according to this view, can be based on three perspectives: integration, differentiation, and fragmentation.
- Researchers differentiate between culture and climate. Culture is reflected in institutional artifacts and deeply held values and assumptions, while climate is less entrenched and represents organizational members' current *perceptions* of the total organizational context.

——————————————— CASE CONTEXT ———————————————

Organizational Culture at Metro West Community College

Sharane Lindale had worked for eight years in the instructional technology department of a small, liberal arts college in the Northeast. However, when her spouse's company relocated, Sharane had to search for a new job in a different part of the United States. Fortunately, she was appointed associate director of instructional technology at Metro West Community College, not far from her new home.

She was pleased to be able to continue her work with faculty members, helping them use technology in their courses and assisting those attempting to teach online for the first time. She found her coworkers to be talented, and her director had given her a glowing review after her first six months. But some of the things that she noticed in the workplace generated a bit of confusion.

"I've never been in a place where people use nearly the same words to describe such very different things," she told her director over coffee. "*Everybody* talks about the 'open access' mission and the commitment to be a student-centered college. But it's like people are from two different worlds."

"Maybe three," joked the director.

"At least three," Associate Director Lindale continued. "You've got people who talk about open access as a way to promote economic development for the state; we bring in students and get them trained for the workforce. I hear that mostly from administrators. Then, you have faculty who talk about open access as a social justice thing: we've got to get these kids into the pipeline to a four-year college, or we'll lose them. And those faculty are in a different camp from the vocational faculty who think that the other faculty don't care about preparing good dental hygienists and auto mechanics. I've heard them say to other faculty, 'What do you have against working people?'

"Even their offices are different," continued Associate Director Lindale. "The vocational faculty have these small little offices that are filled with pictures of their students and letters from them saying what a great teacher they are. Usually, there is a line of students outside their office, waiting to meet with them. It can get a little noisy. And then you go to the faculty offices for the transfer programs, and they are bigger and filled with books and artwork and plants. They have a separate room for students to wait to see their faculty, and it's quiet . . . quiet like a doctor's office."

"It is a complex little place," responded the director. "Faculty around here certainly don't speak with one voice. And you didn't even mention the folks who teach in our corporate training programs. They teach at the job site, so we hardly ever see them on campus. And, yes, administration and faculty don't always see eye-to-eye, and that's putting it diplomatically."

"Right. When I talk with faculty about some new technology initiative that the administration is promoting, they are just so resentful and alienated," Associate Director Lindale explained. "They keep asking, 'Who is promoting this?' 'What strings are attached?' and 'Will I be punished if I don't do it?' It's sad. But when they talk about their students, they are so engaged and open to try new things. It's like you are talking to a completely different person."

"I suppose this place is a lot different from where you worked before," noted the director.

"Well, that place wasn't all roses; it had its problems. But this place has almost the same number of students and faculty as where I worked before, but it's so much more intense and political. And there's so much more emphasis on what the state thinks. Back at my old institution, they could vote everyone out of the legislature, and I don't think anyone would notice. But here it's like, 'How will this play with the governor?' and 'Which legislators do we bring in to talk about this?' And there's a much greater emphasis on working with employers and being responsive to their needs. Back at my old institution, you couldn't get faculty out of their offices, let alone get them to teach a class at some company."

"So is there anything that you actually like about this place?" asked the director with a laugh.

"Absolutely! This place is so much more student-focused than my old institution. And that really is what people agree on. But as I said, they agree for different reasons. So if I'm with a faculty member who hates the administration, I try to get him to see that instructional technology benefits the students, and that it's not some attempt by the administration to control his teaching. But if I'm talking with the administrators to get more funding for my project, I talk about state workforce goals and meeting the technology expectations of employers."

"It took me five years to learn that strategy," laughed the director. "You're going to do just fine, here."

Introduction

How is Harvard different from Yale? How is Borough of Manhattan Community College unlike Broome County Community College in upstate New York? The University of Pennsylvania compared with Penn State University? What does it mean to be a faculty member, administrator, or student at each of these institutions? How do people feel about themselves and their work in these different contexts? The answer lies in part in understanding the culture of organizations. Symbols, norms, values, and rituals are elements of culture that connote much about what kinds of choices people make in different academic institutions, and what rewards and penalties accompany the behavior. What is condoned at Harvard may be unacceptable at Yale (and the reverse). What it means to be a student in a busy, urban community college could differ significantly from the perceptions and interpretations of student status on a rural campus. And the culture of a public institution may value different modes of behavior from a private institution.

Culture in academic organizations, then, informs stakeholders, both inside and outside, about the values and goals to which the institution and its members attach greater or lesser importance. Being able to detect and evaluate these often informal clues to a college or university's character is important for understanding what the institution stands for and how and why its members behave in different ways.

Culture, for many organizational members, is (to borrow a cliché) like water to the fish that swim in it—usually unobserved and accepted as a fact of life. But the profound influence of culture on behavior cannot be underestimated. A culture with a strong value of trust in others, for example, can result in dramatically different motivational forces and resultant behaviors from those of a culture based on fear and suspicion (Mayer, Davis, & Schoorman, 1995).

Each organization's culture is unique in certain characteristics, while similar to others in many ways. Indeed, some institutions strive to be unique, while others attempt to model themselves on the more established institutions among their competitors. Some cultures are clear and strong; others ambiguous and weak (Peters & Waterman, 1982). For some organizational members, the culture of their institutions is profoundly influential; for others, it is not. Some are affected more strongly by other cultures to which they belong, such as the culture of their profession or the culture of their family.

A further consideration is that organizations comprise many subcultures, some in competition with one another for resources, status, and power. Joanne Martin (1992) suggests that the complexities and ambiguities of culture require that organizational observers consider three perspectives: an **integration** perspective, which views culture as clear, consistent, and homogeneous; a **differentiation** perspective, which sees culture as made up of a number of subcultures, sometimes coexisting harmoniously, sometimes in conflict, and sometimes unrelated to one another; and a **fragmentation** viewpoint, which argues that there is no clear and consistent culture or group of subcultures that is meaningful to organizational members, and where consensus and conflict rise and fall with specific issues. We examine these perspectives in this chapter.

Conceptualizations of Culture

Most definitions of culture (Table 11.1) incorporate the idea of a shared philosophy or ideology, or a set of values, beliefs, expectations, and assumptions

TABLE 11.1
Sample Definitions of Culture

- "the system of . . . publicly and collectively accepted meanings operating for a given group at a given time. This system of terms, forms, categories, and images interprets a people's own situation to themselves" (Pettigrew, 1979, p. 574)

- "the behavioral patterns, concepts, values, ceremonies, and rituals that take place in the organization" (Daft, 1983, p. 482)

- the "pattern of basic assumptions that a given group has invented, discovered, or developed in learning to cope with its problems of external adaptation and internal integration, and that have worked well enough to be considered valid, and, therefore, to be taught to new members as the correct way to perceive, think, and feel in relation to those problems" (Schein, 1992, p. 12)

that guide behavior in a social system. Early research in anthropology provided detailed accounts of cultural phenomena, "such as rites, rituals, customs, habits, ceremonies, material artifacts, and patterns of thinking and behaving" (Sackmann, 1991, p. 8). Culture is usually implicit in daily life and not regularly or systematically examined by organizational members. If the culture is strong enough, however, new organizational members learn it in their daily routines, and management intentionally (or sometimes unintentionally by omission) promulgates it throughout the organization.

Why Study Culture

What will organizational leaders be able to do differently after they acquire this knowledge? Consider the following example. An admissions counselor, Kathy Kwan, stays at her office late each night. Kathy is highly productive, and her supervisor, the vice president for enrollment management, wants to understand her behavior and determine how to get others in her department to act similarly. Organizational theorists suggest that the concept of culture can explain Kathy's behavior. They might ask, is it because at Kathy's institution:

1. Though there are no written rules, virtually every admissions counselor stays late.
2. A dedication to high-quality performance is shared among admissions counselors.
3. Admissions counselors feel it is necessary to "appear" to be working hard, regardless of their actual workload.

4. There are many admissions colleagues with whom Kathy is friendly, and they stay late to engage in social conversations.

The choice among these answers calls for alternative interventions by leaders, so it is important to determine which are true. For example, departmental norms for productivity, the range of acceptable work hours in Kathy's unit, and the strength of the value that admissions counselors attach to deviance from informal expectations (Masland, 1985) may drive Kathy's behavior. Such knowledge enables leaders to take more informed courses of action that are based on cultural knowledge of the organization.

Paradigmatic Assumptions About Organizational Culture

So how can organizational leaders develop cultural knowledge about a college or university? Positivist social scientists (Deal & Kennedy, 1982; Denison, 1990; Kotter & Heskett, 1992) attempt to develop conceptualizations of culture that can be generalized across institutions and used to identify some of the more frequently observed types of culture. With those in hand, they claim, it is possible to predict which cultural attributes will enhance organizational effectiveness (Wilkins & Ouchi, 1983). Institutions with different cultural types can be compared on a range of performance indicators.

Some allege, however, that positivist analysis can force essentially different systems into categories that do not fit their unique characteristics (Martin, 1992; Tierney, 1992). Social constructionists question whether a single cultural descriptor, such as bureaucratic, collegial, or political, can represent the complexities and nuances of an organization's culture. The social constructionist argument is that each system must be studied as a unique entity through qualitative inquiry. Researchers following the social constructionist approach use qualitative methods to get "thick" descriptions of organizational life (Geertz, 1973). Such researchers believe that it is necessary to study culture from the perspectives and voices of the participants in order to appreciate fully the meanings of their behaviors, interactions, and sentiments.

In the following sections, we first explicate the positivist perspective on culture by examining the work of one of the major theorists, Edgar Schein. Then we describe other perspectives on culture, which are based in a social constructionist paradigm.

Schein's Framework

Edgar Schein (1992), a former management professor at MIT, has provided one of the most prominent conceptualizations of organizational culture. He suggests that culture exists at three levels. The first is at the observable level, which he calls **artifacts**. The second and third levels exist as inferences about how workers believe and feel, and the assumptions on which those beliefs and feelings are based. He calls these categories **values** and **basic assumptions**. Schein breaks down each of these into categories that allow useful diagnosis of college and university cultures.

Artifacts

Schein's first level, artifacts, is composed of the somewhat overlapping categories of (a) physical environment, (b) social environment, (c) technological output of the group, (d) written and spoken language, (e) overt behavior of members, and (f) symbols.

Physical Environment

Both exterior and interior space can convey symbolically much about the culture of an organization. Contrast, for example, a spare, lean workplace with an opulent and luxurious one. As Coaldrake (1996) notes:

> Architecture affects thoughts and actions, both as a tangible expression of ideas and as a tool for ordering the places where human activity and interaction occur. One illustration of this is the way people feel and act differently in square as opposed to rectangular buildings because of the absence of a dominant direction. A square plan generally affords greater opportunity for human interaction, whereas a rectangular plan automatically creates a spatial hierarchy, which can be articulated to serve the ends of authority. (p. 4)

Architecture frequently says much about the general character of an institution as well as its specific image. Commercial banks, for example, may adopt the style and feel of ancient Greece, with symmetrical columns fronting a secure-looking interior space. The interiors of college and university buildings are also indicative of culture at work. Faculty offices—how big they are, whether they are shared, how clean they are, how they are appointed—may shape the communication patterns that emerge among faculty colleagues and between faculty and students. Another example is the physical layout of a college cafeteria. If faculty members have a separate dining area from students, observers can discern a characteristic of the college culture that reveals deep-seated institutional values about status distinctions.

The fact that culture is reflected in the physical arrangements of offices can be illustrated by the use of space in Japanese corporations. Commonly, there are few private offices, even in very large corporations. Instead, many workers at different levels of status and responsibility sit at closely clustered desks within a large room. The symbolic emphasis on ease and importance of communication is reflected in the desk arrangement. Further, large, attractive conference spaces signify the organization's commitment to easy, impromptu exchanges of information and ideas. Academic department space in colleges and universities, on the other hand, is typically carved up into small cubicles that signify a barrier to cross-faculty communication within departments and suggest a focus on individualized work.

Social Environment

In this category, Schein asks, what is the nature of the relationships that workers have with one another? Are they formal or informal? Trusting or suspicious? Long-term and caring, or short-term and exploitive? Also included here is the culture of communication. Do people address each other by their first names? Do people communicate through written memos, faxes, and e-mail, or do they more frequently deal directly face-to-face? To what extent do people use interactive electronic communications such as web logs (blogs) and video conferencing?

Technology

The technology of an organization refers to the transformation processes that workers use to convert inputs (e.g., an entering student or data used in research) into finished outputs (an educated citizen or a research breakthrough). As we noted in chapter 6, on organizational design, the teaching technology of a college may vary from large-batch processing (giant lecture halls) to craft work (small seminar formats). The types of technologies that an organization uses reflect choices made by its members over time. That is, technology is determined not only by the general nature of the higher education industry, but also by the more specialized role that the institution manifests. Technological choice means that different institutions can decide to adopt different technologies, even if they admit similar students and occupy parallel locations in the Carnegie classification system.

Over time, many colleges and universities have developed distinctive approaches to teaching students. They have adopted their own unique technology for using their physical and human resources. In these cases, technology is a product of organizational history, mission, and leadership, and has a significant impact on the institution's culture. The notion that culture derives from technological choice has a long history, most prominently perhaps in the work of Karl Marx and his followers, as well as Lewis Mumford (1963) and Marshall McLuhan (1965).

Written and Spoken Language

The vocabulary of an organization says much about its values and assumptions. Whether people address each other with formal titles or first names, for example, reveals values of formality or informality, respectively. To understand how language reveals an organization's culture, visit a college's web site. Notice the words used to describe the institution: "selective," "excellent," "affordable." Look for words that convey the outcomes that the college values: "opportunity," "mobility," "career training," "workforce development."

Cultural values are often passed along to newcomers through the telling and retelling of organizational myths or sagas. Burton Clark (1983) defined a **saga** as "a collective understanding of current institutional character that refers to a historical struggle and is embellished emotionally and loaded with meaning" (p. 82). This type of narrative may refer to the founding of the institution or to the accomplishments of a previous college president or senior administrator. The saga reveals values held deeply by current organizational members, and identifies acceptable behaviors that are likely to contribute to the desired direction for the future of the organization. A narrative describing a previous college president who used to ride a motorcycle to campus and go rock climbing with faculty and students communicates values of adventure, risk taking, and camaraderie. The saga of a pious clergyman who founded a college on the basis of religious liberty may convey a different set of values: tradition, seriousness, and public service.

Overt Behavior

This dimension of culture in the Schein typology reflects the idea that culture is revealed and reproduced in the observed behaviors of individuals—both the required formal role behaviors and the emergent behaviors that characterize much of the informal life of the organization. Seemingly innocuous behavior may be quite relevant in understanding culture. For example, the frequency with which staff members get together for coffee and whether faculty tend to eat lunch alone in their offices are illustrations of behavior that reveal cultural values. Other examples include how often faculty and staff stay late to complete work, and how much collegial, help-giving behavior there is (Bess, 1988).

Norms are ritualized behaviors that are endorsed by the culture of the organization. Norms are implicit, and newcomers may not learn what the norms are until they violate them. A newcomer to a religiously affiliated institution, for example, may not realize that most meetings begin with a prayer—until she forgets to offer one at the beginning of a meeting that she chairs. Through repeated observation of organizational behavior, newcomers learn the norms and the sanctions for violating them.

Symbols

A symbol is a tangible representation of some idea or concept that carries meaning for organizational members and constituents of the organizational system. Symbols provide information about what organizational members view as important.

Symbols can be powerful tools for organizational leadership. In a now classic article, Meyer and Rowan (1977) proposed that the formal structure of organizations connotes symbolic meanings and directs patterns of behavior over and above what the formal authority structure would suggest. In addition to goal-oriented pronouncements, leader language generates symbolic meanings relevant to the organizational values that they seek to promulgate.

Positivist theorizing suggests that the management of culture—the development and nurturance of values and their continual symbolic promulgation—is key to organizational effectiveness (Sergiovanni, 1984). As Van Maanen and Kund (1990) note, "[W]e regard conscious managerial attempts to build, sustain, and elaborate culture in organizations as a relatively subtle yet powerful form of organizational control" (p. 238). Critical theorists, however, caution that such forms of symbolic control may conceal the manipulation and exploitation of organizational members (Deetz, 1992).

A number of categories of different symbols characterize an organization's culture (Daft, 1983). College logos on flags, stationery, coffee mugs, and souvenirs in the bookstore tend to engender a feeling of unity. On the other hand, they may also communicate messages of exclusion or insensitivity. Consider the example of college sports teams that retain Native American names and mascots (e.g., Braves, Indians, Savages). They portray images that marginalize and trivialize the experience of native peoples. It is important, therefore, for college leaders to understand how symbols may simultaneously promote unity and exclude underrepresented groups.

In addition to logos, rituals and ceremonies are important symbols that are elaborated and sustained by tradition. The pomp and circumstance of college and university graduation ceremonies, for example, are symbolic manifestations of the rites of passage of students, but also of the age, wisdom, and security of a powerful social institution that can convey honor and potential power on others. The conveyance of honorary degrees serves manifestly to recognize persons of stature in society, but latently, to capture some of the aura of the magnitude of the honored person for the granting institution.

Rituals are like ceremonies, but are often conducted within a smaller unit in the organization. A dean of students, for example, may serve coffee and juice to students on the first day of class. This ritual communicates the college's student-centered approach, and also indicates an informality of leadership, revealing that even the dean will attend to the needs of students.

Values

Earlier we noted three categories in Schein's conceptualization of culture: artifacts, values, and assumptions. We now consider the second dimension. Schein asserts that values reflect deeply held feelings of a person toward particular things, people, or actions. They are not readily evident through direct observation, but, instead, must be inferred through an analysis of cultural artifacts, which *are* directly observable. For example, overt collegial behaviors (such as discussing a workplace issue over coffee with a colleague) and rituals of prosocial behavior (a department chair passing along relevant journal articles to a new faculty member) communicate values of caring and compassion for others.

Schein notes that values emerge on the basis of profound assumptions about human nature and life in general. Recall McGregor's (1960) Theory X versus Theory Y dichotomization of basic assumptions about human motivation (see chapter 9). Theory X asserts that most people are lazy and unmotivated, while Theory Y assumes that they have innate drives for mastery and achievement. Values about organizational life emerge from such assumptions. A value for control may emerge from Theory X assumptions, but a value for autonomy and free expression is more likely to form around Theory Y assumptions.

Collectively, values constitute an important part of the organizational culture. As organizational members become aware of the set of values that characterize the organization as a whole, the values can then be said to be **beliefs**—the cognitive side of values. That is, one can say that "affect" (values) becomes institutionalized as "belief."

Institutionalized beliefs reflect the shared values of organizational members. Schein indicates that values that become embodied in an organizational belief system "can serve as a guide and as a way of dealing with the uncertainty of intrinsically uncontrollable or difficult events" (1992, p. 20). When organizational members are in doubt, they can act according to a set of shared values.

Organizational members, however, are usually unable to express clearly what their organization stands for, partly because of the amorphousness of organizational values and partly because the values are latent and not articulated openly. Moreover, reports of institutional values must be viewed with caution, since there is often a gap between what people say and what they do. What people say is sometimes called their "espoused values," which is in contrast to their "theories in use" (Argyris & Schön, 1978; Deutscher, 1973). Indeed, since many values have a "social desirability" component, respondents are inclined to report them, rather than the less savory value characteristics that may truly represent the organization.

If organizational members are carefully recruited and effectively socialized, values can lead to commitment and motivation to work hard for the organization. Organizations can seek to employ persons who will "fit" into the prevailing culture, and they further indoctrinate members once hired. Several questions, however, can be raised about the wisdom of such socialization. First, too great a homogeneity of values may lead to some degree of insularity, if not groupthink. Second, some of the socialization may be insidiously coercive.

Assumptions

Following our discussion of artifacts and values, we move to a third, deeper dimension of culture, the level of assumptions. These are unconscious driving forces that collectively guide behavior. They are different from values, since most people are not consciously aware of them. That is, although people often act on the basis of their values, when asked, they can defend their actions and values. On the other hand, they also act on their assumptions but have difficulty articulating them, because assumptions are more abstract than values.

If we wanted to look for an organization's assumptions, we might start with five basic underlying assumptions that are manifested in organizational culture: (1) the organization's relation to its environment, (2) the nature of reality and truth, (3) the nature of human nature, (4) the nature of human activity, and (5) the nature of human relationships (Schein, 1983, 1992).

Organization's Relation to Its Environment

This assumption reveals how members of an organization view its involvement with its economic, political, and social environment. Is the organization dominant and in control of its own destiny, or is it passive and controlled extensively by outside forces? (We considered this issue in chapter 5.) Is the college in "peaceful coexistence" with other institutions or under siege by competitors? Keep in mind that positivist theorizing emphasizes the impact of assumed objective external forces on an institution's culture (e.g., the impact of state regulation on a college's culture), while social constructionist theorizing emphasizes the proclivity or planned decisions of institutional actors to enact the organization's relationship to its environment for its own benefit (e.g., promoting discourse on collaboration with other institutions, rather than viewing them as threats).

Undoubtedly, both objective external forces and internal constructions and interpretations shape the assumptions that people have about the organization's environment. These assumptions are likely to affect how and to what extent organizational members engage in boundary-spanning behaviors that seek to manage or regulate relations with external actors. Those who assume that the environment is a threat may be more likely to close off the organization to cross-boundary interaction ("circling the wagons"); those who view external actors as potential collaborators may be more likely to span organizational boundaries.

Nature of Reality and Truth

Just as researchers and organizational analysts have ontological preferences, so, too, do organizations. People in organizations may tend to approach problems from an analytical perspective of positivism. They may believe that truth is revealed through empirical investigation. Alternatively, the first impulse of organizational members with social constructionist assumptions may be to engage in dialogue in order to construct through interaction a common understanding of the problem from a variety of perspectives. The purpose of the dialogue may or may not be to solve a particular problem. Instead, generating new understandings may be sufficient—at least as a starting point for sharing and respecting diverse views.

Of course, all organizations contain members with preferences for positivist or social constructionist perspectives. But Schein argues that organizational cultures are characterized by a more prominent tendency toward one set of assumptions about reality and truth. Uncovering these kinds of organizational assumptions may come from observing how the organization attempts to solve its problems. Is the pattern to engage in systematic investigation in a search for a singular truth, or to emphasize dialogue, uncover multiple interpretations, and make sense of them?

Nature of Human Nature

Are people basically good or inherently bad? This question harks back to ancient conundrums and debates and to philosophic and associated religious arguments stemming from the writings of Aquinas, Luther, Rousseau, and Hobbes. Does the organization have to protect itself against the self-interest of individual workers, or can it assume that all (or at least most) will work toward the greater good of the organization? As we mentioned earlier,

Theory X and Theory Y assumptions, especially of those in leadership positions, say much about the way that people are treated in an organization (McGregor, 1960).

Nature of Human Activity

Is the prevailing assumption in the organization that people grow and develop in diverse ways, and, if so, does the organization have a role in facilitating that growth? Or is personal growth not an organizational concern? How does work fit into the basic assumptions about what people should be doing with their lives? Is it fun? Is it a burden? (Dubin, Champoux, & Porter, 1975). Does the organization consider work to be an essential part of life that can be enjoyed, or is it simply instrumental to pleasures to be derived away from the job? Newer movements toward "flex time" working hours and split faculty appointments (spouses sharing one faculty line) may reveal an institution's values in this regard.

Nature of Human Relationships

What is the appropriate way for the organization to structure its authority relationships? Is asymmetrical power perceived to be legitimate and proper? Are hierarchical reporting relationships necessary to structure communication and ensure accountability? Should competition or collaboration (or both) be encouraged in the organization?

We summarize Schein's framework in Table 11.2. Each dimension of this framework—artifacts, values, and assumptions—can have a profound effect on organizational life in colleges and universities.

Organizational Culture and Organizational Functions

Next we consider how organizational culture affects various organizational functions.

As noted in chapter 4, Talcott Parsons (1951) suggested that to be effective over the long run, all systems must attend to four essential functional

TABLE 11.2
Summary of Schein's Organizational Culture Framework

Artifacts	Values	Assumptions
• physical environment • social environment • technology • language • overt behavior • symbols	• institutionalized as beliefs	• relation to environment • nature of reality • nature of human nature • nature of human activity • nature of human relationships

prerequisites: adaptation, goal attainment, integration, and latency (motivation). The organization's culture affects each of these prerequisites.

Culture and Adaptation

Adaptation refers to the ability of an organization to secure adequate resources and to distribute them efficiently in the organization. When parts of a complex organizational culture are in conflict, however, institutional identity is unclear to outside constituencies, and an institution's ability to secure resources may be impaired. Consider, for example, a university's image for recruitment of students. If the institution's culture is ambiguous or in conflict, students, parents, and institutional supporters (e.g., donors, government agencies, community organizations) may be confused about what the institution represents and what it offers to prospective applicants. Admissions staff members themselves may also be confused about priorities assigned to various strategies for attracting students.

Culture and Goal Attainment

Empirical research has found reasonably strong correlations between culture and organizational goals and objectives. Certain kinds of outputs are produced more effectively when there is a fit between culture and goals (Wilkins & Ouchi, 1983). Consider, for example, the culture needed for a college whose goals include not only the acquisition of knowledge in a liberal arts education, but also the psychosocial development of students. Contrast that culture with one required for a college in which the primary goal is the professional or vocational preparation of its students (Fox, 1983; Tiberius, 1986). Failure to achieve goals (in this case, student success) in each institution may be traced in part to lack of fit between the existing culture and the college's mission, or to inconsistencies in the college's culture or mission, or both. If, for example, in a college with strong psychosocial development goals, faculty, administration, and staff are caught up in an internal atmosphere of distrust, defensiveness, and intolerance of others, it is unlikely that significant gains in student affective development will occur. Psychosocial development requires trust, patience, and support. On the other hand, a college or university with clear, strongly promulgated goals and the leadership to marshal support for them may engender an enveloping culture that matches its goals. Such a culture will reinforce the goal orientation of organizational members (Sergiovanni, 1984).

Culture and Integration

The internal functional prerequisite of integration must also be attended to in viable organizations, and culture can play a role in ensuring this. Integrative mechanisms for encouraging collaboration and cooperation among members of different departments must be in place, lest each department operate too autonomously and focus on its own, rather than the larger institution's, objectives (Balderston, 1995). On the other hand, the overall institutional culture may become too strong and become coercive. It may not permit sufficient variation among organizational units or groups. It may tend to encourage organizational groupthink, breeding an imperviousness to outside stimuli and little constructive internal dissent. Hence, colleges and universities must seek to develop both a stable culture that links disparate segments and a culture that promotes diversity and ready adaptability to changing environmental conditions.

Culture and Latency

Culture is also related to the necessity to sustain high motivation among organizational members. Culture sets the normative context for groups and individuals, and indicates which rewards the organization deems important (i.e., the valence that the organization wishes its workers to attach to alternative rewards) and which kinds of work will be rewarded. A college that builds a high cultural value for good teaching will find ways to demonstrate that teaching will be rewarded consistently, and that the rewards made available are those that are desired by the faculty. Part of the strategy for selecting appropriate rewards is also recruiting faculty who value the intrinsic rewards of good teaching. In an organization with such a culture, there will be more security, less tension, and more motivation among faculty.

Parsons notes that organizations move through phases in which one of the four functional prerequisites receives more attention than others, as the organization experiences different external and internal stresses. Cultures are often built on the predominant phase, with various cultural artifacts addressing the particular needs of that phase (Denison, 1990; Thompson, 1990). Thus, during a period in which adaptation is the prime focus (e.g., a fundraising campaign for a college) the culture will focus on the importance of this function.

Parsons's analysis suggests that an organization's culture reflects its current phase of development. As other organizational variables—such as the external environment and technology—change, culture eventually "catches up" to reflect values and assumptions consistent with the new conditions. Since culture tends to "lag behind" other changes in the organization, without appropriate analysis and intervention by organizational leaders, culture may remain out of sync with a changing organizational context. It would be problematic, for example, if a rigid, bureaucratic culture did not change in response to new developments in information technology. And a workplace culture that tolerates sexist, racist, or homophobic jokes is inappropriate given an increasingly diverse workforce. Under conditions of change, therefore, organizational members may need to assess the current culture and identify discrepancies between the old way of doing things and the perspectives that are necessary for success in a changed environment. Assessing the effectiveness of different organizational cultures under varying organizational conditions is a primary goal of positivist research.

Positivist Research on Organizational Culture

Positivist researchers seek to explain the effects of culture on other organizational outcomes. Here, culture is viewed as an independent variable that can affect a number of dependent variables (outcomes), such as effectiveness, efficiency, job satisfaction, employee turnover, and student retention. In their studies of for-profit corporations, Deal and Kennedy (1982) found that a "strong" organizational culture was associated with higher levels of organizational effectiveness. According to these researchers, cultural strength is determined by the degree to which organizational members share a common set of core values. When the degree of values consistency among members is high, then the culture is strong and the organization is more likely to be effective.

Subsequent research, however, presents a more complex view of the relationship between cultural strength and organizational effectiveness. Kotter and Heskett (1992), for example, found that cultural strength is more likely to contribute to effectiveness when shared values embrace adaptive behaviors and responsiveness to the external environment. When organizational values do not support adaptation, then cultural strength can actually decrease effectiveness. Similarly, Denison (1990) found that the relationship between culture and effectiveness is contingent on environmental conditions. When the environment is turbulent and changing rapidly, values that favor flexibility and extensive participation in organizational decision making become important to effectiveness. But when the environment is stable, values that favor tradition, consistency, and mission clarity contribute to effectiveness.

The basic approach of positivist research can be summarized as follows:

- Step one: develop a typology of the organizational cultures commonly found in an industry or sector.
- Step two: examine the relationship between each cultural type and measures of effectiveness.
- Step three: incorporate intervening variables such as the external environment into the analysis in order to obtain a more accurate picture

of the relationship between culture and effectiveness (e.g., certain cultures are more effective when the external environment is stable, but other cultures perform better when the environment is turbulent).

An example of the relationship between culture and effectiveness is displayed in Figure 11.1, where the external environment serves as an intervening variable. Keep in mind that positivist researchers use organizational culture as one of several independent variables that predict organizational effectiveness (see Figure A in the Introduction). Other independent variables such as organizational design would also account for additional variation in organizational performance.

Cultural Typologies in Higher Education

Higher education researchers have followed similar lines of thinking in their studies of organizational culture in colleges and universities. Specifically, Birnbaum (1988) suggests that colleges and universities can be understood in terms of four cultural models.

1. A **collegial culture** is characterized by shared power and nonhierarchical relationships. People engage in a high degree of personal

FIGURE 11.1
Relationship Between Organizational Culture and Organizational Effectiveness

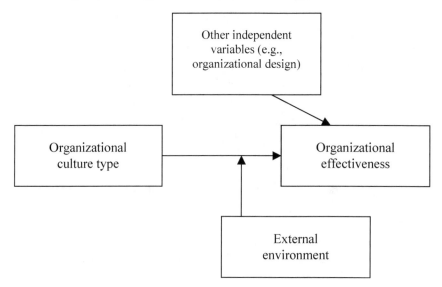

interaction, decisions are typically made through consensus, and organizational behavior relies heavily on tradition and precedent.

2. A **bureaucratic culture** adheres to formal rules that attempt to ensure efficient performance. Organizational behavior is guided by a system of specified roles and reporting relationships. Decision makers value rationality and seek to reduce uncertainty and ambiguity for the organization.

3. A **political culture** is identified through its reliance on negotiation and bargaining among interest groups and coalitions within the organization. Organizational behavior is described in terms of social exchange where people support particular initiatives expecting that they will receive similar support for their own plans at some point in the future.

4. An **anarchical culture** reflects the characteristics of an "organized anarchy" as initially defined by Cohen and March (1974)—goals are vague and often in conflict, transformation processes (technology) are not clearly understood, and participation in organizational decision making is fluid. According to Birnbaum, "There are probably few, if any, occasions on which decisions on two related issues are made by the same people" (1988, p. 156).

Birnbaum argues that one of these four models may have more relevance for a particular institution than the other three, but each institution's culture will have some of the elements of all four models. Similarly, Bergquist (1992) identified four cultures of the academy, which characterize institutions to varying degrees. Three of Bergquist's cultural types parallel those offered by Birnbaum:

1. **Collegial culture** emphasizes consultation and shared decision making.

2. **Managerial culture** (similar to Birnbaum's bureaucratic) is based on rules and hierarchy.

3. **Negotiating culture** (similar to Birnbaum's political) is characterized by conflict, compromise, and bargaining among coalitions.

Bergquist's fourth cultural type—the **developmental culture**—is found in organizations that promote human growth and professional development. The primary valued outcome of organizational behavior is ongoing learning, not just for students, but for faculty, staff, and administrators as well.

These typologies are useful for identifying the predominant cultural orientation of a college or university, and researchers have examined the relationship between different cultural types and important outcome variables such as institutional effectiveness and job satisfaction. Smart and Hamm (1993), for example, examined the relationship between community college organizational cultures and institutional performance on eight indicators. They collected data from a national sample of faculty and administrators, and identified four cultural types:

1. A **collegial culture** is one where people place a great deal of importance on tradition and shared values. Colleges with this culture tend to be reactive to external events, and their leaders are viewed as mother/father figures.

2. An **adhocracy culture** is one where decisions are often made on an ad hoc basis. Organizational members value entrepreneurial behavior and place a high priority on boundary-spanning communication. Colleges with this culture tend to be innovative when confronted with environmental change, and their leaders are viewed as risk takers.

3. A **hierarchy culture** is one where the emphasis is on bureaucratic order, uniformity, and consistency. People place a high priority on following rules. These colleges tend to be reactive when confronted with external change, and their leaders are viewed as coordinators and organizers.

4. A **market culture** is one where colleges seek competitive advantage vis-à-vis their rivals. These colleges place a high priority on customer satisfaction, and they tend to approach environmental change through market analysis. Their leaders are viewed as productivity oriented.

Two of these cultures (collegial and hierarchy) are internally focused—that is, the college's primary value orientations are directed toward people and groups within the boundary of the organization. The other two cultures (adhocracy and market), in contrast, are externally focused. These cultures value connections with external actors.

The cultural types also differ in their orientations toward flexibility and stability. Two cultures (collegial and adhocracy) value flexibility; the other two (hierarchy and market) seek stability. These cultural orientations are displayed in Table 11.3. A summary of all three typologies—Birnbaum, Bergquist, and Smart and Hamm—is offered in Table 11.4. In this table, we note the overlap among the typologies, as well as the unique features that each offers.

Smart and Hamm's research suggested that perceived organizational effectiveness is strongly related to the community college's culture type. Adhocracy cultures had the highest scores on seven of the eight effectiveness

TABLE 11.3
Typology of Organizational Culture*

	Internal Focus	External Focus
Flexibility	COLLEGIAL • cooperation • participation • cohesion • loyalty	ADHOCRACY • creativity • risk taking • change • growth
Stability	HIERARCHY • efficiency • predictability • harmony	MARKET • competition • achievement • winning

*Based on Smart and Hamm, 1993.

indicators. Respondents from colleges with adhocracy cultures had the highest scores on student educational satisfaction, student career development, student personal development, and ability to acquire resources. Adhocracy and market cultures essentially tied for the highest scores for student academic development and community interaction. Adhocracy and collegial cultures tied for the highest score on faculty quality. Collegial cultures also had the highest scores for faculty and administrator job satisfaction. Community colleges with a dominant hierarchy culture had the lowest scores on most of the dimensions of effectiveness.

Based on these results, Smart and Hamm recommended that institutions seek to develop more attributes of an adhocracy culture if they are having difficulty with external forces (e.g., difficulty in acquiring resources). They also suggested that if an institution is experiencing problems of internal integration (e.g., lack of trust, dissatisfaction, lack of commitment to the organization), then the college should work to establish the attributes of a collegial culture.

It should be noted that Smart and Hamm's conclusions are based in the positivist tradition of contingency theory. Specifically, the best organizational culture for a particular institution is contingent on the circumstances that the college is currently experiencing. If circumstances dictate attention to external forces, then an adhocracy culture is likely to be more effective. Instead, if internal conditions are problematic, then the collegial culture probably will produce better results.

Smart and Hamm claimed that the culture that is best for a specific two-year institution is a matter of choice. Leaders can change an organization's

TABLE 11.4
Organizational Culture Typologies

	Birnbaum	Bergquist	Smart & Hamm
Collegial	X	X	X
Bureaucratic, managerial	X	X	X
Political, negotiating	X	X	
Anarchical	X		
Adhocracy			X
Developmental		X	
Market			X

culture (say from hierarchy to adhocracy) to suit the college's circumstances (if, for instance, external forces are problematic). But is organizational culture a matter of choice? Can organizational leaders actually change the culture of an institution?

Organizational theorist Mary Jo Hatch (1997) highlights the difficulties that leaders face when they attempt to change an organizational culture:

> When you attempt to change organizational culture, while it is true that something will change, generally the changes are unpredictable and sometimes undesirable . . . you need to give up thinking of culture as an entity and trying to understand what it does. Instead, think of culture as a context for meaning making and interpretation. Do not think of trying to manage culture. Other people's meanings and interpretations are highly unmanageable. Think instead about trying to culturally manage your organization, that is, manage your organization with cultural awareness of the multiplicity of meanings that will be made of you and your efforts. (p. 235)

Hatch's social constructionist perspective suggests that organizational cultures are not as malleable as Smart and Hamm assume they are. They cannot be bent and shaped easily in ways deemed appropriate by organizational leaders. Cultures are produced and reproduced through elaborate processes of interpersonal communication and sensemaking, which are often beyond the control of managers (Weick, 1995). Cultures reflect deeply held images and identities associated with the organization that are not susceptible to a "quick fix." Instead, social constructionists emphasize the importance of being able to lead within multiple cultural contexts, all existing simultaneously in the same organization.

Social Constructionist Perspectives on Organizational Culture

The social constructionist idea that culture cannot be controlled does not mean that culture is unchanging (Sackmann, 1991). Research by Kezar and Eckel (2002a, 2002b) revealed strong connections between organizational culture and change. They examined 26 change initiatives, which were funded by the W. K. Kellogg Foundation and guided by the American Council on Education (ACE). These initiatives were designed to promote deep and per-vasive transformational change. The plans, developed by senior administra-tors at each institution, ranged from infusing technology into the classroom to revising promotion and tenure guidelines for faculty.

Administrators in many of the institutions in this study expected to cre-ate change through structural processes (e.g., organizational redesign and cre-ation of new policies), but found that they needed to use cultural approaches as well. Specifically, sensemaking was the main vehicle for organizational change in these institutions. Developing a common frame of reference for understanding organizational problems reduced resistance to change and al-leviated anxieties associated with innovation and risk taking. The communi-cative processes associated with sensemaking made organizational members more aware of their shared values and assumptions—that is, more aware of their organization's culture. Through extensive communication about orga-nizational values and beliefs, organizational members arrived at a common understanding of the need for change as well as a more thorough under-standing of how they could work together to achieve common goals. Based on these findings, Kezar and Eckel recommend that institutions conduct or-ganizational culture **audits** before the change process, so that organizational members can identify and understand important elements of their institu-tion's culture.

Tierney (1988) provides a framework around which a cultural audit can be structured. Organizational members seeking to understand better the cul-ture of their college or university can examine six concepts (see Table 11.5).

Organizational members can gather data about each of these concepts by observing institutional rituals and ceremonies. They can look for cultural meanings in the meetings and events that they attend and in the language that people use. They can also interview long-term employees who have his-torical perspective on the organization. Think of the audit process as con-ducting research on your own organization. The findings of this research can provide a rich understanding of the organization and generate a solid foundation for making decisions and engaging in organizational change. As Tierney (1988) noted, many administrators find themselves "dealing with or-ganizational culture in an atmosphere of crisis management" (p. 4) due to

TABLE 11.5
Framework for Studying Organizational Culture*

- **Environment.** How do organizational members define the environment (stable or changing, hostile or accommodating)? How do organizational members interpret the effect of the environment on their organization (tightly controlling or amenable to changes)?

- **Mission.** How is the mission defined? How much agreement is there regarding this definition? Does the mission guide organizational decision making?

- **Socialization.** How do newcomers learn their roles in the organization? What do people need to do to be successful in this organization?

- **Information.** What forms of information are considered valuable? Who produces information, who holds it, and who disseminates it?

- **Strategy.** How does the organization make decisions? Who is involved? What rewards and sanctions are available for good/bad decisions?

- **Leadership.** What do organizational members expect from leaders? Who are the formal and informal leaders of the organization?

*Based on Tierney, 1988.

misunderstandings about key values and assumptions (e.g., when a new college president offends trustees by making decisions without their involvement). Higher education leaders can avoid such crisis management through reflection and study of their institution's culture.

Organizational Subcultures

According to social constructionists, developing an understanding of an organization's culture is not as simple as assigning it to a particular cultural category (e.g., collegial, bureaucratic, political). When we view organizational culture as a social construction, we realize that there will be multiple interpretations of reality and multiple layers of values and assumptions, some of which will be shared rather universally across the organization and others that pertain more directly to certain segments of the institution (Toma, 1997). Therefore, we must seek to understand the multiple subcultures of any organization.

A subculture is the culture of a subsystem within a larger system. Subcultures often overlap with surrounding substructures in an organization. Units such as academic departments or student affairs divisions may have their own subcultures. For example, it is widely noted that the value systems of higher education administrators and faculty members differ in important ways. Administrators have responsibilities for ensuring organizational efficiency and assessing institutional effectiveness, so financial, legal, and managerial issues dominate their work days. As a result, they tend to value clarity, consistency, and accountability to the external environment. Thus, the administrative subculture tends to emphasize managerial or utilitarian values. Faculty members, on the other hand, value collegial communication and expect to play a role in organizational decision making, especially in curriculum and research. Tenure and academic freedom reflect strong preferences for job security and autonomy for the professoriate. Thus, faculty culture reflects many of the cultural attributes of mature professional fields, such as law and medicine.

Differences between faculty and administrative subcultures may manifest themselves in overt conflict, or they may remain latent but still contribute to unflattering perceptions of each group by the other. When these cultural differences become reified, "administrators become identified in the faculty mind with red tape, constraints, and outside pressures that seek to alter the institution . . . Faculty in turn come to be seen by the administration as self-interested, unconcerned with controlling costs, or unwilling to respond to legitimate requests for accountability" (Birnbaum, 1988, p. 7).

Examining the differences between faculty and administrative subcultures is only one way to view subcultural divisions within a higher education organization. The faculty subculture, for instance, is divided even further by differences among the cultures of the various academic disciplines. Biglan (1973) noted that disciplines vary along three dimensions: (1) hard-soft (whether the discipline is unified by a single paradigm or theory base), (2) pure-applied (whether the discipline focuses on practical application), and (3) life-nonlife (whether research in the discipline focuses on living systems). Consider, for example, how the value systems among the following faculty may differ:

- faculty in a chemistry department
- faculty in a humanities department
- faculty in a professional field (e.g., law, medicine, education, nursing)

In addition to viewing subcultures as manifestations of structural differentiation, we can consider the view that subcultures are defined in relationship to the dominant value system in the organization. Hatch (1997) identifies three subcultures in relation to the dominant culture:

1. An **enhancing subculture** is one that strongly supports the dominant values (a faculty senate that unquestioningly embraces every initiative from the administration).

2. A **counterculture** is one that adopts values that contrast with those of the larger culture (a student/faculty coalition protesting administrative decisions).
3. An **orthogonal subculture** is one that maintains a separate value system alongside the dominant one (a faculty subculture that seldom interacts with top-level administrators).

Subcultures that are in conflict are likely to impede the development of the organization and hinder overall organizational effectiveness. A major challenge for organizational leadership, therefore, is to promote dialogue among the different subcultures of the organization (Del Favero, 2003), but not necessarily with the goal of forging common values. Such an effort would likely be viewed as an attempt to dismantle the subcultures and would escalate levels of unhealthy conflict. Instead, leaders can seek to establish **shared commitments** for institutional improvement.

Shared commitments are conscious, intentional, public statements that reveal collectively agreed upon motivations for action (Spender & Grinyer, 1995; Staw, 1980). Through dialogue, different subcultures can arrive at shared commitments, even if the groups do not share the same values and assumptions. For example, faculty may support a university-run health clinic because it is consistent with their values for social justice and because it promotes community-based learning for their medical students. But administrators may support the same clinic because it increases the university's visibility in the community and makes it easier for the institution to lobby for state appropriations. Similarly, student affairs administrators may collaborate with academic affairs leaders to create living-learning communities in residence halls. Student affairs administrators may value the learning community for its effects on college student social development, and academic affairs administrators may value the likely cognitive benefits that come from grouping students in the same academic major together. In this way, different subcultures can work together toward the same shared commitment, even if their commitments are based on different values (Dee, 2006; Spender & Grinyer, 1995).

In the next section, we examine alternative conceptualizations of culture that are based in postmodern perspectives and critical theory analyses. The intent of these theories is to critique organizational cultures, deconstruct assumptions about oppressive characteristics of organizational life, and reconstruct the organization's culture based on a value system that empowers organizational members.

Critical and Postmodern Perspectives on Organizational Culture

Critical Theory and Organizational Culture

Critical theorists examine how the more powerful actors in an organization are able to shape the values and priorities of other organizational members and, hence, determine the overall value system of the organization. According to critical theory, top-level managers control the communication structure of the organization. As a consequence, they have significant influence over the media of culture—the means through which culture is transmitted. On this point, critical theorists agree with positivist researchers; people in positions of authority *can* shape the culture of the organization. Critical theorists, however, raise the concern that the perspectives and values of top management may become the privileged voice of the organization, while alternative voices are silenced—either implicitly or explicitly (Calas & Smircich, 1992; Deetz, 1992; Mumby, 1996).

Ideology, therefore, is an important concept in critical theory; it reflects the dominant, privileged construction of organizational reality (Mumby, 1988). A particular construction of reality is "privileged" when it is endorsed by the dominant class of individuals in a social system, such as a political party, corporation, or higher education institution. Organizational ideology reflects the values, beliefs, and assumptions of the members of that dominant class of people; in work organizations, the dominant employment category tends to be the top-level managers.

Organizational members at lower levels may "buy in" to the dominant ideology for a number of reasons; it may be consistent with how they make sense of organizational life, or they may resign themselves to the fact that they need to "sell out" to get ahead. For example, a faculty member may devote less time to teaching than she would prefer in order to engage in enough research to be awarded tenure.

Critical theorists explain that many workers are not consciously aware of the ideology of the organization in which they work. To a certain extent, this reflects, again, the "fish in water" idea—that is, people are not aware of the medium in which they exist. Many workers, therefore, may unconsciously accept the dominant ideology, even if it conflicts with their own interests and well-being. Instead, attention is drawn to visible, tangible artifacts such as strategic plans, mission statements, and budget allocations. People may fight and disagree over goals and resource decisions, but they may not question the deep-level assumptions that privilege certain goals and allocations over others.

Critical theorists argue that these deep-level assumptions need to be surfaced; that is, the ideology of the organization needs to be made explicit. Once the ideology has been exposed, then organizational members can identify assumptions and values that tend to oppress and marginalize. For example, an ideology that values efficiency may lead to decisions to outsource certain college functions such as food service and janitorial staff. But this decision may lead to marginalization of the college's lowest-paid employees. Similarly, an ideology that values excellence may lead to decisions that solidify an enrollment pipeline from elite preparatory high schools to elite colleges and preclude access to traditionally underrepresented students.

Critical theorists challenge higher education leaders to examine and uncover the ideology of their institution and assess who is privileged and who is disadvantaged by the organization's prevailing value system (Rhoads & Black, 1995). This re-examination of organizational ideology—a key component of culture—is not solely within the purview of formal leaders. Organizational members at all levels can engage in resistance to oppressive ideologies, champion alterative values, and attempt to reframe the structures that emerge from those values. Baez (2000), for example, found that faculty of color in university settings were able to realign institutional values regarding faculty public service; they resisted the notion that community-focused service activities were not viewed as important scholarly work. Instead, they clarified alternative values regarding service and built structures to support those values (e.g., a peer-review process that examined the scholarly components of faculty members' community work). Rather than punishing faculty for noncompliance, institutional leaders listened to voices of resistance and legitimized a new set of assumptions regarding faculty service. One implication of this study is that formal leaders ought not dismiss resistance as intransigence or lack of commitment to the organization. Instead, acts of resistance can help the organization uncover its ideology and assess its deep-level cultural assumptions.

Postmodern Perspectives on Organizational Culture

Postmodern perspectives add another level of complexity to our understanding of organizational culture. Postmodernists focus on the inherent ambiguity of culture (Meyerson, 1991). Culture—at the organizational or subcultural level—is always in flux, according to postmodernists. Cultural connections are transitory—that is, people may share values on one issue, but be diametrically opposed to each other on another. Faculty may unite as a single cultural entity if tenure is attacked by a member of the board of trustees, but after the threat subsides, they may return to heated conflict when discussing the allocation of funds for new faculty positions. In the first instance, faculty share values; in the second, they express competing value systems.

A second key idea in the postmodern perspective is that cultural identities are multiple. In other words, people do not belong to a single subculture; their cultural identity is shaped by their gender, ethnicity, social class, sexual orientation, and age, among many other aspects of identity. Therefore, it is inappropriate to consider the term, "faculty of color," for example, as describing the totality of a single faculty member's cultural identity. A Black, working-class lesbian is likely to have different perspectives and assumptions about organizational life from a heterosexual Latino from an affluent family. A single subcultural category is unlikely to capture the richness and diversity of organizational life in a college or university.

When culture is viewed as transitory and characterized by multiple identities, then we begin to see the inherent fragmentation in organizational life. As organizational theorist Joanne Martin (1992) noted:

> Many organizations lack a clear center. Organizational boundaries are often unclear, as temporary and part-time employees, contractors, and customers blur clear distinctions between insiders and outsiders. Personal ties among employees are often attenuated by physical or social distance. Even face-to-face interactions among organizational members are often fleeting and superficial. (p. 131)

Under these postmodern conditions, organizational culture is inconsistent and ambiguous. Organizational life lacks simplicity and predictability, and organizational experience is fragmented into so many pieces that sensemaking is extremely complex, if not impossible. Alliances and coalitions never solidify into stable subcultures; temporary unity "is the most consensus possible in any context" (Martin, 1992, p. 138).

To a certain extent, postmodernists paint a bleak picture of organizational life, where outsourcing, subcontracting, and impersonal communication mechanisms deaden organizational life and alienate organizational members from their work. Some postmodern theorists, however, argue that new developments in technology and new attitudes about work provide an opportunity to liberate organizational members from oppressive cultures (Bloland, 2005; Wheatley, 1996).

New forms of information technology, for example, enable rapid creation and dissemination of data. When information becomes available almost at the same time it is produced, then top management will find it difficult to control workers' behavior. Formal leaders may not be able to engage in practices of withholding information and accumulating stores of data that are shared only on a "need to know" basis. Broad access to information makes the centralization of power difficult and contributes to a more open organizational culture.

Inclusive attitudes toward diversity also make it difficult to control individual expression in the workplace. The postmodern perspective recognizes cultural identities as multiple. Organizations that adopt this perspective encourage the full expression of the uniqueness of each organizational member. People are valued for the entirety of their identity, not just for one aspect of it. Similarly, diversity is valued not only as an instrumental end (e.g., enrolling a critical mass of students of color), but as a human process that encourages open expression and extensive participation in the leadership of the organization (Ibarra, 2001).

Consider, for example, a director of multicultural programming at a university, who may be appointed routinely to committees that address issues related to students of color. However, she may not be selected for more high-profile committees such as strategic planning or curriculum development. In this instance, the organization considers only one aspect of her identity—her ethnicity. But in an inclusive organizational culture, her diversity would be valued not just for representing a certain group in society, but for her unique identity and potential for contributing to the organization as a whole.

Culture and Difference

The postmodern notion of multiple cultural identities highlights a particular challenge for students, faculty, and staff from minority or traditionally marginalized cultures. Most U.S. colleges and universities are organized around values and assumptions that emphasize competition, individual achievement, and self-reliance. This emphasis on individualism, unfortunately, masks the underlying network of social relationships and connections that create and recreate disparities among social groups (Stanton-Salazar, 1997). Middle-class children, for example, may have a wealth of college choices, not necessarily because of their individual achievements, but because they were born into families with social ties and networks that help these children gain access to important personal and financial resources, such as mentors and scholarships. Poor and working-class children do not have such options and face additional challenges in getting recognition for their individual achievements.

Students from less dominant groups must engage in explicit work to decode the cultures of educational institutions that are organized around the dominant value system. Students must identify and navigate cultural barriers that limit their access to vital resources such as faculty and financial aid counselors. Unlike students from the dominant culture, they must build their own social networks and personal connections. Students become "cultural workers" who attempt to transform their cultural environment (Giroux, 1992; Gonzalez, 2001).

Students who are successful in this work become adept at spanning multiple cultures. They may not abandon their familial culture, but, instead, engage in border-crossing strategies that enable them to succeed across cultures. Similar notions of border crossing have been applied to the study of faculty from traditionally underrepresented groups (Turner, 2003).

Rendón, Jalomo, and Nora (2002) argue that responsibilities for decoding and border-crossing should not be placed solely on the minority-culture student. Institutions are challenged to take active steps to encourage minority-culture students to engage in the academic life of the institution. Specific programs such as first-year seminars or learning communities may help students decode unwritten norms regarding appropriate college behavior, but perhaps most important is the creation of an affirming culture, which communicates that students do not need to give up their familial culture to succeed in the college culture.

Similar arguments can be made regarding institutional responsibilities toward faculty and staff from minority-culture backgrounds. For example, how does the institution assist faculty from working-class backgrounds to negotiate what is often an elite system? Specifically, orientation programs can help new employees decode the cultural system of the organization and facilitate success in multiple cultural contexts.

Using Positivist, Social Constructionist, and Postmodern Approaches

Martin (1992) developed a framework for applying the positivist, social constructionist, and postmodern approaches to studying an organization's culture. She characterized the positivist approach as focused on integration. The *integration* perspective emphasizes shared values and suggests that the goal for organizational leaders is to establish organization-wide consensus. The underlying hypothesis is that shared values produce consensus, which leads to collective action toward organizational goals, which, in turn, enhances organizational effectiveness (Deal & Kennedy, 1982). In contrast, the social constructionist approach is described as a *differentiation* perspective, which emphasizes cultural differences within an organization. Differentiation examines the characteristics of and relationships among subcultures. This perspective "unveils the workings of power in organizations, acknowledges conflicts of interest between groups, and attends to differences of opinion" (Martin, 1992, p. 83). Finally, the postmodern approach is designated as the *fragmentation* perspective, which emphasizes ambiguity and suggests that organizational culture is always in a state of flux.

Martin argues that assessments of culture are limited if they use only one of these perspectives. If we attempt to understand an organization's culture only from an integration approach, then we privilege the voices of top management and overlook alternative perspectives in the organization. Also, by focusing on consensus, we downplay the presence and impact of conflict within the organization.

If we attempt to understand an organization's culture only from a differentiation approach, then we deny the possibility that there are some tacit understandings that nearly everyone in the organization shares. Also the differentiation approach may be too simplistic to represent the complexity of organizational conflict. Organizational disagreements may not be as simple as a "culture clash" between labor and management, or faculty and administration. There are many more cross-cutting fault lines in an organization along which conflict may erupt.

Finally, if we attempt to understand an organization's culture only from a fragmentation approach, then we deny the possibility that organizational members can unite around common concerns. Fragmentation perspectives also downplay the historical context through which professional groups and organizational units have constructed unique subcultural identities (e.g., the unique cultures of a fraternity house or an academic department).

Instead, Martin (1992) argues that the three perspectives should be seen as lenses. Each lens brings some aspects of the culture into focus and blurs others. However, the limitations of one lens are often compensated for by the strength of the other lenses. Together, the three present a more comprehensive picture of the organization's culture.

Analyses of organizational culture can examine questions that emanate from each of Martin's three perspectives. For example, consider the questions offered in Table 11.6. We have also added questions that reflect a critical theory perspective on culture. These questions can be used in conjunction with Tierney's framework (Table 11.5, p. 382) to guide institutional conversations about organizational culture and help organizational members become more aware of the cultural context of their work.

Organizational Climate

Researchers make a distinction between organizational culture and organizational climate. Culture reflects deeply held values and assumptions that are

TABLE 11.6
Questions to Guide an Analysis of Organizational Culture

Integration (positivist)

- What values and assumptions are broadly shared by organizational members?
- On what issues do organizational members easily reach consensus?

Differentiation (social construction)

- What are the subcultures of the institution, and how do their values and assumptions differ?
- How do subcultural differences manifest themselves in organizational conflict?

Fragmentation (postmodern)

- Which of the following contribute to cultural fragmentation in your higher education organization: impersonal communication mechanisms such as e-mail, proliferation of adjunct and part-time faculty, outsourcing of nonacademic functions such as food service and bookstore, others?
- How inclusive is the culture of the organization?

Critical Theory

- What assumptions do organizational members make about culture and control? Does the dominant ideology of the organization privilege certain perspectives and exclude others?

manifested in artifacts and normative behaviors. In contrast, climate is less entrenched and more susceptible to change than is culture. It is socially constructed, so it does not (necessarily) contain some of the characteristics of culture that, from a positivist perspective, exist outside the minds of the perceivers (e.g., "permanent" artifacts, such as long-standing campus buildings). Climate represents organizational members' *perceptions* of the total organizational context. Organizational theorist Renato Tagiuri (1968) described the total organizational context as consisting of four perceptual dimensions:

1. **Ecology** is the physical environment in which work takes place. Perceptions of ecology are affected by the size, age, and condition of the facilities in which people work.
2. **Social milieu** refers to the human dimensions of organizational life. One important measure of social milieu is organizational morale,

the perception of whether organizational members on average are satisfied with their jobs. Other important measures include perceptions of coworkers' motivation, the level of diversity in the workforce, and whether people are paid fairly for their work.

3. **Social structure** refers to elements of organizational design. Do people perceive the organization as hierarchical, or do they see ample opportunities to participate in decision making? Perceptions of centralization, communication, and participation are important measures of this dimension of organizational climate.

4. **Culture** reflects the ways of thinking that are prevalent in the organization. Perceptions of values, assumptions, and artifacts shape impressions of organizational climate.

Organizational members' perceptions of these four dimensions contribute to an overall impression of organizational climate.

It is important to stress once again that measurements of organizational climate are based on the *perceptions* of organizational members, in contrast to studies of organizational culture, which are drawn from direct observations by researchers. Climate, therefore, has come to be seen as what respondents to questionnaires say climate is. An outside observer, then, cannot draw conclusions about climate unless he or she collects perceptual data from the organizational members. Dimensions of the total organizational context (e.g., "closeness of supervision" and "degree of bureaucracy" in the organizational design) are seen as perceptions of the participants in the organization.

Researchers have devoted significant attention to classifying organizational members' perceptions of climate. Halpin and Croft (1963), who developed the Organizational Climate Description Questionnaire (OCDQ) through their research in Chicago public schools, identified eight dimensions of climate, which are described in Table 11.7.

With these dimensions, schools can be differentiated from one another. For example, as Hoy and Miskel (1991) note, six different kinds of school climate can be identified: open, autonomous, controlled, familiar, paternal, and closed. These are presented in Table 11.8. We can focus on some important differences by comparing "open" and "closed" schools. Note how four dimensions are reversed in each climate condition:

- Open climate: high esprit, high consideration, low aloofness, low production emphasis

TABLE 11.7
Dimensions in the Organizational Climate Description Questionnaire
(OCDQ)*

Characteristics of Worker Behavior

- Hindrance: feelings that formal leaders burden workers with routine duties, committee work, and other busywork requirements
- Intimacy: enjoyment of warm and friendly personal relationships among organizational members
- Disengagement: tendency to "go through the motions" without an actual commitment to the organization or to the task at hand
- Esprit: morale growing out of a sense of both task accomplishment and social needs satisfaction

Characteristics of Formal Leader Behavior

- Production Emphasis: close supervisory behavior; leader is highly directive and not sensitive to feedback
- Aloofness: formal and impersonal leader behavior; leader goes by the book and maintains social distance from staff members
- Consideration: warm and friendly behavior by the leader; leader tries to be helpful
- Thrust: dynamic leader behavior in which an attempt is made to move the organization through the example that the leader sets

---

*Adapted from Halpin & Croft, 1963.

- Closed climate: low esprit, low consideration, high aloofness, high production emphasis

Summary

Culture from the positivist perspective is measured through researchers' direct observation of artifacts and behaviors. Based on an analysis of these artifacts and behaviors, researchers make inferences about the values and assumptions shared by organizational members. In contrast, organizational climate typically is measured through surveys that assess organizational members' perceptions about various dimensions of organizational life. Peterson and Spencer (1990) offer an interesting analogy that helps us keep

TABLE 11.8
Organizational Climate Types*

Climate Type	High	Average	Low
Open	Esprit Thrust Consideration	Intimacy	Hindrance Disengagement Aloofness Production Emphasis
Autonomous	Esprit Intimacy Aloofness Thrust	Consideration	Disengagement Hindrance Production Emphasis
Controlled	Disengagement Hindrance Production Emphasis	Thrust Aloofness Esprit	Intimacy Consideration
Familiar	Disengagement Intimacy Consideration	Thrust Esprit	Hindrance Aloofness Production Emphasis
Paternal	Disengagement Production Emphasis	Thrust Esprit Consideration	Hindrance Intimacy Aloofness
Closed	Disengagement Hindrance Aloofness Production Emphasis	Intimacy	Consideration Thrust Esprit

*Adapted from Halpin and Croft, 1963.

in mind the differences between culture and climate: "[C]ulture is the meteorological zone in which one lives (tropical, temperate, or arctic) and climate is the daily weather patterns" (p. 8).

Review Questions

1. Which of the following is an element of organizational culture?
   a. Official dress codes
   b. Office doors closed during meetings
   c. Parking privileges for the college's presidential staff
   d. All of the above

2. Two faculty members talking in the hall are interrupted by students who address them by their first names. In Schein's terms, this phenomenon falls into the category of
   a. Physical environment
   b. Overt behavior
   c. Technological output
   d. Symbol
   e. None of the above

3. A college president repeats a standard speech to the alumni, the faculty, his administrative staff, and students. He is attempting to "manage culture" through the use of
   a. Technology
   b. Manipulation and deception
   c. Interpersonal skills
   d. Symbols

4. In the management of culture, the purpose of logos and slogans is to
   a. Symbolize the institutional culture
   b. Give workers a meaningful standard around which to rally
   c. Give consumers a unified image of the institution
   d. All of the above
   e. a and b only

5. A Midwestern university recently set up a branch campus in a rural area about 50 miles from the university center. For the first six months, the culture of the new branch is likely to be:
   a. Integrated
   b. Differentiated
   c. Fragmented
   d. Some combination of the above

Case Discussion Questions

Consider the Metro West Community College case that was presented at the beginning of this chapter.

1. Use Schein's framework (artifacts, values, and assumptions) to analyze the culture at Metro West Community College.

- Regarding **artifacts**, pay particular attention to language and symbols. What is the vocabulary of the institution? Which words trigger strong emotional reactions? How are office spaces and physical arrangements symbols that reflect the culture of the institution?
- Which **values** are expressed by administrators and by the different segments of the faculty?
- What **assumptions** do administrators and faculty members have about the goals and purposes of education?

2. Consider Smart and Hamm's typology of organizational culture. In which category would you place Metro West Community College?
3. Consider the cultural differences between Associate Director Lindale's former employer and the community college where she now works. Think about these cultures in relation to three dependent variables: faculty job satisfaction, student satisfaction, and environmental responsiveness. On which dependent variables do you think Associate Director Lindale's *former* employer would be effective? On which dependent variables do you think her *current* employer would be effective?
4. Use Martin's three dimensions of culture (integration, differentiation, and fragmentation) to describe Metro West Community College. Which values are shared across the college? How do the college's subcultures differ in their assumptions about education? How do cultural connections shift, depending on the issue or context being discussed (e.g., when state workforce goals are discussed, compared to a discussion of pedagogical improvement)?

References

Argyris, C., & Schön, D. (1978). *Organizational learning.* Reading, MA: Addison-Wesley.

Baez, B. (2000). Race-related service and faculty of color: Conceptualizing critical agency in academe. *Higher Education, 39,* 363–391.

Balderston, F. (1995). *Managing today's university* (2nd ed.). San Francisco: Jossey-Bass.

Bergquist, W. (1992). *The four cultures of the academy: Insights and strategies for improving leadership in collegiate organizations.* San Francisco: Jossey-Bass.

Bess, J. L. (1988). *Collegiality and bureaucracy in the modern university.* New York: Teachers College Press, Columbia University.

Biglan, A. (1973). The characteristics of subject matter in different academic areas. *Journal of Applied Psychology, 57,* 195–203.

Birnbaum, R. (1988). *How colleges work: The cybernetics of academic organization and leadership.* San Francisco: Jossey-Bass.

Bloland, H. (2005). Whatever happened to postmodernism in higher education?: No requiem in the new millennium. *Journal of Higher Education, 76*(2), 121–150.

Calas, M., & Smircich, L. (1992). Re-writing gender into organizational theorizing: Directions from feminist perspectives. In M. Reed & M. Hughes (Eds.), *Rethinking organization: New directions in organization theory and analysis* (pp. 227–253). Newbury Park, CA: Sage.

Clark, B. R. (1983). *The higher educational system.* Berkeley, CA: University of California Press.

Coaldrake, W. (1996). *Architecture and authority in Japan.* London: Routledge.

Cohen, M., & March, J. (1974). *Leadership and ambiguity: The American college president.* New York: McGraw-Hill.

Daft, R. L. (1983). *Organizational theory and design.* Cincinnati, OH: South-Western College Publishing.

Deal, T., & Kennedy, A. (1982). *Corporate cultures: The rites and rituals of corporate life.* Reading, MA: Addison-Wesley.

Dee, J. (2006). Institutional autonomy and state-level accountability: Loosely coupled governance and the public good. In W. Tierney (Ed.), *Governance and the public good* (pp. 133–155). Albany, NY: State University of New York Press.

Deetz, S. (1992). *Democracy in an age of corporate colonization: Developments in communication and the politics of everyday life.* Albany, NY: State University of New York Press.

Del Favero, M. (2003). Faculty-administrator relationships as integral to high-performing governance systems: New frameworks for study. *American Behavioral Scientist, 46*(7), 902–922.

Denison, D. (1990). *Corporate culture and organizational effectiveness.* New York: John Wiley.

Deutscher, I. (1973). *What we say/what we do: Sentiments and acts.* Glenview, IL: Scott, Foresman.

Dubin, R., Champoux, J. E., & Porter, L. W. (1975). Central life interests and organizational commitment of blue-collar and clerical workers. *Administrative Science Quarterly, 20*(3), 411–421.

Fox, D. (1983). Personal theories of teaching. *Studies in Higher Education, 8,* 151–157.

Geertz, C. (1973). *The interpretation of cultures.* New York: Basic Books.

Giroux, H. (1992). *Border crossings: Cultural workers and the politics of education.* New York: Routledge.

Gonzalez, K. (2001). Inquiry as a process of learning about the other and the self. *Qualitative Studies in Education, 14*(4), 543–562.

Halpin, A., & Croft, D. (1963). *The organization climate of schools.* Chicago: Midwest Administration Center of the University of Chicago.

Hatch, M. (1997). *Organization theory: Modern, symbolic, and postmodern perspectives.* New York: Oxford University Press.

Hoy, W., & Miskel, C. (1991). *Educational administration: Theory, research, and practice* (4th ed.). New York: McGraw-Hill.

Ibarra, R. (2001). *Beyond affirmative action: Reframing the context of higher education.* Madison, WI: University of Wisconsin Press.

Kezar, A., & Eckel, P. (2002a). Examining the institutional transformation process: The importance of sensemaking, inter-related strategies, and balance. *Research in Higher Education, 43*(3), 295–328.

Kezar, A., & Eckel, P. (2002b). The effect of institutional culture on change strategies in higher education: Universal principals or culturally responsive concepts? *Journal of Higher Education, 73*(4), 435–460.

Kotter, J., & Heskett, J. (1992). *Corporate culture and performance.* New York: Free Press.

Martin, J. (1992). *Cultures in organizations: Three perspectives.* New York: Oxford University Press.

Masland, A. T. (1985). Organizational culture in the study of higher education. *Review of Higher Education, 8*(2), 157–168.

Mayer, R., Davis, J., & Schoorman, F. D. (1995). An integrative model of organizational trust. *Academy of Management Review, 20*(3), 709–734.

McGregor, D. (1960). *The human side of enterprise.* New York: McGraw-Hill.

McLuhan, M. (1965). *Understanding media: The extensions of man.* New York: McGraw-Hill.

Meyer, J., & Rowan, B. (1977). Institutionalized organizations: Formal structure as myth and ceremony. *American Journal of Sociology, 83*, 340–363.

Meyerson, D. (1991). Normal ambiguity? A glimpse of an occupational culture. In P. Frost, L. Moore, M. Louis, C. Lundberg, & J. Martin (Eds.), *Reframing organizational culture* (pp. 131–144). Newbury Park, CA: Sage.

Mumby, D. (1988). *Communication and power in organizations: Discourse, ideology, and domination.* Norwood, NJ: Ablex.

Mumby, D. (1996). Feminism, postmodernism, and organizational communication studies: A critical reading. *Management Communication Quarterly, 9*(3), 259–295.

Mumford, L. (1963). *Technics and civilization.* New York: Harcourt, Brace & World.

Parsons, T. (1951). *The social system.* New York: Free Press.

Peters, T. J., & Waterman, R. H., Jr. (1982). *In search of excellence: Lessons from America's best-run companies.* New York: Harper & Row.

Peterson, M., & Spencer, M. (1990). Understanding academic culture and climate. In W. Tierney (Ed.), *Assessing academic climates and cultures* (pp. 3–18). San Francisco: Jossey-Bass.

Pettigrew, A. (1979). On studying organizational cultures. *Administrative Science Quarterly, 24*, 570–581.

Rendón, L., Jalomo, R., & Nora, A. (2002). Theoretical consideration in the study of minority student retention in higher education. In J. Braxton (Ed.), *Reworking the student departure puzzle* (pp. 127–156). Nashville: Vanderbilt University Press.

Rhoads, R., & Black, M. (1995). Student affairs practitioners as transformative educators: Advancing a critical cultural perspective. *Journal of College Student Development, 36*(5), 413–421.

Sackmann, S. (1991). *Cultural knowledge in organizations: Exploring the collective mind.* Newbury Park, CA: Sage.

Schein, E. (1983, Summer). The role of the founder in creating organizational culture. *Organizational Dynamics, 12*, 13–29.

Schein, E. (1992). *Organizational culture and leadership* (2nd ed.). San Francisco: Jossey-Bass.

Sergiovanni, T. (1984). Leadership as cultural expression. In T. Sergiovanni & J. Corbally (Eds.), *Leadership and organizational culture: New perspectives on administrative theory and practice* (pp. 105–114). Urbana, IL: University of Illinois Press.

Smart, J., & Hamm, R. (1993). Organizational culture and effectiveness in two-year colleges. *Research in Higher Education, 34*(1), 95–106.

Spender, J.-C., & Grinyer, P. (1995). Organizational renewal: Top management's role in a loosely coupled system. *Human Relations, 48*(8), 909–926.

Stanton-Salazar, R. (1997). A social capital framework for understanding the socialization of racial minority children and youths. *Harvard Educational Review, 67*(1), 1–40.

Staw, B. (1980). Rationality and justification in organizational life. In L. Cummings & B. Staw (Eds.), *Research in organizational behavior* (vol. 2, pp. 45–80). Greenwich, CT: JAI Press.

Tagiuri, R. (1968). The concept of organizational climate. In R. Tagiuri & G. Litwin (Eds.), *Organizational climate: Exploration of a concept* (pp. 11–32). Boston: Harvard University, Graduate School of Business Administration.

Thompson, G. (1990). Fitting the company culture. In T. Lee (Ed.), *Managing your career*. New York: Dow Jones & Company.

Tiberius, R. G. (1986). Metaphors underlying the improvement of teaching and learning. *British Journal of Educational Technology, 17*, 144–156.

Tierney, W. (1988). Organizational culture in higher education. *Journal of Higher Education, 59*(1), 2–21.

Tierney, W. (1992). Cultural leadership and the search for community. *Liberal Education, 78*(5), 16–21.

Toma, J. D. (1997). Alternative inquiry paradigms, faculty cultures, and the definition of academic lives. *Journal of Higher Education, 68*(6), 679–705.

Turner, C. S. (2003). Incorporation or marginalization in the academy: From border toward center for faculty of color? *Journal of Black Studies, 34*(1), 112–125.

Van Maanen, J., & Kund, G. (1990). "Real feelings": Emotional expression and organizational culture. In B. Staw & L. Cummings (Eds.), *Work in organizations* (pp. 193–253). Greenwich, CT: JAI Press.

Weick, K. (1995). *Sensemaking in organizations*. Thousand Oaks, CA: Sage.

Wheatley, M. (1996). *Leadership and the new science*. San Francisco: Berrett-Koehler Press.

Wilkins, A. L., & Ouchi, W. G. (1983). Efficient cultures: Exploring the relationship between culture and organizational performance. *Administrative Science Quarterly, 28*, 468–481.

12

CONCLUSIONS:
UNDERSTANDING THE SHAPE
OF HIGHER EDUCATION

V olume I of *Understanding College and University Organization: Theories for Effective Policy and Practice* is dedicated to the study of alternative ways of theoretically conceiving of the more stable and
persisting conditions that comprise higher education institutions. Our hope
has been to provide different ways of thinking about the more enduring organizational components with which college and university leaders at all levels must contend as a backdrop to dealing with more dynamic elements. To
use a musical metaphor, our contention is that the stable elements act as key
signatures and signposts of harmony and rhythm. The institution must act
harmoniously and within orderly boundaries for propitious and efficient action, yet permit dissonant variation in both that give life and freshness to the
entire educational enterprise. In Volume II, we take up those more dynamic
and dissonant elements directly.

What we pointed out in Volume I is that although organizational problems in colleges and universities may seem unusual, by using theory in the
analysis of these problems, the uniqueness often can be comprehended as
recognizable and common, with repetitive patterns for which there are
known effective remedies. From the theories presented in this volume, therefore, administrators will be able to understand the elements in their institutional dilemmas that have been found to recur across many institutions.
Moreover, administrators will come to know and understand the conditions
that may have caused the problem to arise as well as a variety of solutions
that can be employed to address them.

The primary approach to the use of theory that we have adopted in this
book is a positivist one. That is, we have tried to demonstrate that by assuming that institutional dilemmas constitute "objective" and real situations, rational solutions can be discerned and applied. The reader who follows a

positivist perspective will, therefore, be afforded the opportunity to avail him or herself of the many empirically proven theories that have been shown to be effective (Donaldson, 1996).

There is no shortage of "real" problems at all levels in today's colleges and universities. In many respects, the problems stem from significant changes in the environments outside these institutions. The late 20th and early 21st centuries have seen remarkable social and cultural changes that have shifted and expanded many of the roles colleges and universities have played as well as the ways that they play them. Among many others, the economy, the family, the government, the media, the transforming impact of the use of computers, new modes of communication, changes in the K–12 educational sector, the decline of unions, egalitarianism and its converse, elitism and segregation, the internationalization of life in general, and significant changes in social values and mores, all have put pressure on colleges and universities to adapt quickly and appropriately. Yet, colleges and universities tend to change slowly, and many problems stem from the inertia of using traditional but now somewhat outmoded structures (Allan, 2004). For leaders to think "outside the box" requires not only imagination, but courage. Not only boldness, but sage calculations of risk. It also demands on a moral level the abandonment of egotistic self-aggrandizement and the adoption of a willingness to admit ignorance and to take advantage of wisdom wherever it lies in the organization—not just at the top.

The reader will note again that these conclusions are based on positivist assumptions. In this volume, we presented two alternative paradigms that in some cases may be better tools for institutional change than positivism. The social constructionist perspective recognizes not only the increasingly disconnected nature of work in colleges and universities, but the fact that the more chaotic conditions may now be perceived in idiosyncratic ways that have their own validity. A particularistic, qualitative understanding of the nature of and changes in academia may provide a much more effective guide to action than do positivist theories that attempt a rational prediction of the future from what has happened in the past (Davies, 1999). So, also, one of the claims in the postmodernist paradigm denies the possibility of prediction of the future from the past. As Richard Harvey Brown (1995) notes, postmodernism "eschews the linearity, order, and rationality of modernity . . ." (p. 2). But it can be highly constructive and pragmatic, as Allan (2004) notes:

> [Constructive postmodernism] calls into question the eternal verities that are the hallmark of modernism, the timeless and universal standards by which the fleeting and parochial achievements of the world are measured and judged excellent or deficient. But it also rejects the nihilistic attempt to demolish verities of any and every sort, to deconstruct all the traditional

hierarchies based on truth, goodness, and beauty, on faith, hope, and love. (p. 3)

The need for adjustments in the ways academic and administrative work are conducted, however, derives not only from the demands of outside constituents for products and services of a different quality (e.g., students with different skills and dispositions, research output with both short- and long-term applications), but also from dramatic changes in the technologies that are employed in work in academia. New modes of research collaboration, new technologies for teaching, and new patterns of and locations for learning require new thinking about the ways that colleges and universities pursue their objectives. New organizational models arise out of what is sometimes called "emergent evolution" (Mihata, 1997), which refers to the emergence of new structures and novel modes of behavior (Nagel, 1979). Further, when these novel properties are integrated into a new organizational system, they may not be predictable (Crutchfield, 1994).

Because of the increasing unpredictability of market demands and technological changes, there is a tendency to abandon the belief in the utility of systematic, orderly, rational analysis of organizational behavior. In fact, however, the very uncertainty of conditions in higher education could argue for even more focus on coherent ways of understanding the basic activities of organizations. Our explication in chapter 4 of general and social systems is intended to provide an omnibus framework for analyzing and understanding organizations. Too often college leaders and their staffs put out fires in one sector of their institution without being sufficiently aware of the far-reaching impact of their decisions. The elements of systems theory constitute reminders of how systems are held together—or, in contrast, tend to disintegrate and lose energy. Of particular relevance to colleges and universities is the concept of "boundary" (Marchington, Grimshaw, Rubery, & Wilmott, 2004), which includes many physical, psychological, sociological, and economic boundaries. The degree to which boundaries are open or closed is often left to chance, whereas the definition of their permeability should be part of institutional planning and policy.

We also included in the chapter on systems theory a discussion of "social systems theory." The apparent simplicity of the social systems formula ($B = f[p,e]$) may lead observers to ignore its profundity. Too often we see higher education leaders attaching blame for poor performance to individuals or to circumstances allegedly beyond their control. The social systems formula reminds us that behavior is determined jointly by the interaction of person and environment. This principle applies at all levels of the organization.

In chapter 5, we examined the question of organizational environments in some detail. What comes through strongly in our application of various theories of environment to higher education is the necessity to understand the degree to which the environment of a particular organization is constrained and, conversely, the extent to which institutions are free to exercise strategic choice. A fit between strategy and degree of environmental freedom will likely predict institutional effectiveness. As Donaldson (1996) notes:

> Organizations adopt structures that better fit their contingencies as a result of a process of *incremental adaptation* [emphasis in the original]. They move out of misfit into better fit by changing their structures a little, but sufficiently to attain fit. The new fit allows effectiveness to rise and thereby generate the additional resources necessary to grow a little more. This changes the contingencies incrementally and induces more misfit, that again requires a further incremental change in the structure to gain another new fit. (p. 169)

The failure of institutional leaders to appreciate how much or how little flexibility is available in the environment and how much choice they have within their institutions to make decisions to achieve a better fit with their environment is a significant cause of ineffective policy making. Wishful thinking about opportunities in the environment, coupled with static institutional decision-making structures will yield greater degrees of misfit. This is an old lesson (see Riesman, 1958), but it continues to be forgotten or never learned. Institutional leaders, using environmental theories, would do well to appreciate the niche into which their institutions currently fall and the niches to which they aspire in order to develop realistic strategic plans.

Fit was also a subject of the chapter on organizational design. As we noted, most institutions derive their structure from models that were appropriate in the early part of the 20th century. Admittedly, it is difficult to package organizational work in new and innovative ways. Once again, imagination and courage on the part of leaders are required to embolden their constituents. Needless to say, a restructuring of the reward system must match any new organizational design.

We included in Volume I a complete chapter on bureaucracy, partly because it describes the predominant mode of conducting administrative work in higher education and partly because it has acquired such negative, often undeserved images. When used in situations that call for maximum rationality, bureaucracy is the organizational design choice that provides the most efficiency—and sometimes effectiveness (Walton, 2005). What gives it a bad name is not the design mode itself. Rather, it is the misunderstanding of the situations where its use is appropriate and of the ways it should be employed.

To be sure, human relations problems arise in many bureaucracies, but sensitive leaders can find ways to enrich bureaucratic environments so that organizational members can feel fulfilled while at the same time serving the organization's best interests (Levinson, 1973; Maccoby, 1988).

While bureaucracy addresses macro-organizational concerns, role theory is focused on a different level—interpersonal interactions in organizations as mediated by organizational expectations and constraints. Role behavior is a significant source of both inefficiency and personal dissatisfaction in organizations, largely because the overall organizational structure and culture are inadequate to set specific boundaries of appropriate role behavior, except for the most mundane and routine duties. As we noted in chapter 8, the inevitable interstices in role definition must be (and are) filled in by organizational members themselves, rightly or wrongly. Leaders in higher education have important policy decisions to make with respect to the norms and values of the organization when they set the limits of individual role definition and flexibility. A hierarchical system will leave role definition to top-level administrators (when and if they are able to perceive overlaps and ambiguities). Other, more collaborative systems will encourage—and formally and informally structure—modes for organizational members to adjust roles continually and adjudicate differences.

In addition to understanding roles and role behavior, it is important for organizational leaders to know the mechanisms through which people become motivated to perform their roles. We presented an overview of theories of work motivation, which collectively explain how inner needs and drives, as well as external incentives and constraints, produce different levels of effort and commitment. Various combinations of intrinsic and extrinsic motivators explain individual behavior in organizations. Skillful leaders will design organizations that maximize the potential for organizational members to achieve satisfaction from the work itself as well as create reward systems that ensure equity in the way that extrinsic rewards are allocated.

This volume was also concerned with organizational behavior at the next higher level—groups and teams, which are common modes for decision making and increasingly a structure for conducting work. The effectiveness of groups such as departments and research centers depends importantly on the degree to which members focus on group goals and on their compatibility as coworkers. However, excessive homogenization of personnel types and styles of behavior leaves little room for dissent or encouragement of innovation. Rather, it is the creation of group norms and climates that include both tolerance of and caring for others' personal interests as well as their uniqueness that contributes to group and total organization effectiveness. Effective performance also derives from a group cohesiveness that is based in collaboratively identified goals and agreement on the means to achieve those goals. High-quality goals and commitment to work hard toward those goals will yield both the group effectiveness and personal satisfactions that make work meaningful and intrinsically rewarding.

The final chapter of this volume moved up yet another level of analysis to organizational culture. Institutional leaders at every level can work to make manifest what the organization stands for—what characteristics give it vitality and life and provide meaningfulness to its workers. These characteristics vary widely, from deeply held assumptions about the nature of truth and reality to the ethics of human interaction that are basic to the institution. The classification of different kinds of cultures into four types—collegial, bureaucratic, political, and anarchic (Birnbaum, 1988)—provides useful analytic handles to begin to understand a particular institution's organizational culture, but the reality is that each college and university comprises a unique combination of all four—plus others. Indeed, the saga of each institution is the result over time of the carving out of a colorful, qualitative niche that allows both internal and external constituents to identify what is unique and to decide whether and how to interact with the institution.

Institutions of higher learning are important in the satisfaction of the different needs of the larger society in which they play a part. The systems that evolve to allow them to perform with excellence must be examined analytically and with care. Only by continually and critically reviewing the design of the structures that connect worker to worker, department to department, and total institution to the external environment can higher education perform its roles responsibly and effectively. The theories in Volume I of this book constitute an initial look at extant modes. In the next volume, we take a closer look at some of the reasons why these more traditional views of organization are being reshaped by the fresh stimuli of a constantly changing world both within institutions and in the environments they serve.

References

Allan, G. (2004). *Higher education in the making: Pragmatism, Whitehead, and the canon.* Albany: State University of New York Press.

Birnbaum, R. (1988). *How colleges work: The cybernetics of academic organization and leadership.* San Francisco: Jossey-Bass.

Brown, R. H. (1995). Postmodern representation, postmodern affirmation. In R. H. Brown (Ed.), *Postmodern representations: Truth, power, and mimesis in the human sciences and public culture* (pp. 1–19). Urbana: University of Illinois Press.

Crutchfield, J. P. (1994). Is anything ever new? Considering emergence. In G. A.

Cowan, D. Pines, and D. Meltzer (Eds.), *Proceedings, Santa Fe Institute Studies in the Sciences of Complexity: Vol. 19. Complexity: Metaphors, models and reality* (pp. 515–537). Reading, MA: Addison-Wesley.

Davies, J. (1999). Postmodernism and the sociological study of the university. *Review of Higher Education, 22*(3), 315–330.

Donaldson, L. (1996). *For positivist organization theory: Proving the hard core.* Thousand Oaks, CA: Sage Publications.

Levinson, H. (1973). *The great jackass fallacy.* Boston, MA: Division of Research, Graduate School of Business Administration, Harvard University.

Maccoby, M. (1988). *Why work: Leading the new generation.* New York: Simon and Schuster.

Marchington, M., Grimshaw, D., Rubery, J., & Wilmott, H. (Eds.). (2004). *Fragmenting work: Blurring organizational boundaries and disordering hierarchies.* New York: Oxford University Press.

Mihata, K. (1997). The persistence of "emergence." In R. A. Eve, S. Horsfall, & M. E. Lee (Eds.), *Chaos, complexity, and sociology: Myths, models, and theories* (pp. 30–38). Thousand Oaks, CA: Sage.

Nagel, E. (1979). *The structure of science: Problems in the logic of scientific explanation* (2nd ed.). Indianapolis, IN: Hackett.

Riesman, D. (1958). *Constraint and variety in American education.* Garden City, NY: Doubleday.

Walton, E. J. (2005). The persistence of bureaucracy: A meta-analysis of Weber's model of bureaucratic control. *Organizational Studies, 26*(4), 569–600.

APPLYING ORGANIZATIONAL
THEORY

The authors are most grateful for the critical comments on an early draft of this appendix by Corinna A. Ethington, University of Memphis. The final version, of course, is our own and may or may not reflect the perspective of the reviewer.

I n this book, we have discussed many theories that can be of significant assistance in sorting out and understanding the multiple and diverse problems encountered by administrators in higher education. While using social sciences may not be as precise as experimenting in the physical sciences, the social sciences do have a fairly rigorous set of procedures for analysis and application. For some readers, using social science theory may come easily and naturally. For others, a better understanding of what theory is and how it can best be applied is necessary. This brief appendix addresses that need. We consider the application of theory in all three paradigms. The reader may wish to test his or her understanding of these principles by applying theories to the cases at the beginning of each chapter.

Using Theory in the Positivist Mode

The process of *applying* organizational theory to the "real" world is different from the process of understanding and mastering the theory itself. That is, understanding how concepts are related to one another is not the same as seeing how abstract concepts have relevance to particular events and people in organizations. Applying organizational theories is a skill that requires considerable practice. Hence, first attempts may be difficult, while later efforts will usually proceed more easily.

In principle, it is important to become aware of the different ways of thinking about two distinct levels of analysis that are intertwined in the application of theory: the **level of theory** and the **level of concreteness and action**. At the theoretical level, ideas are always abstract and generalizable and should be applicable to a number of situations and organizations. The concrete level, in contrast, describes particular real, palpable events, situations, persons, and organizational phenomena.

In organizational analysis, the process of using theory connects these two levels and proceeds through nine steps. The first step involves the identification of a problem at the concrete level (identified as "b" in Figure A.1). The second step requires a jump up a level of abstraction to seek relevant theoretical concepts that match the problem (identified as "B"). The third step necessitates a search for "connections" among concepts found at the theoretical level to be meaningfully predictive of the problem—that is, the probable explanation of the problem (identified as "A"). The fourth step involves the statement of a hypothetical relationship between "A" and "B" (e.g., the higher the level of "A," the more severe the problems in "B"). In the fifth step, a leap must be made back down from theory to the level of concreteness in order to find referents to the concepts. These are identified in the diagram

FIGURE A.1
Sequence for the Application of Theory to Practice

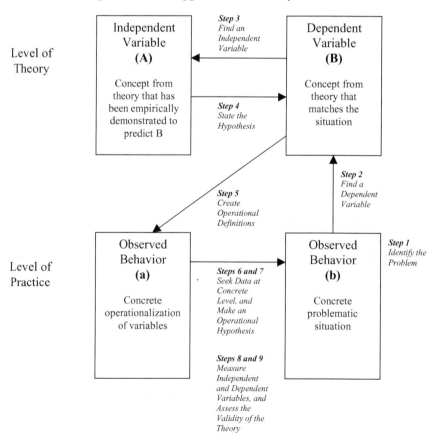

as "a." In the final stages (six through nine), a verification of the predicted connections among real phenomena is made at the concrete level.

Before describing these steps in detail, it is necessary to define some of the vocabulary that is used in the application of theory. Here are some key definitions.

Key Terms in Positivist Approaches

Variables

When college and university leaders use theory to understand issues and problems, they must find ways of scientifically—that is, accurately and validly—assessing the strength of the organizational phenomena they are dealing with in their roles. (For example, though there may be many different opinions among workers, how much power does the dean *really* have?) Each of these phenomena has counterparts at the level of theory; these are called "concepts" or "variables." To use theory, leaders need to match variables from the research literature to the "real" phenomena of interest in their organizations. With these variables, they are able to place a numerical value on the strength of the phenomena. They then can measure them in order to calculate reliably and validly their relationships to each other.

A variable is a property of some phenomenon that may be present in some degree and to which we assign a numerical value. Some of the property may be present, a lot of it, or none of it. Suppose, for example, that, for the purpose of developing retirement policy options for faculty, an institutional researcher was exploring the relationship of faculty age to faculty achievements—such as number of publications. Here, while "age" is a commonplace concept that names one phenomenon of interest and would seem rather obvious, it is nevertheless subject to different interpretations and could be difficult to use as a measure. Hence, as a variable, the concept might be stated more precisely as "*number* of years since birth." If the faculty as a whole is surveyed for their ages, a range of age values will be found. This numerical conceptualization of the phenomenon is called **operationalization**. Variables that can take on a range of values are called **continuous variables**.

Note that some variables are not properties that vary by quantity (such as age), but are, instead, attributes. In other words, the phenomenon being observed either has the attribute or it does not. These kinds of variables are called **discrete** or **categorical variables**. For example, on a survey, the question is sometimes asked, "What degrees do you hold?" While continuous variables can take on a range of values, discrete variables differ categorically, not quantitatively, from one another. Thus, age can range continuously from

0 to 100 or more, but degrees held can encompass A.A., B.A., M.A., Ph.D., etc., which vary descriptively but not quantitatively from one another. The reader might find it interesting and perhaps instructive to ask what kinds of variables the following are: "gender," "imagination," "conflict." Observe that some of these can be either discrete or continuous, depending on how they are defined. In an empirical study, for example, one could look for the existence or absence of different kinds of conflict, or one could look for the extent (within a continuous range) that one kind of conflict is manifested. In the first instance, conflict is a discrete variable; in the second, a continuous variable.

Types of Variables

Many theories propose relationships between independent and dependent variables. An independent variable is the presumed cause of the dependent variable (Van de Ven & Drazin, 1985). Independent is the *antecedent*; dependent, the *consequent*.

Independent variables are presumed to have an effect on the dependent variable, though causality is difficult to claim with certainty. The size of an organization, for example, may have an effect on the organization's culture. Large organizations may tend to have a more bureaucratic culture, while small organizations may be more collegial. Here, size is an independent variable, and organizational culture is a dependent variable. Size (the antecedent) has an effect on culture (the consequent).

Independent variables can be manipulated in experimental situations. Testing the effects of assigning students to specialized residence halls on student grade point average (GPA), for example, requires scientific assignment of a selected sample of students to each residence hall, both the specialized ones and others, then collecting data on their GPAs. In this case, the *type* of residence hall constitutes the independent variable, and the *result* of the treatment (the educational experience) is the dependent variable.

Hypotheses

Positivism is based on hypothetical-deductive research techniques that propose a theoretical connection between concepts. Relationships between concepts are called "hypotheses." A hypothesis is a formal conjectural statement of the relationship between two or more concepts. In other words, a hypothesis is based on informed speculation about the ways in which an allegedly related independent variable changes the value of a dependent variable.

Hypotheses are always in declarative form. For example, "The larger the organization, the more bureaucratic the culture." Hypotheses are never *questions*. "What is the range of salaries among administrators at this institution?" may be a good question to ask, but it is not a hypothesis.

Good hypotheses carry clear implications for assessing or calculating relationships among organizational phenomena. Hypothesized statements contain two or more concepts that are *measurable* or potentially measurable, and they specify how the concepts are related. For example, in a college, "the younger the faculty member, the lower the number of publications will be found on the resume." This is a testable hypothesis. Administrative leaders will find many hypotheses in the research literature that have been shown over time consistently to be valid, hence available for possible application to a new organizational setting. When hypotheses have been found to be valid over time, they tend to be labeled as theories.

Theoretical research permits us to place a statistical probability on the likelihood of our predictions (hypotheses) being accurate over a given number of times that the theory is applied (tested). Statistics are necessary to correct for the possibility that chance variations in the data collection procedures and calculations may distort the findings. Some types of social science research use statistical methods, particularly when applying theories known to be valid. For some other types of research, statistics are not appropriate. Qualitative research, instead, may be needed to address organizational problems that have not been extensively examined previously.

Finding good measures of variables can sometimes be a daunting task for administrators wishing to conduct research on the areas under their control. One reason is that each time the name of a concept appears in a hypothesis, there must be a possibility of substituting for it an empirical indicator—a variable—that measures the value of the concept. For example, if we think again about "age" as a concept, we can substitute an empirical indicator such as "number of years a person has lived" as a measure. This substitution is easy to do with "age," but what about the following: "speed," "fuel efficiency," "accident rate," "absenteeism," "motivation," "conflict," "leadership"? Can measurable empirical indicators be designed for each of these? As can be seen, not all concepts lend themselves easily to measurable definitions—especially to definitions that are valid and will hold up to scrutiny against reality. Good administrators and researchers, however, have learned how to create valid measures of even complex phenomena.

Hypotheses may take a number of forms, including:

- The more X, the more Y (a positive relationship).
- The more X, the less Y (a negative or inverse relationship).
- The less X, the less Y (also a positive relationship).
- The less X, the more Y (also a negative or inverse relationship).
- If X, then Y; or if X, then no Y.
- When X, then Y; or when X, then no Y.

But there are even more complicated hypotheses. For example, "if a university student was a transfer from a community college and enrolls in a writing skills class, he or she will earn a higher GPA than those who are not so enrolled in such a class." Note that there are three, not two, variables in this hypothesis: (1) the transfer/no transfer condition; (2) the enrollment or nonenrollment in a writing skills class; and (3) the earned GPA. Here, the phenomenon of "community college/no community college" is called a condition or a **control variable**. It sets *limits* on the validity of the hypothesis that follows. That is, for the hypothesis to be valid, the university students being tested *must* have come from community colleges. If the students being tested are not from community colleges, then the hypothesis is not verifiable. As another example, there could be a conditional variable that controls for tenure status. This would permit the analysis of the relationship of two other concepts—for example, salary and research output—while holding tenure status constant.

To reiterate, theories are sets of interrelated concepts that present a systematic view of phenomena by specifying relations among variables. The concepts are abstractions from particulars observed, and each concept can be specified in terms of a variable—that is, it can be operationalized so that we can examine it in concrete, not abstract terms.

Above, for example, we took the concept of age and operationalized it as a variable measure—number of years a person has lived. Concepts are related theoretically in hypothetical form. That is, we can specify the theoretical relationships among concepts in terms of hypotheses, which are conjectural statements. To test a theory, then, we translate the concepts into variables whose values can be measured. The variables are stated hypothetically in terms of independent and dependent variables. Independent variables are presumed to have a relationship to a dependent variable (though caution must be exercised in assuming that the relationship is causal).

Analysis Procedures: Application of Theory to Research

As noted earlier, there are nine steps in the procedure of applying organizational theory to practical problems (see Figure A.1).

Step #1: Identify the Problem

The first step is identification of the problem. It may be that a researcher has identified a concrete problematic situation—for example, a person, group, or organizational unit that seems to be functioning poorly. Using organizational theory, it may be possible to explain *why* this is taking place and, thereby, to assist in the creation of policy that may remediate the problem.

To help in the analysis, we can identify this problematic situation as *lowercase* "b" (see Figure A.1).

Step #2: Find a Dependent Variable

This step requires the identification of a concept or dependent variable that has been discussed in the literature that *in the abstract* overlaps or encompasses the concrete problem identified in #1 above—that is, lowercase "b" above seems to be a concrete example. We have, in other words, moved up from the level of concreteness to the level of abstraction. For example, suppose that in #1 above, you had observed at your institution that a worker seemed to be complaining a great deal about his job. Here, in #2, you might recognize that the particular concrete behavior is an example of the abstract concept, called job satisfaction. (Note: The dependent variable is "satisfaction," not "low satisfaction" or "high satisfaction," since variables must have the possibility of having different values when applied to different situations and different people.) We can label this variable *uppercase* "B." Again, refer to diagram A.1.

Step #3: Find an Independent Variable

Now it is necessary to identify and define conceptually a corresponding concept or independent variable that has been shown in previous research to explain or predict the dependent variable identified in #2 above. For example, when studying role theory, we found that there is a hypothesized relationship between role conflict and job satisfaction. Here, role conflict is the independent variable. This may be labeled uppercase "A." In some instances, there may be more than one independent variable in the theory; make sure that each is defined.

Step #4: State the Hypothesis

At this point the hypothesis that *connects* the independent and dependent variables in the theory is presented. Some forms of hypothetical relationships include:

1. The more A, the more B. Here both variables are continuous.
2. If category A exists (rather than alternative categories), then the more B. In this case, the first variable is categorical, the second is continuous.
3. If there is a condition Z, the more A, the more B. Here, the hypothesis is valid only when condition Z is present. In this situation, there must be evidence of the existence of the condition prior to testing

the hypothesis. For example, the condition of the external environment helps determine which kind of organizational design will be most effective. So, it is necessary to establish first what the condition of the environment is; then the hypothesis that exists within that condition can be tested. For instance, if the environment is highly predictable, a bureaucratic organization will be more effective than a loosely structured one. To test that hypothesis, it would be necessary to see whether, in the situation of a predictable environment, the elements of bureaucracy (versus the characteristics of a more organic form) are present, then whether the organization is, indeed, effective.

In our role conflict and job satisfaction example, we can state the hypothesis as an inverse relationship: the more role conflict, the less job satisfaction.

Step #5: Create Operational Definitions

An operational definition of each variable must be presented in order for data to be collected. An operational definition permits the measurement of the value of the variable in the situation at hand, but also must be capable of being used in other, similar organizations that also might be analyzed for comparative purposes. It is not appropriate to create operational definitions that can be applied to data only from the one situation, since, that will preclude the ability to compare findings across other organizations. Units for measuring the variable must be chosen that allow these units to be counted in the organization of interest as well as in other comparable organizations. For example, if the variable is "interaction frequency," it could be defined operationally as the "number of face-to-face meetings of at least five minutes' duration per day between leaders and workers." Clearly, if a comparison of organizations is desired, a count can be made of the number of meetings per day between two similar individuals in other organizations.

For discrete/categorical variables, in contrast to continuous variables, *each* category of the variable must be defined so that in examining the data, the presence or absence of each category can be determined and, later, when applying the theory, a decision can be made as to the category into which the data fall.

Returning to our previous example, we can provide an operational definition for role conflict: the number of times different supervisors provide contradictory instructions to a focal person. Here, our operational definition represents a specific type of role conflict—intersender role conflict. Job satisfaction can be defined operationally as the amount of positive sentiment that an employee expresses toward his or her job. This operational definition applies to all types of jobs and to all types of organizations; it is not limited only to the specific problem that we are trying to solve.

Step #6: Seek Data at the Concrete Level

We have just dealt with the theory level. It is now necessary to move back to the real or concrete level. Just as lowercase "b" at the concrete level required the would-be user of theory to move up a level of abstraction to look for the dependent variable (uppercase "B") at the theoretical level, and uppercase "B" in turn required a search (still at the theoretical level) for the independent variable (uppercase "A"), now the procedure calls for a search for the behavior or phenomenon at the level of concreteness to which the independent variable in the theory ("A") points. For example, if "intersender role conflict" is the independent variable at the theoretical level, it is necessary to look for examples of this at the concrete level. For convenience, these examples can be labeled lowercase "a."

Step #7: Make an Operational Hypothesis

Having identified the independent and dependent variables and their concrete referents, it is possible to restate the theory or hypothesis in operational terms, referring directly to the phenomena of interest in the institution being researched. In other words, an explanation or prediction can be made about what happened (or will happen) to "b"(the original practical problem) if "a"(the concrete manifestation of the independent variable) is present. That is, using theory, it is possible to determine if "b" (in this case, low job satisfaction) is, indeed, the practical resultant of "a" (high levels of intersender role conflict). Had theory not been used, it would have been difficult to identify role conflict as a possible cause of low job satisfaction. Theory pointed to a possible—and reasonable—explanation.

Step #8: Measure the Independent and Dependent Variables

Having defined both the independent and dependent variables above, both conceptually and operationally, it is possible now to find the *value* of each variable. That is, the numeric value of each variable can be assessed, or a determination can be made regarding in which of the specific categories the unit being examined falls. This can be done by counting the data for each variable in the situation, then placing the value obtained on an imaginary scale (based perhaps on personal experience) representing the range of values for each variable. The range of values can be imagined as those you might find in, say, 30 other situations or organizations similar to the one you are analyzing.

For your problematic situation, in other words, compared with 30 other similar situations, approximately where on the scale for each variable (the independent and the dependent) do the data from your institution fall? For continuous variables, you can imagine a range from low to high compared to the mean for the 30 other cases. Thus, if the mean for the 30 other cases is, say, 10, and you find only 3 instances in your situation, the value of the variable for your situation is "low." It is possible, however, to imagine a range of values of the variable in which an "ideal" value is higher than the actual mean for the 30 comparison institutions. For instance, one could imagine in a selected set of 30 "distressed" systems that you choose for comparison purposes, the average level of job satisfaction is itself low. For your institution, then, the value of the job satisfaction variable compared with the 30 distressed institutions may be at about the midpoint, but in the "absolute" or "ideal" sense, your institution's overall level of job satisfaction would be lower than optimum. You must, therefore, decide whether the theory you are using is meant to apply to the "ideal" range. If it is, then you should establish the value for your individual case using that range.

For discrete (categorical) variables, the procedure is slightly different. There will be a relationship between the categories of the independent variable and the value of the dependent variable. (Let us assume here that the *dependent* variable in this case is continuous.) That is, for those organizations where category A (versus B, C, or D) is preponderant, the value of the dependent variable in the hypothesis between the two may be low; where category B exists, the value of the dependent variable may be moderate, while for category C, the value of the dependent variable may be high. For example, if the categorical variable is institutional type, and the continuous variable is number of faculty publications, you may find a difference: low in community colleges (category A), moderate in comprehensive colleges (category B), and high in research universities (category C).

Thus, it is necessary to determine whether, for your organization, the theory or hypothesis you are testing holds true. First, what is the category of the variable that describes your case, and what is the value of the dependent variable? You must then ask whether the relationship of categories to the dependent variable in other organizations is similar to or different from the pattern that you found in your own case.

For example, consider "training" as an independent variable that affects "unit performance"—a dependent variable. The value of the independent variable, training, can be established by reviewing the resumes of unit staff. Based on knowledge of other units in the organization, the training variable for this unit can be assessed as low, medium, or high. Or an aggregate training "score" can be established for the unit, if there is a quantifiable operational definition of training (e.g., number of professional development courses taken). A similar process can be used to measure the dependent variable. Is unit performance highly effective or highly ineffective? Effectiveness could be measured in terms of quantity or quality of output, client satisfaction scores, or level of performance on a particular goal.

In our previous example, we could ask employees to keep a log of the instances in which they received conflicting instructions from different supervisors. This would be our measure of intersender role conflict. In addition, we could have each employee complete a standardized job satisfaction questionnaire from which the overall job satisfaction score for the organization can be compared to national averages for similar organizations.

Step #9: Assess the Validity of the Theory for Your Institution

We are now in a position to draw a conclusion about the relationship of the variables in the theory to the situation at the concrete level. For example, does the relationship between the independent and dependent variables in the theory ("A" to "B") match the relationship ("a" to "b") actually found in the institution? If the independent and dependent variables in the *theory* are positively related, say, was there a similar positive relationship in your institution? Or for discrete/categorical variables, did the category found to be present more than the others correctly match the predicted relationship with the other variable in the hypothesis?

We would expect a positive relationship between training and unit performance. If we found a unit with low levels of training and poor performance, then we could conclude that the hypothesis is valid, and that the unit may benefit from additional training opportunities. However, if we found a unit with high levels of training and poor performance, then we could conclude that the hypothesis was not valid for this case. That is, the predictive relationship between the independent variable and the dependent variable was inadequate. When this happens, researchers *could* reject the theory, claiming that it needs to be replaced by a more robust hypothesis. Or researchers could understand that the situation being examined is more complex than can be accommodated by a bivariate (two-variable) analysis. That is, there may be other variables that affect either the independent variable or the dependent variable (or both), and these additional variables will need to be accounted for in the analysis. In our example, it may be that if we added a control variable—say, "highest level of education"—and tested the theory separately for those at the high and low levels, the theory might, indeed, turn out to be predictive. For example, high levels of training may have improved the effectiveness of staff members who had less formal education (thus confirming the theory for staff with lower education levels), but the training may not have had a significant effect on the performance of staff members with higher levels of educational attainment. In that case, we would need to identify a different theory to explain the poor performance of highly educated staff members.

In our role conflict and job satisfaction example, the theory suggested that high levels of role conflict ("A") are associated with low levels of job satisfaction ("B"). The logs kept by the employees may reveal a surprisingly high number of intersender role conflicts ("a"). The employees noted many more instances of role conflict than we expected, given our knowledge of their work responsibilities. Also, their scores on the standardized job satisfaction survey ("b") were much lower than national averages. Thus, we can conclude that the hypothesis is valid, and that organizational leaders can improve job satisfaction by ensuring that supervisors coordinate the instructions they provide to employees.

Using Theory in the Social Construction Mode

Positivist researchers identify concrete organizational problems and then find concepts from a particular theory that help them explain the phenomenon that they observed. The concepts in the theory are operationalized as independent and dependent variables, and the relationships among the variables are tested empirically to assess the validity of the theory for explaining the organizational problem.

Unlike the positivist researcher, the social constructionist does not begin his or her study with a specific definition of an organizational problem, nor does he or she start the research with specific hypotheses to test. Instead, the definition of the problem and the key explanatory concepts related to the problem emerge from the data that are collected (Kvale, 1996; Stake, 1995). Social constructionist researchers may have a general idea about the phenomenon of interest that they seek to study (e.g., how colleges and universities change over time), but they will not have specific research questions and theories in mind before data collection.

Rather than apply a particular theory to study a problem, social constructionist researchers use inductive methods to produce new theories or explanatory frameworks to understand an organizational context more fully. Theory is an *outcome* of their research. Figure A.2 illustrates this process.

Some researchers refer to this methodology as **grounded theory**, which means that the researcher is attempting to uncover a theory that is "grounded" in the data provided by key informants. Strauss and Corbin (1998) offer a series of analysis procedures that can be used as a guide for social constructionist research.

   1. Develop a "storyline" that explains the organizational issues and problems described by the key informants. Strauss and Corbin recommend that researchers examine their interview data and field notes

FIGURE A.2
Inductive Research Process*

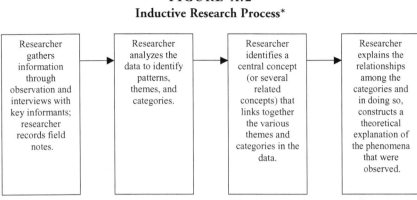

| Researcher gathers information through observation and interviews with key informants; researcher records field notes. | Researcher analyzes the data to identify patterns, themes, and categories. | Researcher identifies a central concept (or several related concepts) that links together the various themes and categories in the data. | Researcher explains the relationships among the categories and in doing so, constructs a theoretical explanation of the phenomena that were observed. |

*Adapted from Creswell, 2003.

to extract general impressions, rather than specific facts. Reflect on questions such as, "What is the main issue or problem with which these people seem to be grappling? What keeps striking me over and over? What comes through, although it might not be said directly?" (Strauss & Corbin, 1998, p. 148).

2. Move from description to conceptualization. Once the researcher has formulated a general impression of the data, he or she is ready to name a central concept that explains the essence of the data. Researchers can use criteria to identify the central concept in their data (see Table A.1). Sometimes researchers identify more than one central concept, depending on the size and scope of their studies.

3. The researcher engages in a process of integration, whereby the different categories and themes identified in the data are explained in relation to the central concept. Integration is more than the sum of the themes and categories identified in the data; it entails specification of how each major category/theme relates to the central concept and to other relevant categories and themes in the data. Without integrating the findings, "there might be interesting description and some themes but no theory because there are no statements telling us how these themes relate to each other" (Strauss & Corbin, 1998, p. 155).

A brief example from the higher education literature illustrates the process of integration. Kezar and Eckel (2002) found that five central concepts emerged in their study of large-scale change in colleges and universities: senior administrative support, collaborative leadership, robust organizational design, staff development, and taking visible action. Additional data analysis revealed how a series of secondary

TABLE A.1
Criteria for Identifying a Central Concept*

Centrality: the other major categories in the data can be related to the central concept.

Internal consistency: the relating of the categories to the central concept is logical, not forced.

Frequency: most or all of the key informants provide data that point to the central concept.

Explanatory power: the central concept is able to explain variation across multiple conditions; that is, when conditions vary, the central concept is still able to explain the phenomenon of interest, though the analysis may look somewhat different.

*Adapted from Strauss and Corbin, 1998.

themes was related to the five central concepts. These secondary themes included incentives, the external environment, effective communication, and holding people accountable to new expectations, among many others. Kezar and Eckel explained how each of the secondary themes was related to one or more of the central concepts associated with change and how the five central concepts were related to each other.

4. Finally, the researcher refines the theory. He or she checks for consistency and appropriate logical development, which can be strengthened by drawing a diagram that displays the relationships among the concepts in the researcher's theory. Diagramming "demands that the analyst think very carefully about the logic of relationships because if the relationships are not clear, then the diagrams come across as muddled and confused" (Strauss & Corbin, 1998, p. 153). Additional steps in refining the theory include fleshing out underdeveloped categories, eliminating extraneous categories that do not have a strong connection to the central concept, and validating the theory by going back and comparing the theoretical explanation to the raw data. The theory should be able to explain most of the raw data that were collected. Another validation technique involves asking the original key informants to respond to the theoretical explanation that the researcher developed. Does the theory inform and/or enhance their understanding of the organization in which they work?

Creswell (2003) noted that researchers may have to engage in multiple stages of data collection to refine relationships among categories. In fact, it is important to keep in mind that, in the social constructionist tradition, research designs evolve and change throughout the course of the study. Even the central concept may need to be re-examined and revised if additional data point in a different direction. This is not to suggest, however, that a social constructionist study is never ending. Social constructionists acknowledge that data collection may cease when the researcher attains theoretical saturation, which means that no new insights relevant to the central concept are created through the accumulation of additional data (Kvale, 1996).

Why go to the trouble of constructing new theory to explain organizational phenomena? Positivists argue that, given the hundreds of existing organizational theories, a researcher should be able to turn to the literature to find a theory that fits his or her data. Social constructionists, however, argue that deductive applications of existing theory might "prevent researchers from arriving at new perspectives and approaches, and these are important to the advancement of knowledge in every field" (Strauss & Corbin, 1998, p. 155). Existing theories may only partially fit the local circumstances that the practitioner-as-researcher is investigating. A particular organizational theory may not be sensitive to the contemporaneous local context. Positivist methods of theory application "even though they are remarkably effective in reducing complexity and chaos into manageable concepts, rarely provide a picture that reflects the reality of a particular place and particular people" (Bensimon, Polkinghorne, Bauman, & Vallejo, 2004, p. 107).

Also, the positivist approach assumes that the researcher has identified the organizational problem correctly. If the researcher has misread the organizational context, then he or she may frame the problem in a way that is not relevant to organizational members, and the subsequent application of theory to address the problem may not improve organizational performance. If organizational members do not have an opportunity to socially construct an understanding of organizational problems, then researchers may attempt to solve organizational problems that people do not believe exist. Therefore, even if researchers have determined that a positivist approach is appropriate given the aims of their study, they may be wise to invest some time in an initial round of inductive data collection, which would allow key informants to help them frame the research questions.

Estela Bensimon's (2004) Diversity Scorecard Project illustrates the importance of having organizational members socially construct shared understandings of organizational problems. Bensimon and her colleagues worked with 14 institutions in Southern California to examine student outcomes disaggregated by race and ethnicity. Each campus formed an "evidence team" to examine student outcome data. Rather than impose a uniform set of outcome measures, Bensimon and colleagues allowed the campus teams to identify their own indicators of student success. "The fact that the evidence teams of 14 institutions developed 58 fine-grained measures of educational outcomes indicates why it is so difficult to translate generalized research findings into practice" (Bensimon et al., 2004, p. 114). The team members socially constructed their own understandings of the student outcome data and developed collaborative strategies for addressing their institution's challenges.

To summarize, the primary difference between positivist and social constructionist theory use is that positivists apply theory to address specified organizational problems, while social constructionists engage in a process of "theorizing" to construct new explanations of the organizational context. Theorizing, however, should not be equated with mere speculation; it is based on extensive data collection and an iterative process of continually refining categories and delineating relationships among categories.

Using Theory in the Postmodernist Mode

Postmodernism is a philosophical position that rejects the idea that events take place in linear modes, from which future events can be predicted from prior ones. Whereas positivism directs attention to events or problems that have concrete, objective referents, the postmodern position urges only the recognition of "incongruous events"—events that are not sensible using traditional tools of analysis and that require methods for making sense of the "blooming, buzzing confusion" of organizational life, to borrow from William James's (1890) famous phrase. Rather than apply theories to reduce complexity or clarify ambiguity, postmodern researchers use different lenses that attempt to illuminate what was initially hidden or marginalized.

Theory use in postmodern interpretations of organizations, therefore, involves the selection of modes of orientation toward events and toward the observer. For example, the researcher may utilize the lens of race, ethnicity, gender, or social class to guide a particular study. The lens identifies "what issues are important to examine (e.g., marginalization, empowerment) and the people that need to be studied (e.g., women, homeless, minority groups)" (Creswell, 2003, p. 131).

The research itself may take the form of community organizing or participatory action research (Reason, 1994; Rossman & Rallis, 1998), where local and political dimensions of organizational life are front and center in the inquiry. This type of research produces new knowledge that empowers people and whole organizations through an authentic collaborative process.

Collaboration is an important characteristic of the postmodern research process. Collective action in the collection and analysis of data is likely to stimulate long-term commitment for change. As Bensimon discovered in the Diversity Scorecard Project, through extensive participation in all aspects of the research, team members felt empowered to become campus change agents. In this way, institutional data were transformed into "actionable knowledge" (Bensimon, 2004, p. 52).

Postmodern research transforms not only perspectives on data, theory, and knowledge; it also transforms individuals and the frames of reference that they use to interpret and address future organizational challenges. Regarding the educational equity goals of the Diversity Scorecard Project, Bensimon et al. (2004) indicated that "change of this nature requires that the individuals who are responsible for decisions affecting the education of African American and Latino students must, themselves, go through a process of change" (p. 115).

It is not surprising that learning how to use postmodern theory is a different kind of activity from learning positivist theory. Indeed, the learning procedure is itself postmodern in form and technique. That is to say, not only is postmodern theory different from positivist theory, but learning about it takes place in different ways from learning about positivist theory. Moreover, the human values and assumptions buried in the two approaches may be quite different.

If, for example, positivist theory represents formalized knowledge, and knowledge is a mode of power and control (as Foucault suggests), then theory can be viewed as a tool to maintain the status quo and preserve inequalities. In response, postmodern researchers can deconstruct the concepts associated with a particular theory; they can challenge the assumptions on which a theory was constructed.

One example of this approach involves the critiques that emerged around Vincent Tinto's (1975) theory of student integration. Tinto theorized that when students are more highly integrated into the academic and social life of their college, they are less likely to drop out. However, the theory may "hold potentially harmful consequences for racial and ethnic minorities" (Tierney, 1992, p. 603). Tierney deconstructed Tinto's interpretation of the "integration" concept by arguing that minority students may struggle to become integrated into an institution that does not value diversity. Students of color may feel that they have to give up part of their personal identity to "fit in" with the majority culture; they may have to be willing to de-emphasize their cultural identities to become fully integrated into a particular college community. Tierney claimed that Tinto's theory contributed to cultural dominance in higher education by privileging the existing power relations that caused students of color to feel like outsiders at the colleges they attend. Initially, Tinto framed integration as "fitting in" with a particular institutional culture. Now, other researchers have reframed the concept to emphasize how institutions can integrate diverse perspectives into their curricula and pedagogical practices. Instead of assuming that the institution represents an unchanging context to which students must adapt, these more recent conceptualizations emphasize how institutions must change to integrate increasingly diverse perspectives (Ibarra, 2001).

In sum, research guided by postmodern principles serves as an important check on traditional assumptions about the phenomena being studied and the methods used to study the phenomena. Further, it recognizes the fragmented world we live in and the increasing difficulty of making projections about the future based on patterns of the past. Finally, postmodern research increases sensitivity to hidden intellectual, social, and ethical biases that distort both methods and findings.

References

Bensimon, E. (2004). The diversity scorecard: A learning approach to institutional change. *Change, 36*(1), 45–52.

Bensimon, E., Polkinghorne, D., Bauman, G., & Vallejo, E. (2004). Doing research that makes a difference. *Journal of Higher Education, 75*(1), 104–126.

Creswell, J. (2003). *Research design: Qualitative, quantitative, and mixed methods approaches* (2nd ed.). Thousand Oaks, CA: Sage.

Ibarra, R. (2001). *Beyond affirmative action: Reframing the context of higher education.* Madison, WI: University of Wisconsin Press.

James, W. (1890). *The principles of psychology.* New York: H. Holt and Company.

Kezar, A., & Eckel, P. (2002). Examining the institutional transformation process: The importance of sensemaking, inter-related strategies, and balance. *Research in Higher Education, 43*(4), 295–328.

Kvale, S. (1996). *Interviews: An introduction to qualitative research interviewing.* Thousand Oaks, CA: Sage.

Reason, P. (1994). Three approaches to participative inquiry. In N. Denzin & Y. Lincoln (Eds.), *Handbook of qualitative research* (pp. 324–339). Thousand Oaks, CA: Sage

Rossman, G., & Rallis, S. (1998). *Learning in the field: An introduction to qualitative research.* Thousand Oaks, CA: Sage.

Stake, R. (1995). *The art of case study research.* Thousand Oaks, CA: Sage

Strauss, A., & Corbin, J. (1998). *Basics of qualitative research: Techniques and procedures for developing grounded theory* (2nd ed.). Thousand Oaks, CA: Sage.

Tierney, W. (1992). An anthropological analysis of student participation in college. *Journal of Higher Education, 63*(6), 603–618.

Tinto, V. (1975). Dropouts from higher education: A theoretical synthesis of recent research. *Review of Educational Research, 45,* 89–125.

Van de Ven, A., & Drazin, R. (1985). The concept of fit in contingency theory. *Research in Organizational Behavior, 7,* 333–365.

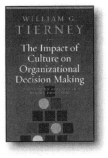

The Impact of Culture on Organizational Decision-Making
Theory and Practice in Higher Education
William G. Tierney

"At a time when institutions recognize the need for change but may be unsure of how to make that change happen, I found *The Impact of Culture on Organizational Decision-Making*, by William G. Tierney, a must-read. I would recommend it to business officers and other leaders engaging their campuses in improvement and prioritization processes. Understanding the culture of the institution—and of higher education in general—is vital to the success of any change plan, particularly for business officers coming from private industry. Tierney's call to look beyond the structure of American research institutions and use a cultural model to understand organizational decision making is a needed wake-up call to college and university administrators who wish to lead their organizations to success and excellence in the 21st century."—***Business Officer Magazine***

Community College Leadership
A Multidimensional Model for Leading Change
Pamela L. Eddy
Foreword by George R. Boggs

"Pamela L. Eddy's *Community College Leadership: A Multidimensional Model for Leading Change* deserves our time for two simple reasons: first, the multidimensional model for leading change transcends community colleges and is applicable broadly within and beyond education; and, second, the author's thoughtful inclusion of vignettes and case studies provides the day-today grounding to make her model relevant to readers of all professions. Yes, community college readers have the advantage of knowing many of the leadership challenges firsthand and will be more interested than most in sections such as 'Challenges of Community College Leadership,' but this book adds sufficiently to leadership literature that it should find itself on the bookshelves of professionals across education and the private sector."—***The Department Chair***

Sty/us

22883 Quicksilver Drive
Sterling, VA 20166-2102

Subscribe to our e-mail alerts: www.Styluspub.com

Also available from Stylus

Cautionary Tales
Strategy Lessons from Struggling Colleges
Alice W. Brown
With Elizabeth R. Hayford, Richard R. Johnson, Susan Whealler Johnston, Richard K. Kneipper, Michael G. Puglisi and Robert Zemsky

"A roadmap for organizational health, for spotting and avoiding problems before they become overwhelming, and for becoming sustainable, not just surviving. There is rich material here for all the key players: trustees, presidents, faculty members, and administrative staff on the roles they play and the responsibilities they often share for both the onset of survival threats and for their successful (or unsuccessful) resolution."—*Patrick T. Terenzini*

"Alice Brown's new study of colleges on the brink of closure provides a fascinating resource for college planners. The book's case studies of a half dozen such colleges, told from the vantage points of key participants in the decisions that proved most critical, gives texture to our understanding of the ways in which institutional histories actually unfold. The accompanying essays by several informed observers provide a broader context for the case studies. In a field that is often dominated by jargon, Brown's clear prose makes for engaging reading."—*Richard Ekman, President, Council of Independent Colleges*

"This volume could be useful for students as they prepare for careers in higher education. The essays in this book focus on small private institutions, but they contain useful lessons for students who will often be working in larger universities or community colleges."—*Elizabeth Hayford, former President of the Associated Colleges of the Midwest*

Rethinking Leadership Practices in a Complex, Multicultural, and Global Environment
New Concepts and Models for Higher Education
Edited by Adrianna Kezar

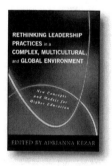

"Indeed *Rethinking Leadership Practices* is an excellent compilation of the concepts, models, and good practices to develop the contemporary leadership capacity so needed in a new generation of college leaders. . . . The audience for this book is any administrator accountable to develop talent and capacity for faculty and staff in the leadership pipeline. With the admonition that old models of training will not develop leadership capacities so needed in today's times, Kezar and her authors present successful models that have developed women and professionals of color over the years. . . . Each chapter is well written, rich in context and detail, well researched with useful resources, and anchored by direct practical applications. The chapters are uniformly of high quality. Many students tell me they usually skip the 'preface', but in this book, that would be a big mistake! This preface is a substantive contribution to the evolution of leadership development programs and framework for the argument for the book."—*The Review of Higher Education*

"Many resources on higher education leadership are of only passing relevance to department chairs. Not this one. While not all of the chapters will be of interest to the typical chair, most of them will, particularly the introductory overview and the chapters on complexity, activism, and ethics. Here even the most jaded consumer of 'airport leadership' books will find provocative and maybe even inspiring material."
—*The Department Chair*